PRACTICAL HANDBOOK OF STAGE LIGHTING AND SOUND

# PRACTICAL HANDBOOK OF STAGE LIGHTING AND SOUND
BY W. EDMUND HOOD

ROBERT E. KRIEGER PUBLISHING COMPANY
MALABAR, FLORIDA
1989

Original Edition 1981
Reprint Edition 1989

Printed and Published by
ROBERT E. KRIEGER PUBLISHING CO., INC.
KRIEGER DRIVE
MALABAR, FLORIDA 32950

Copyright © 1981 by Tab Books Inc.
Reprinted by Arrangement

All rights reserved. No part of this book may be reproduced in any form or by any means, electronic or mechanical, including information storage and retrieval systems without permission in writing from the publisher.
No liability is assumed with respect to the use of the information contained herein.
Printed in the United States of America.

Library of Congress Cataloging-in-Publication Data

Hood, W. Edmund.
 Practical handbook of stage lighting and sound.

 Reprint. Originally published: Blue Ridge Summit, Pa.: Tab Books, c 1981.
 Includes index.
 1. Stage Lighting.   2. Theaters-Sound effects.   3. Amateur theater.   I. Title
PN2091. E.4H66 1989   792'.025   85-19730
ISBN 0-89874-901-8

10   9   8   7   6   5   4   3   2

Preface To The Reprint Edition

In the eight years since the first edition of this book was published, the state of the art has expanded tremendously, particularly with regard to electronics. When the first edition was written, there were still quite a few vacuum-tube amplifiers being used in ameteur theatrics. Consequently, a chapter of the original book was written to apply to that otherwise obsolete technology. Today vacuum tubes are no longer to be found in any but the more ancient sound equipment. Furthermore, today's solid-state electronic theory covered herein is still applicable as far as it goes.

Except for sound equipment, the more state-of-the-art theatrical accessories are priced beyond the reach of the average amateur or group of ameteurs, and there is where *we feel this book can still be a great asset*. The home-made lighting devices can still be built, the techniques for mixing sound systems still work, and the principles of light and color mixing will always be valid.

With all this in mind, we offer this book for a second time, and we are convinced that the lover of the performing arts who wants to do his thing on a shoestring will find it an indispensable tool.

Contents

	Introduction	7
1	**Basic Rules and Principles**	9
	How to Read an Electrical Diagram—Electrical Measurements—Transformers—Basic Lighting and Optics	
2	**The Importance of Sound**	33
	Human Hearing—Sound Propagation—Acoustics—Speaker Location—Speaker Installation	
3	**Speakers and Speaker Systems**	57
	Loudspeaker Types—Baffles—Horn Installations—Cross-Over Networks—Filters—Loudness Controls	
4	**Amplifiers and Amplifying Systems**	79
	Vacuum Tube Versus Solid-State Equipment—Amplifier Inputs—Volume, Gain and Loudness Controls—Tone Controls—Amplifier Outputs—Power Supply—Troubleshooting Choosing Your Equipment	
5	**Microphones**	109
	Impedance—Output Level—Microphone Types And Their Applications—Selecting a Microphone—Using a Microphone	
6	**Putting the Sound System Together**	127
	Program Mixers—Outdoor Installations	
7	**Lighting the Stage**	149
	Tungsten Incandescent Lamps—Arc Lamps—Strip Lights, Flood Lights and Spotlights—Light Controls	

8 Optics, Lenses and Projection   171
Reflectors—Lenses—Light Projection—When You Have to Make Do—Projected Scenery

9 Electrical Power Distribution   207
Typical Electrical Requirements—Non-Metallic Sheathed Cable—Plastic-Sheathed Cable—Flexible Armored Cable—Thin-Wall Conduit—Fixtures and Wiring Devices—Installation of Cable—Control Systems

10 Color and Its Magic   223
The Light Spectrum—How the Human Eye Responds to Color—The Addition and Subtraction of Light—Moods and Special Effects—Colored Lights on Colored Objects—Crossing Lights—Special Effects—Makeup—Costumes—Scenery

11 Psychedelic and Special Lighting Devices   235
Flashtubes—Fluorescent Lighting—Sequential Flashing Lights

Glossary   251

Appendices

- A—Electronic Symbols   285
- B—Manufacturers of
  Theatrical and Public Address Sound Systems   288
- C—Manufacturers of
  Theatrical Lighting Equipment   290
- D—Dealers in
  Theatrical Sound and Lighting Equipment   293

Index   303

Introduction

Supplying lighting and sound to the amateur stage is an extremely challenging field to say the least. It requires a rather broad range of knowledge and experience in several professional areas. At the professional level, the person who determines the manner in which the stage is lighted does not necessarily install and maintain the wires that bring power to the lighting units; he or she does not necessarily rig the cables that support those fixtures, and he or she certainly has little or nothing to do with the sound system. Still, the person responsible for lighting must be familiar with the many types of light units and where they are best applied. He or she must be artistically sensitive to the effects of combining various colors in the light sources and in the objects to be lighted. The sound system operator has his or her particular set of problems. It is essential that a sound system operator be proficient in the operation of the electronics equipment used, well practiced in the precise control of the equipment and sensitive to the acoustics of the hall and stage area.

At the amateur level, there is a real possibility that one person will be responsible for all these operations. That responsibility is often further complicated by limited facilities and the necessity to improvise. Moreover, the less professional the setting, the more challenging the problem and the more jobs one person might have.

It is plain, that to provide a comprehensive textbook covering all these problems at a professional level would be a tremendous undertaking, well beyond the capabilities of this writer or even a team of writers who have not been closely involved in professional production for a long time. What I can do, and what I try to do well here, is give you a starting point. I feel that whether you are involved with a church, a fraternal lodge, or a school (where the facilities might even approach a professional level), this book will at least supplement what you might already know with enough information to raise your task from an ominous challenge to a truly rewarding experience.

Twenty years ago, the best available amateur stage facility had minimal sound and lighting equipment. It was necessary to either make do by improvising or do without. Now, while there are still a great many auditoriums with relatively spartan lighting and sound equipment, newer buildings, especially public schools, have nearly professional setups. Moreover, every major city has a nearby agency or other source of rental equipment. The dissemination of electronic knowledge has become sufficiently widespread that at least one person with those capabilities can be found in almost any community.

Nonetheless, it goes without saying that a person proficient in all the key related fields would be a rare find indeed. Hence this book, which hopefully will fill in the gaps where expertise is deficient or absent. Practically every reader will find some information herein that is old hat. But, he or she should also find material to fill the empty spaces. Because of the increasing availability of professional equipment, I have devoted much of this book to coverage of that equipment. However, I hope that the professional techniques will cause the amateur to look around and apply those same principles, to enhance the potential of improvising with what is available.

W. Edmund Hood

Chapter 1

Basic Rules and Principles

The ability to handle stage lighting and sound re-enforcement requires some general knowledge in those fields related to electricity and electronics. This chapter will provide enough general reference data to enable you to answer the majority of questions the beginner will have. If you are already versed in the electrical sciences, you'll find nothing new here. Indeed some parts will be quite basic. But review never hurt anybody.

HOW TO READ AN ELECTRICAL DIAGRAM

In stage lighting and sound work, there are two types of electronic circuit diagrams. One shows how different pieces of equipment are connected. In this type, a whole unit, such as an amplifier or a mixer, is shown simply as a block labeled to show its function. Therefore, it is called a *block diagram*. With the coming of age of integrated circuit chips, block diagrams are even more widely used than ever.

The second type of circuit diagram shows each wiring connection between each circuit component in a piece of equipment. Each component is depicted by a standard symbol. Such a diagram, called a *schematic*, is much more informative as to the operation of the circuits in a piece of equipment.

Sometimes a diagram may be part block and part schematic. Consequently, it is important that you be familiar with both types. Either type is nothing more than an orderly way of showing how a device is wired. For instance, a simple light circuit might be drawn in block form as shown in Fig. 1-1. The same connections are shown schematically in Fig. 1-2. In both cases, the electrical connections shown are identical. However, in the latter case the circuit is much more clearly detailed. Also, it is much easier to draw, and the symbols can be understood anywhere in the world.

The wiring of a simple transistor amplifier might look like the drawing in Fig. 1-3. A schematic of this same amplifier appears in Fig. 1-4. The schematic clearly shows the type of transistor and the electrical values of individual components.

Now let's compare schematic and block diagrams for a more complex circuit. Figure 1-5 is a schematic of a monaural record player amplifier. Each component is represented by a symbol. However, it is possible to buy an amplifier as a separate unit and it is possible to buy a power supply as a separate unit. Consequently,

Fig. 1-1. Block diagram of a simple light circuit.

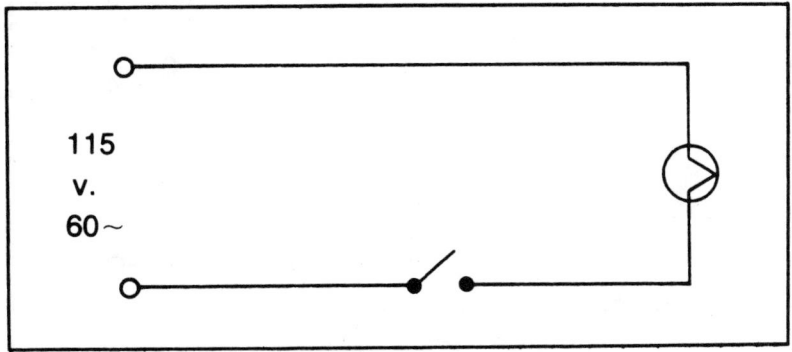

Fig. 1-2. Schematic of the circuit in Fig. 1-1.

in Fig. 1-6 the circuit is shown as a block diagram. Note that the cable to the pickup and the cable to the speaker are shown as if they were single conductors. It is assumed that the reader of the diagram is aware that each of these devices is connected by two conductors which are often physically bound together in a single cable. In a block diagram the lines show how each section relates to other sections, not how each section is actually connected to the other.

Block diagrams using integrated circuit chips show the chips as the complete units they are. However, one or two discreet

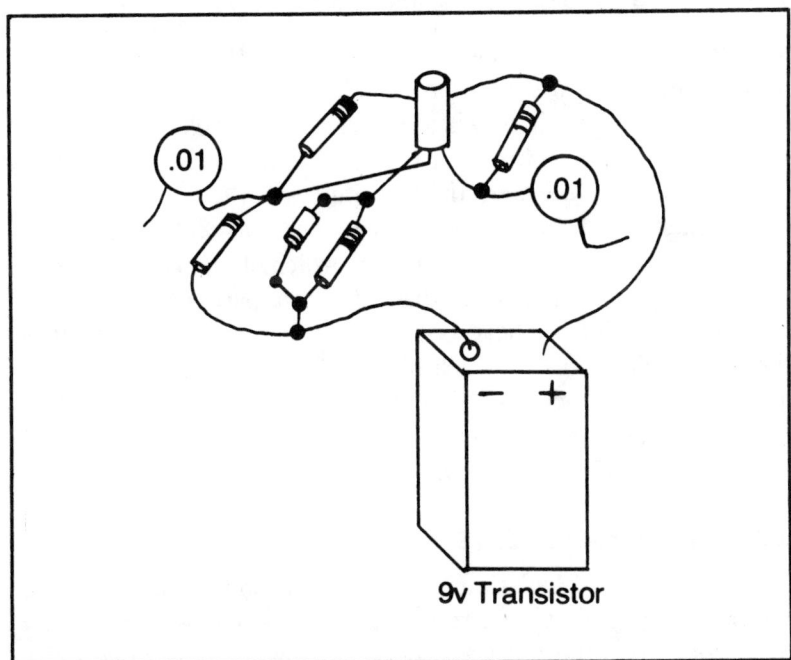

Fig. 1-3. A transistor amplifier circuit.

11

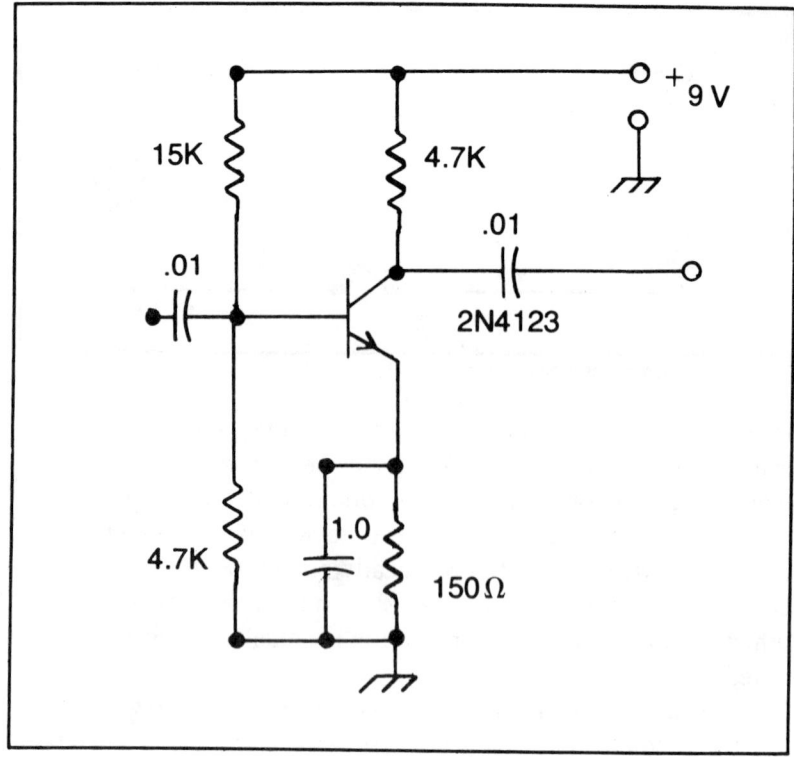

Fig. 1-4. Schematic of the amplifier shown in Fig. 1-3.

components are often connected externally to ICs. These and the power connections are shown in a single composite drawing. Since each integrated circuit chip is made as a single, solid piece and is not intended to be repaired, it is drawn as a discreet component rather than a complete operational module.

Sophisticated switching devices such as calculators and computers use digital logic techniques which often may utilize one portion of a given chip in an entirely different part of the operation from other portions. There is a set of standard symbols used in digital logic diagrams in which blocks of a specific shape indicate specific circuit functions (Fig. 1-7). Except for special effect devices, you are not too likely to run across digital logic in the field of theatrical lighting and sound.

ELECTRICAL MEASUREMENTS

All electrical calculations consider some or all of the following four quantities: voltage, current, resistance and power. If any two are known, the others can easily be calculated. If any two exist together, the others are always present.

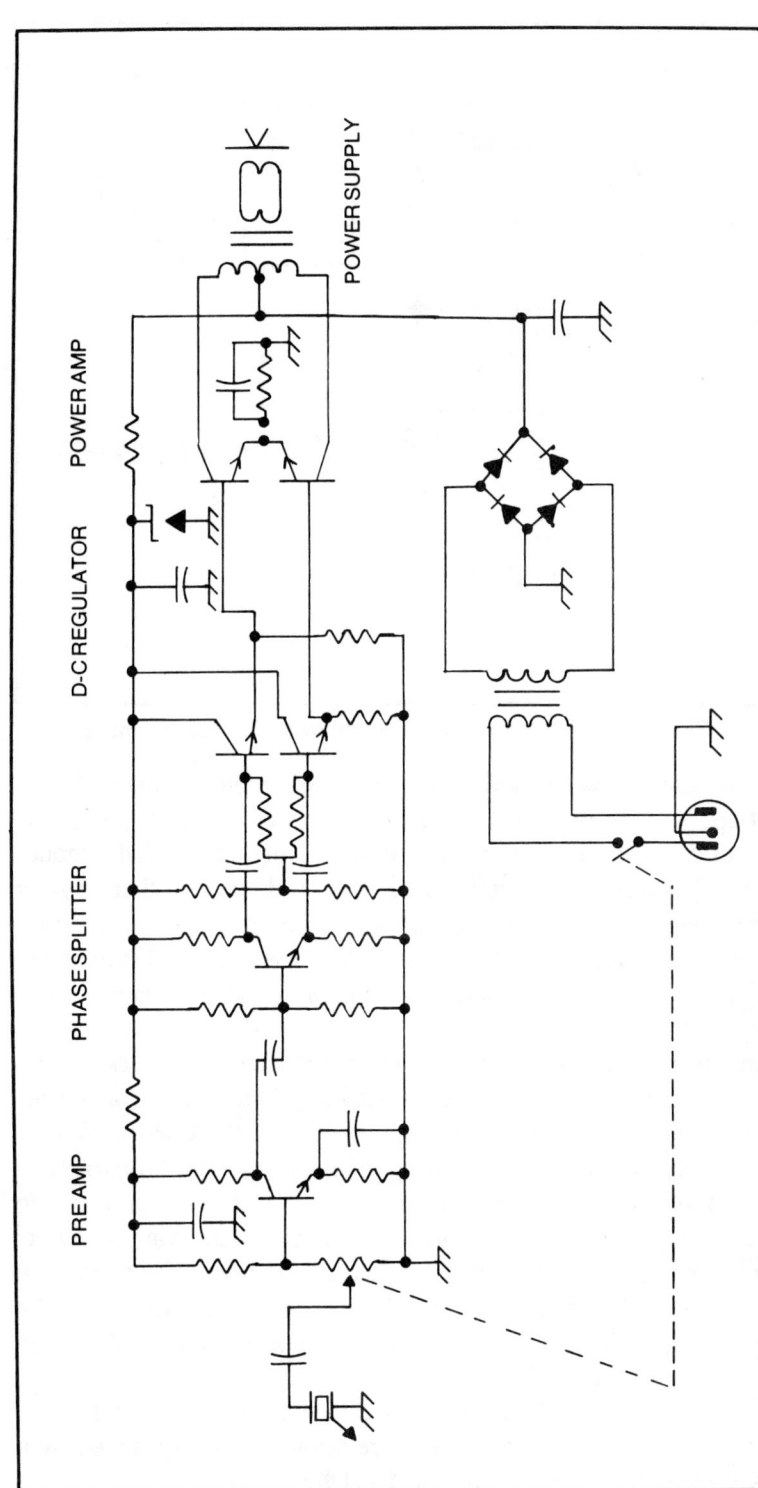

Fig. 1-5. Schematic of a typical monaural phono amplifier.

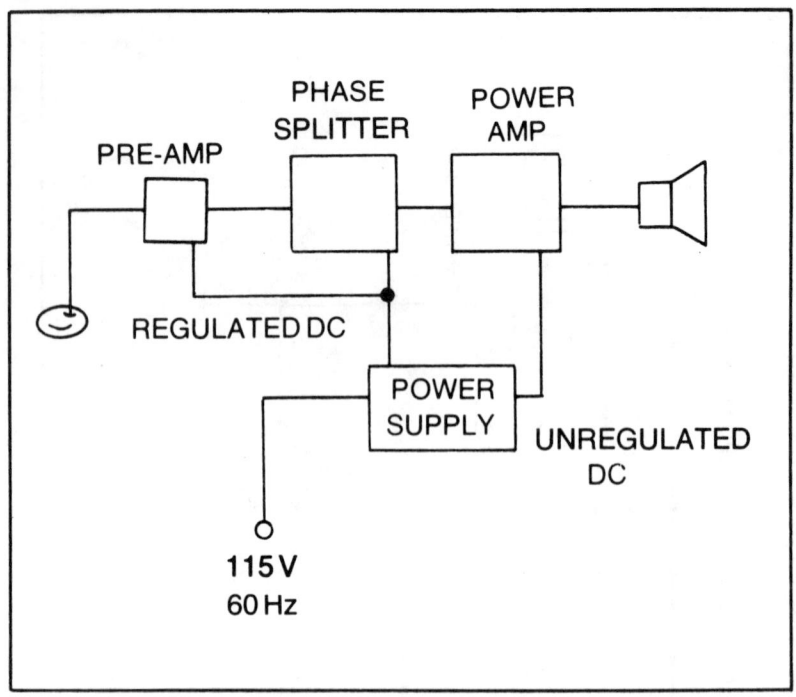

Fig. 1-6. Block diagram of the phono amplifier shown schematically in Fig. 1-5.

Resistance is defined as the quality of an electrical conductor that opposes the flow of electrical current. All materials resist the flow of current, some more than others. Substances that conduct electricity well are called conductors. Substances that greatly oppose electricity are called insulators. Silver and copper are two of the best conductors. Rubber and glass are two good insulators. Because a material has some amount of resistance, current can flow only if some pressure or electromotive force is applied. Therefore, whenever current flows, some amount of work is done and consequently some power is expended. Electrical pressure, called electromotive force, is expressed in *volts*. Current flow is expressed in *amperes* or, with very small amounts, *milliamperes*.

Power is expressed in watts. An electromotive force of one volt moving a current of one ampere dissipates one watt of power. If this continues for an hour, it is called a watt-hour. The resistance of a piece of conductive material is expressed in *ohms*. An electromotive force of one volt will move one amphere of current through a resistance of one ohm.

Voltage, current and resistance have a certain mathematical relationship to one another. This relationship is expressed by a series of algebraic equations based on Ohm's Law.

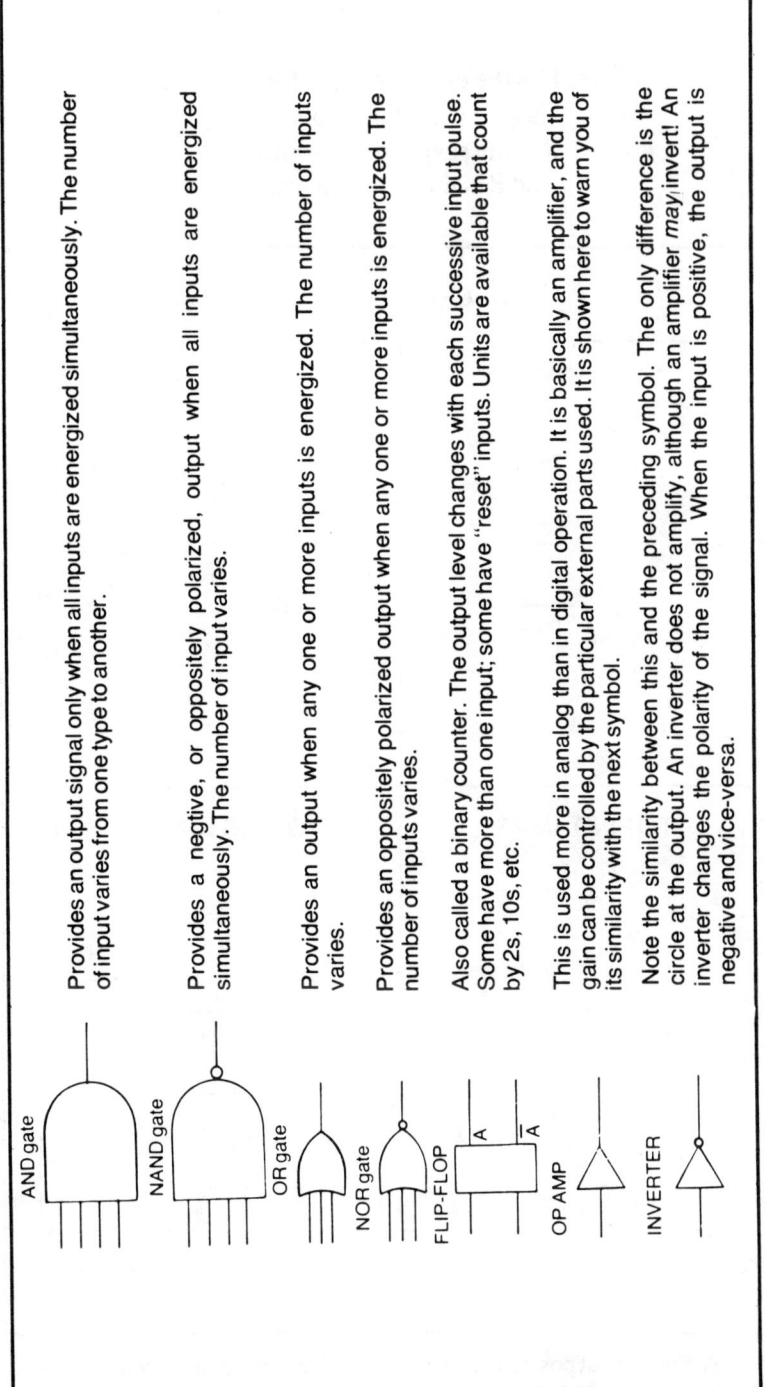

Fig. 1-7. Standard digital logic symbols.

$$E = I \times R$$
and
$$P = E \times I$$

where: E is the electromotive force in volts,
I is the current in amperes,
R is the resistance in ohms,
and P is the power in watts.

OHM'S LAW	
TO FIND VOLTS: $E =$ $I \times R$ $\dfrac{P}{I}$ $\sqrt{P \times R}$	**TO FIND OHMS:** $R =$ $\dfrac{E}{I}$ $\dfrac{E^2}{P}$ $I^2 \times P$
TO FIND AMPS: $I =$ $\dfrac{E}{R}$ $\dfrac{P}{E}$ $\sqrt{\dfrac{P}{R}}$	**TO FIND WATTS:** $P =$ $E \times I$ $\dfrac{E^2}{R}$ $I^2 \times R$
E = VOLTS I = AMPS R = OHMS P = WATTS	

Fig. 1-8. Four variations of the mathematical relationships between current, voltage, resistance and power.

If any two of these are known, the others can be calculated using the variations of the basic Ohm's Law equations shown in Fig. 1-8.

Series and Parallel Circuits

When two or more electrical devices are operated from the same source, they can be connected either in series or in parallel. A *series* circuit is one in which the current path goes through each part of the circuit in turn (Fig. 1-9). Therefore, the current is the same in all parts of a series circuit. But the voltage drop across any given part is proportional to the resistance of that part as compared with the total resistance. The sum of all the voltage drops will always equal the source voltage.

Series circuits are rare in modern lighting circuits. However, loudspeakers are often connected in series where it is necessary to match a certain number of loudspeakers to a particular impedance. In a series circuit, the resistances of all speakers add. As far as lighting is concerned, series circuits were once commonly employed in products such as Christmas lights. The disadvantage of series-wired lights is that none light if only one burns out.

In a *parallel* circuit (Fig. 1-10), each part has the same voltage (that is, the full source voltage) across it. The current through any given part, however, depends only on the resistance of that individual part. Parallel circuits are the most common for lighting, since the failure of one will not affect operation of the others. In loudspeaker systems, parallel circuits are fine when just a few units are involved. Beyond that, impedance matching can be a

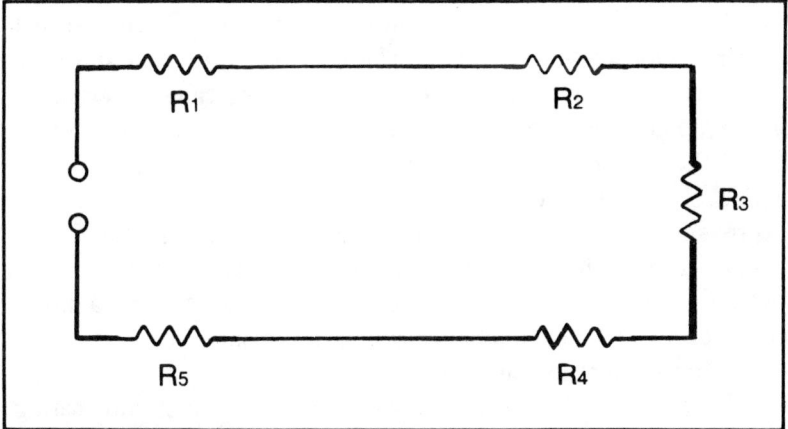

Fig. 1-9. Five resistors connected in a series circuit. The same current flows through each of the resistors.

17

problem. Combined series and parallel circuits are often used. These are covered later.

In either a series or a parallel circuit, the resistance of the wiring itself becomes significant and must be considered as if it were a resistor connected in series with the load. If any significant amount of power is being used, there will be a significant voltage drop through the wire with a consequent loss of power.

Source Resistance

There is no such thing as a perfect source of any kind of electrical energy. Whether the source is a battery, a generator, the output of an amplifier, a microphone or phono pickup, there is a finite amount of internal resistance in each case. This resistance behaves as if it were connected in series with the load. When power is being consumed by a circuit load, the current flowing through the source causes a voltage drop. Consequently, the more current coming out of a source, the lower the voltage at the terminals. There is a point beyond which less and less power will be delivered as the load current is increased. The point of greater power transfer is that at which the load resistance equals that of the source. This is very important to remember in audio work.

AC and DC

Current from a battery flows from the battery, through the load and back to the battery. As long as the circuit remains complete, the current flows steadily in this direction. This is called *direct current*.

Electrical power coming into the home is rarely direct current. More often it moves briefly in one direction and then reverses. This constantly reversing current is called *alternating current*. The rate at which the current reverses direction of flow is called the frequency. Frequency is expressed as so many cycles per second. One cycle per second is called one *hertz*. Such units are expressed in metric terms. A thousand Hertz is called one kiloHertz, a million is called a megaHertz. Each cycle represents two complete reversals of direction. It is possible to have a direct current flowing which fluctuates regularly. In such a case, it is said to have an AC component.

Practically all domestic power sources deliver alternating current. This current alternates at a frequency of 60 Hertz. In order to operate an amplifying device such as a transistor, integrated

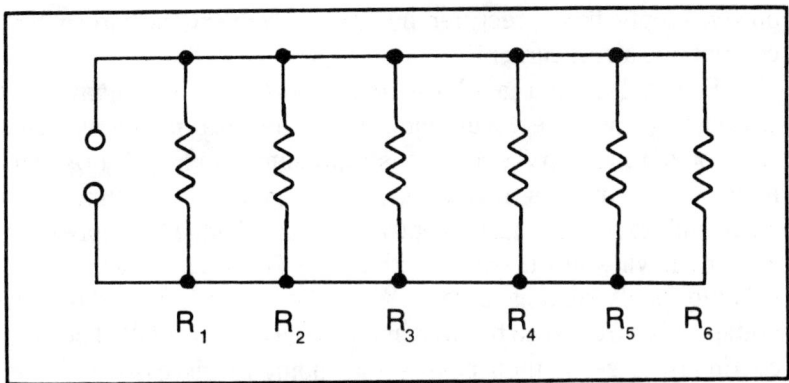

Fig. 1-10. Resistors in a parallel circuit connection. The current flow through each resistor is independent of the others.

circuit or vacuum tube, you must have direct current. You can make the necessary conversion with an electronic device called a *rectifier*. Every electronic device that plugs into the domestic

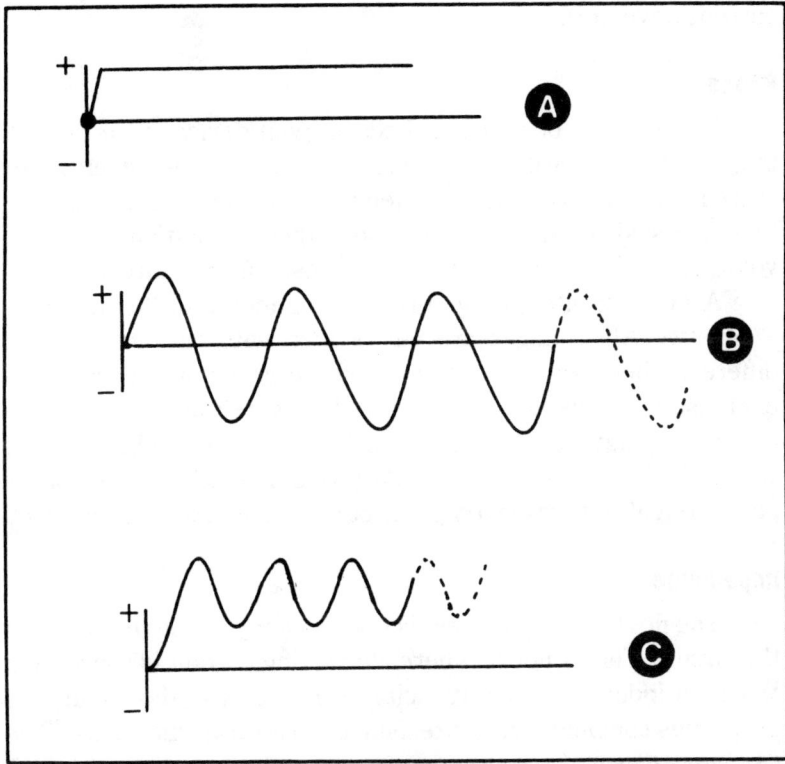

Fig. 1-11. Direct current (DC) is steady; it does not vary (A). Alternating current is constantly changing from positive to negative (B). Direct current with an AC component, called pulsating DC, varies in magnitude but does not change polarity.

power supply has a rectifier built in to convert the alternating current into direct current.

Figure 1-11 is a graphical representation of the behavior of alternating and direct currents, with the current shown as a function of time. Direct current is represented in Fig. 1-11A. The moment the power is turned on, the voltage rises to its maximum value and stays there until the power is turned off. This represents current flowing only in one direction. See Fig. 1-11B. Consider the behavior of alternating current. When the power is turned on, the voltage rises from zero to a maximum, then begins to fall. The drop continues to zero, then passes that point to increase with the opposite polarity. It continues to a maximum in that polarity, then again returns to the zero point where it reverses and begins the whole process all over again.

Figure 1-11C, direct current is shown with an AC component. Note that the voltage polarity doesn't actually reverse as it does with AC. However, the fluctuations resemble an alternating current waveform.

Phase

If more than one source feeds a given device, their outputs might not necessarily be in step with one another even if the currents are the same AC frequency. If the currents are in step, they are said to be in phase. Under those conditions, the two voltages reinforce one another and the result is the sum of the two.

A cycle of alternating current is divided into 360 degrees. When two AC voltages are out of step with one another, the difference between the two is called the phase difference and is expressed in degrees (Fig. 1-12). If they were a quarter of a cycle out of step, they would be said to be 90 degrees out of phase. If they were a half-cycle out of phase, they would be 180 degrees out of phase. Equal voltages 180 degrees out of phase cancel one another.

Impedance

The flow of direct current is opposed only by the resistance of the circuit. This is not so where alternating current is concerned. When an inductance or a capacitance is a part of the circuit, its properties combine with the resistance to form an impedance. The (AC) impedance of a circuit is not necessarily the same as the (DC) resistance. Impedance is the combined effect of resistance and reactance. Reactance is the opposition to alternating current introduced by either an inductance or a capacitance. Reactance is

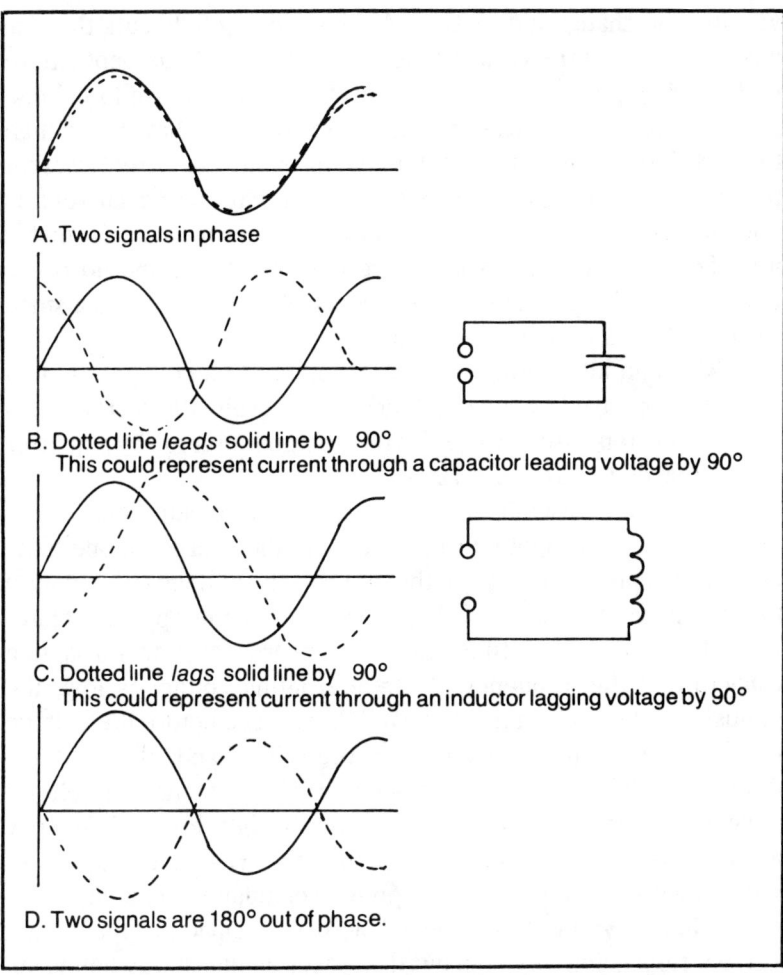

Fig. 1-12. These drawings illustrate phase difference. In the first diagram (A), the two signals are in phase. This could represent two voltage waves or it could represent the voltage and current through a resistance. In the second (B), the dotted line leads by 90 degrees, while the third (C) it lags by the same amount. If the dotted line represents current and the solid one voltage, these diagrams might indicate the relationships of voltage and current in reactances. At D, a 180-degree phase difference is shown.

expressed as being either inductive or capacitive. The two reactances are opposite and tend to cancel each other. Whether the characteristics of a circuit are primarily inductive or capacitive depends on which reactance (inductive or capacitive) is greater.

Inductive reactance is the result of an electromagnetic field. An electric voltage is produced whenever a wire moves through a magnetic field or vice versa. As an alternating current flows through a wire it produces a magnetic field that is constantly

21

varying and changing direction. As this moving field cuts through adjacent turns in the coil, it tends to induce a voltage opposite to that producing the current. This reactance is expressed in ohms. Inductive reactance varies directly with AC frequency, being high for high frequencies and low for low frequencies. Direct current flows easily through an inductance, but alternating current is opposed. If the wire used for the coil were made of a material that is a perfect conductor, it would have only reactance and no resistance. Since there is no perfect conductor, there is always a small amount of resistance in the circuit.

When an alternating voltage is applied to a coil, the flow of current is opposed by the reactance. As a result, the current does not vary in step with voltage. It trails behind, or *lags*, by a quarter cycle or 90 degrees (Fig. 1-12C).

Capacitive reactance is the result of an electrostatic field. When a voltage is applied to a capacitor, the charge on one plate attracts an opposite charge to the other. If the voltage is constantly reversing, an alternating voltage appears on the opposite plate. Therefore, an alternating current appears to flow through a capacitor. If the frequency of the alternating voltage is low, the opposite plate might run out of available charge before the voltage reverses. At high frequencies, on the other hand, this problem diminishes. Therefore, a given amount of capacitance will offer a very low reactance to high frequencies, but lower frequency apparent currents are opposed. Capacitive reactance varies inversely with the frequency, the opposite of inductive reactance.

When a voltage is imposed across a capacitor the circuit current flow is initially high but decreases as the charge builds up. If an alternating voltage is used, the current flow will *lead* the voltage by a quarter cycle, or 90 degrees (Fig. 1-12B).

Since there is no such thing as a perfect conductor, all inductive and capacitive devices have a certain amount of internal resistance. Furthermore, any practical device operated by alternating current will have resistive components in addition to the trivial resistance of a capacitor or inductor. These quantities all combine to form an impedance.

Let us first examine the reactances. As previously mentioned, they oppose one another. The resultant reactance is the difference between the inductive and the capacitive reactance. With DC resistance also in the circuit, the picture gets more complex. Remember that the current through the resistor wants to be in phase with the applied voltage. However, it wants to lead through a

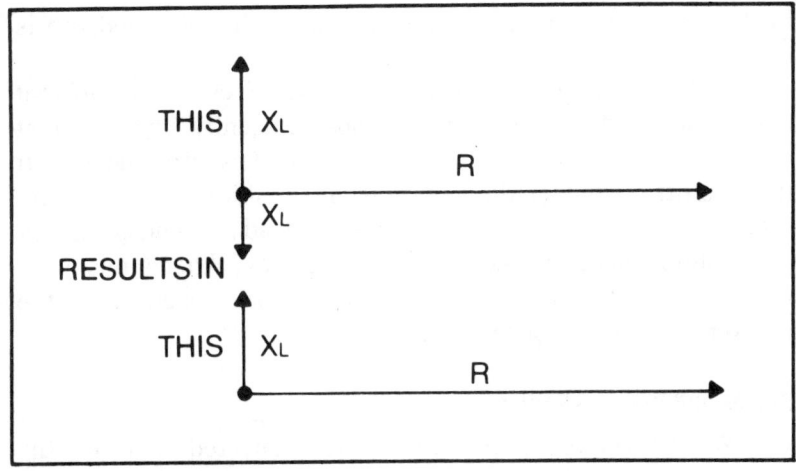

Fig. 1-13. Impedance is the result of the combination of inductive and capacitive reactances and resistance.

capacitor or lag through an inductor. In either case, it is 90 degrees out of phase. Referring to Fig. 1-13, the length of the arrows labeled X_L and X_C represents the magnitude of the current. The direction represents phase. The arrow representing current through the resistor is horizontal. The arrow representing current through the reactance is vertical, either up or down, depending on whether it is leading or lagging. If the length of the arrows is proportional to the number of ohms in the resistance or reactance, you can calculate the impedance by making the arrows two sides of a right triangle and calculating the hypotenuse. The angle between the hypotenuse and the resistance arrow is the phase angle of the circuit (Fig. 1-14). While phase angles do not apply to the material

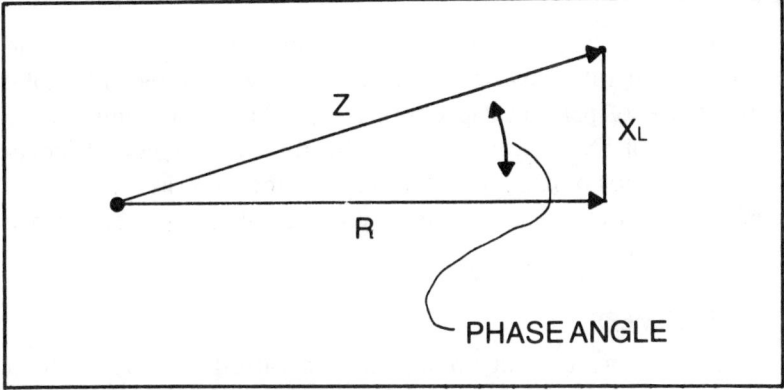

Fig. 1-14. If the resistance and reactance arrows are used to form two sides of a right triangle, the relationship of impedance is revealed. Impedance is expressed as $Z = \sqrt{X^2 + R^2}$.

23

in this book, an understanding of the principles of impedance is needed.

Just as it is important to match the source resistance with that of the load in order to deliver power most efficiently, it is important in audio devices to match the impedance of the source and load. It matters little whether the source is an amplifier output or a microphone and it matters little whether the load is a loudspeaker or an amplifier input. The same principle applies. When a mismatch must exist, it is less consequential if the load impedance is the greater than it would be the other way around.

Series and Parallel Resistance

When a number of resistances are connected in series, the total resistance of the circuit is the sum of all the resistances. When they are connected in parallel, however, it is the conductance, that is, the reciprocal of the resistance, that adds. To calculate the total resistance of a series resistance circuit, use the formula:

$$R = R_1 + R_3 \ldots$$

To calculate resistances in parallel, use the formula:

$$\frac{1}{R} = \frac{1}{R_1} + \frac{1}{R_2} + \frac{1}{R_3} \ldots$$

or, for only two,

$$R = \frac{R_1 R_2}{R_1 + R_2}$$

The total capacitance of capacitors in series is calculated the same as the total resistance of resistors in parallel. The total capacitance of parallel capacitors is calculated the same as the resistance of resistors in series. The total inductance of inductances in series or in parallel is calculated the same as if they were resistances. Remember that here you are calculating capacitance and inductance, not reactance.

TRANSFORMERS

Alternating current voltage can be raised or lowered by a transformer. A transformer consists of two coils of wire in close proximity to each other. When alternating current flows through one coil, it creates a magnetic field around that coil. This magnetic field cuts through the other coil, producing an alternating current in that coil (Fig. 1-15). The proportion of currents is inverse to the turns ratio. That is, if the primary coil has twice as many turns as the secondary, the secondary current will be twice that in the primary but only one half the voltage. Power can neither be created nor destroyed. Therefore, if the current is doubled, the voltage will be halved. In this way, the same amount of power is maintained.

Since the magnitudes of voltage and current are changed, the impedance is also changed. With a two-to-one turns ratio as previously described, the current doubles, indicating half the impedance. The voltage halves, again indicating half the impedance. Half of a half equals one quarter. A two-to-one turns ratio produces an apparent four-to-one impedance transformation. The impedance changes proportionally to the square of the turns ratio.

Power is transmitted over long distances at a very high voltage and relatively low current level to minimize power losses. At its destination, a transformer drops it to more usable levels. Power coming into the average house enters the building at a potential of 220 volts. The 220-volt line divides to provide two 110-volt lines for domestic use (Fig. 1-16).

Some commercial buildings have what is called a three-phase power system. In this system, three separate sources, 120 degrees out of phase with one another, enter the building on three wires. This makes much more power available with less wire. The three circuits can be used independently or together, depending on the type of equipment they operate. There are two kinds of three-phase systems, *delta* and *wye* (Fig. 1-17).

Alternating current used to power lighting systems can be controlled either by a variable transformer or by an electronic

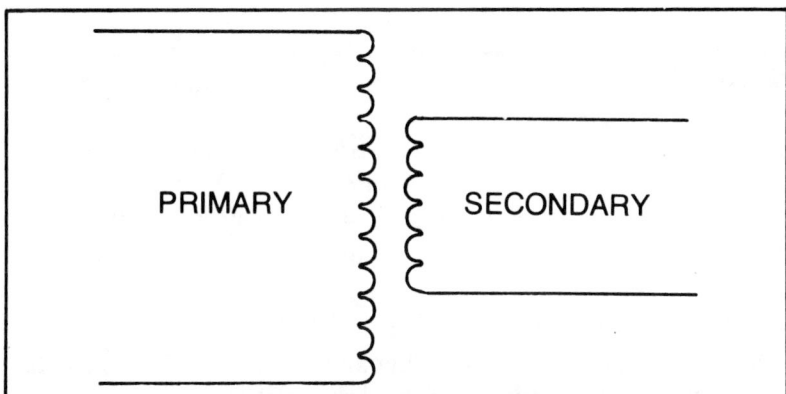

Fig. 1-15. Schematic symbol of an air-core stepdown transformer.

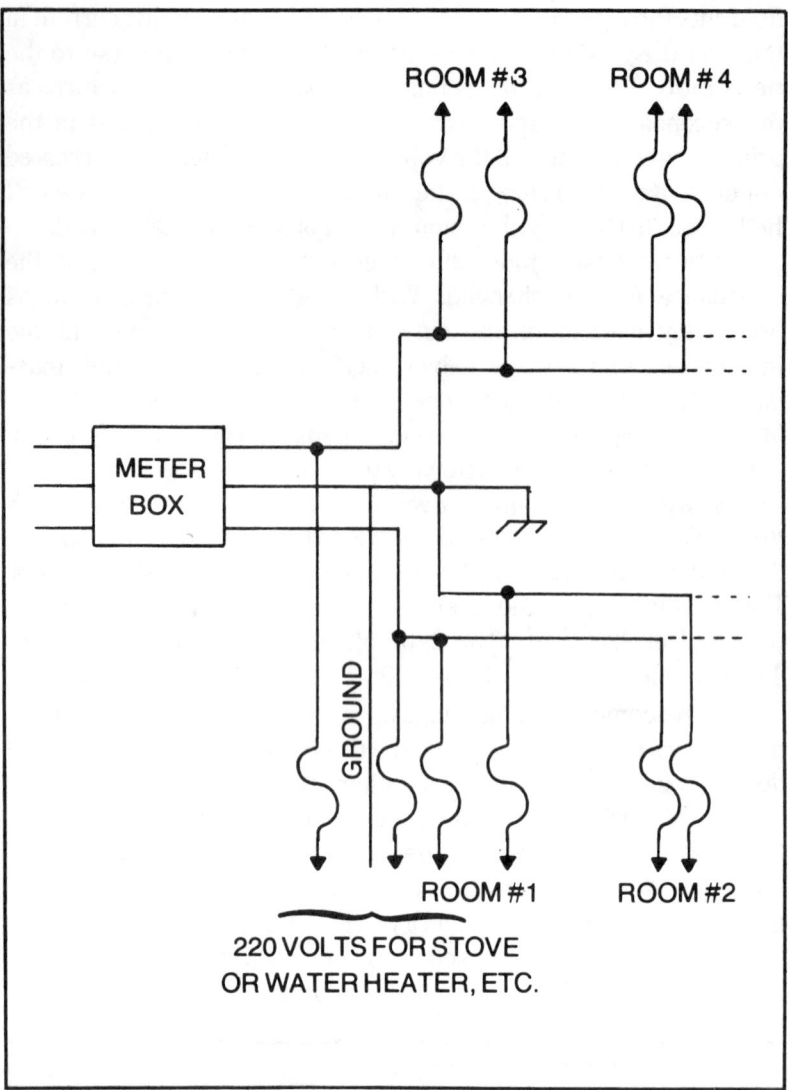

Fig. 1-16. Schematic representation of a typical home electrical power service.

circuit. Older systems use variable transformers, or autotransformers (Fig. 1-18). Such a device is often called a Variac. Variac is a trade name for a General Radio Co. autotransformer, but its use has become so universal that the name is often applied by the user to other makes.

Today, many types of electronic devices are replacing the bulky autotransformer for light dimming. Two such devices are the silicon controlled rectifier and the Triac. Schematic symbols and simplified circuits are shown in Fig. 1-19A and Fig. 1-19B.

26

BASICS LIGHTING AND OPTICS

In order to best command and hold the attention of an audience, the performing area must be well lighted. Lighting should be so arranged as to prevent confusing shadows. In addition, lighting should augment the colors used in the scenery and costumes, except where special effects are needed.

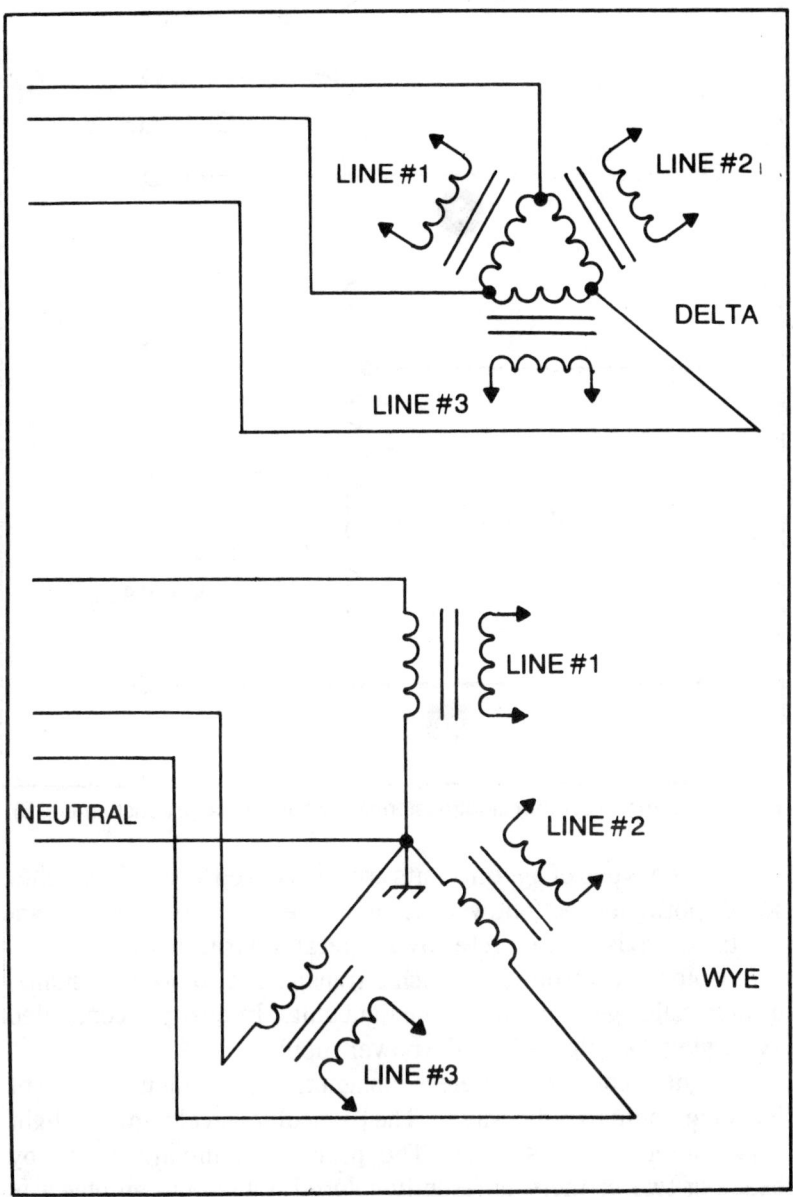

Fig. 1-17. Schematic symbols used to represent 3-phase transformers.

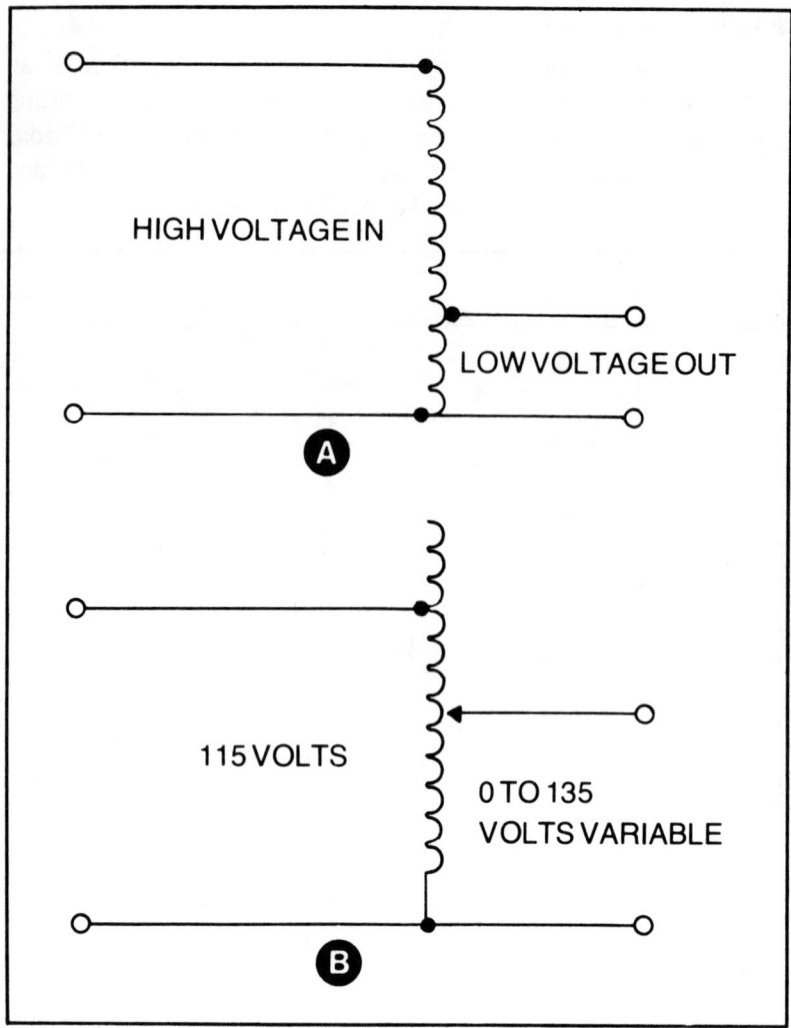

Fig. 1-18. Symbols used for autotransformers (A) and variable transformers (B).

Three types of lighting units are considered basic: floodlights, fixed spotlights and follow spotlights. The first two are preset and the third needs to be directed by an operator during use.

Color is controlled by placing transparent colored mediums, usually called gels, in front of the light units. Intensity is controlled by varying the voltage from the power supply.

Light is composed of electromagnetic waves, identical except for wavelength to radio waves. The particular wavelength of a light beam determines its color. The process of mixing colors by beaming two or more differently colored lights onto an object is called additive color mixing. Mixing colors by mixing two or more differently colored pigments, or by placing two or more differently colored gels in succession is called subtractive color mixing.

Any color can be produced by combining the correct quantities of three primary colors. The primaries used for additive mixing are red, green and blue. The primaries used for subtractive mixing are cyan, yellow and magenta. A uniform mixture of the three additive primaries results in white light. The use of all three subtractive primaries in uniform amounts results in neutral gray or black. Black is the total absence of light. Combining any two additive primaries uniformly results in a subtractive primary. Uniform

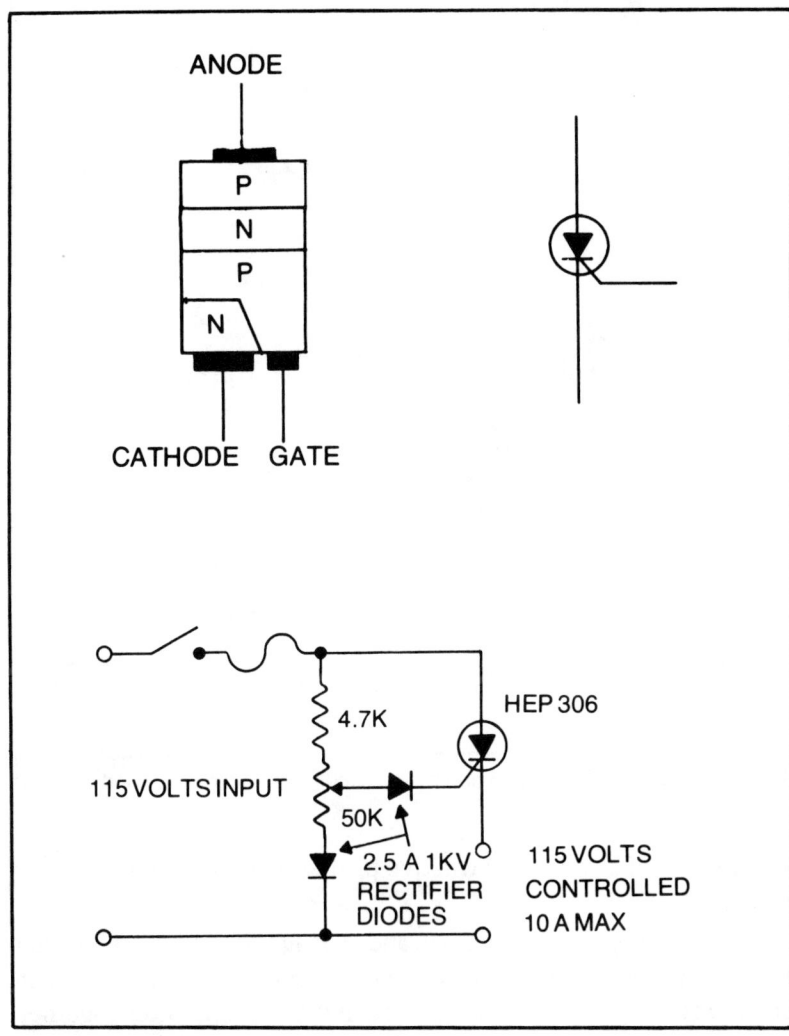

Fig. 1-19A. Schematic symbols and typical circuits for silicon controlled rectifiers (SCRs).

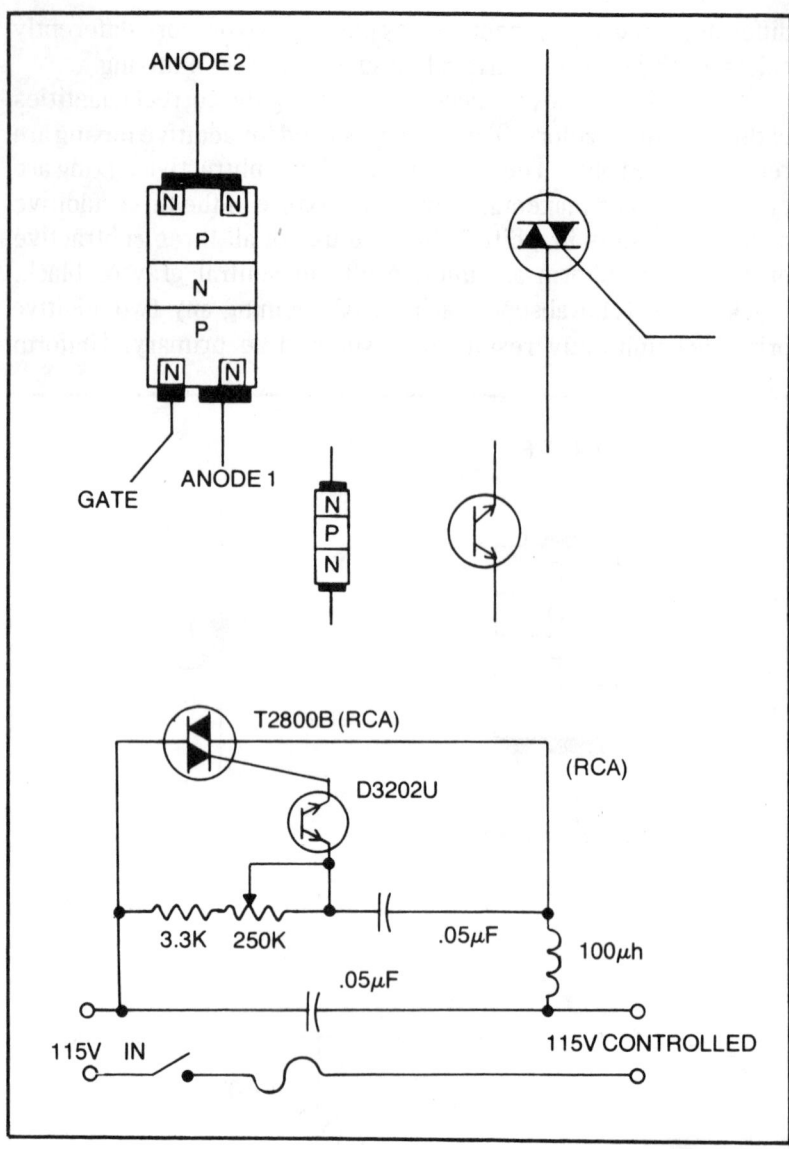

Fig. 1-19B. Schematic symbols and typical circuits for silicon controlled Trac light dimmers.

elimination of any two subtractive primaries produces an additive primary.

For example, if a yellow and a magenta filter are placed together the result is red. Place a yellow and a cyan filter together and the result is green. Place a cyan and a magenta filter together and the result is blue. Shine a red light and a green light on the same spot and the result is yellow.

Shine a red and a blue light on the same spot and the result is magenta. Shine a green and a blue light on the same spot and the result is cyan.

Place filters of equal density at all three subtractive primaries together in the path of a light beam and the result is either black or neutral gray, depending on the total density. Shine light of each of the three additive primaries onto the same spot and the result is white.

In a yellow light a red or a green object will appear in its correct color. A cyan object illuminated with yellow light will appear green and a magenta object will appear red. A blue object will appear black in yellow light.

Magenta light will show a red object or a blue object in its correct color. A yellow object will appear red and a cyan object will appear blue. A green object will appear black in magenta light.

Under cyan illumination a blue or a green object will show in its correct color. A magenta object will appear blue and a yellow object will appear green. A red object will appear black in cyan light.

Red light will show red objects in their correct color. Magenta or yellow object will appear red while blue, cyan or green objects will appear black in red light.

Green light will show green objects in their correct color. Yellow or cyan objects will also appear green while red, magenta or blue objects will appear black in green light.

Blue light will show blue objects in their correct color. Magenta or cyan objects will appear blue while green, yellow or red objects will appear black in blue light.

Light travels in a straight line until it is reflected or until it is refracted. When light enters a more dense medium, its path is bent toward a path perpendicular to the junction of the two mediums. Then light enters a less dense medium, its path is bent away from a path perpendicular to the junction of the two mediums. A concave lens makes light diverge. A convex lens makes light converge.

The foregoing covers the basic rules of electricity and optics and is not intended to be anything more than an encapsulation. All the laws mentioned here are covered in greater detail later in the book.

Chapter 2

The Importance of Sound

Any program in which people appear before people is, in reality, a combination of two programs—one that the audience sees and one that the audience hears. If the audible portion is to be effectively delivered, certain natural rules must first be known and observed.

HUMAN HEARING

Sound waves, travel in all directions from the source, diminishing in power as they go. The power of a sound wave varies inversely with the square of the distance. If the distance from the sound source to the ear doubles, the ear receives only one fourth as much sound. If the distance triples, one ninth as much sound power is heard by the listener.

The human ear responds to vibrations ranging from roughly 20 vibrations per second (cycles or Hertz per second) at the low end to over 15,000 Hertz per second at the high end of the audible spectrum. It does not respond uniformly over this entire range. There is a definite peak in hearing at 3,000 to 4,000 Hertz.

Of the fairly wide sound range to which the ear responds, only about half is really used. The average frequency range of human speech is 300 to 3,000 Hertz (Fig. 2-1), while the piano keyboard covers a range between 27.5 and 4186 Hertz (Fig. 2-2). The remaining portion of the sound spectrum serves only to give what is called character or realism to the particular voice or musical sound.

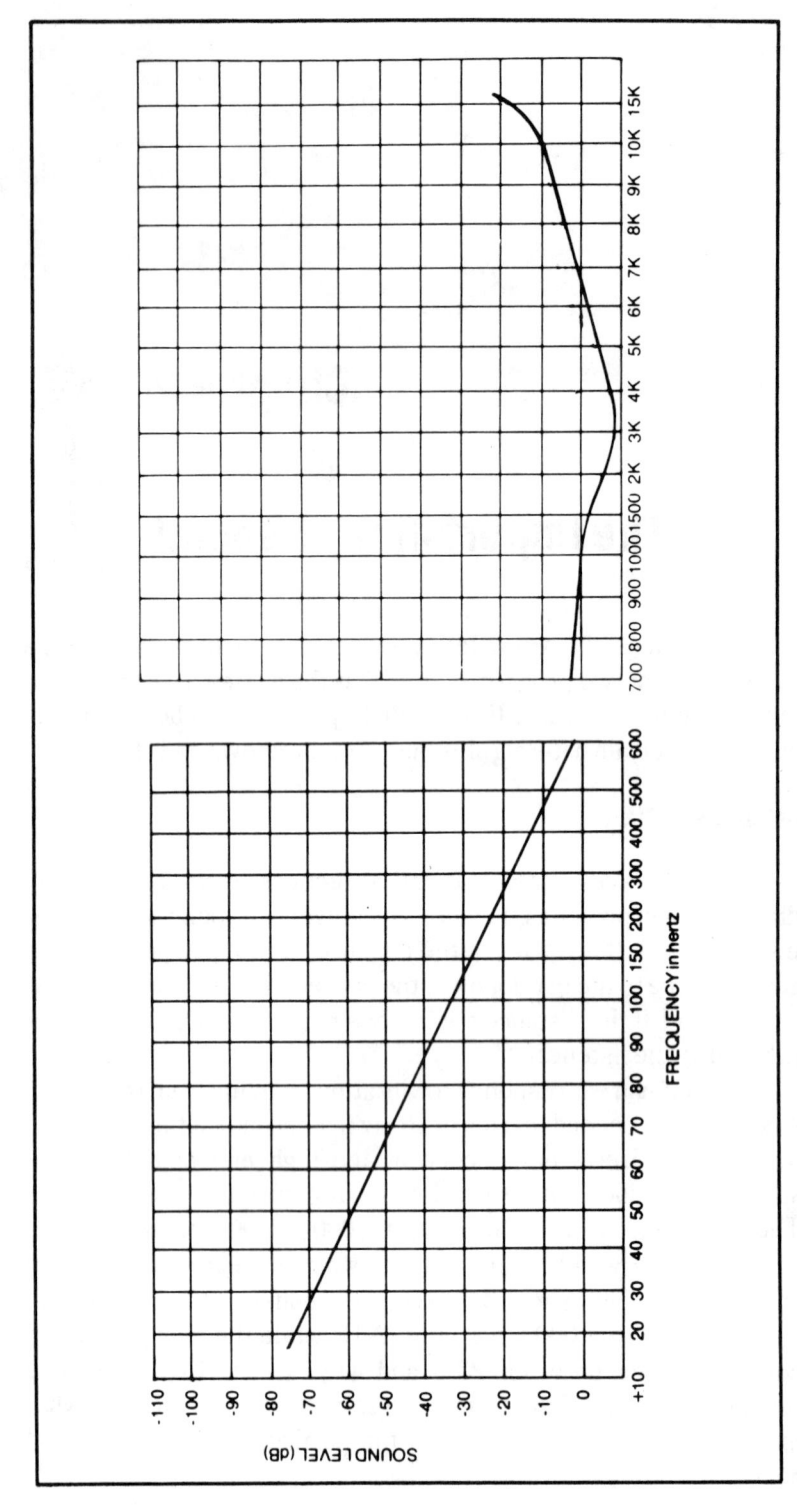

Fig. 2-1. Curve showing the threshold of hearing for an average ear.

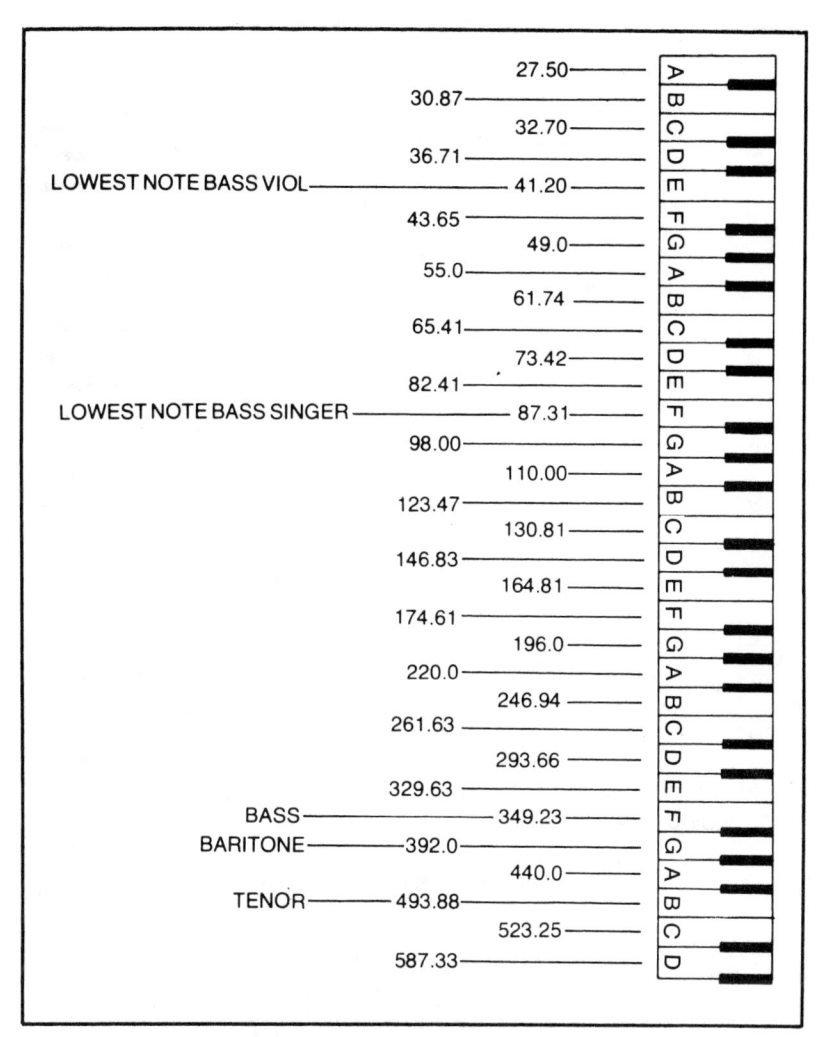

Fig. 2-2. This musical tone scale compares the range of human hearing with the piano scale (continues on page 36).

The intelligence conveyed by the human voice is contained not only in variations of frequency or pitch, but in variations of loudness. The human ear can distinguish only variations of loudness within a certain range. If variations occur above that range, the ear fails to recognize them. Beneath that range, the sound level drops below the threshold of hearing and is lost. Too loud a sound is as unintelligible as too soft a sound.

SOUND PROPAGATION

Sound travels through dry air with a temperature of 70 degrees F at a speed of 1129 feet per second. Upon reaching an

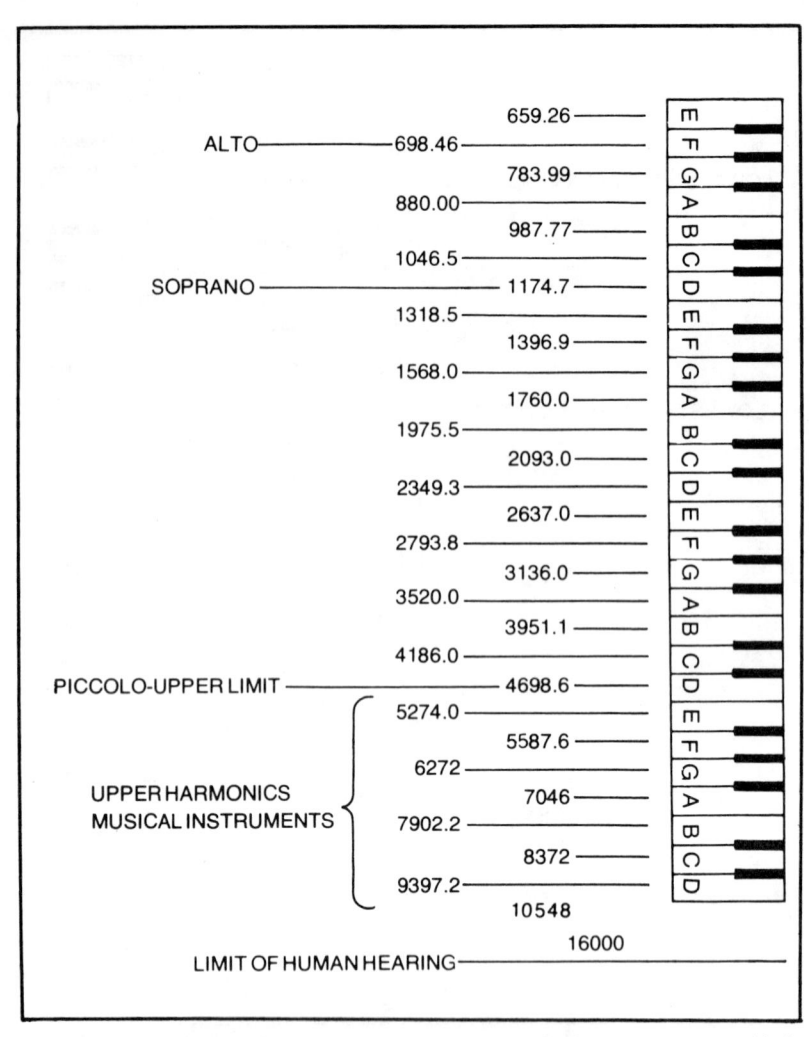

```
                            659.26 ──── E
         ALTO ──── 698.46 ─────────────── F
                            783.99 ──── G
                   880.00 ─────────────── A
                            987.77 ──── B
                   1046.5 ─────────────── C
         SOPRANO ──────────── 1174.7 ──── D
                   1318.5 ─────────────── E
                            1396.9 ──── F
                   1568.0 ─────────────── G
                            1760.0 ──── A
                   1975.5 ─────────────── B
                            2093.0 ──── C
                   2349.3 ─────────────── D
                            2637.0 ──── E
                   2793.8 ─────────────── F
                            3136.0 ──── G
                   3520.0 ─────────────── A
                            3951.1 ──── B
                   4186.0 ─────────────── C
PICCOLO-UPPER LIMIT ──────── 4698.6 ──── D
                   5274.0 ─────────────── E
                            5587.6 ──── F
                   6272 ─────────────────── G
  UPPER HARMONICS            7046 ────── A
  MUSICAL INSTRUMENTS 7902.2 ──────────── B
                            8372 ────── C
                   9397.2 ─────────────── D
                            10548
                            16000
         LIMIT OF HUMAN HEARING ────────────
```

Fig. 2-2. This musical tone scale compares the range of human hearing with the piano scale (continued from page 35).

obstacle, a sound wave may reflect or bounce away at an angle equal to the angle of incidence (the angle at which the sound wave strikes the surface). Some materials reflect quite well. Some absorb more than they reflect.

All the above-mentioned factors can come into play, either to enhance or to deteriorate the quality of the sound program your audience receives. However, much of it can be condensed into one or another kind of echo. Echos out of doors usually involve objects a considerable distance away and often involve so long a time delay as to render them inconsequential. Indoors, however, it's another matter.

In has been demonstrated experimentally that when a person's voice is fed back to him or her with a time delay of approximately one tenth of a second, it produces such confusion as to completely interfere with the ability to speak. As long as the condition exists, one can utter nothing but an incoherent babble. This was the cause of a serious problem in one theatrical auditorium. A balcony formed a graceful curve about 55 feet away from the stage. It focused echos on one certain spot (Fig. 2-3). The conditions were perfect. The balcony, being 55 feet away, returned the echo with a one-tenth second delay. Anybody unlucky to be standing at the focus point on the stage was completely unable to deliver any speaking part. He or she would always break down in utter confusion.

Many people complain that voices have an unnatural sound out of doors. The truth may well be the other way around. Our culture has been indoors for centuries, and we have long since adapted to hearing sounds as they are distorted by the reverberations from walls and ceilings. Consequently, a certain amount of echo is desirable. In fact, some recording studios add a little artificial echo in all their recordings for that very reason.

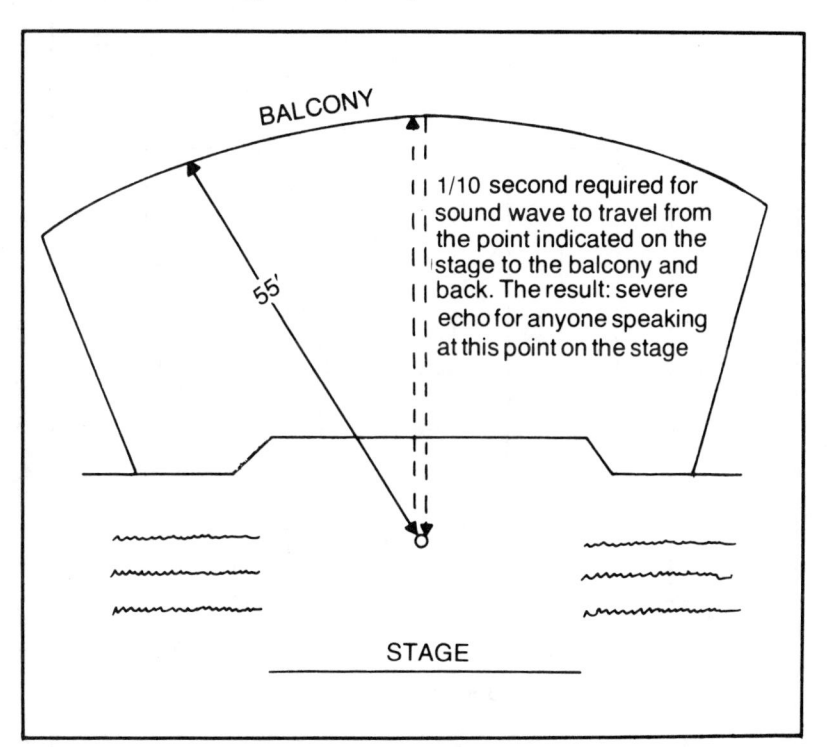

Fig. 2-3. Poor layout of an auditorium can cause a severe echo problem.

37

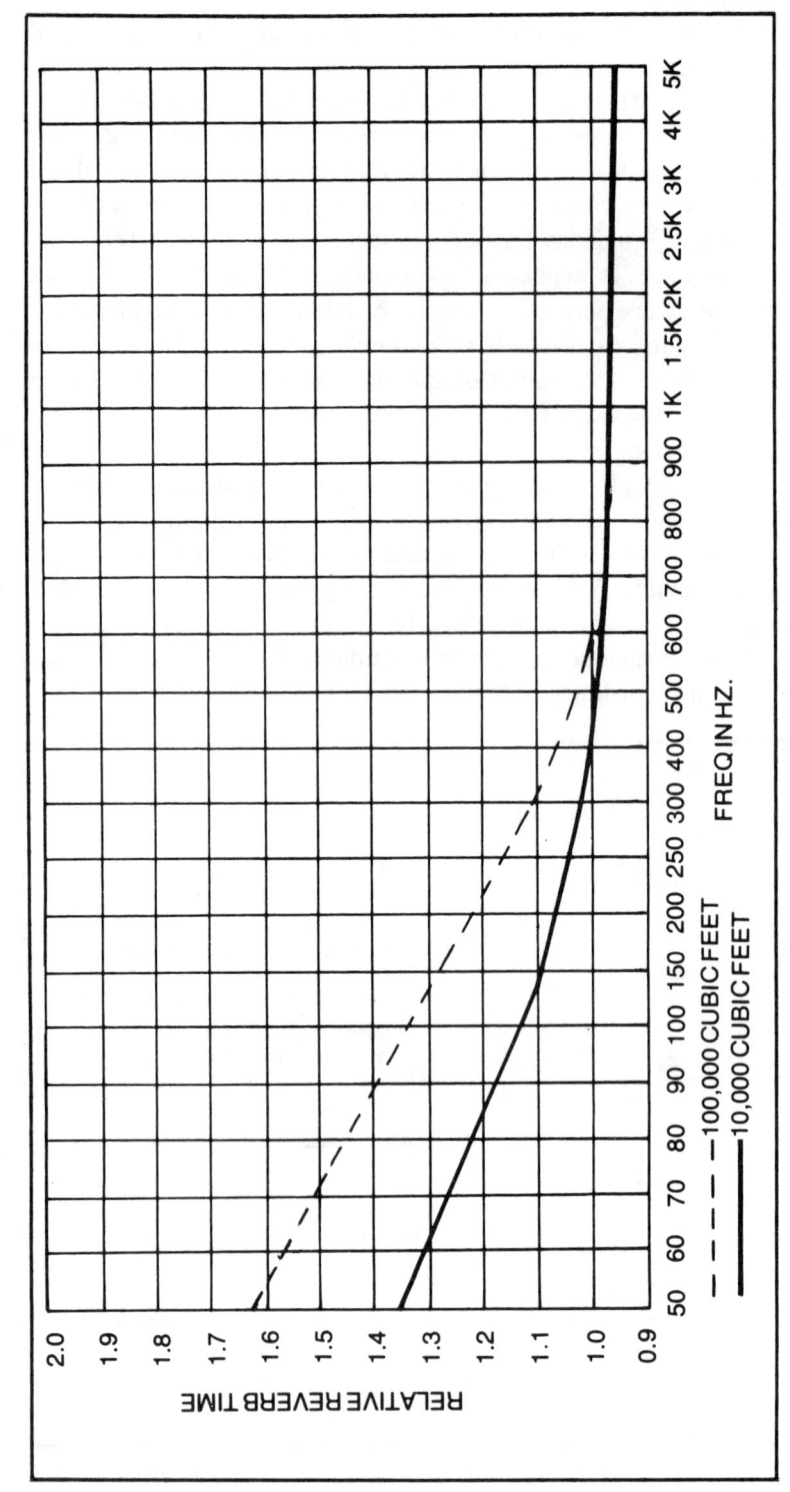

Fig. 2-4. These curves show the reverberation times versus frequency for two different size rooms.

ACOUSTICS

When a sound originates within any closed space, it echoes and reechoes from the walls, floor and ceiling until the combined effects of absorbtion and dissipation cause it to die away. Therefore the sound appears to sustain itself for a short period. This period is called the reverberation time of the room (Fig. 2-4). For precise measurement, it is taken as the time required for the sound level to drop 60 decibels (dB).

Every pure sound has a definite wavelength. A room with highly reflective walls and ceiling can, if its dimensions are just right, be resonant to (sustain) sounds of certain frequencies (Fig. 2-5). This can cause problems, too. In an ideal auditorium, all the factors of room volume, absorption, reflection and ratios of its various dimensions Table 2-1 have been taken into consideration. One very well known place designed for acoustical perfection is Symphony Hall in Boston, MA (Fig. 2-6).

From Fig. 2-4, Fig. 2-5 and Table 2-1 it can be seen that certain combinations of room dimensions and architecture can be undesirable. However, the amateur producer doesn't always have much to say on those qualities, unless a number of potential locations are available. The next question is what to do if the hall has poor acoustics. First of all, let's see what can be done with a small room. The first object is to eliminate echo. If the room is to be used on a permanent basis, carpeting on the floor and acoustic tile on the walls and ceiling will make it sufficiently "dead" to use for a recording or broadcast studio. For temporary use, carpeting on the floor, drapes along the walls and acoustic "clouds" on the ceiling are as effective as they are attractive. If the room is not

Table 2-1. Chart Showing Ideal Room Dimensions Ratios for Good Acoustical Quality.

SIZE & SHAPE	H	W	L
SMALL 3,000-10,000 CUBIC FEET	1	1.25	1.6
AVERAGE SHAPE 10,000-30,000 CUBIC FT	1	1.6	2.5
LARGE, LOW CEILING 30,000-100,000 CUBIC FT	1	2.5	3.2
LARGE, LONG OVER 100,000 CUBIC FT	1	1.25	3.2

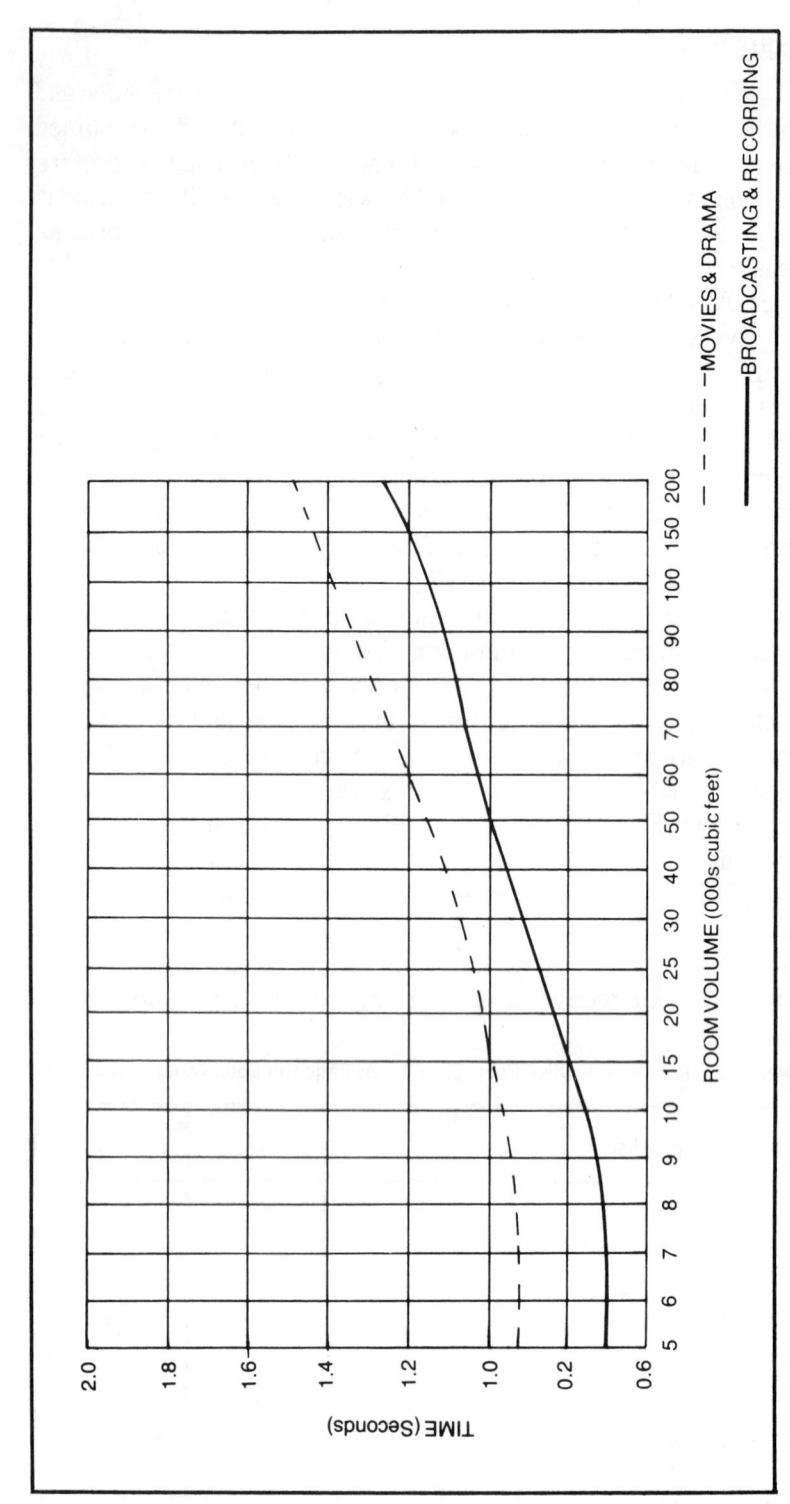

Fig. 2-5. Optimum room reverberation times for two uses.

Fig. 2-6. Symphony Hall, Boston, Massachusetts. Since its opening in 1900, Symphony Hall has been widely known for its design. It is the first building designed with known principles of acoustics in mind and is to this day one of the three finest concert halls in the world. The auditorium is completely isolated from the outside by surrounding corridors and rooms at all three floor levels. Its mid-frequency reverberation time is 1.8 seconds when all seats are occupied. It seats 2631 people in winter. In the summer, when tables and chairs replace the orchestra-level seats, seating capacity is 2335.

going to be seen by the audience, that is, if it is to be used for recording or broadcasting with only the announcer in the room appearance is not important. Those TV shows where studio walls are lined with egg-crate liners are as sound from an engineering standpoint as they are funny. Such things are cheap and effective for short-term use.

Large halls can best be deadened by draperies around the walls. As to the floors, the mere presence of an audience has a tremendous sound-absorbing quality. However, if there is to be considerable floor area not occupied by an audience, carpeting (preferably deep pile) goes a long way toward softening echoes. About the only thing that can be done with the ceiling is the hanging of acoustic clouds, such as are used in numerous offices.

For permanent conversion of a large room, such as a gymnasium, into any kind of assembly hall, much can be done with various types of wall panelling. Table 2-2 gives the absorbing quality of some materials.

SPEAKER LOCATION

As we have mentioned before, the ultimate object is to deliver the sound program to the audience. Contrary to what seems to have been the popular belief years ago, sound doesn't necessarily have to come from just one speaker. Until recent years, every school

Table 2-2. Chart Showing Sound-Absorbing Qualities of Various Materials.

Material	Sound-Absorption Coefficient	
	350 Hz	3 KHz
Unpainted brick wall	0.027	0.06
Painted brick wall	0.015	0.024
Painted plasterwood lath	0.027	0.034
Painted plastermetal lath	0.055	0.05
Unpainted concrete	0.014	0.031
Painted concrete	0.013	0.0175
Carpet on concrete	0.014	0.32
Carpet on 1/8 in. felt	0.25	0.26
Draperies	0.19	0.37
Audience (per square foot)	0.91	1.00
Each person seated	2.5	6.8
Glass surface	0.035	0.02

assembly hall I ever went into had a nice matching set of loudspeakers, one on each side of the stage, even though that stage might jut out closer to the audience than the speakers. Such installations were invariably plagued with problems of feedback and inadequate distribution to the audience.

The ideal system would so deliver the sound that none of it would return to the speaker on stage. Under these conditions, the amplifier gain can be raised, resulting in better microphone sensitivity and thereby allowing the microphone to be further away from the speaker's mouth. This in turn gives the audience a better view of the speaker, further enhancing the program. Nothing really looks more amateurish than a speaker or singer who appears as though he or she is swallowing the microphone.

Much of the solution lies in the use of numerous loudspeakers, operating at a relatively low level, each delivering the sound to a specific portion of the audience area. None of these ought to be anywhere near the stage. People close to the stage can hear the show best without loudspeakers. Of course, the architecture of the hall is the final determining factor as to how it must be done, but the idea is to *deliver* the sound to the audience, rather than *throw* it at them.

One of the better systems I have had a hand in designing was at the old Methodist campmeeting ground at Asbury Grove, MA. Places of that nature are breeding grounds for amateur performances of all kinds, ranging from religious revival meetings to dramatics. The focal point of such activities at Asbury Grove is an architectural monstrosity which the people there fondly call the tabernacle. It is a large, open-walled, circular building about the size of a circus tent. The interior is a hundred feet or more in diameter, with a seating capacity close to 500. The stage is at the far side from the entrance. The audience area is liberally sprinkled with wooden posts that support the roof.

It took 16 loudspeakers (Fig. 2-7) to distribute the sound throughout the audience area. None of the speakers were less than 20 feet from the stage. Once the loudspeakers were properly phased, a performer could stand almost an arm's length from the microphone, talk in a normal, conversational tone and be clearly heard all through the audience area. He never could hear any of the sound *from* the loudspeakers, and often one unfamiliar with the system would ask the audience if it was working!

If there are pillars in the hall (as there are in many churches) they can serve as natural positions on which to mount loudspeakers

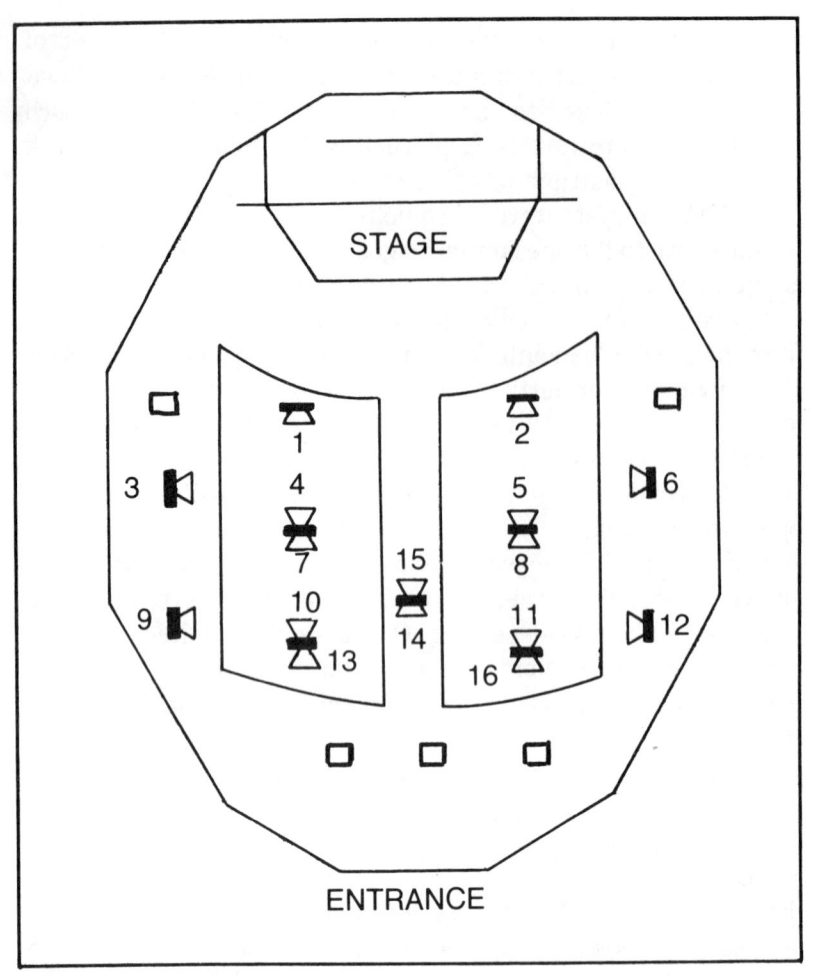

Fig. 2-7. A typical arrangement of loudspeakers in an odd-shaped auditorium.

in situations where small units are justified. In other installations, loudspeakers can often be mounted around the walls, each covering a portion of the audience. The whole effort can be wasted, however, if the loudspeakers are not correctly phased. Figures 2-8, 2-9 and 2-10 show various speaker installations.

SPEAKER INSTALLATION

By phasing I mean connecting the loudspeakers so that all cones are moving in the same direction at any given instant. A loudspeaker consists of a coil of wire suspended between the poles of a powerful permanent magnet (Fig. 2-11). A cone made of specially treated paper is fastened to this coil. Currents in the coil cause the cone to vibrate. The direction in which the coil moves the

44

cone depends on the direction of the current through the wire. Normally the current in the coil is alternating, that is, periodically reversing direction. Therefore, the coil vibrates the cone. When several loudspeakers are used together, they must all move in the same direction at the same time. Otherwise, they oppose one another and the sound is distorted.

Speaker Phasing

On most loudspeakers there is a colored dot adjacent to one of the terminals or some other visible difference between the two terminals. Most wire used to connect speakers to the amplifier carries some mark to distinguish one wire from another. Depending on the type of wire, the two conductors could have different colored insulation. For example, one might be copper-colored and the other silver. In the case of common two-conductor lamp cord, the insulation for one of the conductors is marked by one or more grooves running lengthwise along the insulation (Fig. 2-12). However it is marked, practically all types of two-conductor wire have some means of differentiating between the two strands. It then is simple to always connect the same side of the wire to the

Fig. 2-8. Photo showing how speakers can be mounted in a basement auditorium. The rafters block the sound from the stage. Sound is directed downward and away from the stage.

Fig. 2-9. When the architecture of the room provides no natural means of shielding the speakers from the microphone, satisfactory performance can be had by simply mounting them in the rear of the hall where the most amplification is needed.

Fig. 2-10. Here is an example of a sound system in a church, intended only to deliver the preacher's voice to the congregation. The small speakers are adequate for that purpose. Note that there are no speakers covering the front rows. They are close enough to hear directly. All speakers face away from the microphone (located in the pulpit). The speakers are further isolated by the columns to which they are fastened. Feedback with this system is almost non-existent, unless the gain is raised much higher than necessary. Of course, if a system is to be used to present recorded or vocal music, higher quality speakers would be in order.

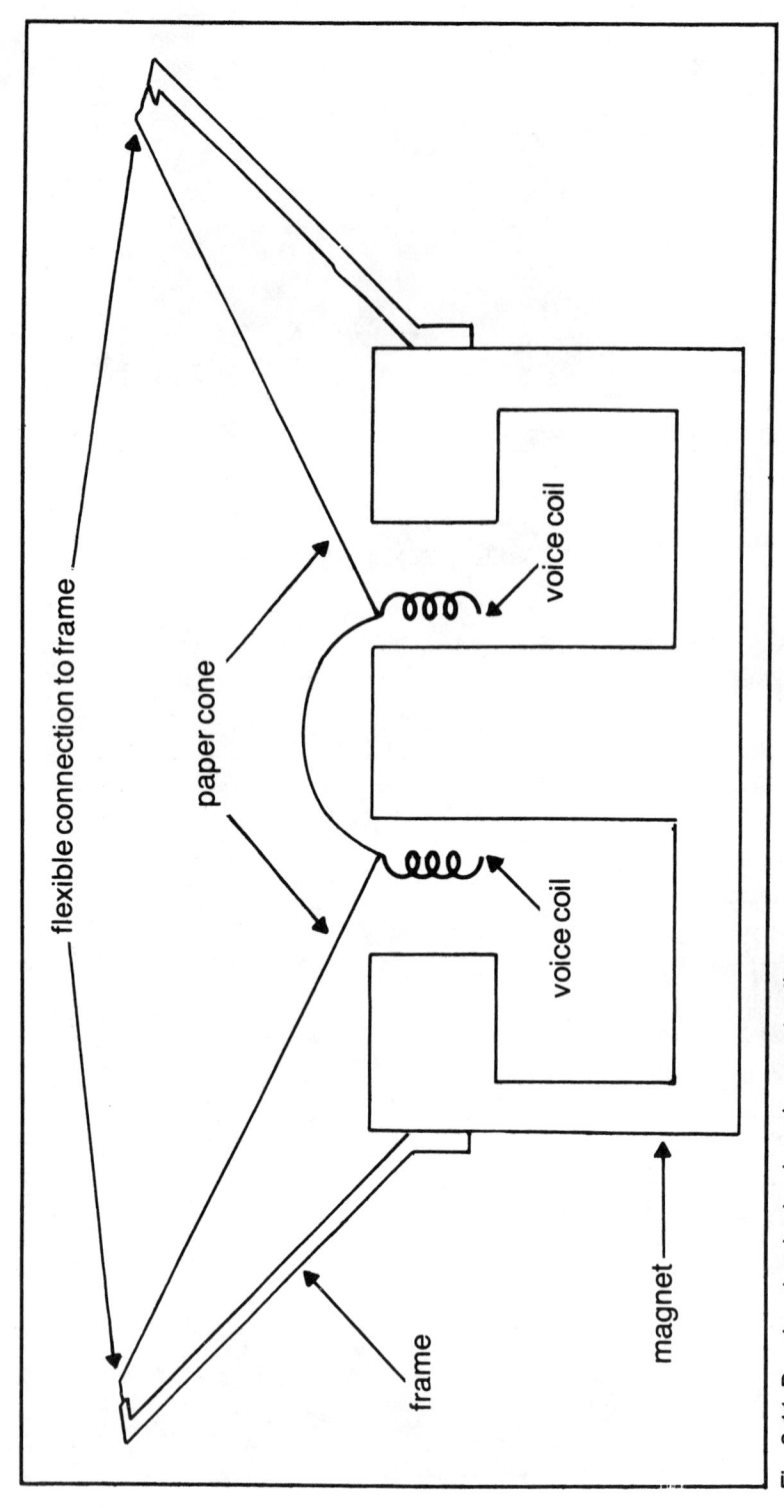

Fig. 2-11. Drawing showing loudspeaker construction.

marked speaker terminals for in-phase operations. If the speakers are phased oppositely, the connections are reversed (marked terminal to unmarked terminal).

As mentioned earlier, the louspeakers must be connected so that, at a given moment, all speaker cones are moving in the same direction at a given instant for in-phase operation. Where loudspeakers face each other, they must be *oppositely* phased. When one cone is moving in, the other (if they are to both go in the same direction) must be moving out (Fig. 2-13A and Fig. 2-13B). By the same token, loudspeakers that are side-by-side must be similarly phased. This applies whether they are on the wall on either side of the stage, or mounted on the ceiling, as in supermarkets and discount stores.

Loudspeakers that are mounted at right angles to one another work independently to each other. Therefore loudspeakers are mounted on each of four walls, each speaker must be in phase with those mounted on the same wall and out of phase with those on the facing wall. The relationship to those on the adjacent wall (at a right angle) does not matter.

Speaker Wiring

When running the wires to the loudspeakers, consideration must be given to power loss in the wire itself. Loudspeakers are generally rated by their impedance. Impedance is the opposition to alternating currents presented by a given device and it varies with the frequency of the alternating current. Audio device impedances are generally measured at a frequency of 1000 Hertz. This number being chosen for engineering convenience.

In order to secure the most efficient delivery of power from the amplifier to the loudspeaker, it is necessary to match the

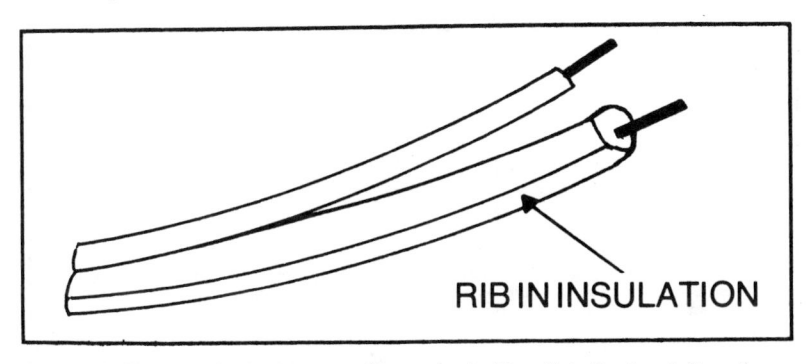

Fig. 2-12. Two-conductor lamp cord is marked with a rib in the insulation of one of the conductors.

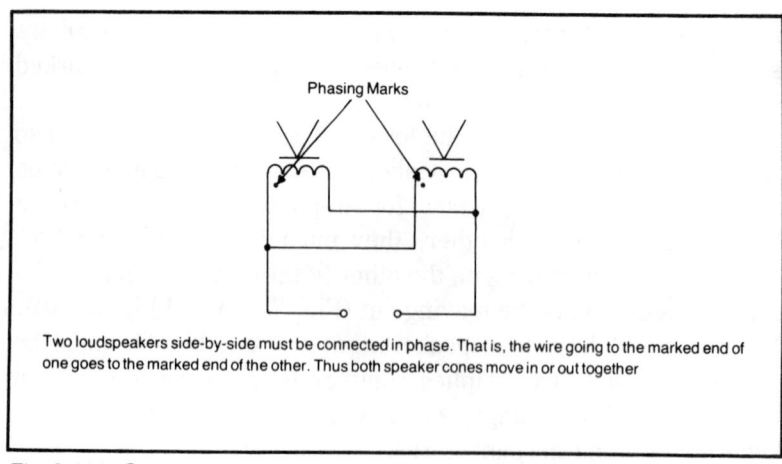

Fig. 2-13A. Correct speaker connections for in-phase operation.

Two loudspeakers side-by-side must be connected in phase. That is, the wire going to the marked end of one goes to the marked end of the other. Thus both speaker cones move in or out together

source to the load. That is, the output impedance of the amplifier must match the impedance of the load. Loudspeakers are designed with standard impedances of approximately 4, 8 and 16 ohms. The impedance of the less expensive varieties, such as found in low-cost radios, is generally 4 ohms (sometimes 3.2 ohms). Most of the better-grade units have an impedance of 8 ohms and the high-quality units run at 16 ohms. However, these three grades are not exclusively confined to the three. There is often a considerable amount of overlap.

Amplifiers are designed with output terminals for each of the more common impedance levels. It then becomes a simple matter

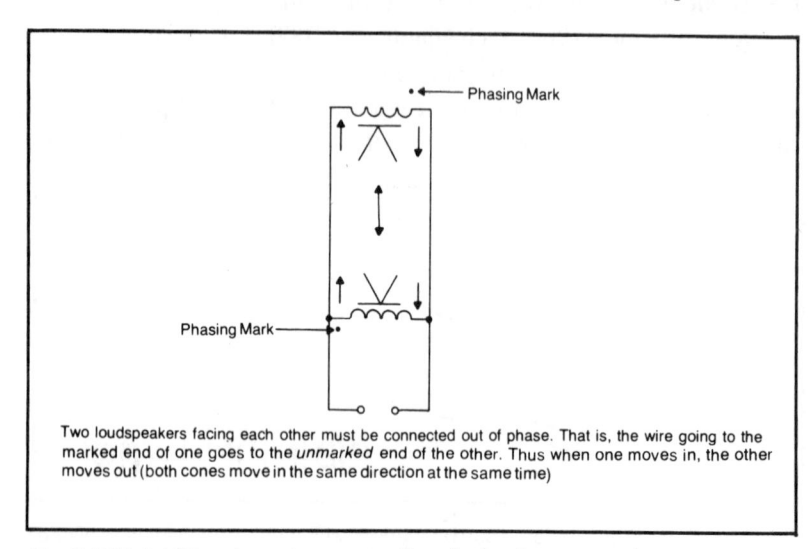

Two loudspeakers facing each other must be connected out of phase. That is, the wire going to the marked end of one goes to the unmarked end of the other. Thus when one moves in, the other moves out (both cones move in the same direction at the same time)

Fig. 2-13B. Additional speaker connections for in-phase operation.

Loudspeakers connected in series.
If one quits, none will operate.

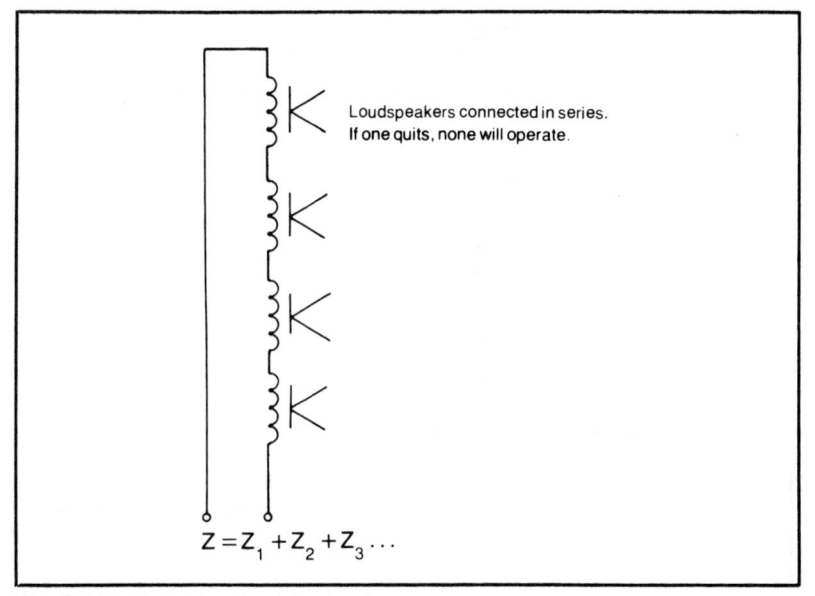

$$Z = Z_1 + Z_2 + Z_3 \ldots$$

Fig. 2-14A. Series loudspeaker hookups.

to match the loudspeaker with the correct pair of terminals. However, when two or more loudspeakers are connected to the same amplifier, the total impedance of the load must match one of the impedances available at the amplifier terminals.

Loudspeakers can be connected either in series (Fig. 2-14A) or in parallel (Fig. 2-14B). When connected in series, the

Loudspeakers connected in parallel.
If one quits, the others keep going

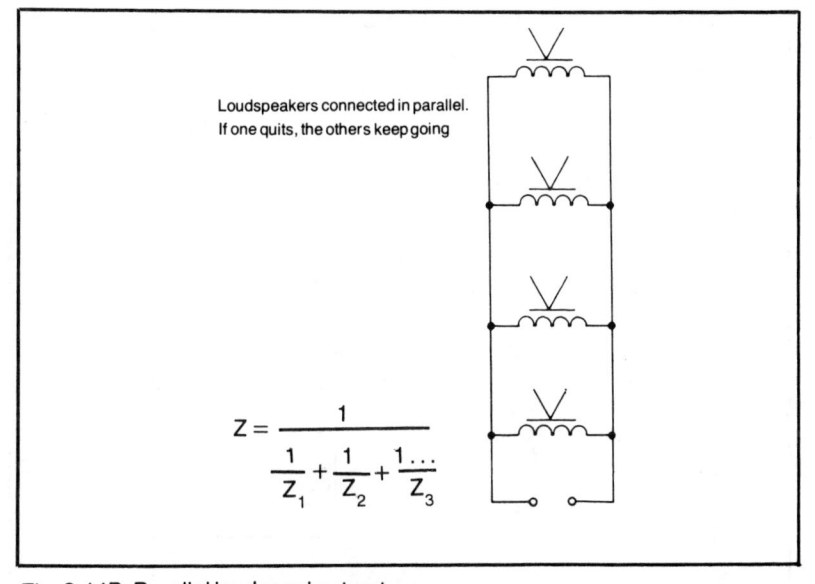

$$Z = \cfrac{1}{\cfrac{1}{Z_1} + \cfrac{1}{Z_2} + \cfrac{1}{Z_3} \ldots}$$

Fig. 2-14B. Parallel loudspeaker hookups.

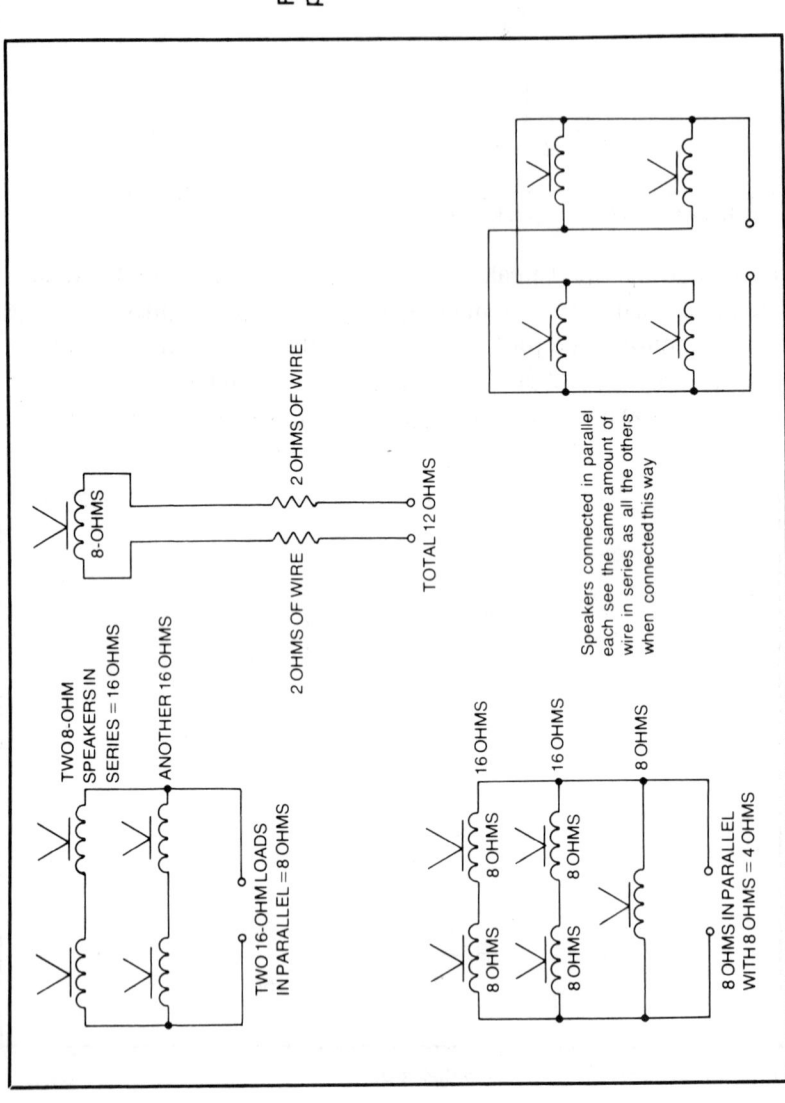

Fig. 2-15. Several possible series / parallel speaker connection schemes.

impedances of each add. Two 8-ohm speakers connected in series presents a total load of 16 ohms. When the loudspeakers are connected in parallel, they combine, if all are of the same impedance, according to the reciprocal of the number of loudspeakers. That is, two 8-ohm loudspeakers connected in parallel present a total load of ½ of the impedance, or 4 ohms. Three units would present a load impedance of 2 ⅔ ohms. Four would present a load of 2 ohms. If the amplifier output offers only a choice of 4, 8 or 16 ohms, where are you going to get an amplifier to match such an odd-ball load? Simple. If you use an even number of loudspeakers, you can always find a series/parallel combination to match one of the output impedances (Fig. 2-15).

TAP ON TRANSFORMER ALLOWS LESS POWER TO BE DELIVERED IF NECESSARY

70-VOLT LINE

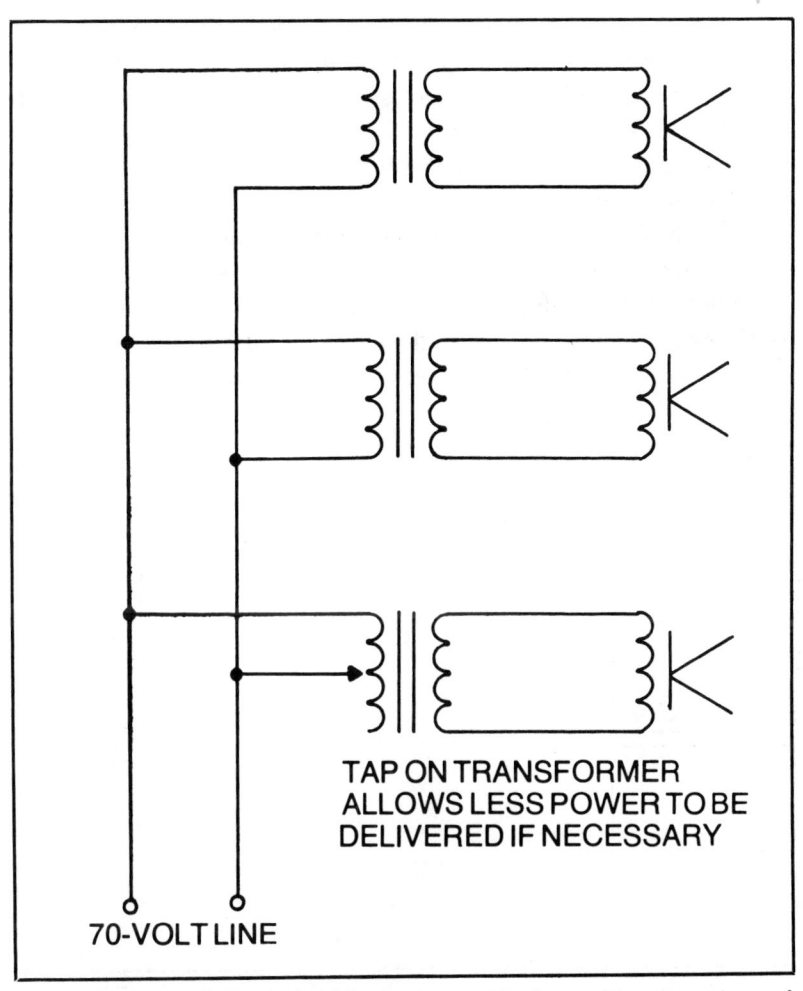

Fig. 2-16. A 70-volt line is best for long runs of wire and large numbers of loudspeakers.

Table 2-3. Wire Resistance Table.

WIRE SIZE	DIAMETER	OHMS PER 100'
12	0.081"	0.162
14	0.064"	0.26
16	0.051"	0.41
18	0.040"	0.65
20	0.032"	1.03
22	0.025"	1.65
24	0.020"	2.6

Finally, you must determine how long a run of wire you're going to have from the amplifier to the loudspeaker. From the Table 2-3 you can see that the resistance of the wire itself can, if the run is long enough, have a significant effect on the load impedance presented to the amplifier and can waste a significant amount of power.

There is a way of solving that. When the run of wire will exceed several hundred feet, you will want to go to an entirely different scheme of delivering the sound to the loudspeakers. Most of the better grade amplifiers designed for auditorium use have a 70-volt output. This presents an impedance high enough to make

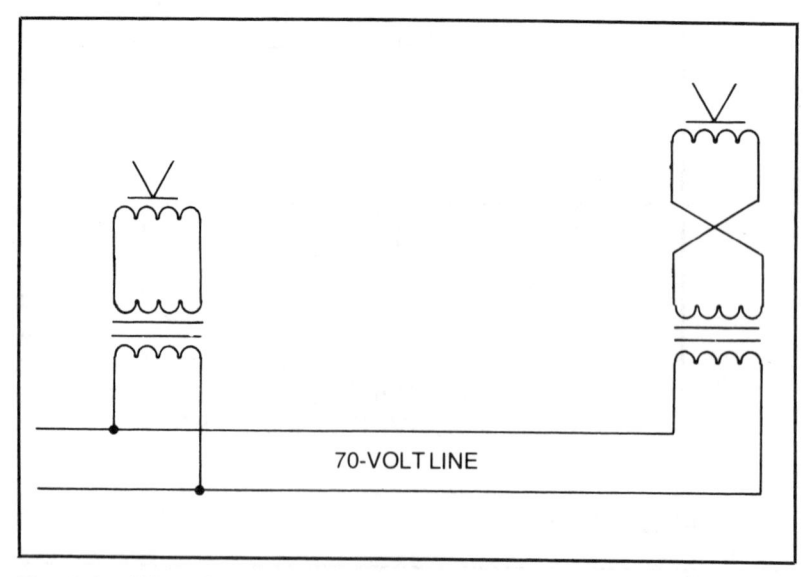

Fig. 2-17. With 70-volt line connections, phase reversal can occur if the transformer connections to the loudspeaker are reversed as shown on the right.

the resistance of the wire insignificant. The loudspeakers are then connected in parallel, each being matched to the amplifier with its own matching transformer (Fig. 2-16). These transformers, called line-to-voice-coil transformers, have several taps on the primary to apportion a discreet amount of the audio power to each speaker. To determine which tap to use, simply divide the amplifier power by the number of loudspeakers, then use the tap for the next *lower* power level.

Generally speaking, the 70-volt line is used for public address installations in large buildings. In theatrical applications, especially in large halls and where high-fidelity audio is required, large diameter wire, or high-quality transformers must be used. If the wire used is large enough, a run of several hundred feet can be made without seriously affecting the impedance match or without a significant loss of power. Loudspeaker phasing is just as important with a 70-volt line as with direct speaker connection to the amplifier. Furthermore, the phase between the line and transformer must be watched, or two reversals of phase (Fig. 2-17) result. This would put you right back where you started with the consequent deterioration of audio quality.

Chapter 3

Speakers and Speaker Systems

The basic construction and operating principles of a loudspeaker are explained in the preceding chapter. However, the speaker as described is only a part of the system used to convert the amplifier output into sound waves. Numerous other factors, such as the size and construction of the loudspeaker, the cabinet in which it is contained, even the architecture and furnishing of the room in which the sound is being reproduced, all lend to the quality of the final product.

In situations where you are simply providing background music or a speech program, many of these details can be overlooked. However, if you are after the highest possible quality, you must take all into consideration. Room acoustics are discussed briefly in the preceding chapter. Here they will be given a little further consideration.

LOUDSPEAKER TYPES

Loudspeakers can be considered in two general categories, direct radiators and horns (Fig. 3-1). The most simple is the direct radiator. This category covers all loudspeakers in which the vibrating cone sends sound waves to the listener's ears with little or no further modification. Horn loudspeakers use the acoustical effect of the horn's flare to couple the diaphragm or cone to the air, thereby giving greater efficiency and power output. The active elements of several theatrical speaker systems appear in Fig. 3-2,

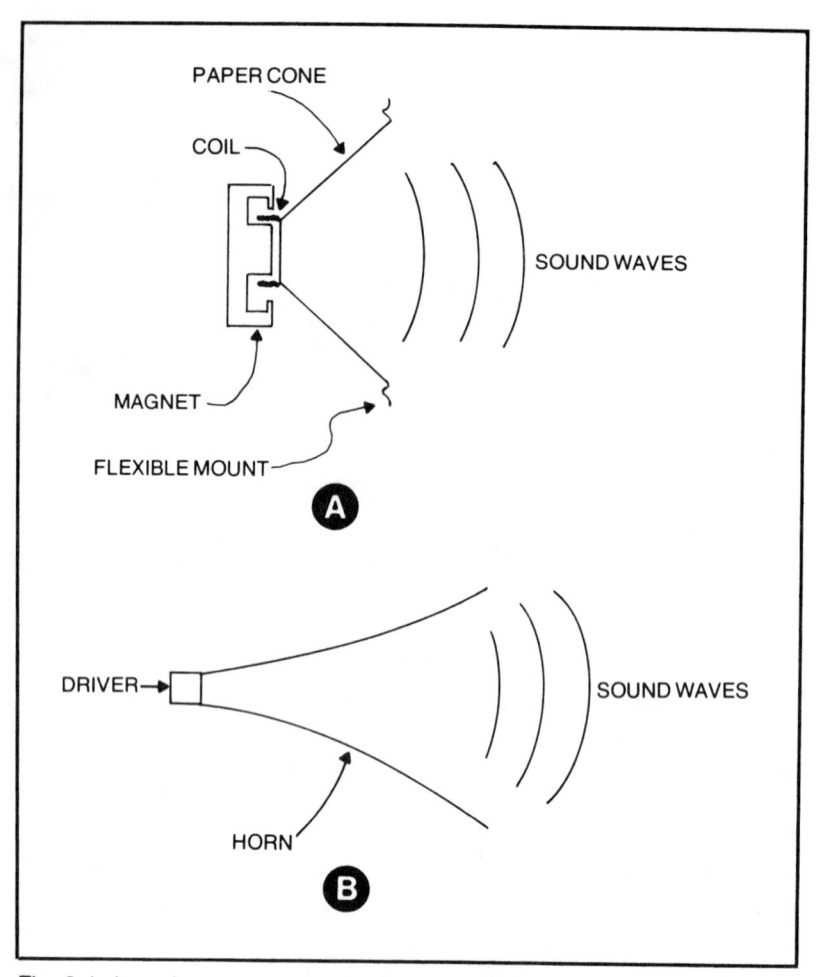

[Figure 3-1 diagram: (A) Direct radiator with labels PAPER CONE, COIL, MAGNET, FLEXIBLE MOUNT, SOUND WAVES. (B) Horn type with labels DRIVER, HORN, SOUND WAVES.]

Fig. 3-1. In a direct radiator (A), the driven diaphragm (paper cone) alone couples to the air. In a horn type (B), the driver is much smaller and is coupled to the air by a horn.

Fig. 3-3A, Fig. 3-3B and Fig. 3-4. As explained later in this chapter, it is quite possible for a single unit to fall into both of these categories.

Direct radiators are used almost universally in the less expensive indoor applications. Horns are used in most outdoor applications and in high-noise areas. Direct radiators are the less efficient, but in low-cost systems they give better quality. On the other hand, the higher priced horns are way ahead of the higher priced direct radiators where quality is concerned.

A direct radiator cannot operate on its own. It must be mounted in a suitable cabinet or be properly baffled if any kind of good quality sound is to be obtained. Horns can often be used without any kind of cabinet. However, in some systems the cabinet is itself a horn.

Many different factors are taken into consideration when the relative quality of a loudspeaker unit is examined. One of these is the impedance. There is a more detailed explanation of the nature of impedance in the first chapter, where the function of the frequency of the applied signal is explained. Since the audio-frequency spectrum covers a pretty wide range, the impedance of a loudspeaker unit can vary considerably. However, the industry has adopted standard ways of expressing this particular quality.

Loudspeakers for AM broadcast radios generally have an impedance of 3.2 ohms measured at "the first frequency above resonance that gives a minimum value when tested without a baffle." This standard applies to loudspeakers intended only for AM radios. These small speakers have a pole piece less than one inch in diameter.

Loudspeakers for sound systems are measured in a different way. The standard impedances, 4, 8, and 16 ohms, actually represent pure resistance values (specified by the manufacturer) that are used to measure the available power to the unit.

Fig. 3-2. Shown here are active elements of a theatrical speaker system. Low frequencies are covered by the large direct radiator. The driver for the high-frequency horn is in the bottom center (photo courtesy Altec).

Fig. 3-3A. A baffle forms a horn to distribute sound. The high-frequency unit is a multi-section exponential horn (photo courtesy Altec).

In direct radiators, the type of cone used reveals the relative quality of the unit. In general, inexpensive units have a thinner, stiffer cone and persons with a well trained ear can simply tap very lightly on the cone with a finger and get a rough idea of the resonant

60

frequency of the cone by the sound that results. Inexpensive units will have a higher resonant frequency than a quality unit of the same size.

Fig. 3-3B. The baffle is a bass-reflex exponential horn cabinet (photo courtesy Altec).

Loudspeakers for AM radios have a built-in resonance in the neighborhood of 4000 Hz. This helps compensate for the limited frequency range broadcast by AM stations. Paging and background music systems use direct radiators with cone diameters of roughly six to eight inches. Low-priced home music systems and public address systems use anywhere from eight-to-10 inch speakers. Twelve-to 15-inch speakers are used mostly for the low-frequency portion of multi-speaker systems.

High-frequency "tweeters" are often horn type. If they are direct radiators, they will be four inches or less in diameter and have a fairly stiff cone. The so-called "wide-range" units have two cones. The wider one handles the low end of the audio spectrum and a smaller stiff cone reproduces the high frequencies. The high-frequency cone is mounted concentric with the bass cone at the small end while the wide end is independent of any fastening (Fig. 3-5). The less expensive wide-range loudspeakers have either a flexible cone or one that is divided into two or more sections by means of corrugations midway between the voice coil and the mouth. This allows the inner portion to vibrate at high frequencies, while the whole cone can still vibrate as a single unit at low frequencies.

Fig. 3-4. At bottom left is a simple direct radiator. A dual-cone unit is in the center. In the back center and left are two units which include horn tweeters and direct radiator bass cones (photo courtesy Altec).

The size and weight of the magnet betrays a loudspeaker's worth. Inexpensive units have a much smaller magnet than the more expensive ones. The larger magnet produces greater cone movement without distortion. While this is noticed only at the higher volume levels, it nonetheless must be considered when you're setting up for a large audience.

Loudspeakers for the bass (Fig. 3-6) portion of the spectrum (and those used for musical instruments) should be well damped. Damping means that when the cone is vibrated by a signal, it won't keep vibrating once the signal is removed. Poorly damped speakers will vibrate for a fraction of a second after the signal impulse passes. This makes certain sounds, such as a roll of drums, come out muddy.

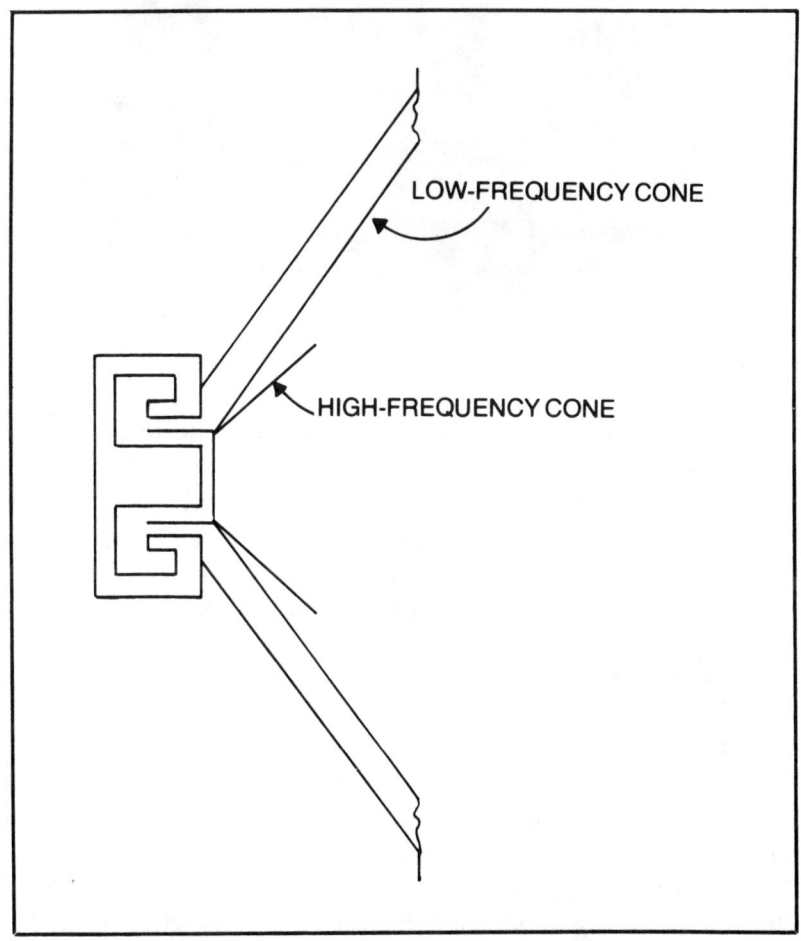

Fig. 3-5. A dual-cone direct radiator. The paper cone radiates the low frequencies, while the highs are handled by the stiff, smaller cone.

Fig. 3-6. An Electro-Voice vented base speaker system.

    All loudspeakers, except those in specially designed enclosures, have a particular directional pattern of radiation. As a general rule, these patterns are much more restricted at high frequencies than at low frequencies (Fig. 3-7). In fact, many of the better systems have several high-frequency horns oriented to spread the high-frequency radiation to approximately equal that provided for the low frequencies.

    Some systems take advantage of directional radiation patterns and deliberately arrange those patterns to better suit the user's needs. Loudspeaker columns are an excellent example of this. This arrangement radiates a wide plane of sound with relatively little vertical spread (Fig. 3-7 and E), thereby eliminating unwanted echoes from the ceiling. Portable columns, consisting of a number of oval-shaped speakers, are very popular with square-dance callers. These people frequently have to set up in gymnasiums or other accoustically poor places where they must be clearly heard in all parts of the room.

Here are the qualities to look for in a good loudspeaker:
- Sufficient power-handling capability
- Satisfactory sensitivty
- Sufficient damping at the bass resonant frequency
- Good transient response
- Smooth frequency response
- Low distortion over the frequency range
- Broad directivity

Any loudspeaker is a compromise. When you reduce the thickness of the cone material to increase the sensitivity, you

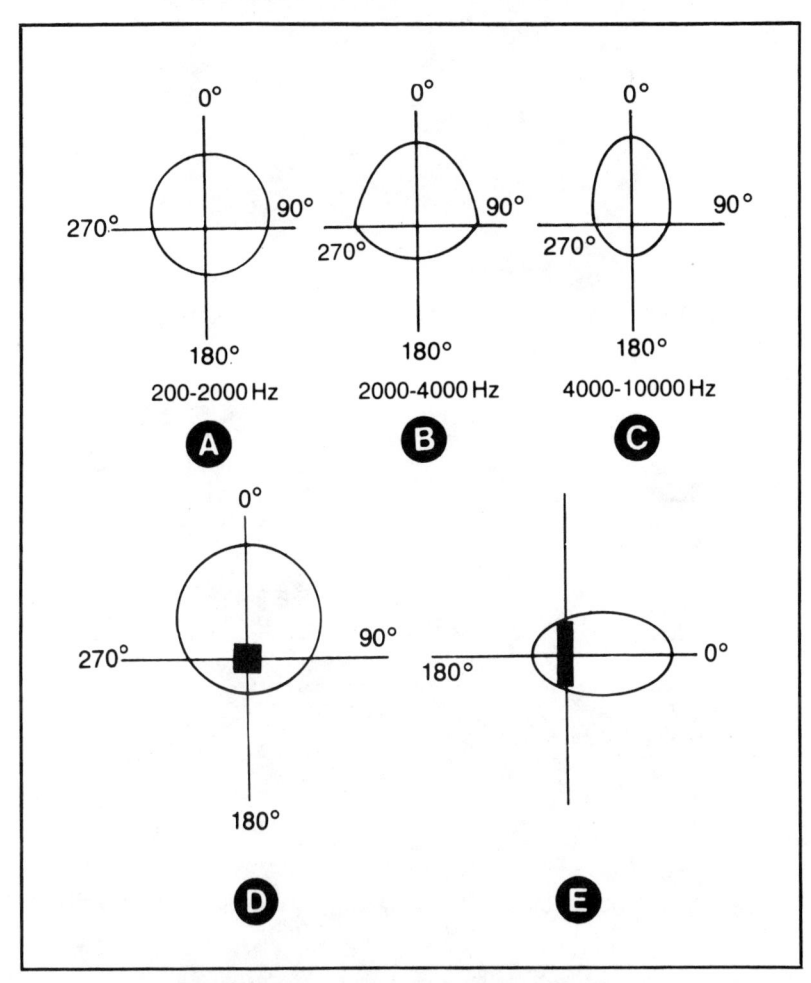

Fig. 3-7. Typical speaker radiation patterns. The first three (A, B and C) show typical sound radiation from a loudspeaker unit at various ranges. Note that the higher the frequency, the narrower the pattern. The remaining two drawings show the sound dispersal pattern of a column unit as seen from above (D) and as seen from the side (E). Note that the horizontal spread is almost negligible.

Fig. 3-8. A two-way multiple speaker system (photo courtesy Electro-Voice Inc.).

Fig. 3-9. A three-way multiple speaker system. The baffle openings improve response uniformity (photo courtesy Electro-Voice Inc.).

increase distortion and increase the bass resonance, and the bass response deteriorates. A larger, heavy cone is excellent for bass reproduction. A thin, light cone is excellent for highs. Neither of the two will work well in the other's "territory." That is, the large cone is very poor at reproducing highs and the small cone is poor at the low end. Hence the invention of multiple-speaker systems (Fig. 3-8).

A direct-radiator loudspeaker will not sound right unless it is mounted on a baffle or in an enclosure of some sort. Without the baffle, air pressure from the front of the unit is out of phase with that from the back at a frequency depending on the front-to-back distance. At this frequency, there is a definite dip in the response. The use of a baffle lowers this dip to a frequency below the range needed for a particular installation.

BAFFLES

Most of the engineering charts concerning baffles are plotted with respect to a flat baffle, which is seldom used in practice. Furthermore, to make the resonance less pronounced the loudspeaker is usually mounted off center in the baffle. For example, a 10-inch loudspeaker with a 4-foot square baffle may be mounted 18 inches from two adjacent sides. Figure 3-9 gives some idea of baffle size with respect to minimum frequency.

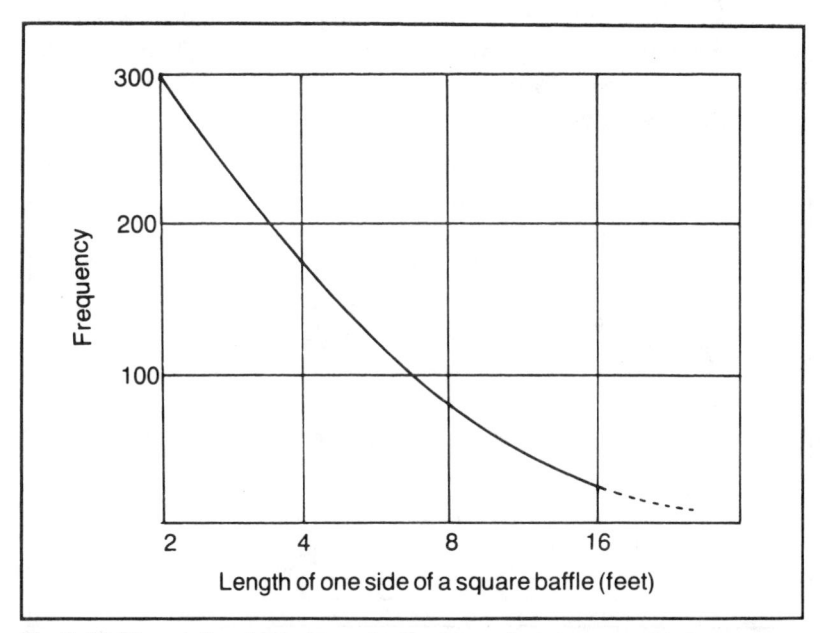

Fig. 3-10. The relationship between baffle size and minimum usable frequency.

The ideal flat baffle is the wall of a room with the back of the cone radiating into the adjacent room. Open-back cabinets can be looked at almost as if they were flat baffles with the sides folded over, provided they aren't deep enough to exhibit significant resonance characteristics. Even shallow cabinets, however, can produce a resonance at least 6 dB above the average response. Deeper cabinets can have peaks twice as high. For these reasons, they are not too desirable where excellence in fidelity is concerned. If they must be used, they should be eight inches or more from the wall, with as little accoustical obstruction as possible.

The opposite extreme is a cabinet that is totally enclosed (Fig. 3-10). While there is no real critical rule concerning the volume of the enclosure, it should be noted that such an enclosure does increase the resonant frequency of the speaker (Fig. 3-11). The larger the volume of the cabinet, the less that resonant frequency is increased. However, there are practical limits beyond which the enclosure begins to resemble a small room. The behavior of the system is similar to that of a nearly infinite flat baffle.

The best of two worlds can be had in the vented baffle, also called the acoustical phase inverter, or bass reflex baffle (Fig. 3-12). It is an enclosed cabinet with a rectangular opening beneath the speaker opening. In the better cabinets, this rectangular opening is one end of a short "tunnel" into the cabinet. Cabinet volume, tunnel length and vent opening area all play a part in determining the overall performance of the system. Their relationship and effect on performance is very complex—too much so for a comprehensive coverage in this book.

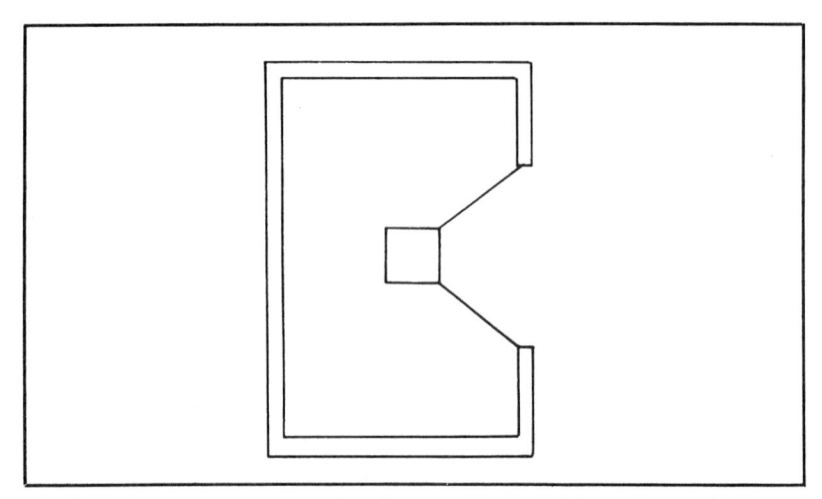

Fig. 3-11. An enclosed cabinet. There is no outlet except from the speaker cone.

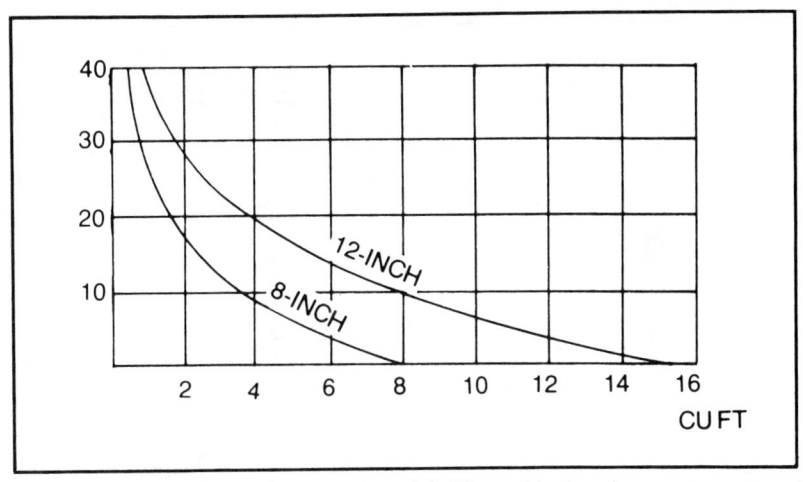

Fig. 3-12. The effect of an enclosed baffle cabinet volume on resonant frequency.

The next step in loudspeaker system evolution is the *acoustical Labyrinth* (Fig. 3-13). This a trademark term of the Stromberg-Carlson Co. system consists of a cabinet interior that is a long, folded tube lined with sound-absorbing materials. Some people compare it with a vented baffle having the longest possible tunnel, but this is perhaps a poor analogy. While its behavior is similar to that of a vented baffle, it does have the unusual characteristic of lowering the resonant frequency of the

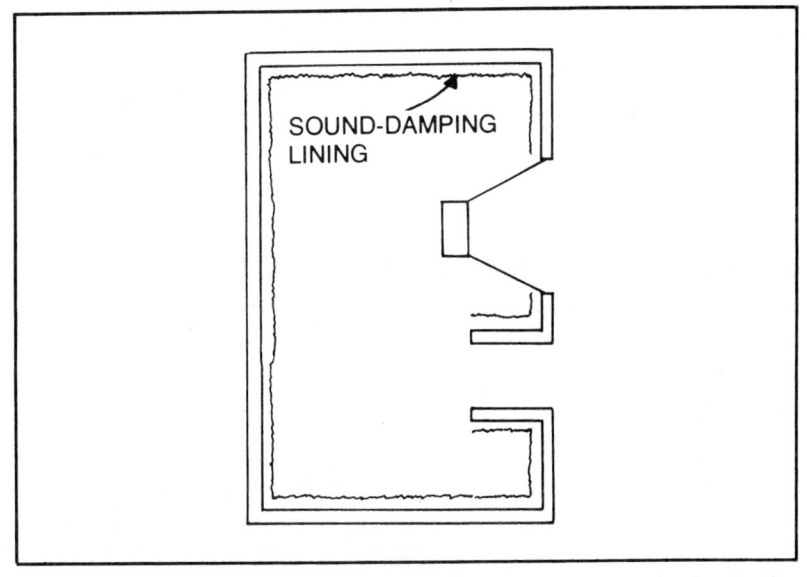

Fig. 3-13. A vented baffle or bass-reflex cabinet. In the lower priced units, the "tunnel" is omitted, leaving just an opening.

69

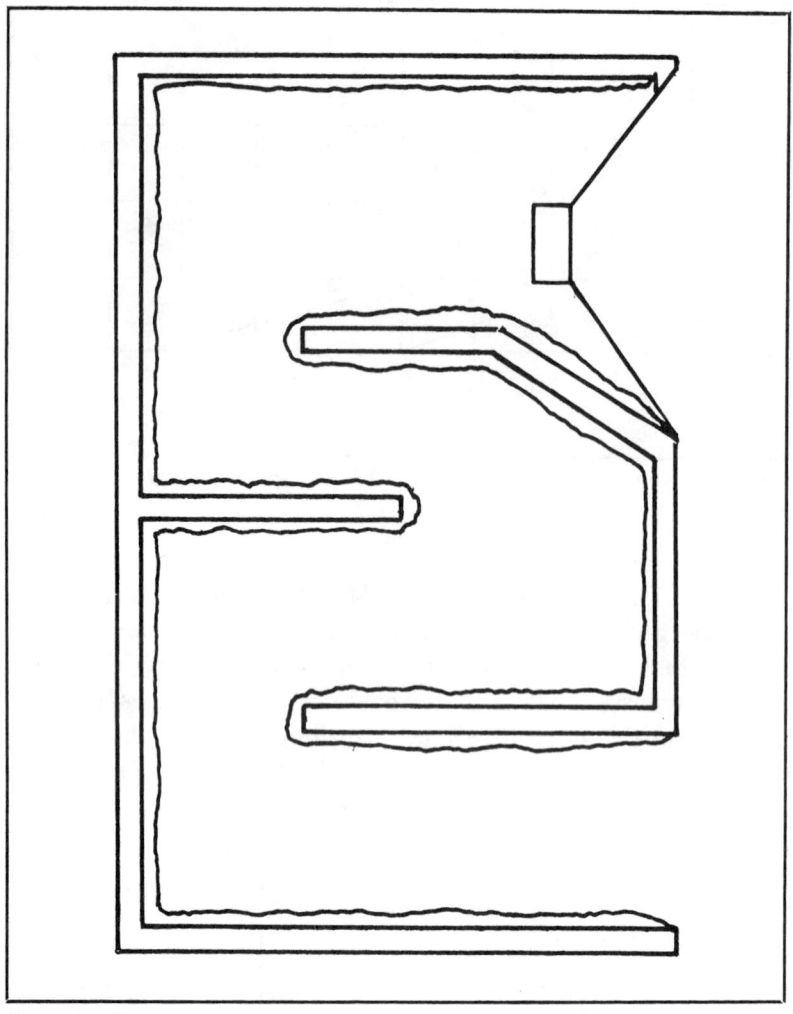

Fig. 3-14. Cross-sectional view of an acoustical Labyrinth cabinet, just a step from a folded horn.

loudspeaker element. In the opinion of this writer, the acoustical Labyrinth represents something halfway between a direct radiator and a horn loudspeaker.

HORN INSTALLATIONS

This brings us to the more interesting of loudspeaker systems, the general category of horn units. While nearly everyone is familiar with the horn loudspeakers used out of doors, and while you may never have considered quality a prime factor in a bull horn, horns can be both the most efficient and can offer the highest quality in the loudspeaker family.

There are two major classes of horns: conical and exponential. A conical horn is one having straight sides and a uniform rate of spread or horn flare. These are sometimes used with cone-type loudspeakers to give directional characteristics. Also, exponential horns are sometimes approximated in "economy" units by joining together a number of cones of varying degrees of taper. Such an arrangement is nowhere near as effective as an exponential horn.

In general, the high-frequency response of a horn loudspeaker is limited by the design of both the transducer and the relationship of the diaphragm to the area of the throat opening (Fig. 3-14). This is a very complex relationship of interest only to those who design the units. The low-frequency response is related to the throat area and to the length and final diameter of the horn. The transducer can be a specially designed device similar to an earphone, or it can be a well designed direct-radiator loudspeaker.

Horn loudspeakers can be as high as 80% efficient over a limited frequency range, which makes them so popular in high-noise areas and outdoors. Cinema-quality units have a wider frequency range, but are a bit less efficient (30% to 45%). The Klipsch corner horn is 50% efficient over its useful range.

Once in a great while, you may see a straight horn, but most horn loudspeakers are folded as shown in Fig. 3-15. An exponential

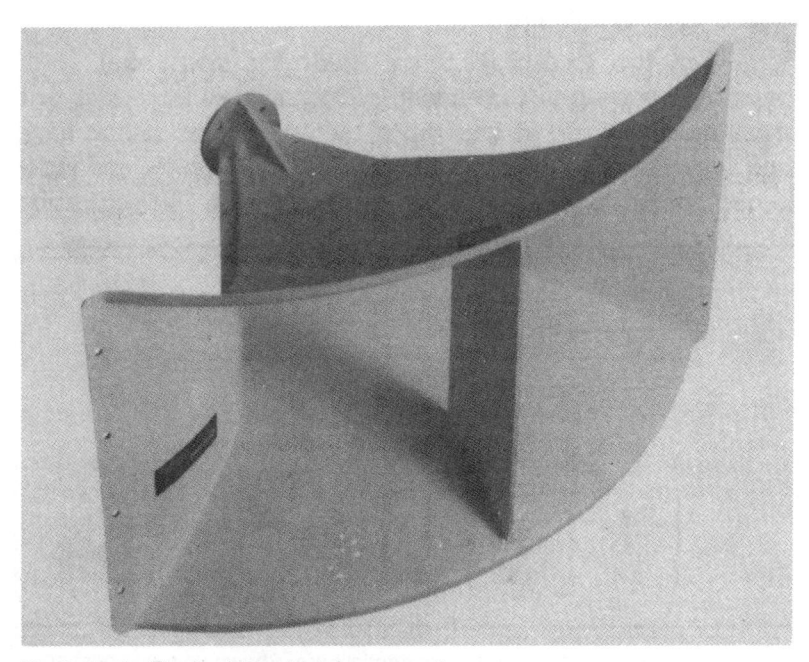

Fig. 3-15. An Electro-Voice high frequency horn.

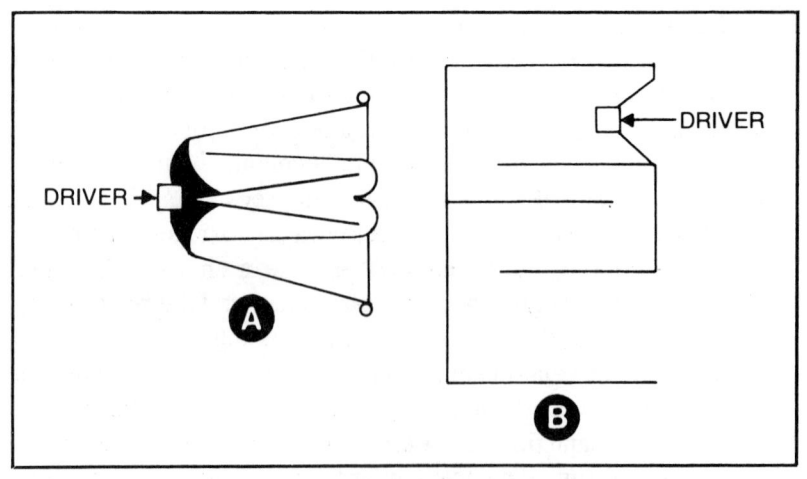

Fig. 3-16. Two kinds of folded horns. One is designed for outdoor use (A) and the other (B) is designed for indoor applications.

horn is one in which the flaring of the horn follows a particular mathematical relationship to its length and throat area (Fig. 3-16 and Fig. 3-17). While an ideal one is impractical (30 feet long and made of cement), it can be made of less than ideal materials, folded into a small volume by comparison and still be the highest quality loudspeaker on the market.

CROSS-OVER NETWORKS

When two loudspeakers are used as a single unit, each covering a portion of the audible spectrum, it is important that signal meant for one be kept out of the other. Bass signals have sufficient power to burn out a high-frequency tweeter and high-frequency signals are often distorted in a bass unit. The separation

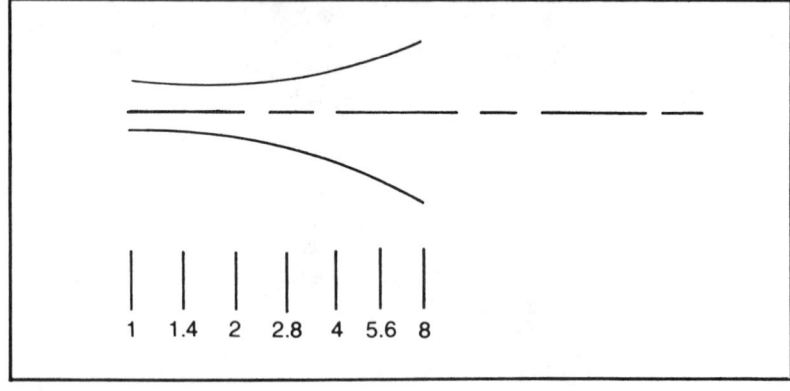

Fig. 3-17. Flare ratios for an ideal exponential horn. Shown as a rate of change in diameter versus unit length.

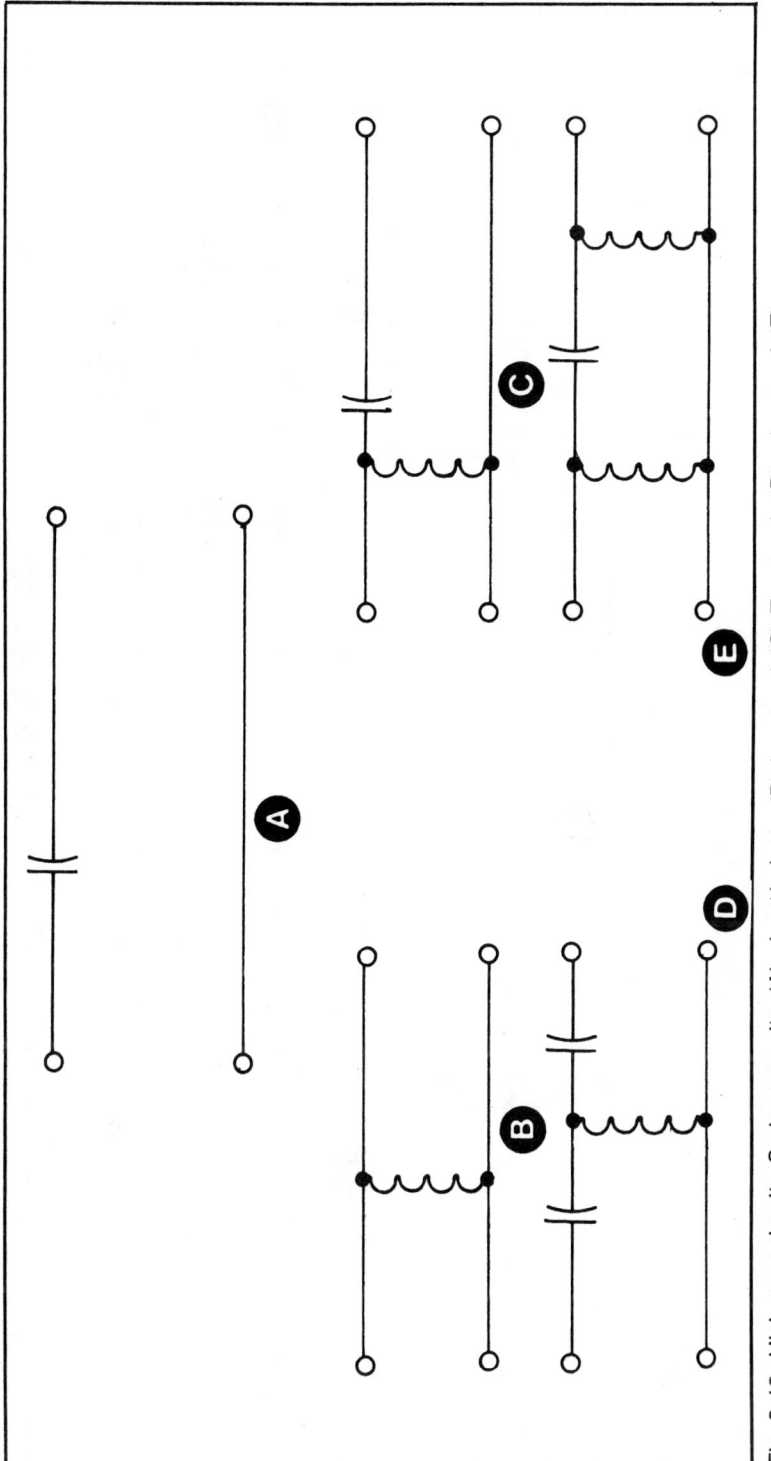

Fig. 3-18. High-pass circuits. Series capacitor (A), shunt inductor (B), L-network (C), T-network (D), pi-network (E).

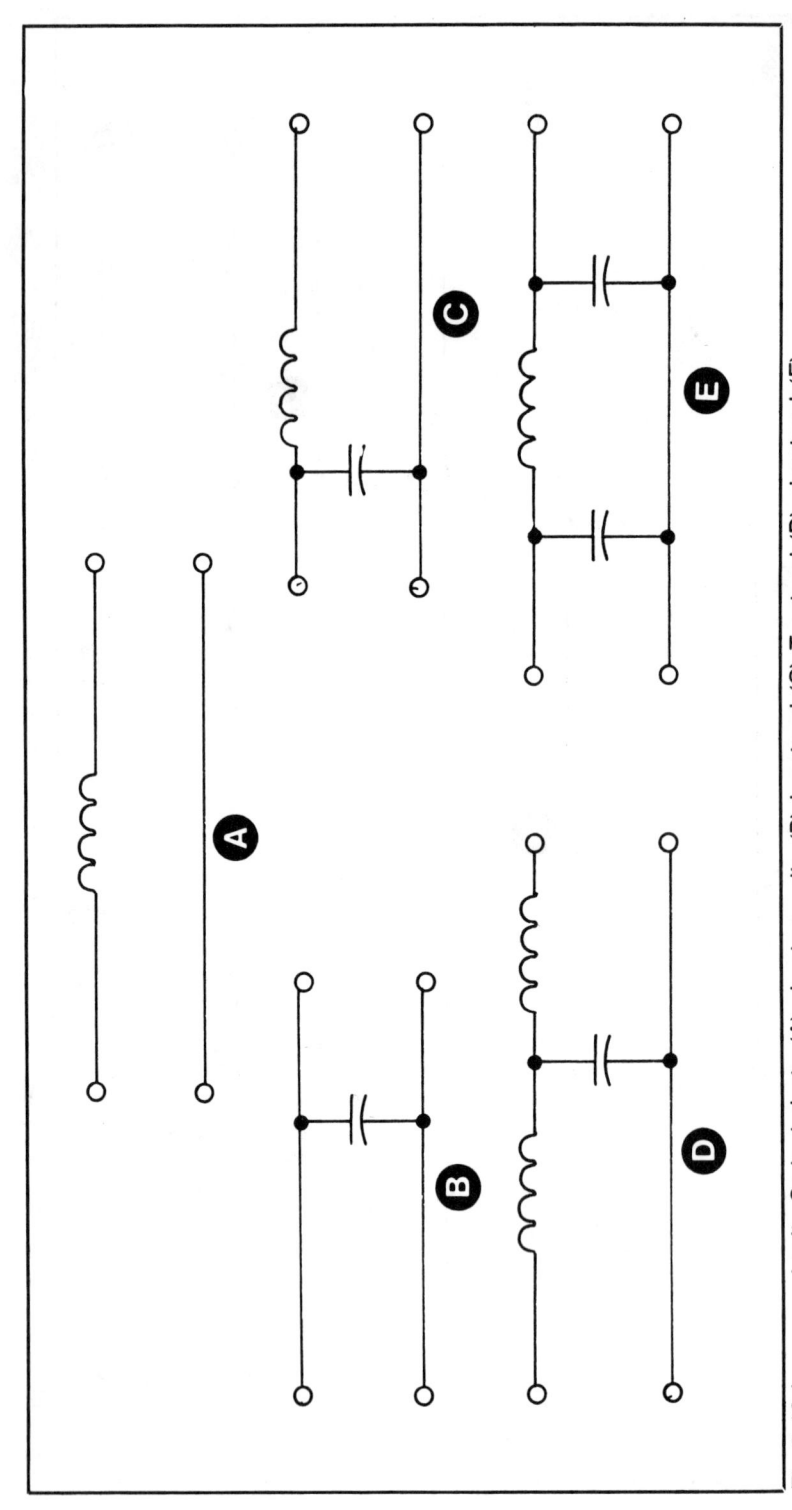

Fig. 3-19. Low-pass circuits. Series inductor (A), shunt capacitor (B), L-network (C), T-network (D), pi-network (E).

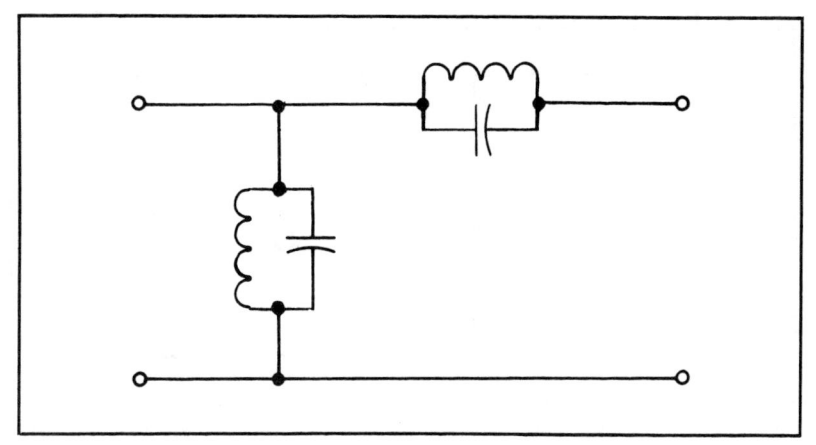

Fig. 3-20. Shunt and series band-pass filter circuit.

of the portions of the audible spectrum and the isolation of the speakers from one another are accomplished by a crossover network. A crossover network is a system of filters that allow only the desired signals to be fed to a given load. In these instances, the load is the loudspeaker.

FILTERS

Basically, there are three kinds of filters: high-pass, low-pass and band-pass. A high-pass filter allows signal frequencies above its cutoff point to pass, while lower frequency signals are attenuated. A low-pass filter allows signal frequencies below the cutoff point to pass, while high frequencies are attenuated. A band-pass has two cutoff points. It allows frequencies between two

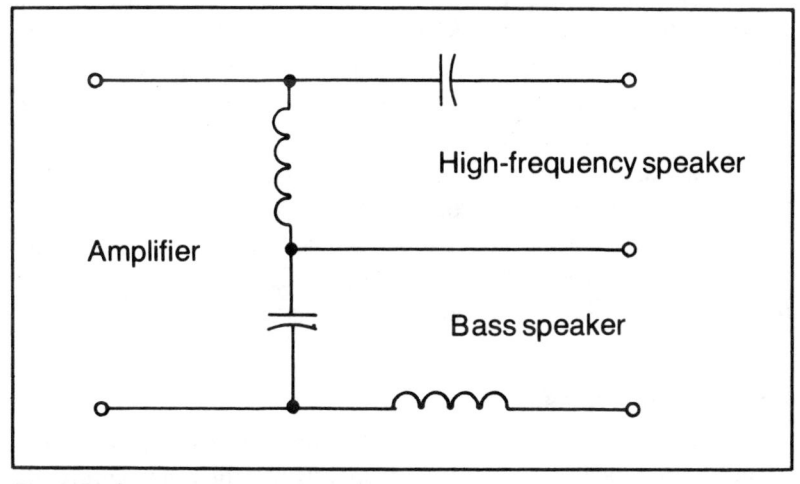

Fig. 3-21. Series frequency dividing circuit.

75

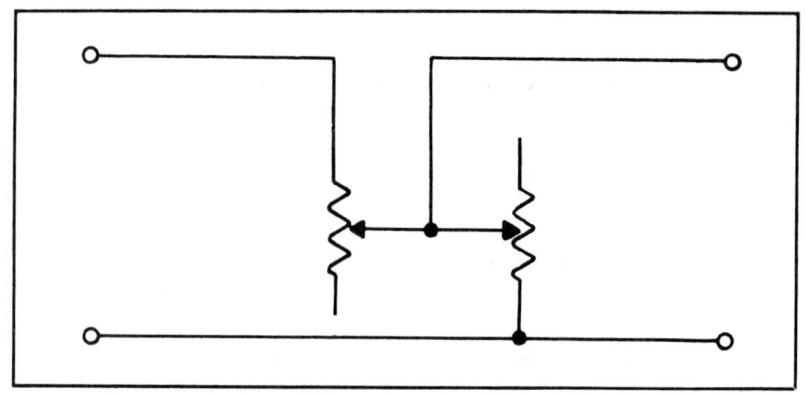

Fig. 3-22. Circuit of an L-pad level control.

points to pass, while all others are attenuated. In each case, the amount of attenuation depends on the design of the filter and the difference between the frequency being attenuated and the cutoff frequency. It is generally expressed as being a certain number of decibels per octave (6 and 12 being common attenuation rates).

The simplest high-pass filter circuit is a series capacitor (Fig. 3-18A). Improved attenuation characteristics can be obtained by adding one or more shunt inductors and series capacitors (Fig. 3-18B through C).

The simplest form of a low-pass circuit is a series inductor (Fig. 3-19). Additional attenuation is obtained by adding one or more shunt capacitors and series inductors. Note that the two types of filters, high-pass and low-pass, are complementary look-alikes.

A bandpass filter is no more than a high-pass filter and a low-pass filter combined into the same circuit (Fig. 3-20). In its design, different cutoff frequencies are selected, one for the high pass and one for the low pass. The result is a unit that passes only a desired band of frequencies.

In actual installation the loudspeakers appear to be connected in series. However, when you realize that each is getting only its intended portion of the spectrum, each sees the full output of the amplifier. The series connection in (Fig. 3-21) is preferred because it offers the least power loss due to filter insertion.

LOUDNESS CONTROLS

When loudspeakers of different impedances are used for separate portions of the audible spectrum, they are likely to reproduce sounds at different loudness levels. In such a case, an

L-pad level control (Fig. 3-22) on one unit can achieve balance by varying the loudness of one of them. To achieve this balance, operate first one, then the other, at the crossover frequency. Then adjust the pad until both produce the same sound level.

It is important that the loudspeakers be correctly phased in this kind of installation. Phasing requirements for multiple-speaker installations are shown in Chapter 2.

Chapter 4

Amplifiers and Amplifying Systems

The development of the transistor was a major step forward in the electronics industry, not only because of its small size and mechanical ruggedness, but also because it does not need a filament which consumes a great deal of power in vacuum-tube circuits. Today there are very few applications where tubes still hold the edge over solid-state devices, and this number is growing ever smaller. However, it still pays to be aware of the similarities and differences between the two.

VACUUM TUBE VERSUS SOLID-STATE EQUIPMENT

Both vacuum tubes and transistors have a principle input element, a grounded element, and a principle output element. However, a tube operates with current flowing through a vacuum, while a transistor operates with current flowing through a solid. A tube amplifies voltage, while a transistor amplifies current. A tube can withstand accidental high-voltage input surges and accidental momentary overloads without ill effect, while a transistor will blow instantly under those same conditions.

While vacuum-tube equipment is outmoded for the most part, there is still quite a bit of it in use. Chances are you may run across some that will still do a good job if you know what to do with it.

A vacuum tube contains a *filament*, similar to that in an incandescent lamp, which heats a small, metal tube that surrounds it (Fig. 4-1). This tube, called the *cathode*, emits electrons when

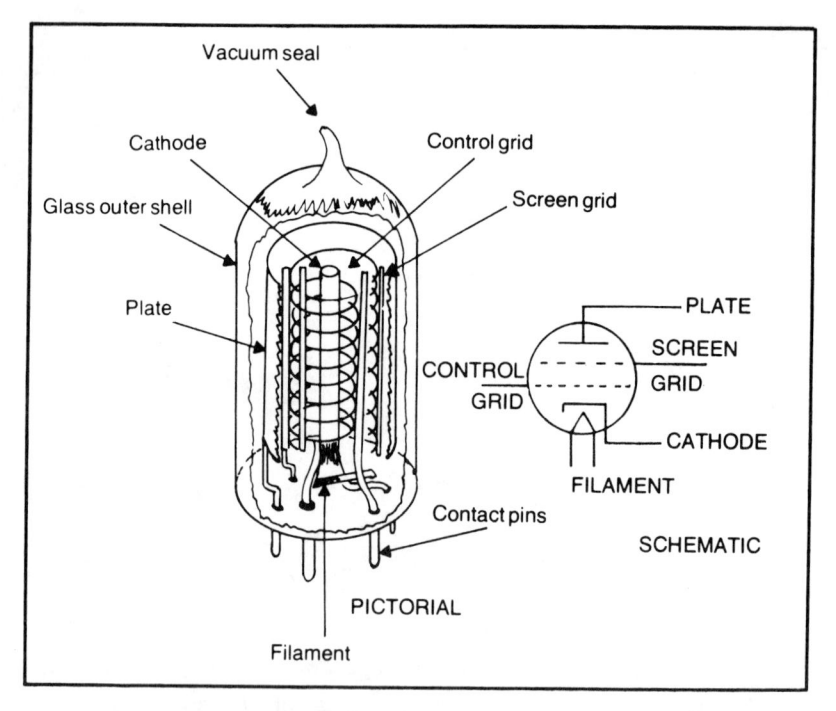

Fig. 4-1. Pictorial and schematic of one type of vacuum tube.

hot. A metal *plate* surrounding the tube contains a positive charge that attracts the electrons emitted by the cathode. Therefore, electrons flow through the tube from cathode to plate. Between the cathode and the plate (or anode) there is an element consisting of a wire *grid*, upon which the signal to be amplified is imposed. Variations in signal voltage on the grid cause large variations in the electron flow to the plate. Therefore, the tube amplifies the signal applied to the grid.

Junction transistors are the most common type used in audio work. A junction transistor consists of a tiny "sandwich" of germanium specks (Fig. 4-2), each doped with impurities to give it the desired electrical characteristics. Germanium so doped in either P type or N type. A transistor can be either a P-N-P or an N-P-N sandwich. Either kind works equally well, although one sequence requires operating voltages of opposite polarity to the other. The three specks of germanium in a junction transistor form two junctions. One is called the *emitter*, and the other, the *collector*. Minute variations of signal current between the base and the emitter cause large variations in the current flowing between the emitter and collector. Therefore the transistor amplifies.

The basic vacuum-tube circuit requires a positive high voltage on the plate and a small negative charge on the grid to ensure linear operation (Fig. 4-3). The grid bias is usually obtained by inserting a resistor of a few hundred ohms between the cathode and the ground (Fig. 4-4A). This holds the cathode at a slight positive potential with respect to the ground, therefore keeping the grid, which is at or near ground potential, negative with respect to the cathode.

The plate circuit has a load resistor between the plate and the high-voltage source, in the order of a few hundred thousand ohms. The amplified signal voltage appears across this resistor. In a power output stage the output transformer primary winding serves in place of the plate load resistor. In order to avoid negative feedback (development of an out-of-phase signal voltage in the cathode circuit), which would result in a loss of gain, the cathode resistor is bypassed with a capacitor of several microfarads (Fig. 4-4).

If the tube is a tetrode (4-element), it will have a screen grid, which is connected to the high-voltage source through a resistor of several thousand ohms. (The 3-element tube in Fig. 4-4A is called triode.) In addition, a pentode (5 element) will have a suppressor

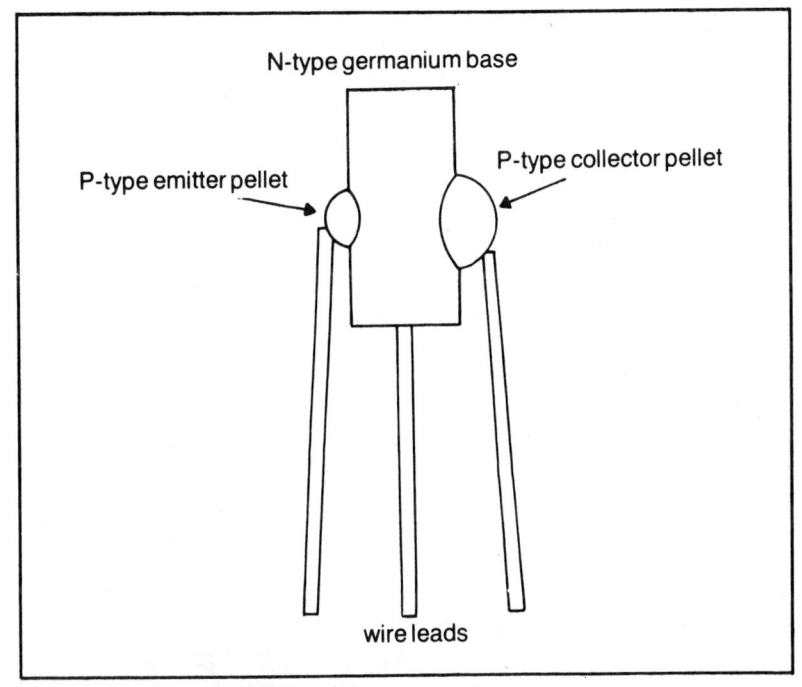

Fig. 4-2. Drawing of a PNP transistor.

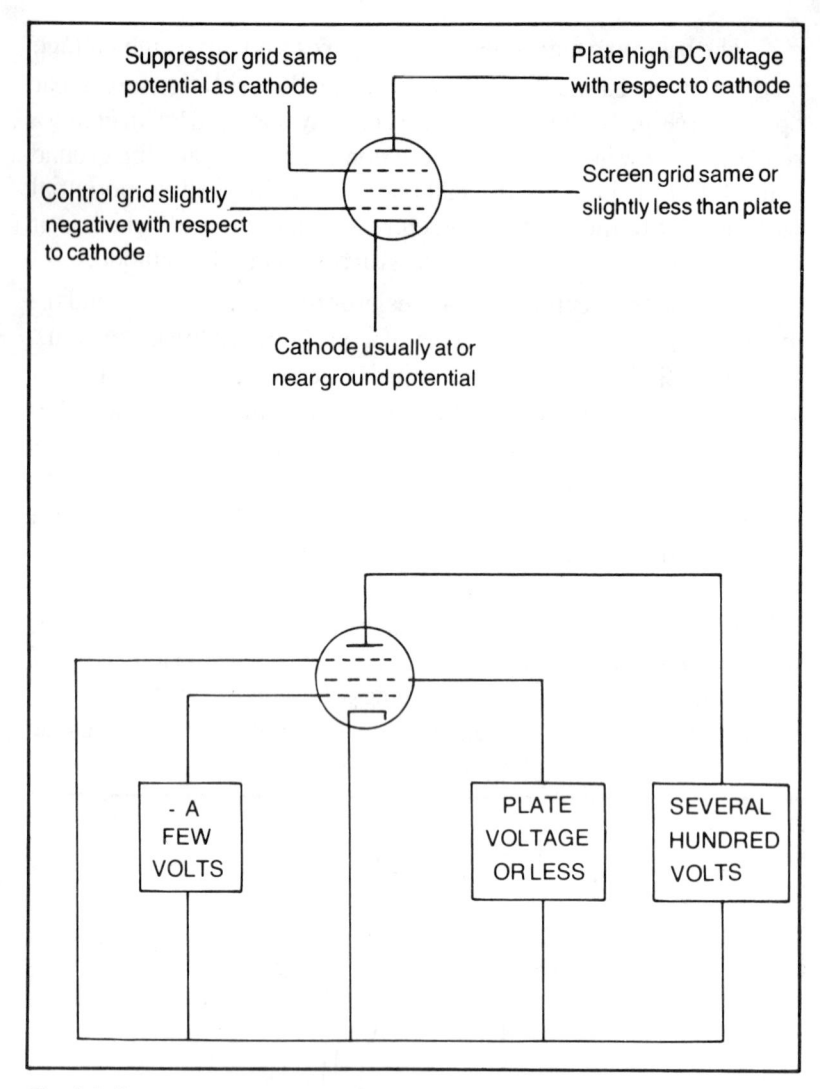

Fig. 4-3. Power supply requirements for a vacuum tube amplifier.

grid connected either to ground or to the cathode. If the screen grid high voltage is lost, the tube will not operate. The screen grid in a vacuum tube serves as a helper to the plate (attracting electrons from the cathode), and the suppressor grid functions as a shield to prevent electrons from escaping from the plate once attracted to it.

Transistor amplifier circuits are considerably simpler than those of vacuum tubes. The emitter, like the cathode of a tube, is connected to ground through a small resistor (Fig. 4-5A). However, its purpose is different from that of the vacuum-tube counterpart. The emitter sets the level of current flowing through the base-emitter junction. The voltage on this junction is set with a simple voltage divider. The base-emitter junction is negative if a PNP transistor is used and positive if an NPN transistor is used. There is usually a 0.7-volt difference between the emitter and the base terminals. Like the plate of a tube, the collector circuit of a

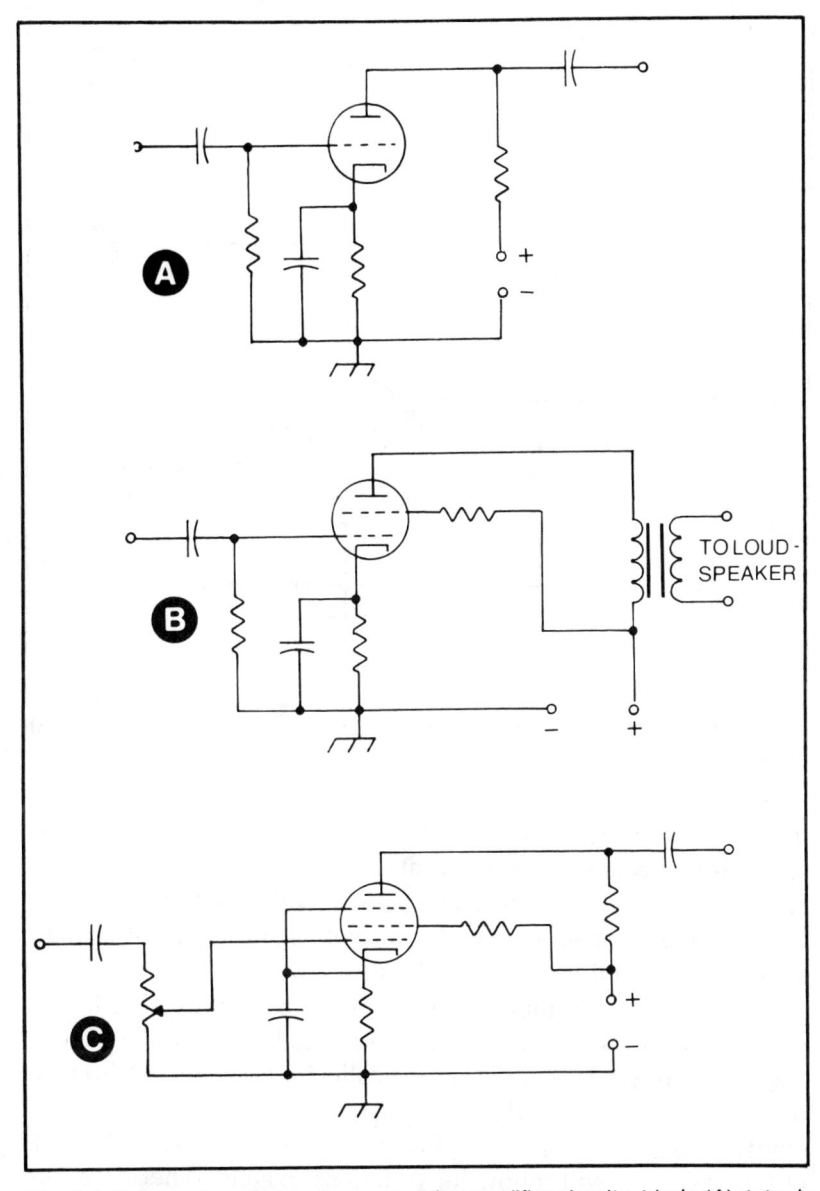

Fig. 4-4. Schematics of typical vacuum tube amplifier circuits: triode (A), tetrode (B), pentode (C).

83

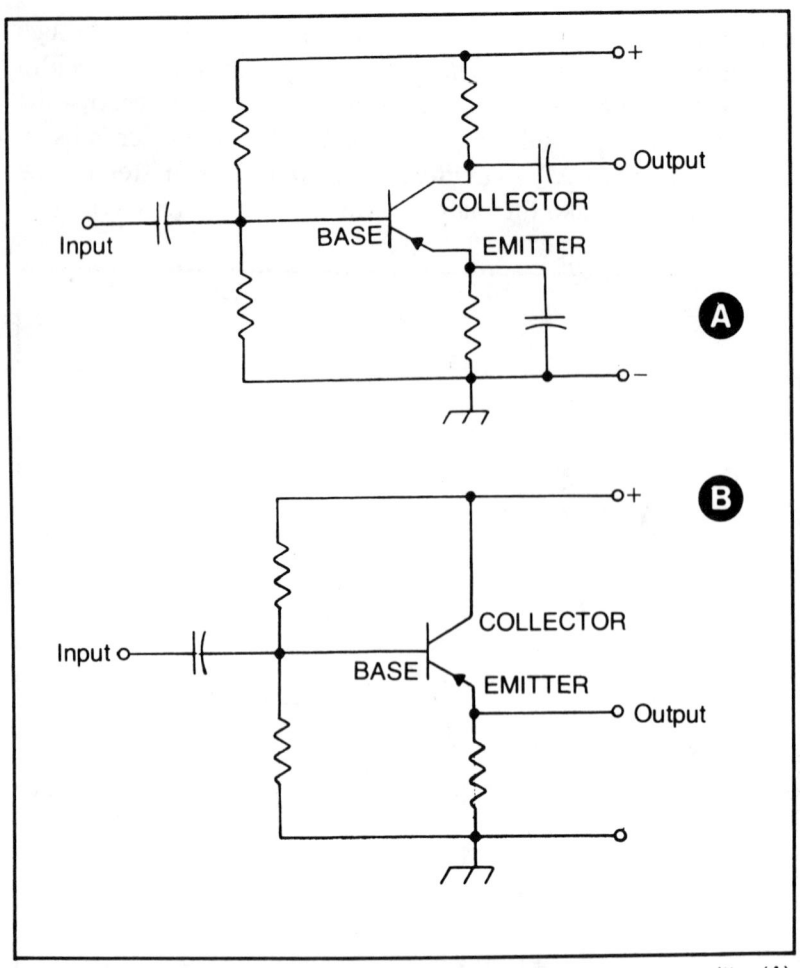

Fig. 4-5. Schematics of typical transistor amplifier circuits: common emitter (A) and emitter follower (B).

transistor has a load resistor, but it is much lower in value than its vacuum-tube counterpart. Current flow in the collector circuit is higher then current flow in a tube plate circuit. Therefore, a lower value load resistor produces a higher voltage drop (signal voltage amplified) in a collector circuit ($E = I \times R$).

Solid-state amplifiers often avoid the use of a bulky, heavy output transformer by using an emitter follower for the output stage (Fig. 4-5B). In this circuit, the collector is connected directly to the power source and the load resistor is connected between the emitter and the ground. The emitter voltage will not rise above that of the base, but will follow its variations exactly. Therefore, an emitter follower has a voltage gain of unity, but has a high current gain. The emitter circuit of a transistor is generally quite low in impedance, allowing the speakers to be driven directly.

Because of the complementary characteristic of transistors, they can be made to drive successive stages directly (Fig. 4-6) without coupling capacitors. This not only saves the cost of parts, it greatly extends the bass response of the circuit.

AMPLIFIER INPUTS

There are a great many types of audio input connectors in use, although a few are found more frequently than others. Phono inputs frequently consist of the "RCA"-type phono connectors—about a quarter-inch across, looking like a little silver doughnut on the back panel of the amplifier. The male connector can be a bit tricky to put on the cable, but it is well shielded and doesn't have to be threaded onto the female, it simply plugs in.

On the older units, microphone connectors were threaded with a small solder dot for the center contact. These had the advantage that the male connector could be quickly changed to a female connector simply by unscrewing the ground-contact ring. It would then mate with another male cable end, making it possible to connect a series of cables end-to-end. When it comes to putting one of these on the end of a cable, I'd prefer to work on any of several other connectors.

More up-to-date amplifiers have microphone connectors consisting of two prongs on the male end that mate with the chassis

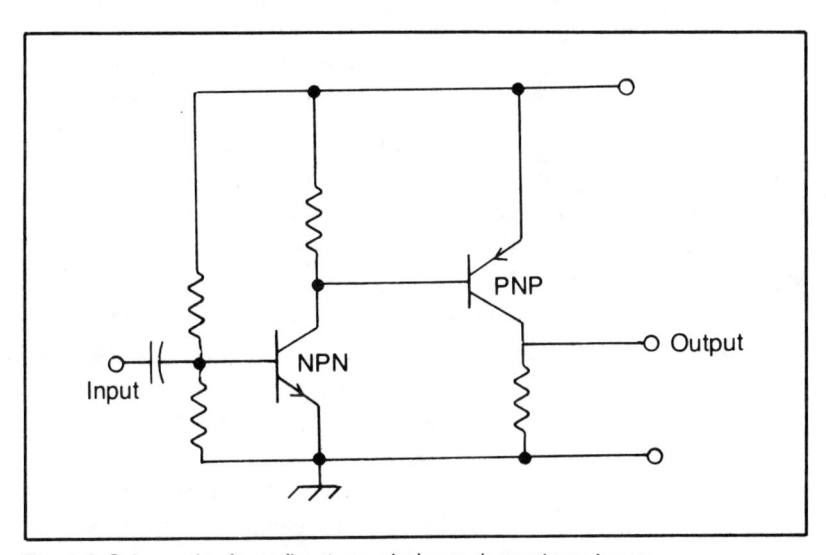

Fig. 4-6. Schematic of two direct-coupled complementary stages.

connector and a threaded retainer ring similar to the older type. These are easier to install and have the mechanical strength of the older type. Of course, there are many other types, but these are the most frequently encountered with amateur equipment.

Input circuitry depends on the kind of device intended to feed into the amplifier. High-impedance microphone inputs sometimes feed through a frequency-response equalizing network, directly to a gain control potentiometer and then to the grid of the tube or the base of the transistor. In the more expensive amplifiers low-impedance microphone inputs have a transformer between the connector and the first amplifier stage.

Phone inputs, like high-impedance microphone inputs, feed directly to the gain-control potentiometer. Some amplifiers have a PHONO 1 and PHONO 2 input, served by a single gain control potentiometer. In the center of its rotation, the control allows no signal to enter from either input. Rotating it one way opens one input and rotating it on the other way opens the other input. Inputs for the better grade, low-impedance phono inputs have an equalizer network, often with a switch to select the desired frequency-response characteristics.

VOLUME, GAIN AND LOUDNESS CONTROLS

You would be almost correct in insisting that volume, gain and loudness controls all produce the same end result. However, there is a slight technical difference. A volume control is what you're most likely to see. It simply raises or lowers the level of the signal going into the amplifier. However, since the human ear responds differently to low sound levels, sound quality appears to change with the setting of a simple volume control.

To compensate for this, some of the better amplifier units have a resistance-capacitance network which boosts the bass response at low-level settings, thereby making the sound quality appear to remain constant as the volume is reduced. Such a compensating control is known as a loudness control (Fig. 4-7).

Audio compressors work by controlling the actual amount of gain in the amplifier stage. Controls that accomplish this are more properly known as gain controls. As front-panel controls, however, gain controls are more common in radio communication than in audio work.

A well constructed public address system may use attenuator pads such as those described in a later chapter as part of their mixing system. Generally speaking, however, the more economi-

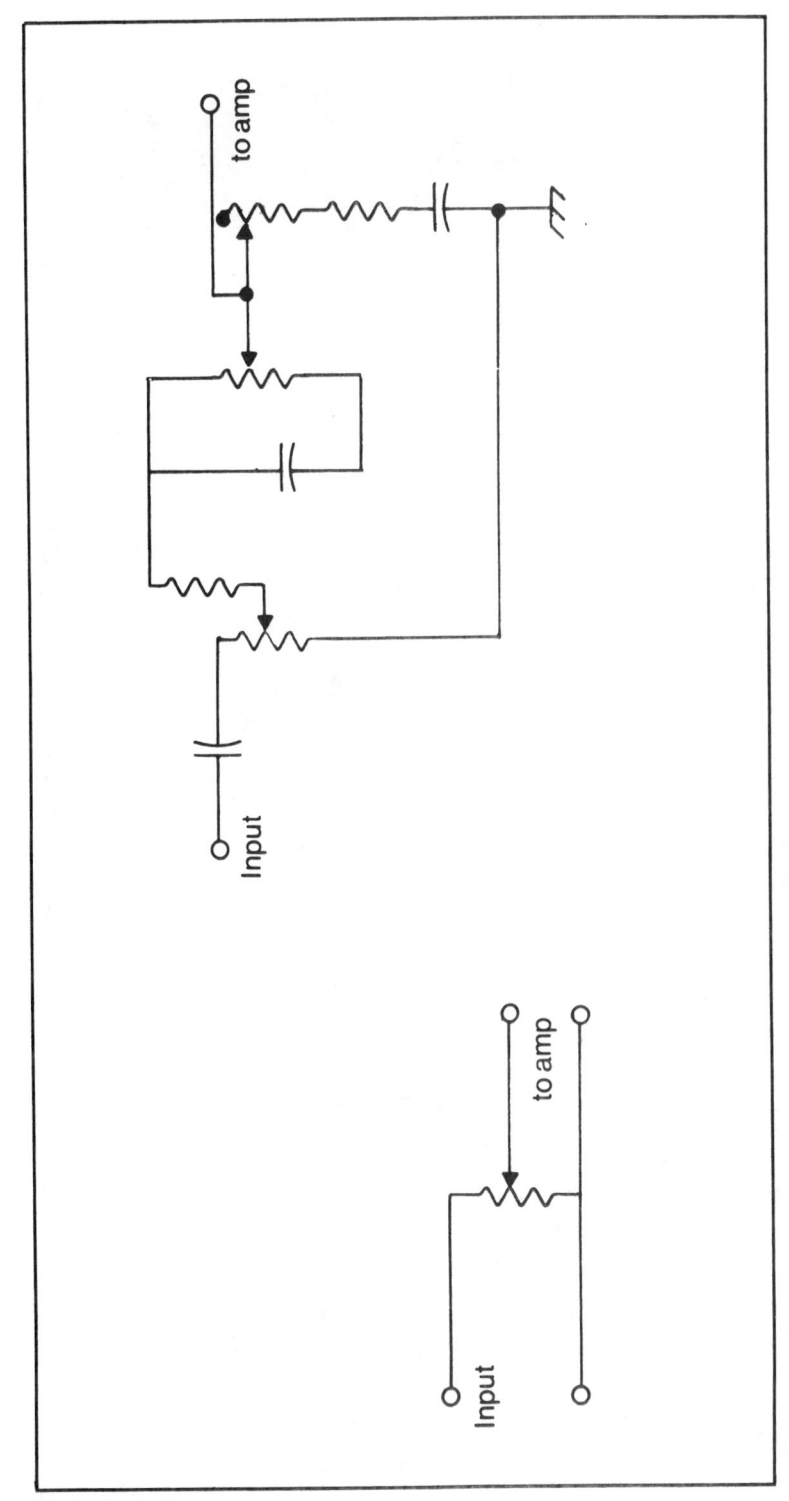

Fig. 4-7. Volume control circuit (left) and loudness control circuit (right).

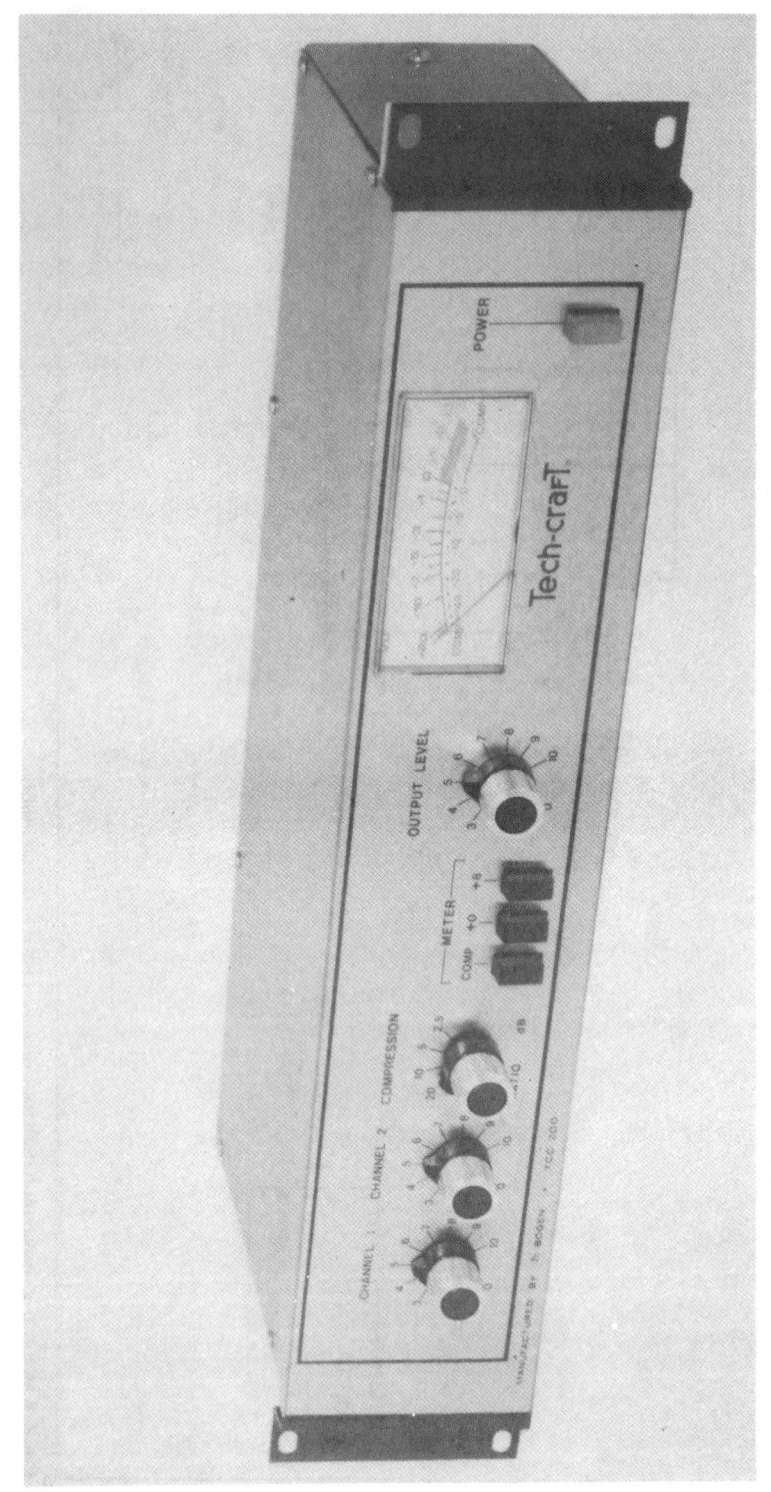

Fig. 4-8. Bogen Tech-Craft TCC-200 compressor used to automatically maintain constant loudness levels (photo courtesy Bogen).

cal amplifiers will have just a simple volume control. Commercially produced compressor units are available to provide stable audio levels at all frequencies (Fig. 4-8).

TONE CONTROLS

All amplifiers have one kind or another of tone control. The exact circuit depends on the quality and price bracket of the system. There are a great many circuits for accomplishing tone control and a complete coverage of them would take up an entire chapter considerably larger than this one. Generally speaking, the following grouping can be considered.

The lowest-priced units have a fixed shunt-capacitor tone control (Fig. 4-9). Medium-priced sets will have a single (Fig. 4-10) control often labeled *tone*, which will be one of the following circuits:

- Variable resistance and fixed shunt capacitor.
- Bass boosting.
- Continuously variable control giving bass boosting in one direction and treble boosting in the other.
- Step-type control in the form of a "quality" switch.

Better amplifiers may be fitted with two separate controls, one giving bass control, and the other, treble. In addition, there may be a switch for compensating for the frequency response variations of various types of microphones, tape decks and phono pickups. See Fig. 4-11 and Fig. 4-12.

The simplest form of tone control consists of a capacitor shunting the output of the last tube or transistor. In the cheapest

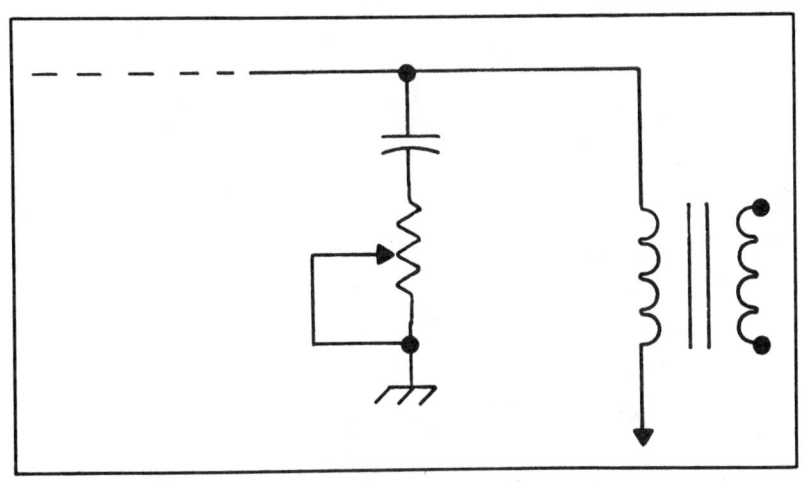

Fig. 4-9. Tone control circuit featuring a shunt capacitor.

89

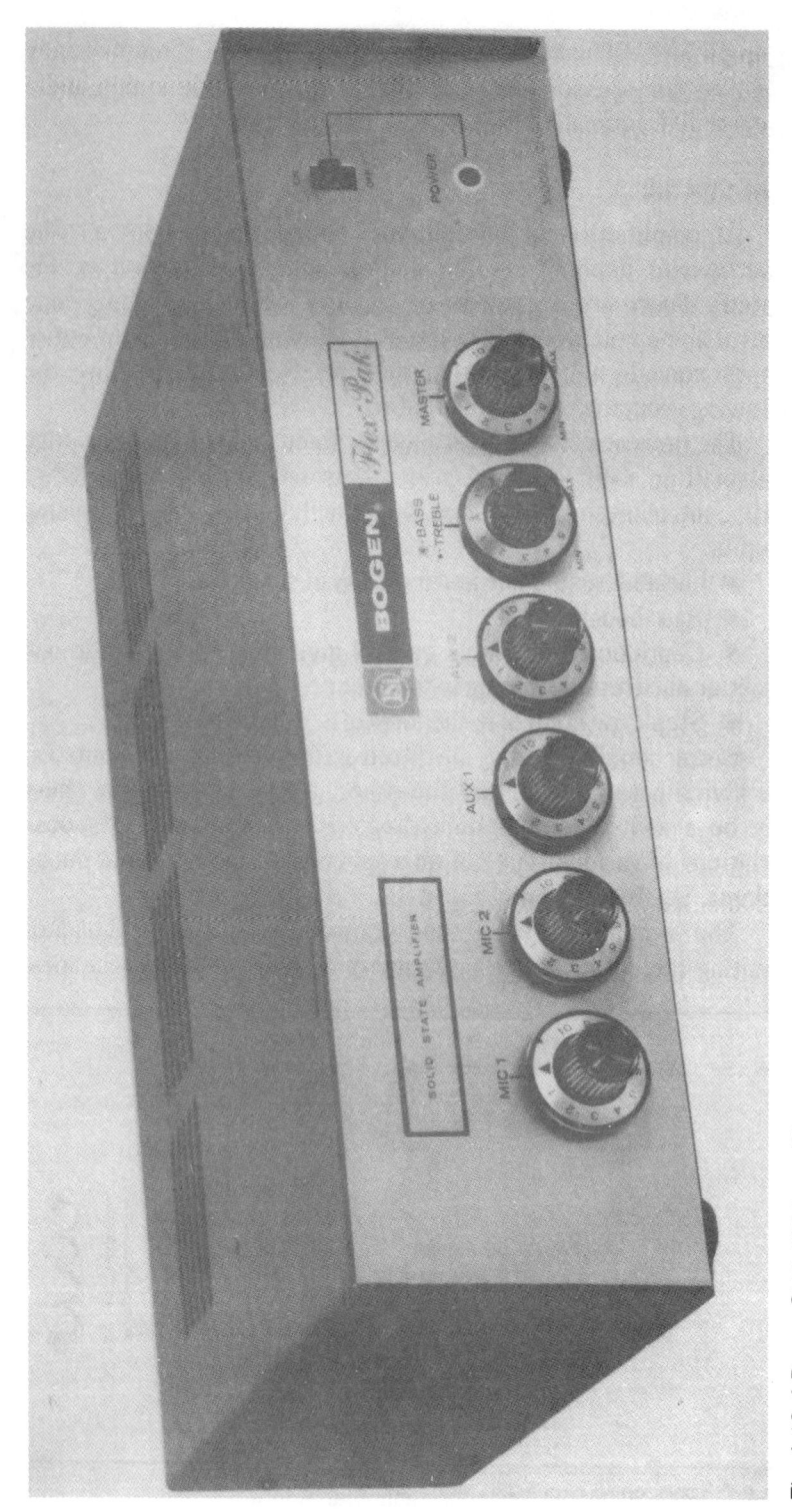

Fig. 4-10. A Bogen CHS-100A amplifier.

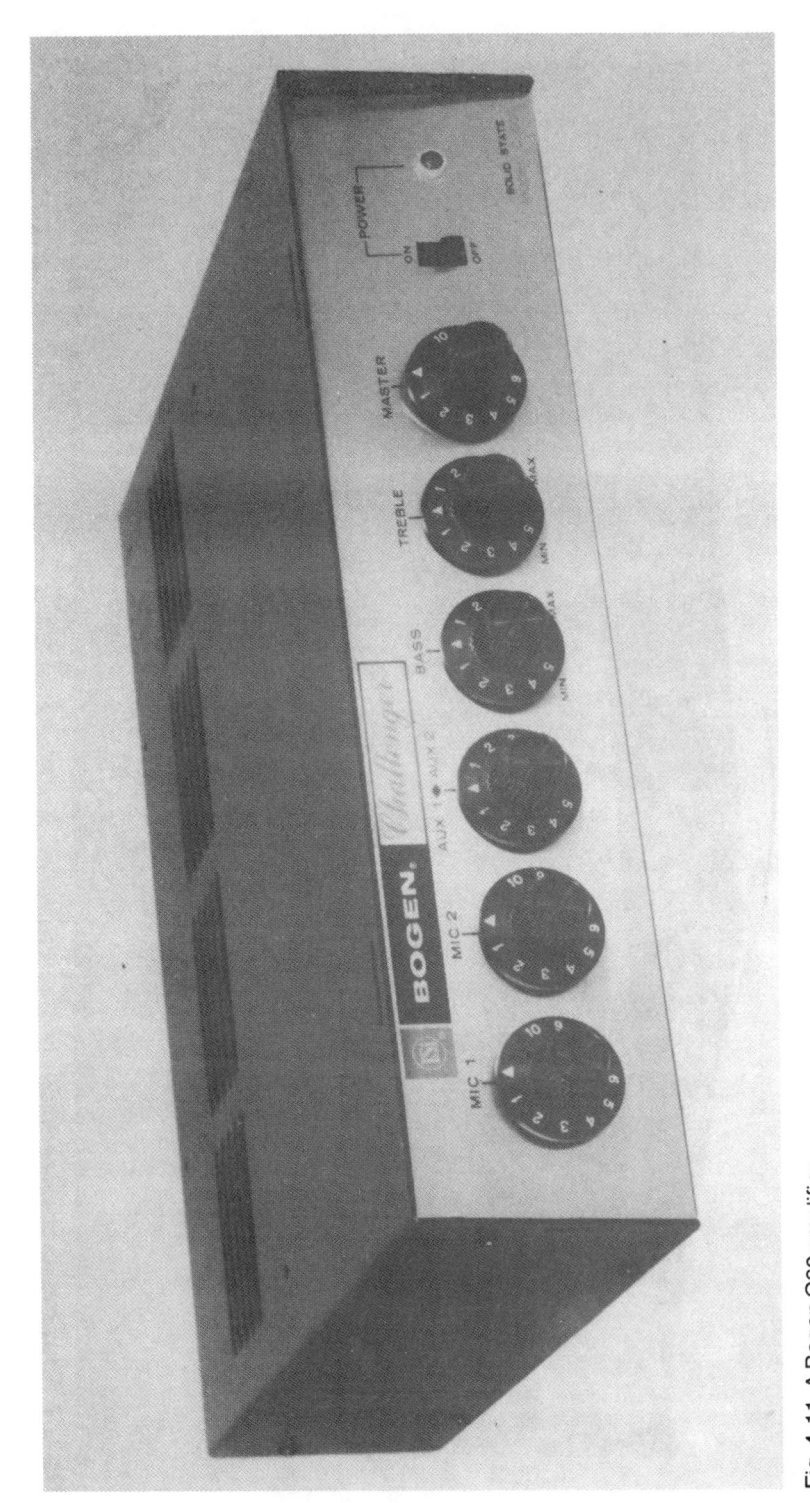

Fig. 4-11. A Bogen C60 amplifier.

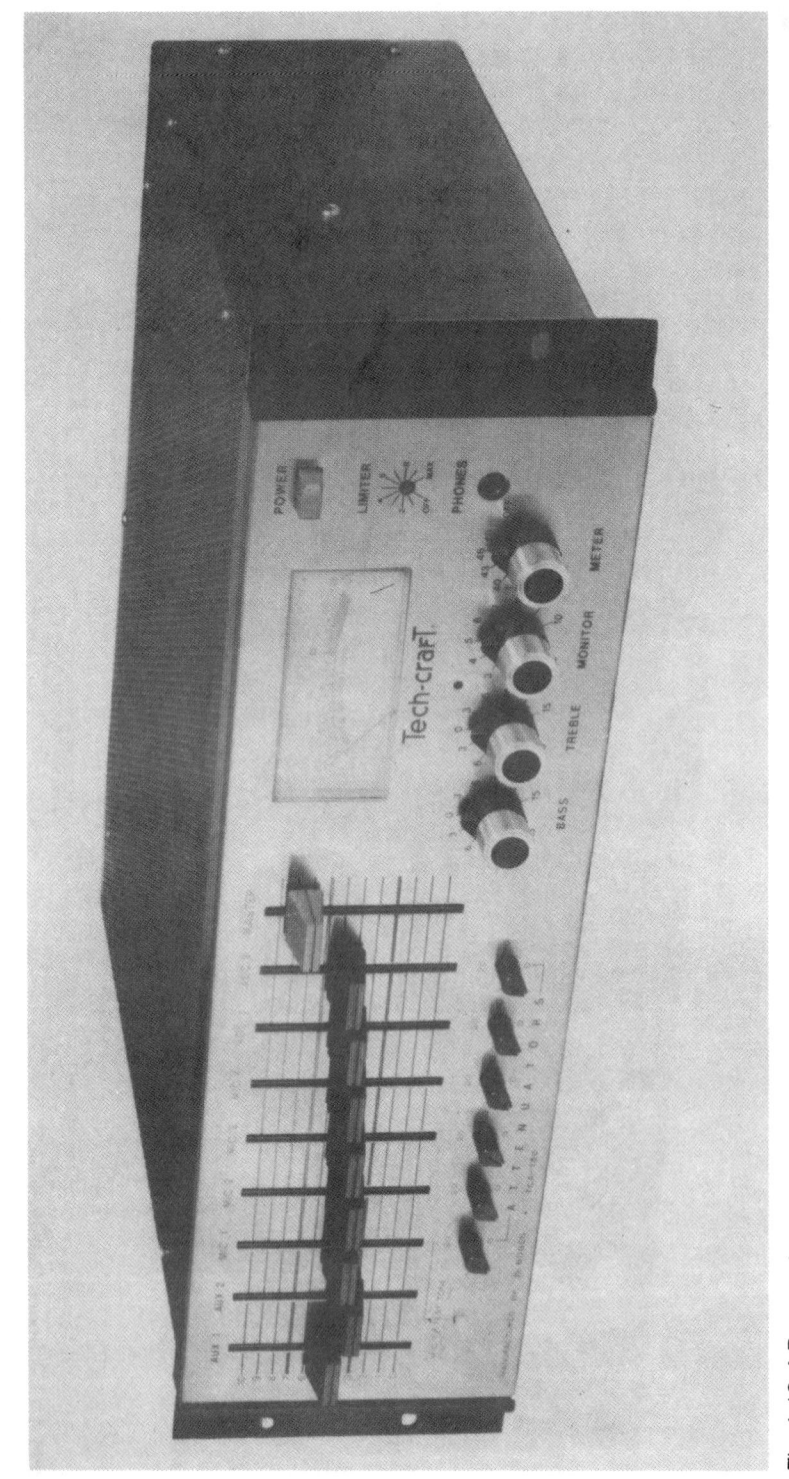

Fig. 4-12. A Bogen mixer-power amplifier.

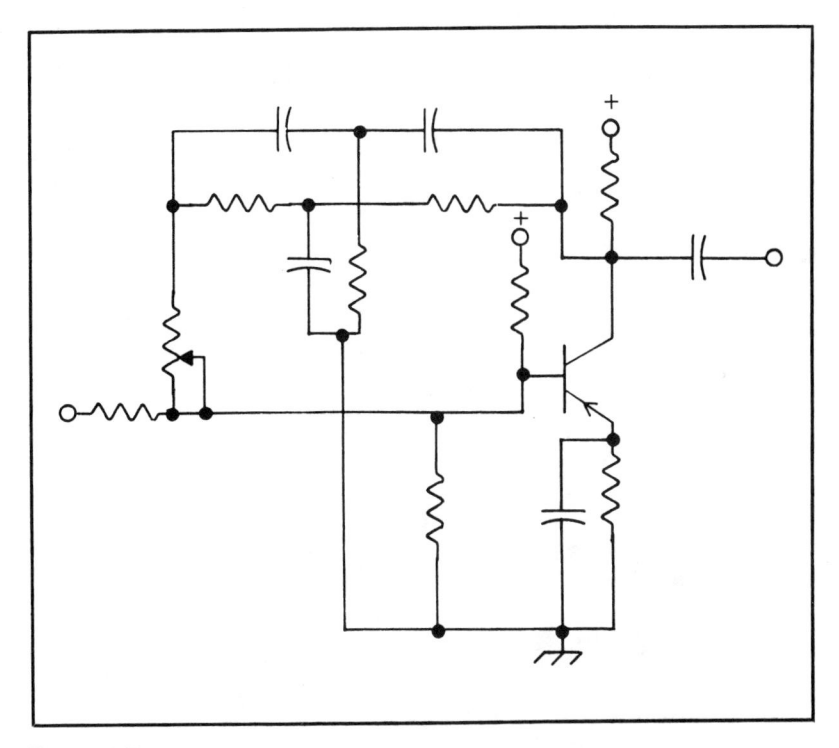

Fig. 4-13. Bass-boosting circuit.

units it may be simply switched in or out of the circuit with a simple slide or toggle switch. In the next higher price bracket, a potentiometer is inserted in series with the capacitor, allowing a continuously variable control (Fig. 4-9).

Bass boosting controls (Fig. 4-10 through Fig. 4-13) operate by feeding some of the output signal in a stage back to the input. A resistance-capacitance network controls the range of frequencies that are fed back. When a portion of the signal is fed back in phase, the tube or transistor tends to reinforce itself at the particular frequencies involved.

Late model amplifiers have tone controls that consist of half dozen or so individual controls (Fig. 4-14 through Fig. 4-16), each controlling a narrow portion of the audio spectrum. Such systems might have their controls marked "60, 300, 1000, 3K, and 10K." These numbers refer to the center of the passband for each control. They are so designed that, when set at equal levels, the overall passband is flat. By careful manipulating, any conceivable amplifier passband can be achieved.

Of course, these are just a few of the possible circuits. The number of circuits available are approximately equal to the number

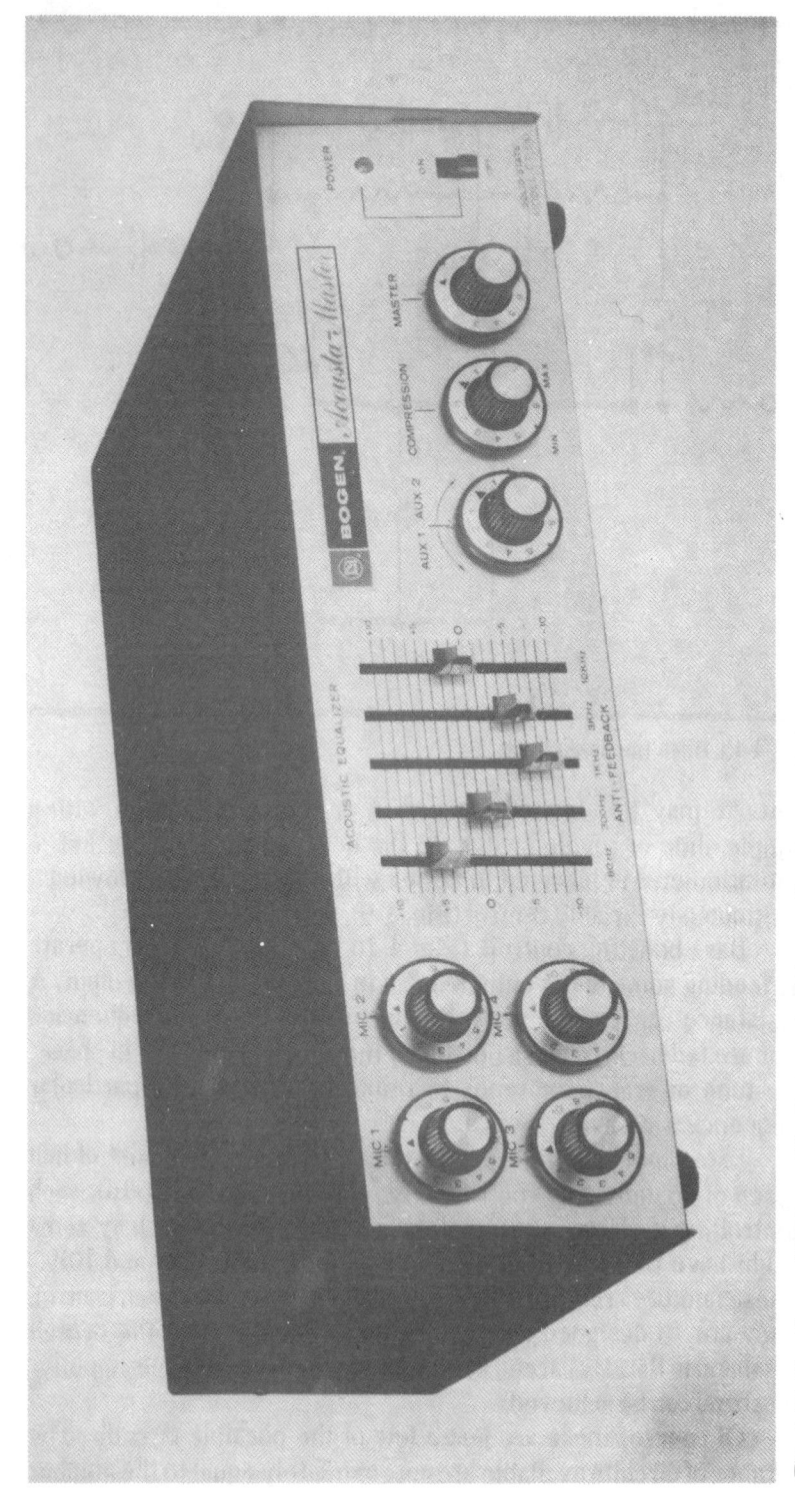

Fig. 4-14. The Bogen CT60 amplifier features built-in equalizer tone controls.

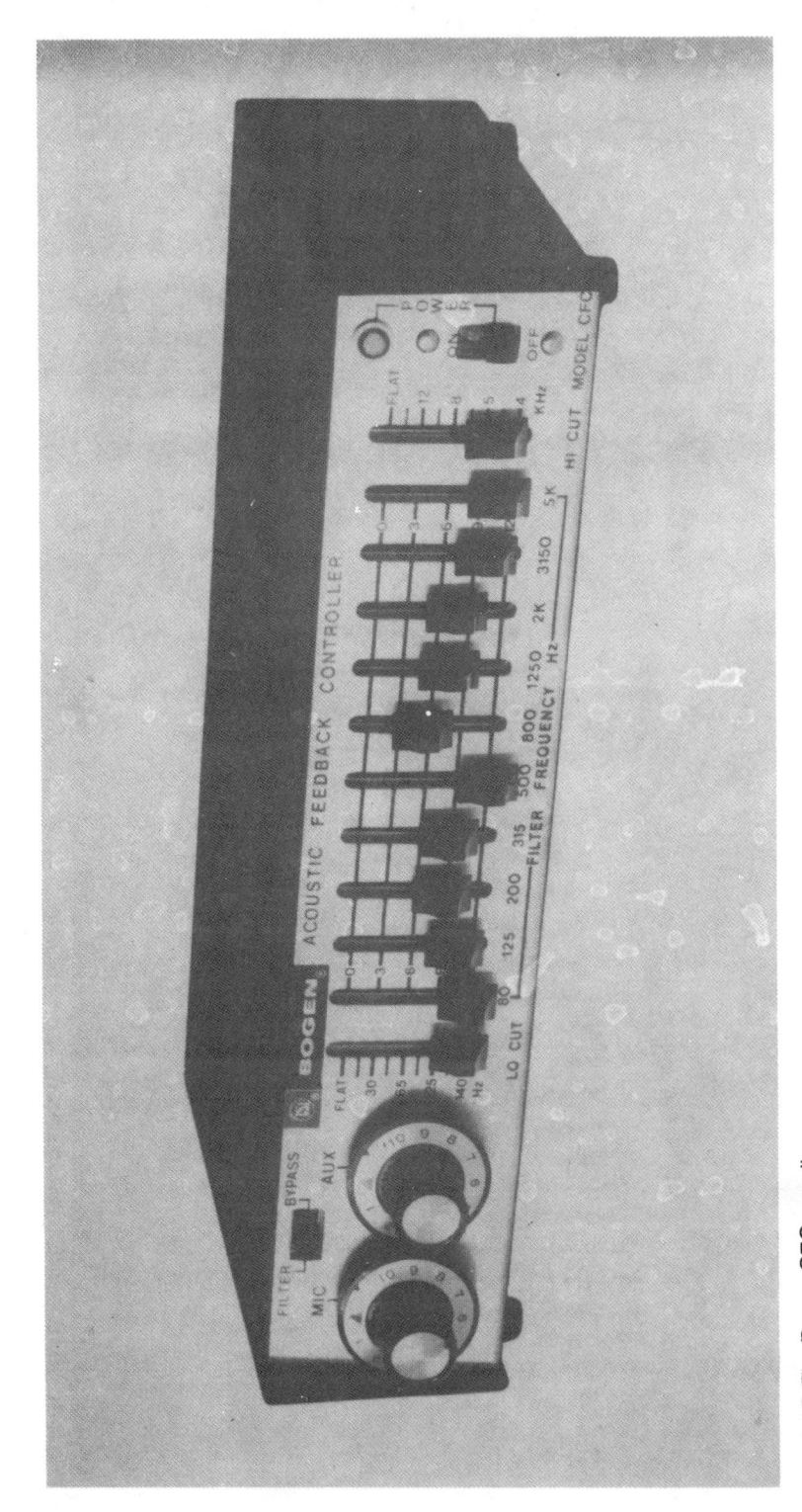

Fig. 4-15. The Bogen CFC equalizer.

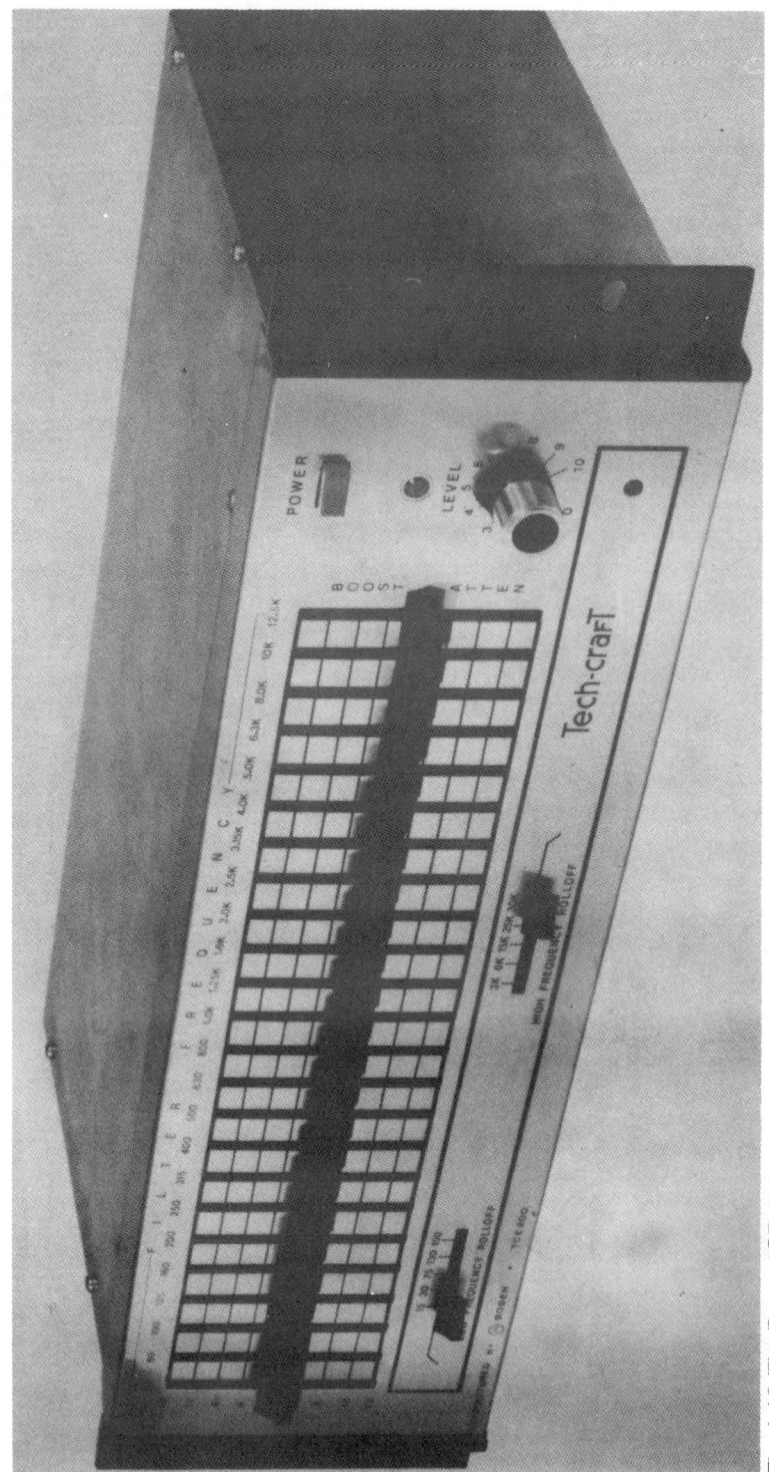

Fig. 4-16. The Bogen ICE-200 equalizer.

of engineers. The few shown here are among the most common, however, and will serve to give you some idea of the way tone control works.

Contrary to popular belief, the ideal sound system need not necessarily have a "flat" response over the entire audio range. The most desirable setting depends on the acoustics of the hall and on the program input. There are times when it is highly desirable to cut down on some portions of the spectrum and boost others.

Human speech is understood with the greatest intelligibility when only the range between 300 and 3000 Hz is amplified. The remainder of the spectrum serves to provide body and tonal quality only. A program consisting of dialog without music can be helped by cutting in somwhat on either end of the spectrum. Also, a speaker with a very bass voice or one with a relatively high-pitched voice can be helped out with the tone control.

On one occasion, the same microphone was being used by a singer and a guitarist. The guitar tended to override the singer's voice. The amplifier in use had six separate tone controls covering the audio range. A guitar is way down in the bass end of the range, so cutting way back on the 60 and 300 Hz controls while boosting the 1 kHz and 3 kHz controls very effectively boosted the singer while keeping the guitar audible but at a pleasing level.

These are just a couple of examples that should serve as a guide. The combination that is perfect for me might not work at all for you. There is no better indication than your own ears (provided you have no hearing loss). Just one note of caution: Never fool with the tone control unless you can hear the results. Some phono inputs have switchable compensators that select response curves for a variety of recording characteristics. If the characteristics of the recording you are using is known, select the desired characteristics, but use the tone control for the final touch.

AMPLIFIER OUTPUTS

Until the development of solid-state electronics, the output circuit of any audio power amplifier consisited of a transformer with several taps in the secondary winding to enable matching with the various loudspeakers (Fig. 4-17). These transformers were very heavy. It was generally felt that the more iron in the core, the better the quality.

The invention of transistors, which operate at a pretty low voltage to begin with, made possible high-power, low-impedance amplifying devices that allowed direct coupling. The emitter

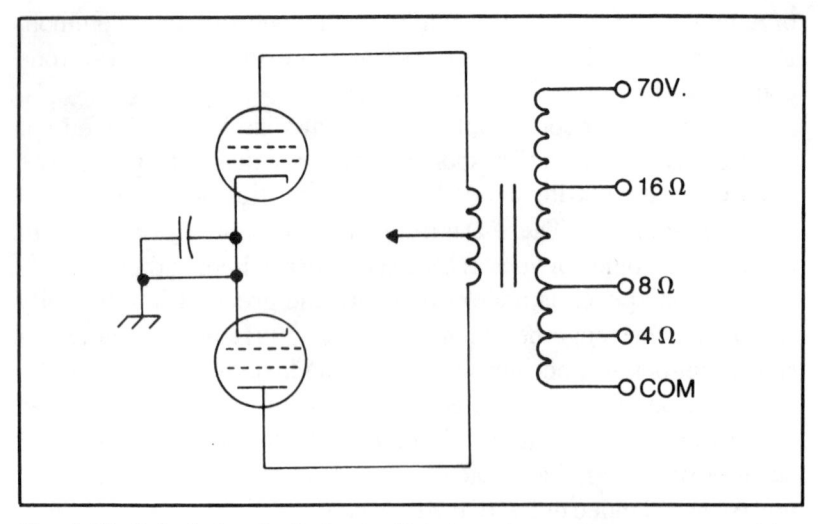

Fig. 4-17. Output circuit offering multiple impedences from a vacuum tube amplifier.

follower circuit, shown in Fig. 4-5 can eliminate the need for the bulky output transformer. Even with solid-state amplifiers that use an output transformer, the lower impedance of the transistors permits a smaller primary-to-secondary ratio, therefore less metal to deliver good audio quality.

POWER SUPPLY

The power supply portion of audio equipment has undergone radical change since the advent of solid state. Previously, it was

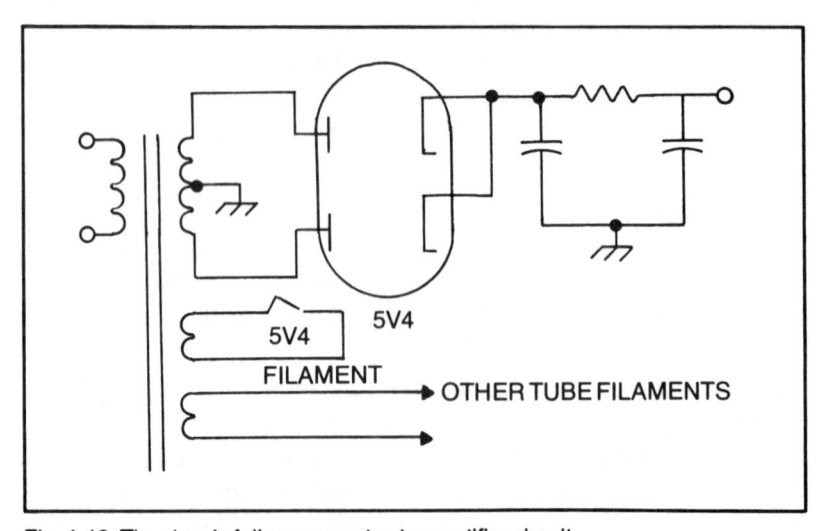

Fig. 4-18. The classic full-wave center-tap rectifier circuit.

relatively simple. A single transformer changed the domestic AC power into the several voltages needed to light the tube filaments, bias the grids (if a separate grid-bias supply was used) and deliver high voltage to the tubes (Fig. 4-18). Where solid-state bridge rectifiers are used today to provide the plate voltage, full-wave and center-tapped vacuum tube circuits were used then. This supplied a plate voltage about equal to half the transformer secondary voltage. Large electrolytic capacitors were used for filtering and they frequently broke down, especially in the spring, with the resulting hum in the amplifier output.

Some of the more expensive amplifier power supplies had a gas-discharge tube to regulate the plate voltage. A gas-discharge tube has a known "breakdown voltage" at which the gas inside ionizes and begins to conduct (Fig. 4-19). Once the gas is ionized, the voltage across the tube remains constant regardless of the current through it (within practical limits). A series resistor limits the current through the tube to that current required to drop the raw supply voltage to the ionization voltage of the regulator. Any load connected in parallel with the tube will see a constant source voltage in spite of variations in current, so long as the current drawn does not drop the series resistor voltage beyond the capabilities of the circuit.

Today there is a solid-state version of the gas-discharge regulator. It is called the zener diode (Fig. 4-20). Zener diodes work in exactly the same manner as gas-discharge tubes, except that they use a solid-state breakdown phenomenon instead of gas ionization. They are available in any voltage rating you can imagine and in an equally wide range of power ratings. Solid-state regulator circuits often go one step further, applying the zener diode voltage

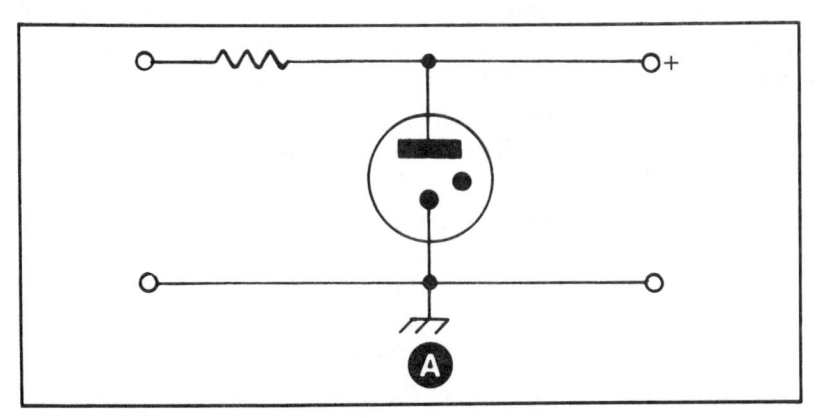

Fig. 4-19. Gas discharge regulator circuit.

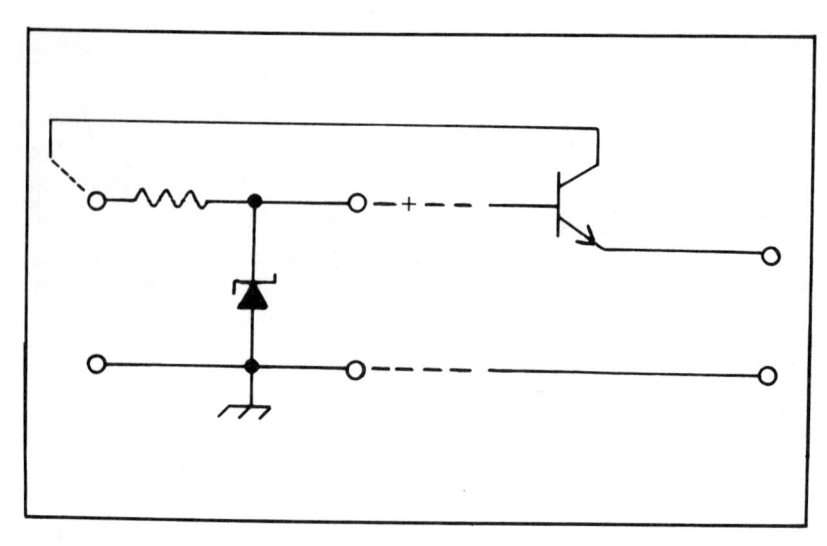

Fig. 4-20. Solid-state regulator circuit.

to an emitter follower. This allows the use of a diode on smaller ratings since the transistor does the bulk of the voltage dropping.

TROUBLESHOOTING

Space does not permit complete coverage of all the possible problems that might impair the operation of audio equipment, especially where many problems could be idiosyncrasies peculiar to the particular make of equipment. However, we can cover a few of the most common. Some basic steps for troubleshooting and repair are included.

Hum

Hum in the output of an amplifier can come from any of several sources. Most frequently it is caused by a defective filter capacitor in the power supply. This can often be recognized by the fact that the volume control does not affect the loudness of the hum. Only if the volume control is defective can a similar condition be realized. If you have a vacuum-tube amplifier, you can pin down a defective filter capacitor by turning off the power and measuring the resistance of the suspected part with a voltohmmeter. A normal capacitor reads a momentary low resistance followed by a rapid rise in resistance up to or exceeding several hundred thousand ohms. This reading can be modified by circuit parameters, so it's best to temporarily disconnect the positive lead when taking the reading.

Another cause of hum is a defective ground connection in the cables leading to the amplifier input. This can be quickly identified, since lowering the volume control will lower the hum level.

In solid-state equipment, hum can also be caused by a defective rectifier diode. To check the diodes, turn the power off and measure the resistance of each diode, first with the red lead at the cathode end and the black lead at the anode end (Fig. 4-21). Then switch the meter leads, red for black, and measure again. What you are doing is sending a current through the diode, first in one direction, then in the other. A diode that is in good condition will show a low resistance in one direction and a high resistance in the other. If the diode shows low resistance in both directions, or if it shows high resistance in both directions, replace it.

Loss of Signal or Low Gain

If the gain of the amplifier seems way down, check first that all input devices are functioning correctly. Next, check the gain of each successive stage. To do that you will need an electronic voltmeter. Measure first the input voltage, then the output voltage of each stage. A properly working grounded-emitter stage will show an increase of about ten to one or more in voltage. A grounded-cathode vacuum tube stage will show about the same. An emitter-follower stage will show no voltage gain.

Once you determine the stage in which the signal is lost, you are more than halfway to the solution. If you are working with a vacuum-tube stage, try substituting the tube. If that doesn't work, or if you are working with solid state, you must then measure the DC voltage on each of the principle elements of the tube or transistor.

Vacuum-tube units ususally have a diagram in the accompanying instructions that shows the voltages to expect at strategic points in the circuit. Transistors usually follow a common rule. The collector will have a DC voltage of from half to three quarters that of the supply voltage. The base voltage will be about 0.7 volts higher than the emitter voltage (Table 4-1). The polarity will depend on whether it is a PNP or NPN transistor.

Of course, this volume does not afford room for anything more than generalities. Detailed troubleshooting is an art in itself. These steps should help to at least get the reader started. Anything more extensive will require some degree of skill on the part of the person doing the troubleshooting.

Table 4-1. Typical Tube and Transistor Operating Voltages.

Tube	Plate	Positive with respect to ground 100-350 volts (Depending on equipment design)
	Grid	Ground potential or slightly negative
	Screen	⅔ plate voltage to full plate voltage
	Cathode	Ground potential to slightly positive
Transistor	Collector	About half the supply voltage
	Base	0.7 volts to about 1½ supply voltage
	Emitter	0.7 volts less than the base
		Polarity of transistor voltages is negative with PNP transistors, positive with NPN transistors

Replacing Transistors

Solid-state amplifiers are usually marked to indicate that they contain no user-serviceable parts. By this they mean that anybody attempting to repair the device had better be a qualified technician or he's likely to get in deeper than he realizes. If you once determine without question that a transistor in your amplifier is defective, here is a general procedure for replacing it: Usually the transistor will be soldered into a printed-circuit board. To release it, you must exercise extreme care. Desoldering is greatly simplified with solder wick or a solder sucker. Use a small iron-20 to 50 watts at the most. Heat the foil at the point where the wire from the transistor comes through, applying the solder wick or sucker. Once all wires from the device are cleared of all solder, it can easily be removed.

Power transistors are usually fastened to a heat sink or to the chassis with a heat-conducting insulator. Remove the insulator or heat sink with extreme care and secure it to the new unit. Some power transistors use a mica insulator, aided by a pasty, heat-conducting compound. It may be necessary for you to buy some of this compound, available at most electronic supply houses.

Radio Interference

Two-way radio equipment, such as amateur and CB transmitters, will sometimes be picked up by audio wiring in public auditorium sound systems. This is especially true if there are long cable runs between the microphone and the amplifier. Such

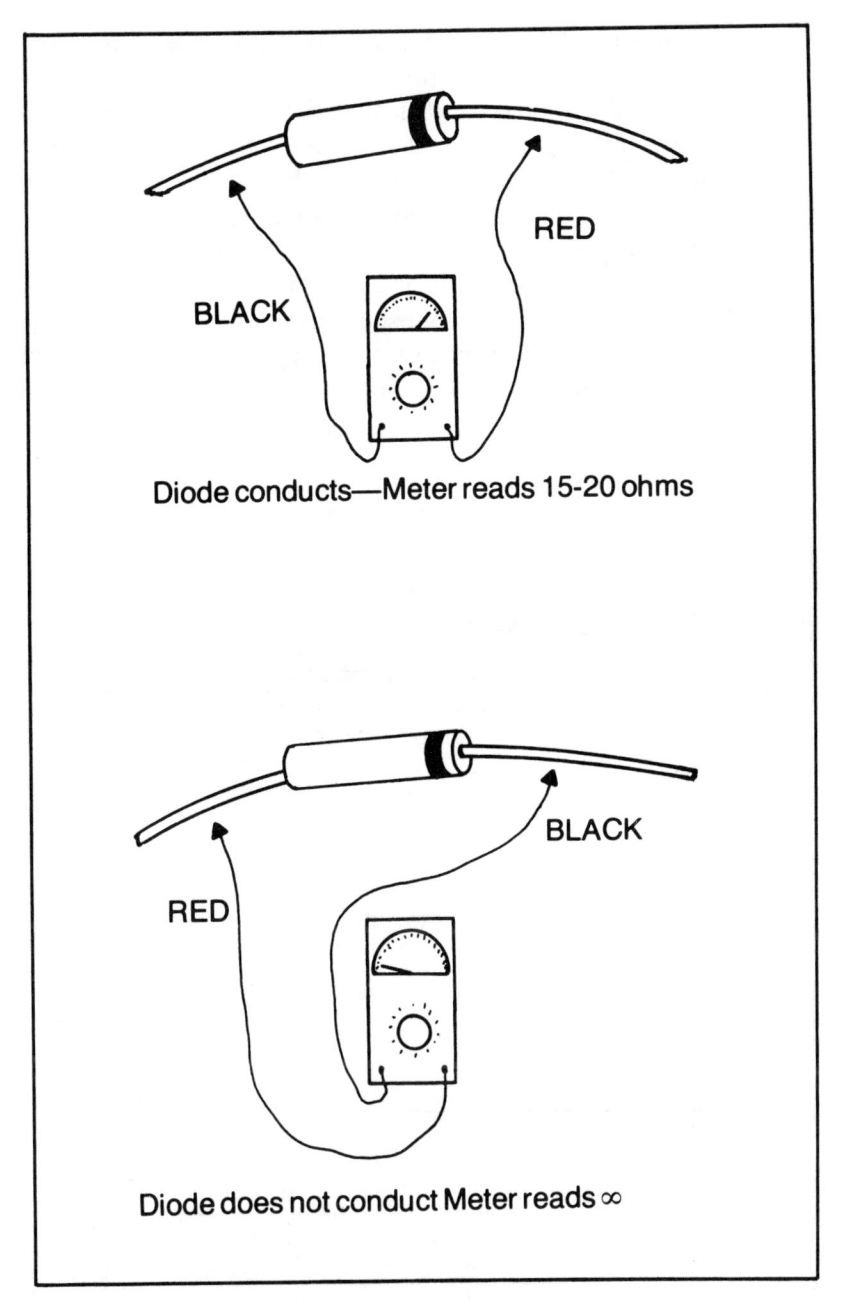

Fig. 4-21. A diode can be tested with a multimeter.

interference is *not* the fault of the transmitting station, and there is nothing the owner can do to his equipment to prevent it. Preventive measures must be taken by the owner of the sound system.

The cure for this problem is a fairly simple one. But before doing any work on your equipment, be sure all connectors are properly assembled and securely fastened. If they are, and you still get the interference, connect a .001 microfarad, disc ceramic capacitor across the input as shown in Fig. 4-22. Connect the capacitor between the grid and ground of the input tube. Or if you are using solid-state equipment, connect the capacitor between the "hot" lead of the input connector and ground.

If you are planning a setup, especially one near a strong radio signal source, you might want to select very low-impedance input devices (microphones, etc.). Low-impedance circuits are far less susceptible to radio pickup than high-impedence circuits.

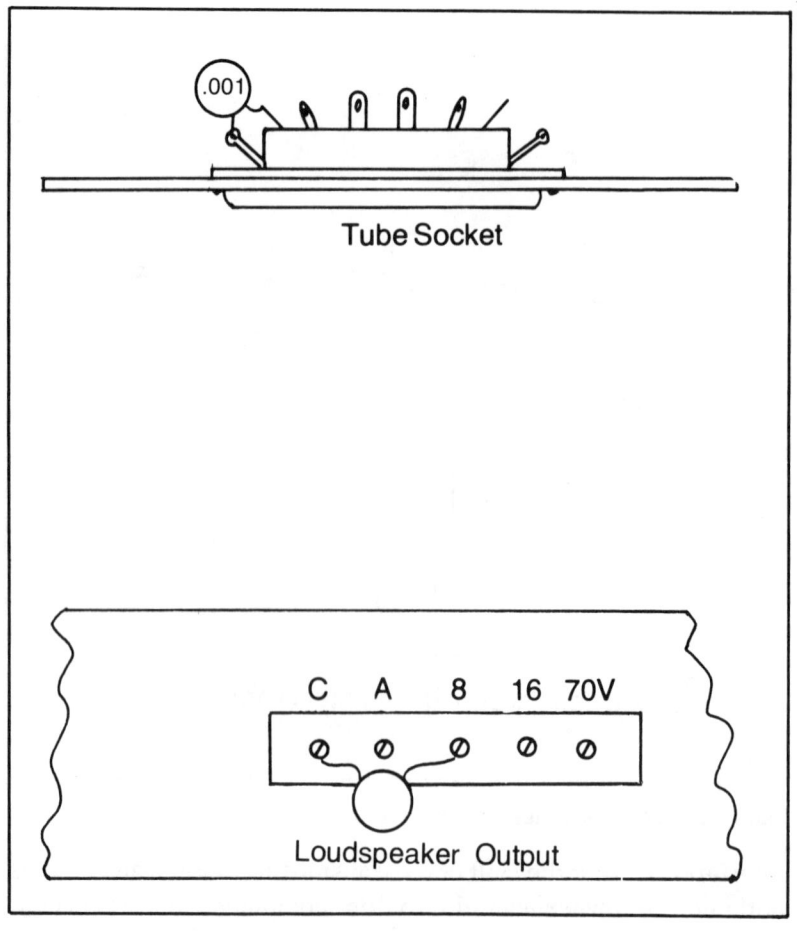

Fig. 4-22. Two ways to connect a .001 mfd disc capacitor to eliminate interference from amateur or CB transmitters.

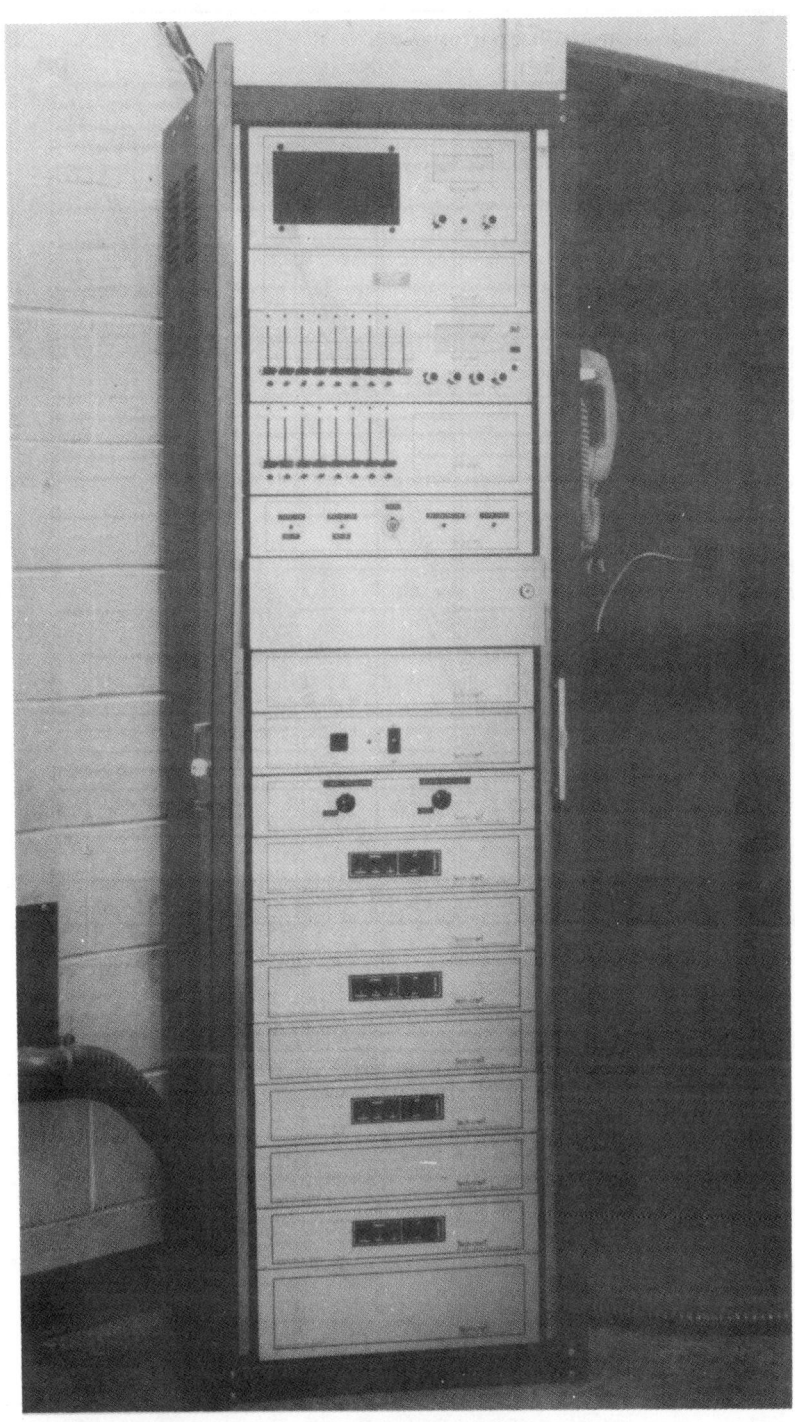

Fig. 4-23. This Bogen Tech-Craft rack serves as the public address system for the Sussex County Vocational School, Spartan, NJ.

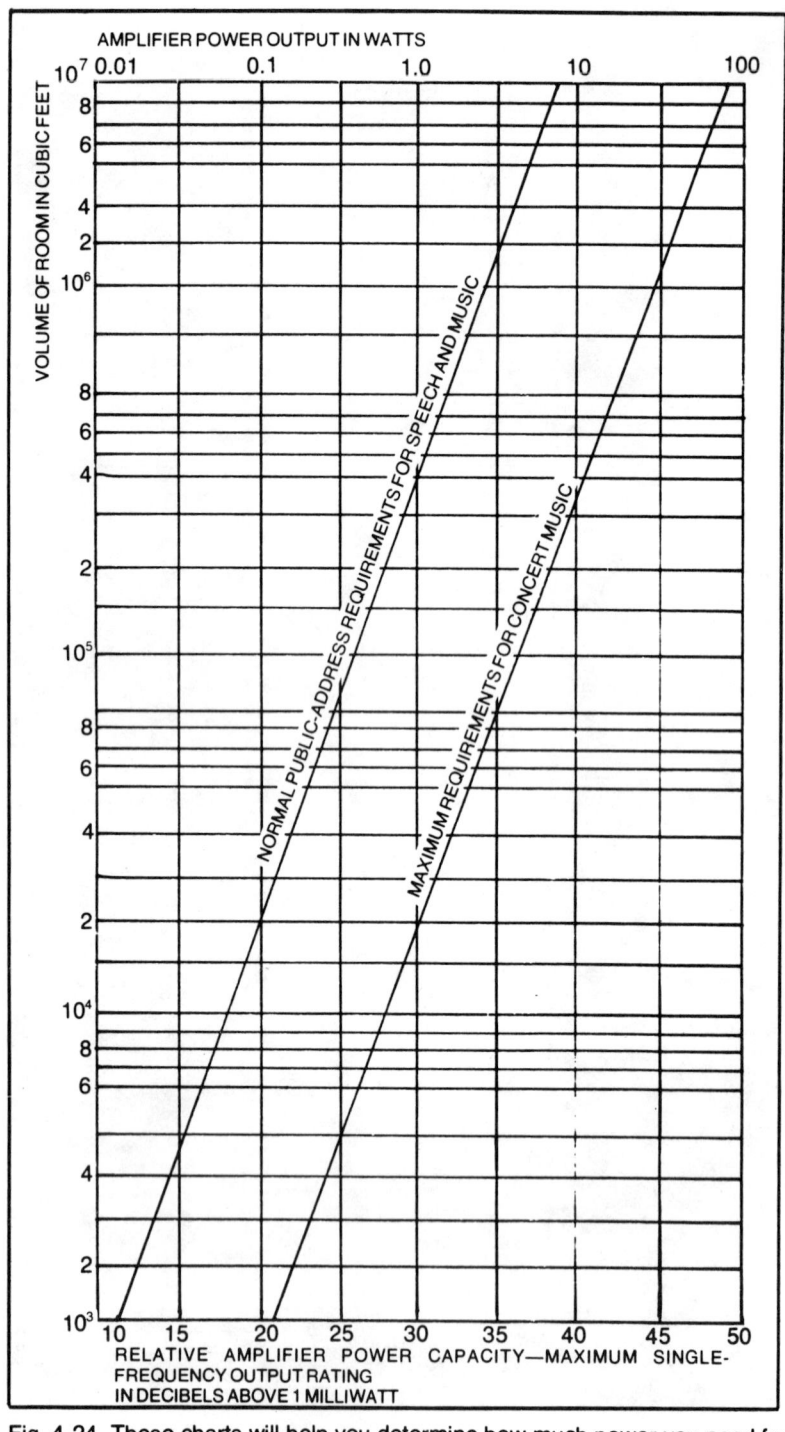

Fig. 4-24. These charts will help you determine how much power you need for any public address system installation.

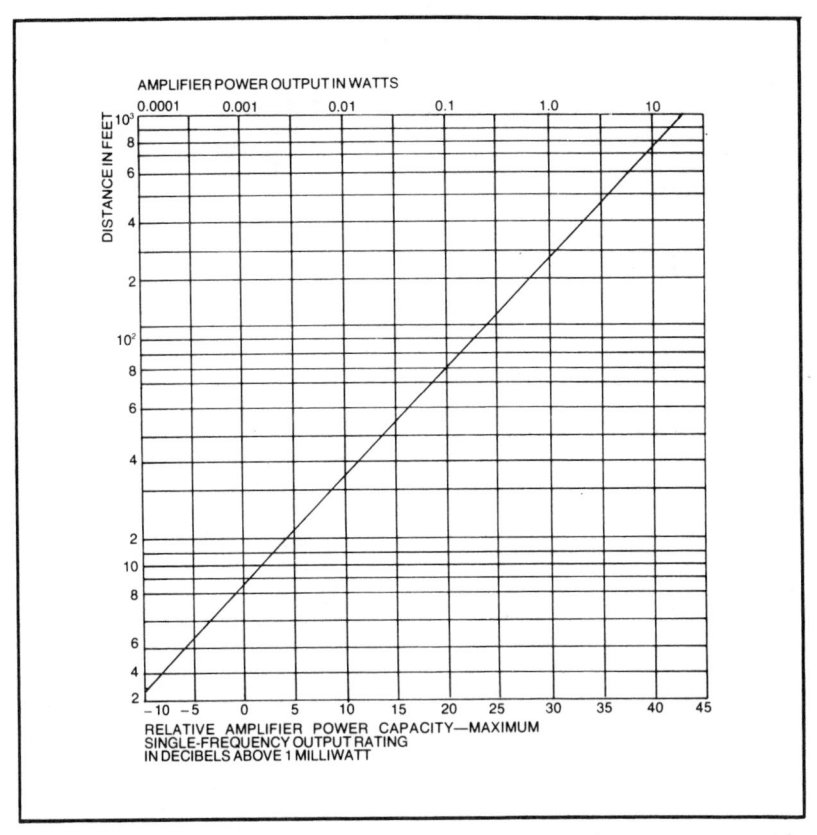

Fig. 4-24. These charts will help you determine how much power you need for any public address system installation (continued from page 106).

CHOOSING YOUR EQUIPMENT

If you are planning a new setup, the first thing you must do is determine the amount of sound power needed to fill your hall. (Fig. 4-23 is a typical school public address installation.) This is not something you can guess at when you're in a store with a salesman breathing down your neck. He's out to make the biggest possible sale (unless he's an unusual person) and you may end up buying a much more powerful unit than you need. Conversely, if you scrimp on cost you might end up with insufficient power. It might sound fine in an empty hall. But without enough power the sound will come out of the loudspeakers and drop when the hall is full of people. Figure 4-24 will help you to determine how much power you need.

Be sure the input connectors on the amplifier you buy are mates for the connectors on the microphones, or be sure mating connectors are available at a reasonable price.

Chapter 5

Microphones

In the recording and reinforcing of sound, microphones are at least as important as loudspeakers, if not more so. The finest amplifying system and the finest loudspeakers made can do no better than faithfully reproduce the signals applied to them. The input must be right to begin with. In other words, garbage in, garbage out.

Microphones come in a wide variety of shapes, sizes, types and prices. Each type is designed for specific applications. A little care and a little understanding of the operation of the microphone to be selected can spell the difference between success and failure. Therefore, you should first understand the electrical rules that apply, first to microphones in general, and then to specific types.

IMPEDANCE

Impedance is the total amount of opposition an electrical device offers to the flow of alternating current. It varies with frequency, and special equipment is needed to measure it. The impedance of audio devices is generally measured at a frequency of 1000 Hz.

Best results are obtained when the impedance of the microphone is the same as that of the circuit it is feeding. This rule, however, has a fairly wide tolerance, with mismatches up to two to one being acceptable in most cases. In situations where a mismatch cannot be avoided, it is of lesser consequence to connect a microphone to a load impedance higher than that of the mike than to connect it to a lower load impedance.

The amount of power dissipated in an impedance depends upon the resistive portion of the circuit. A pure reactance consumes no power. In microphones as in loudspeakers, the reactive component is usually quite small—almost to the point of being insignificant with respect to some power measurements.

OUTPUT LEVEL

Output level is an important factor when it comes to matching a microphone to an amplifier. It is generally expressed as a negative number of decibels. Decibels must be expressed in relationship to a specific reference level, called O dB. In most cases, microphone output is expressed with respect to a power level of one milliwatt (MW). Since the level is far below one milliwatt, the greater the number of negative dB, the *lower* the output level.

Manufacturers of inexpensive microphones seldom tell the amount of sound used to produce the stated amount of output. Those that do usually express it as a certain number of microbars. For convenience, some leave out the "micro" prefix and just use the word "bar."

"Bars" or "microbars" refer to the amount of sound pressure being exerted on the diaphragm of the microphone. A pressure of one bar is equal to the average sea-level pressure of the atmosphere. Sound producing a variation of one full bar would destroy the diaphragm of any microphone made. When the word "bar" is used with regard to microphone sensitivity, it can be assumed to mean microbar.

MICROPHONE TYPES AND THEIR APPLICATIONS

Microphones are usually identified by the type of material from which they are made or the use for which they are designed. In selecting microphones, it is wise to carefully match the requirements of the job with the characteristics of the mike. Following is a description of each type.

Carbon

The carbon type is one of the oldest and simplest microphones. It is best used in communications work, being reserved almost exclusively for telephones and some two-way radios. A carbon microphone consists of a small container of carbon granules with a diaphragm at one end (Fig. 5-1). Sound striking the diaphragm causes it to vibrate, thereby alternately compressing

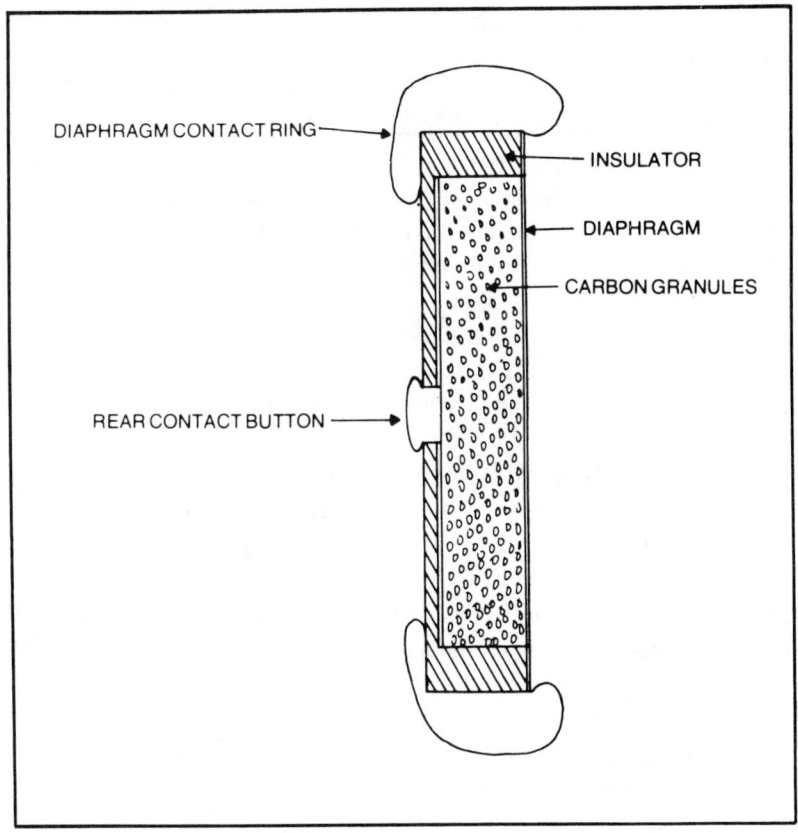

Fig. 5-1. Cross-sectional drawing of a carbon-button microphone.

and loosening the carbon granules. A direct current, usually in the order of 100 to 300 MA, is applied between the diaphragm and the other end of the container. The compression and loosening of the carbon granules causes the current to fluctuate. These fluctuations can be converted to an AC voltage by coupling them through a transformer or other suitable circuit.

In telephone applications, a carbon microphone is simply connected in series with the earphone and a battery or other DC source connected across the whole circuit (Fig. 5-2). In radio communication circuits, the carbon microphone is often capacitively coupled to the circuit in Fig. 5-3.

Crystal and Ceramic

Prior to the widespread popularity of solid-state devices, ceramic and crystal microphones were the most widely used of the various types among hobbyists. Today, dynamic units have the lead. They are extremely rugged, simple to use and can, in some self-powered telephone circuits, be used as both microphone and earphone.

A crystal microphone consists of a thin piece of quartz crystal mechanically coupled to a diaphragm. Quartz (and some ceramic material) has the property of producing electrical voltages when mechanically stressed. Sound waves striking the diaphragm mechanically vibrate the crystal or ceramic element. The resulting electrical impulses are taken off through a metallic plating on either side of the element (Fig. 5-4).

Microphones of this type have a very high internal impedance, on the order of a million ohms or more. Consequently, the circuits into which they couple are very sensitive to hum pickup. The cable between the microphone and the amplifier should not be over ten feet or so and must be well shielded.

The frequency response is somewhat better with a ceramic than with a crystal element, although the output is slightly lower for the ceramic unit. Both types have a relatively poor bass response. Ceramic and crystal mikes are used most widely in communications, PA systems and some of the older tape recorder circuits. They are very easy to couple into a high-impedance circuit, simply by direct connection. As in most self-powered microphones, the output level is proportional to the area of the diaphragm, all other factors being equal. Most manufacturers try to strike a happy medium between size and output.

Dynamic Microphones

Dynamic microphones presently hold the limelight as general purpose units of fairly good quality. The impedance characteristics

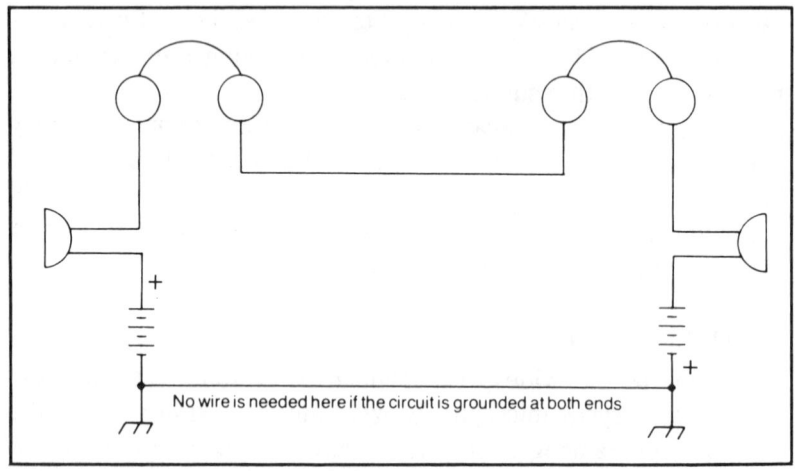

Fig. 5-2. Typical telephone circuit using a carbon microphone.

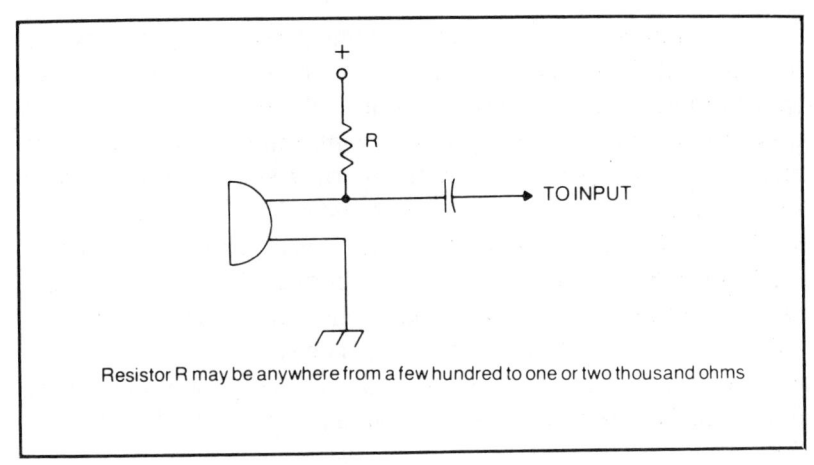

Resistor R may be anywhere from a few hundred to one or two thousand ohms

Fig. 5-3. A capacitor isolates DC from the amplifier input but passes the variations produced by a carbon microphone.

make it easy to match a dynamic mike into most solid-state equipment, and the audio is of a better quality than that produced by either crystal or carbon microphones. For most middle-of-the-road entertainment applications, they offer the best compromise between cost and quality.

The construction of the basic dynamic microphone element is very similar to that of a loudspeaker, similar enough that loudspeakers are often used as microphones in intercoms and inexpensive walkie-talkies. A lightweight coil of wire is bonded to the diaphragm and suspended between the poles of a magnet (Fig. 5-5A). Sound waves cause the diaphragm to vibrate, which moves the voice coil with it. This movement of the coil between the poles of the magnet generates electrical currents in the coil which are easily coupled into the equipment (Fig. 5-5B, C and D).

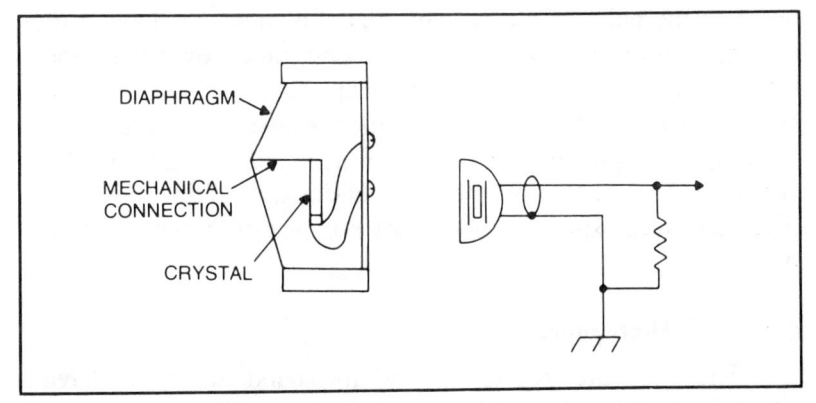

Fig. 5-4. Cross-sectional drawing of a crystal microphone and schematic of a typical coupling circuit.

The impedance of a dynamic element alone is quite low—in the order of 30 to 50 ohms. However, most microphones have transformers built in to match them to the equipment for which they are intended. Some varieties even include a switch or other means of selecting a tap on the transformer secondary in order to set the microphone to one of several standard impedances (Fig. 5-5B). In some of the low-to-medium priced dynamic microphones, the "cheapness" is mostly in the transformer. In many cases this can be rectified by removing the transformer and replacing it, either at the amplifier or by installing a new, higher-quality one in the microphone housing. Several dynamic microphones in differing mounts and price ranges are pictured in Fig. 5-6, Fig. 5-7 and Fig. 5-8.

Some broadcasting stations still use dynamic microphones with no internal matching transformer at all. The element is connected directly to the output cable, neither side being grounded. A ground wire is run directly to the microphone housing. This results in a very low impedance balanced circuit. Circuits of this type are insensitive to most hum pickup problems. Only the resistance of the cable conductor limits the distance from mike to equipment input. The impedance is raised to match the equipment by a transformer at the equipment end, rather than in the microphone housing.

Velocity Microphones

Velocity microphones are used where higher quality is wanted, both in broadcasting and in recording. They work on a principle that is only slightly different from dynamic microphones. A thin strip of corrugated metal ribbon is suspended between the poles of the magnet. Sound is imposed along, rather than directly on, the ribbon. As the sound travels over the ribbon, the velocity of the sound waves sets up vibrations which are then translated into electrical signals by the action of the magnetic field. Velocity microphones have a very low impedance, and need not only the matching transformer but additional amplification as well. They are quite expensive, and so are not generally available to the amateur.

Condenser Microphones

These are the "top of the line" for sound quality and have a very wide angle of pickup. They are exactly what the name implies. The diaphragm is one plate of a capacitor. Microphones of this type

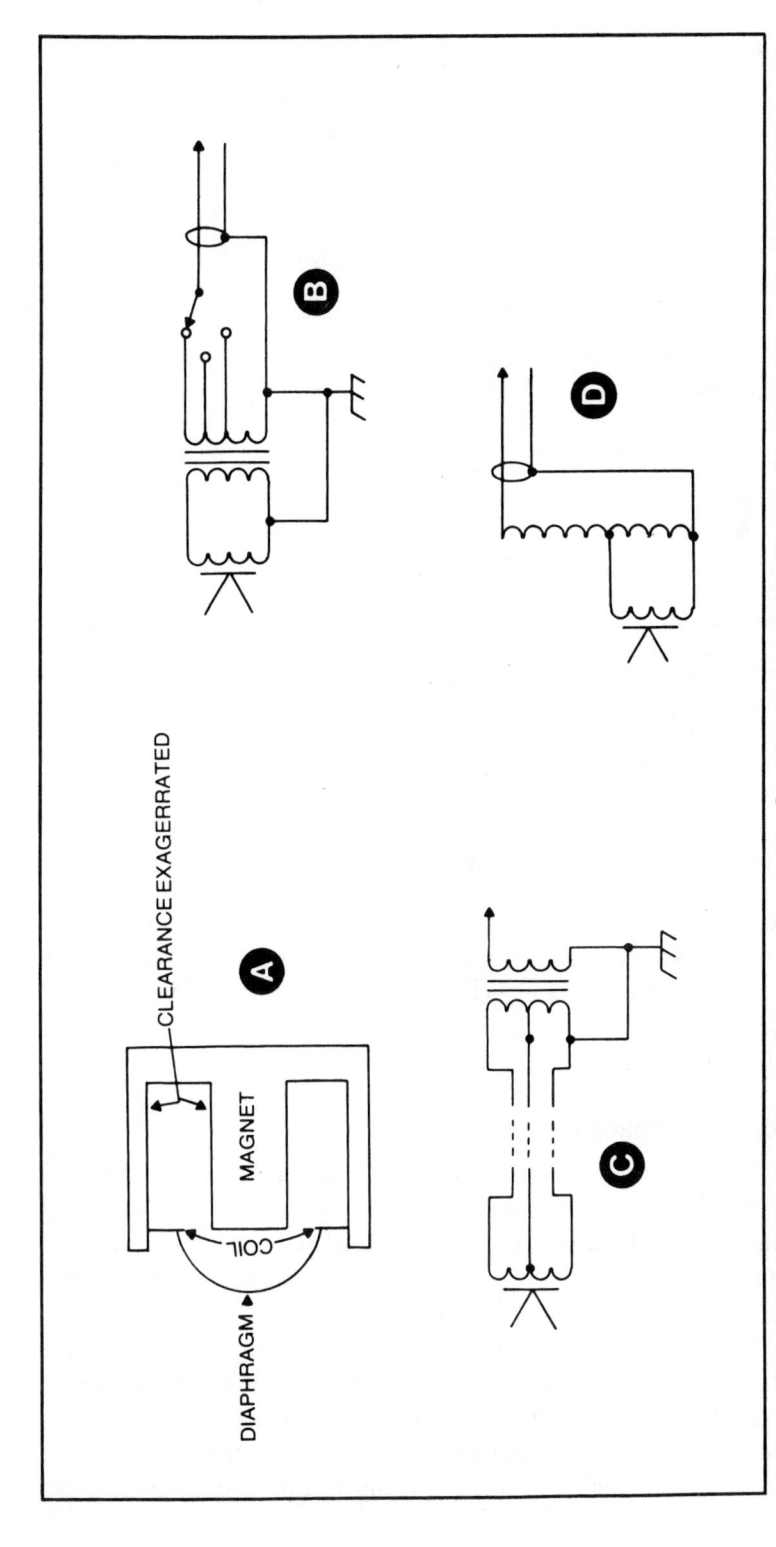

Fig. 5-5. Cross-sectional drawing of a dynamic microphone (A). Coupling to an amplifier is usually achieved by a transformer. Shown are selectable impedance circuit (B), a low-impedance balanced microphone arrangement (C) and a high-impedance connection (D).

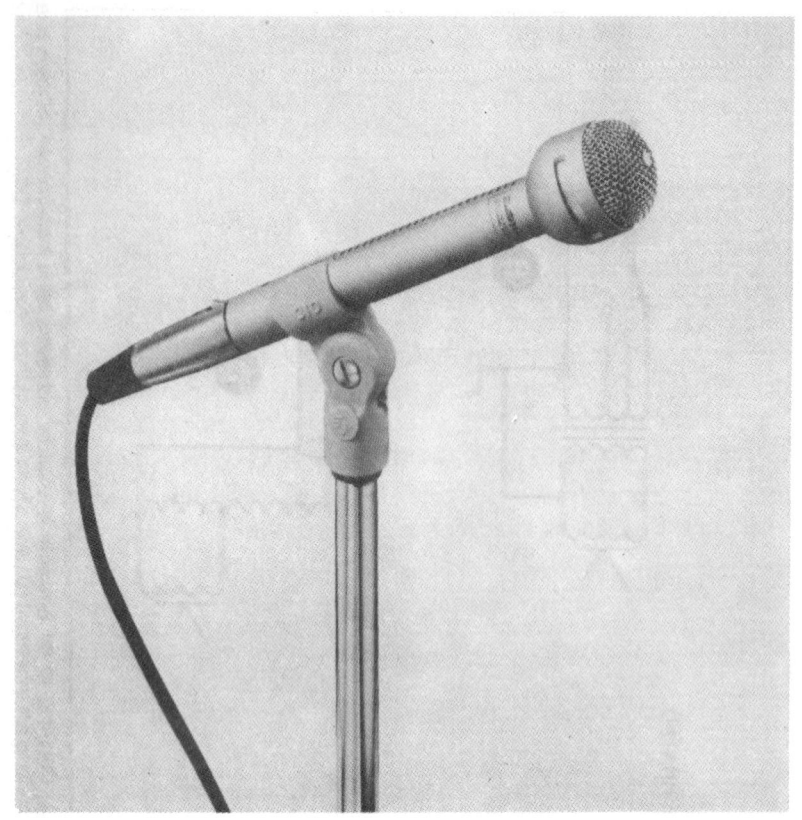

Fig. 5-6. An Electro-Voice model RE-10 microphone.

require a large DC bias. The impedance approaches infinity, and the output is so low that a preamplifier is generally contained inside the microphone housing (Fig. 5-9). Typical condenser microphones and power supply units are pictured in Fig. 5-10, Fig. 5-11 and Fig. 5-12.

Cardioid Microphones

The cardioid microphone is a specific kind of dynamic microphone. It is so named because of the shape of its sensitivity pattern. A cardioid is a two-dimensional figure that can best be described as resembling a cross-section of an apple, the microphone being roughly at the position of the stem (Fig. 5-13).

Very early in the history of sound reproduction, it was realized that microphones were needed which would be sensitive to sound coming only from one direction. Random noise, reverberation and acoustical feedback limited the effective pickup range of most microphones. If sound pickup could be eliminated from

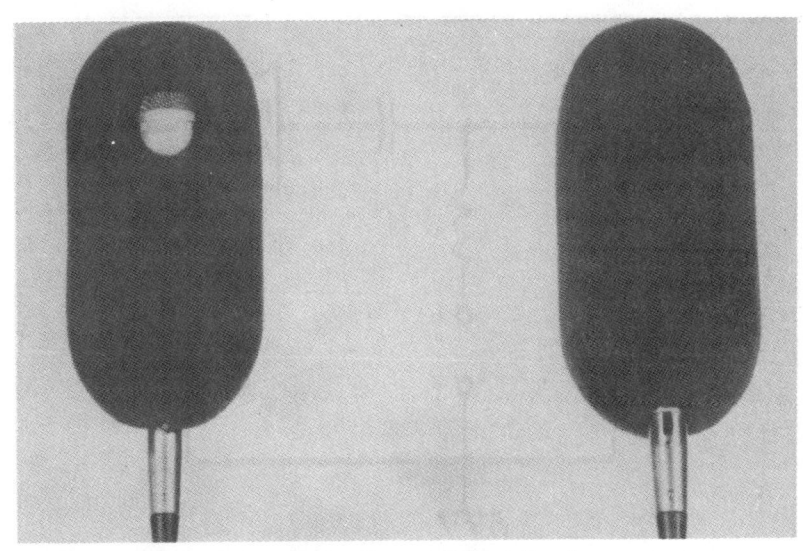

Fig. 5-7. A stage-mount model 411 Electro-Voice microphone.

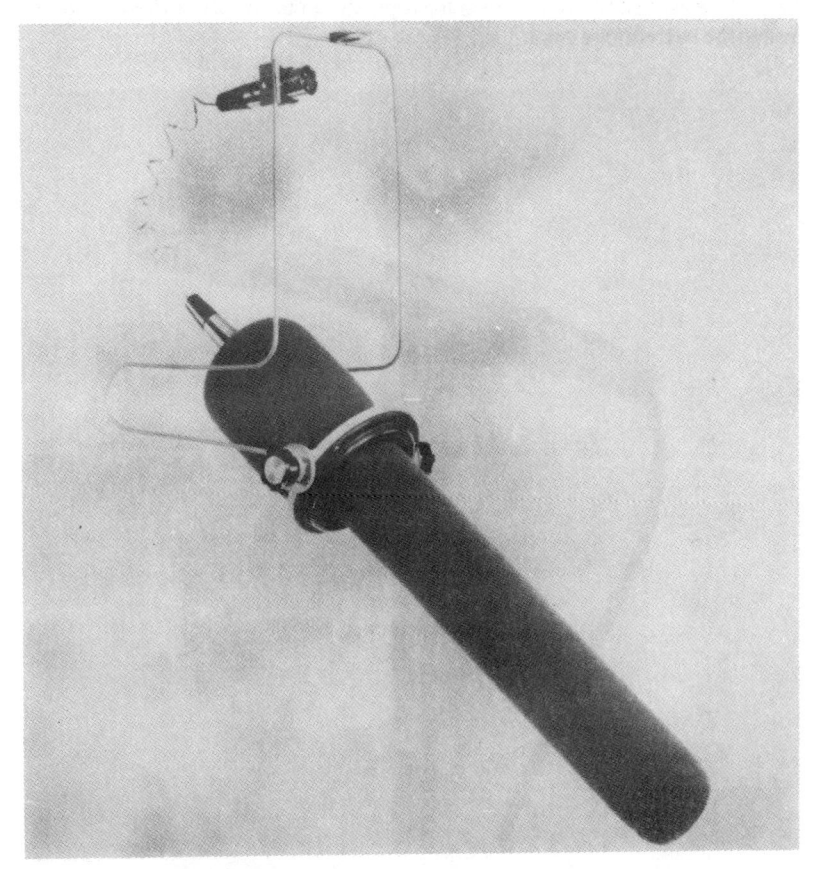

Fig. 5-8. A boom mount DL-42 Electro-Voice microphone.

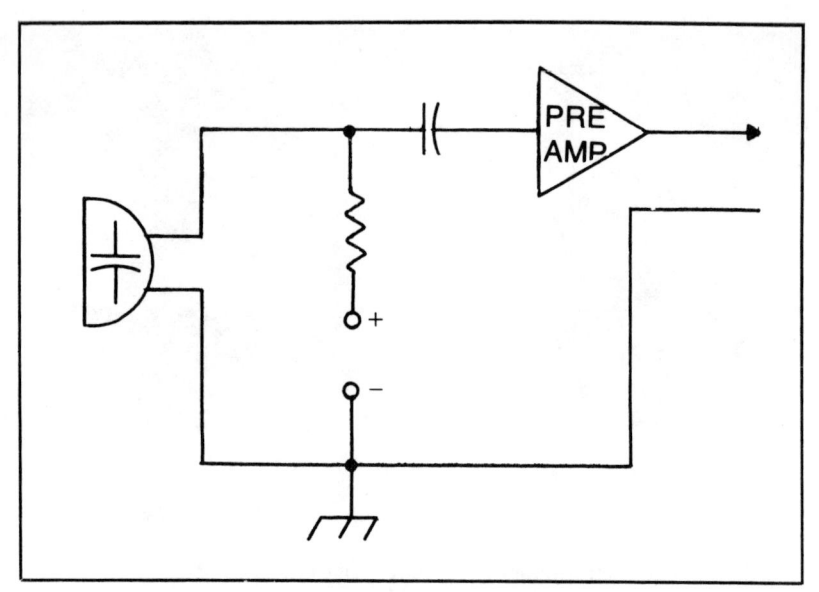

Fig. 5-9. Schematic of a condenser microphone circuit. All of it is often contained within the microphone case.

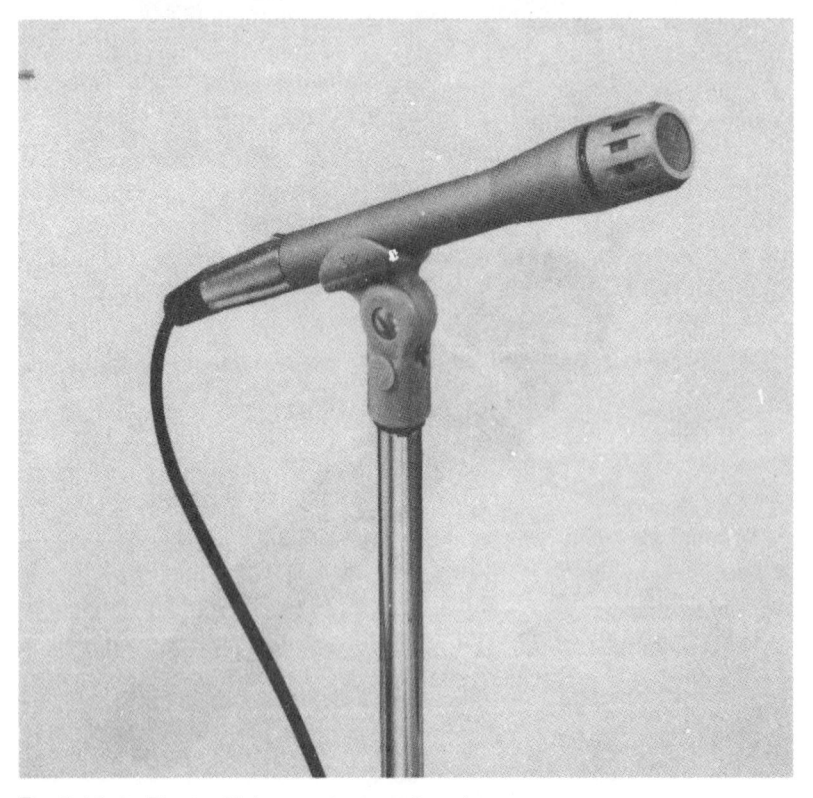

Fig. 5-10. An Electro-Voice condenser microphone.

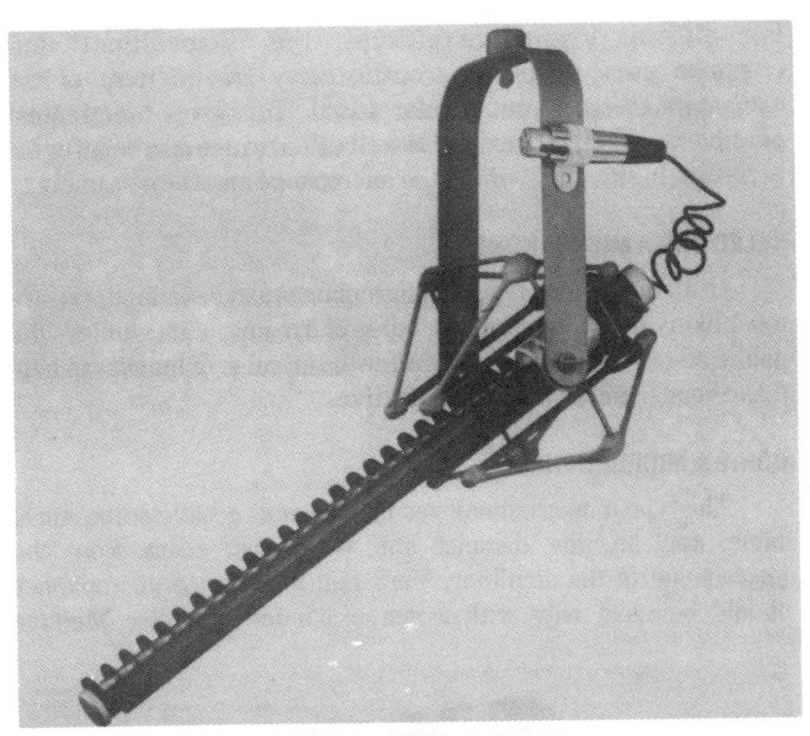

Fig. 5-11. Electro-Voice boom mount condenser microphone.

directions other than that of the source, the usable distance between the microphone and the speaker could be increased without the loss of sound quality (Fig. 5-14). Over the years, several ways of accomplishing this have been developed. In one scheme, developed by Electro-Voice, a ribbon element is connected in series with the dynamic element. The ribbon element is directionally sensitive only toward the front and back. Moreover, the phase is opposite with opposite directions. Sound waves coming from the front have the same phase from either element, so the two reinforce one another. However, sound coming from behind is opposite in phase from the ribbon to the dynamic elements, and so they cancel (Fig. 5-15). This is the oldest form of cardioid microphone.

Crystal cardioids are also available and have been for quite a few years. These use two separate diaphragms, one of which is coupled to the element through a mechanical delay so that sound coming from behind is mechanically cancelled (Fig. 5-16).

Another form of cardioid microphone uses an acoustic delay chamber to phase out the back sound. These have the advantage of greater uniformity in the cancellation with respect to frequency.

For difficult long-range pickups, the "Sound Spot" microphone uses a tapered acoustic delay line in front of the diaphragm to cancel out angular sound. This gives the greatest possible working distance and is well suited to use on a boom or for recording in situations where the microphone must be off camera.

SELECTING A MICROPHONE

Of all the various types of microphones just described, you are most likely to use one or more types of dynamic units—unless the public tastes change radically. A few basic rules of thumb can help make your sound pickup most effective.

USING A MICROPHONE

The type of microphone you use depends greatly on the run of cable, that is, the distance the wire must reach from the microphone to the amplifier. Very high impedance microphones should be used only with a run of 25 feet or less. Medium

Fig. 5-12. An Electro-Voice AC24M slave power supply (top) and a Model AC24M master power supply.

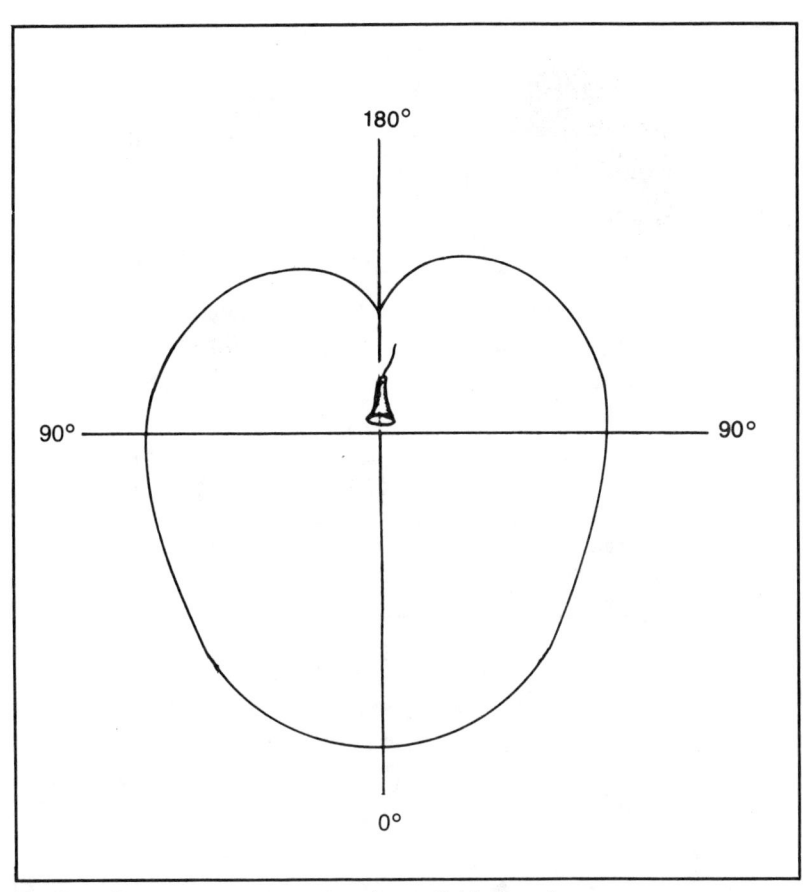

Fig. 5-13. Relative response patter of a cardioid microphone.

impedance (20,000 to 50,000 ohms) will tolerate a run of 25 to 50 feet without excessive hum pickup, unless the wire runs adjacent to a power wire carrying heavy current. For runs of more than 50 feet or so, use a low-impedance mike and match it to the amplifier at the amplifier end of the cable with a suitable matching transformer.

    Few things are more revolting to this writer than the spectacle of an announcer in a public place or a solo performer who appears to "swallow" the microphone with the resultant distorted garble coming out of the loudspeaker. To those who are unfamiliar with the use of sound systems, this is almost understandable. Perhaps there is a quirk of vanity that makes some experienced performers desperate to hear their own voices coming back amplified, no matter how distorted, or maybe it is a distrust of the sensitivity of the things. At any rate, this characteristic alone demonstrates the need for the sound technician to be present at

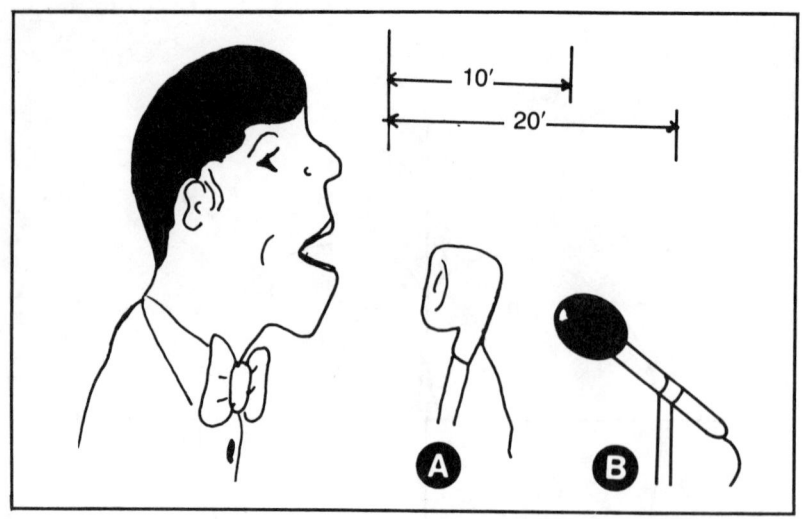

Fig. 5-14. A comparison of the useful distances between the old dynamic and the cardioid microphone.

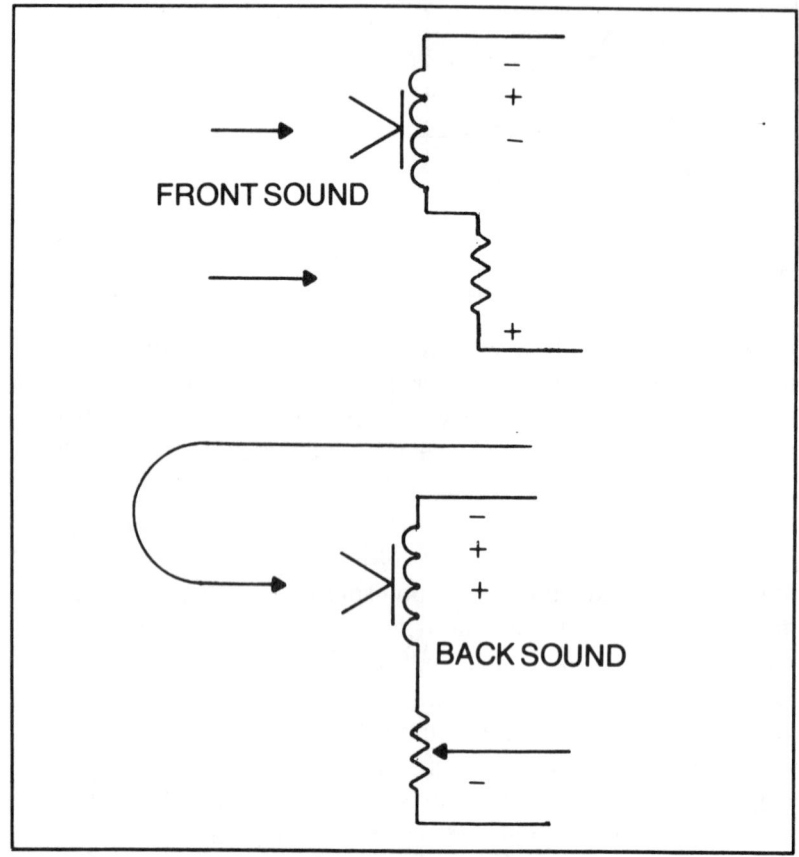

Fig. 5-15. A schematic for the principle of a two-element cardioid microphone.

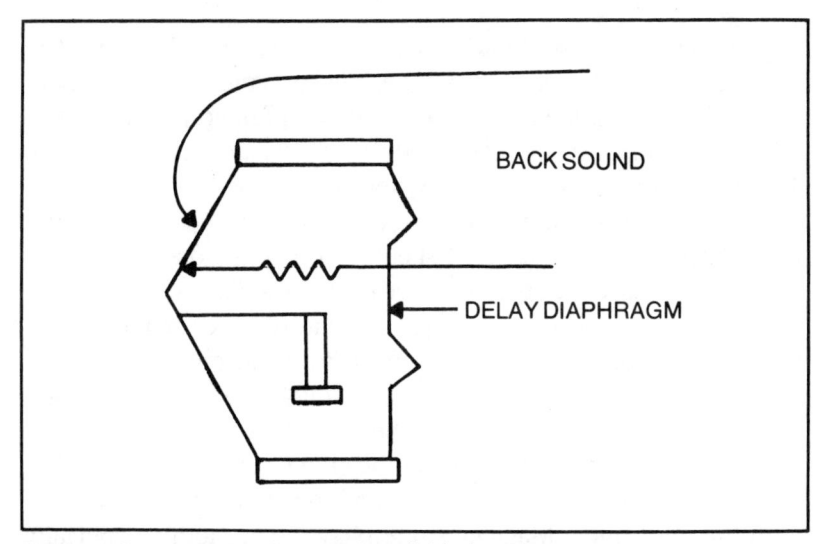

Fig. 5-16. Cross section of a crystal cardioid microphone.

dress rehearsals and the need for a speech compressor when it is known that such performers will be let loose with a microphone in hand. There are some solo speakers and performers who simply feel more comfortable with a hand-held microphone. Of these, a certain percentage simply don't know how to use a mike. For these persons, a few discreet words at rehearsal are sufficient.

A microphone is a sensitive instrument. It can hear you, and it can hear you well. However, it does not have the miraculous built-in features that the human ear has. It does not automatically adjust itself for differences in distance to your mouth. If it is too close, your voice sounds very bassy; too far away and your voice sounds hollow. If you move it around while performing, the voice level goes up and down over a tremendous range.

Fig. 5-17. The recommended position of a microphone with respect to a user.

An omnidirectional microphone should be about 10 inches to a foot (25 to 30 centimeters) from the speaker's mouth and not more than 45° to one side or the other. A cardioid microphone is most effective 18 to 24 inches (40 to 60 centimeters) away (Fig. 5-17). These figures apply to solitary speakers. Microphones can be greater distances from choral or orchestral groups. Whichever type of microphone is used, it should not be positioned or held so high as to obscure the speaker's face from the audience.

A singer or performer whose routine requires him or her to move about the stage will often prefer a hand mike, unless the routine calls for use of the hands, as might be the case with a magician. In the latter case, either a lavalier or a sound-spot operated so as to follow him about the stage would be preferred. If you want to use a microphone fastened to his clothing, check first with the performer. Magicians often have their clothing specially prepared and if the microphone should pick up extraneous sounds that reveal some or part of his secrets he may prefer some other arrangement.

When a number of speakers will follow one another, all presenting their contributions from the same position on stage, a microphone on a stand is preferred. If the speakers are reasonably close in height, set the height of the stand for the shortest speaker and leave it alone. If both children and adults will be speaking, use two or more microphones for the several height ranges. Nothing appears in poorer taste than having somebody run up and readjust the microphone in the middle of the program. Of course, if there is no alternative, readjustment is the preferable solution.

One of the biggest problems of public performers, especially amateurs or those not accustomed to public appearance, is what to do with the hands. This might explain the popularity of hand-held microphones among performers. When the mike is on a stand, the performer usually takes a death grip on the stand while speaking. It is a kindness in such cases to use a lectern if at all applicable. For small auditoriums, some lecterns even have build-in sound systems. The lectern gives the nervous speaker something to lean upon.

Choral groups are best covered by a number of microphones, each doing a portion of the work. In such cases, be sure the microphones are in phase with one another, applying the same rules you would use for loudspeakers. The microphones can be a greater distance away from the singers, since the sound level will be louder, of course. They can either be hung from overhead or, preferably, be on floor stands. Some stages have microphones concealed in the footlights, but in that position they are likely to pick up all the sounds of foot movement. Even that can be desirable in a tap dance routine.

Small groups, such as trios or quartets, often use individual microphones for each of the members. While this requires some elaborate control, it does allow for the most effective blending of sound.

In dramatic performances, there is always the possibility of concealing the microphone in one of the props, but only if the performer will be close to that prop during the entire routine. Back in the late 40s and early 50s, singer Kate Smith had a very popular television show. Much of the time she spoke while seated at a table. The microphone was concealed in a large arrangement of flowers on the table in front of her. More than one of the old-time Grade B movies used a telephone containing a line mike as a prop.

The "sound-spot" microphone is in a category all by itself. Recording companies have used it at considerable distances to record marching bands. It has been used by the press, even at Presidential inaugurations and it can be used quite effectively in dramatic presentations when aimed by a technician off stage.

All the preceding paragraphs have assumed that microphones are wired to the amplifying or recording system. One type of microphone contains a miniature radio transmitter. These units transmit in the FM broadcast band and the quality is no better than the transmitting and receiving apparatus used with them. Called wireless mikes, they come in price ranges as wide as do conventional microphones. The greatest use for wireless mikes is with performers who might be moving around the stage and in outdoor presentations.

Outdoor presentations often pose problems with microphone pickup, especially when the wind is blowing. Wind can produce a roaring sound in the microphone which can be detrimental to the most professional-sounding quality. The more expensive microphones have optional screens, called blast filters, wind screens and a variety of similar names. These minimize the wind problem, but they are often available only for the more expensive models. Some of the medium-priced models have wind screens built in.

Echoes outdoors pose an entirely different problem than those indoors. They are either absent altogether, making the sound a bit unnatural, or echoes arrive sufficiently long after the original sound to make it unpleasant. The latter of these two problems can be eliminated by using a directional microphone. If the echoes come from behind the speaker, a backdrop can be very helpful. Many outdoor concerts are staged in a half-dome structure which provides enough echo at the proper timing to make the sound more natural. An excellent example of this is the Hatch Memorial Shell on the bank of Boston's Charles River, where the famed Boston Pops Orchestra puts on its summertime programs.

Many amplifiers have a phono turntable of one kind or another built in. For those that do not, it is an easy matter to use an external turntable and pickup, feeding the output of the pickup into one of the amplifier's auxilliary inputs. It is a good idea to include a separate on-off switch for the phono motor to enable precise timing of the music with the rest of the program. Square-dance callers like to use a turntable with a speed control. Beyond this, the quality of the turntable should be consistent with the quality of the amplifying system which is, in turn, dependent on the quality of programming.

Phone pickup cartridges are electrically similar to microphones. Mechanically, they are different in that the element is vibrated by the needle riding in the grooves of the record, rather than by sound waves impinging on a diaphragm. In quality, they nicely parallel microphones of similar type—crystal, ceramic, dynamic or reluctance. Crystal pickups are inexpensive. They are best suited for general public-address systems where the main objective is simply boosting the sound. Ceramic pick-ups are the best compromise between low price and fairly good quality. They are used in many schools, stores and club auditoriums. Some of the equipment used by square dance callers use ceramic pickups. Professionals use magnetic pickups, which are the higher priced and better quality. As a general rule, you can expect the higher quality pick-ups to have a lower output level.

Chapter 6

Putting the Sound System Together

In the preceding chapters, the various components of a sound system have been discussed individually. Now it's time to assemble them into a system you can use. No two systems are exactly alike. After all, no two systems have exactly the same layout and use. A system that is just barely adequate in one case will be ridiculously overdone in another.

There are very few applications for the most basic system, which consists of one microphone, one amplifier and one loudspeaker (Fig. 6-1). However, the concept of the basic system can be used to better understand even the most complicated of systems. The microphone represents the program source, which can be either a single microphone, a combined microphone and turntable, or the output of a mixing console combining any number of microphones, turntables, tape decks and any other assorted bric-a-brac. About the only applications I know of for the most basic system are electrified lecterns, electric bullhorns and toys. Any other system uses more than one loudspeaker or has more than one program source. Most public address systems have several loudspeakers (rather than one). School and church auditoriums fall into this category, as do sound systems in church sanctuaries, paging systems in department stores, etc. Multiple speaker installations require attention to proper impedance matching and phasing. A decision must be made on whether to connect the loudspeakers directly to the output terminals of the correct

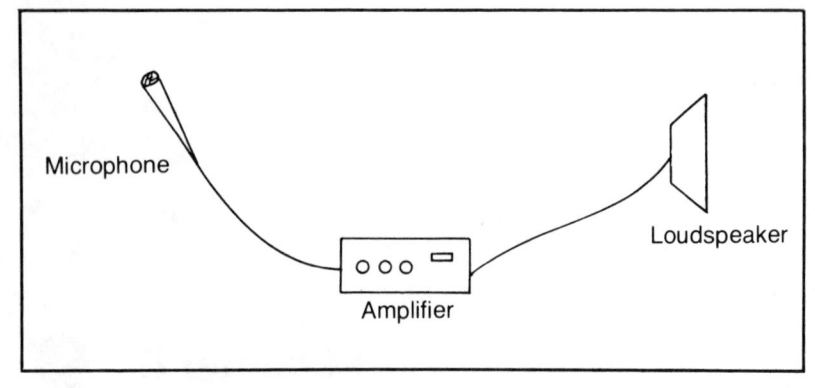

Fig. 6-1. The most basic PA system contains a microphone, an amplifier and a loudspeaker.

impedance or to use the 70-volt line and matching transformers. That choice is largely up to you. I recommend the 70-volt line if more than four loudspeakers or more than a hundred total feet of line is contemplated (Fig. 6-2).

PROGRAM MIXERS

Many systems, particularly those in school auditoriums and department stores, have a phono turntable, tape deck or fm tuner, in addition to a microphone. These are usually connected into the amplifier through separately controlled, high-impedance inputs. Such a system will meet the needs of a wide range of applications, ranging from factories, stores and building paging systems to the rudimentary needs for amateur theatrical presentations.

Systems that have more than one program source need some form of mixer, that is, a device to combine the two program sources into one line (Fig. 6-3). In the system described in the preceding paragraph, a mixer was a built-in feature of the amplifier. Most basic public address amplifiers have this feature. However, especially in the less expensive models, this feature allows only one or two extra channels. If more are needed, an external mixer is needed (Fig. 6-4). These are available quite economically at most electronic supply houses (Fig. 6-5). Generally, they are only needed for recording or for theatrical presentations. The built-in features of the amplifiers usually suffice for most other applications.

Here is a simple scheme to mix several microphones when it isn't necessary to have independent controls for each (Fig. 6-6). It simply ensures that each microphone feeds into the correct impedance and that the amplifier input is fed from a source of the

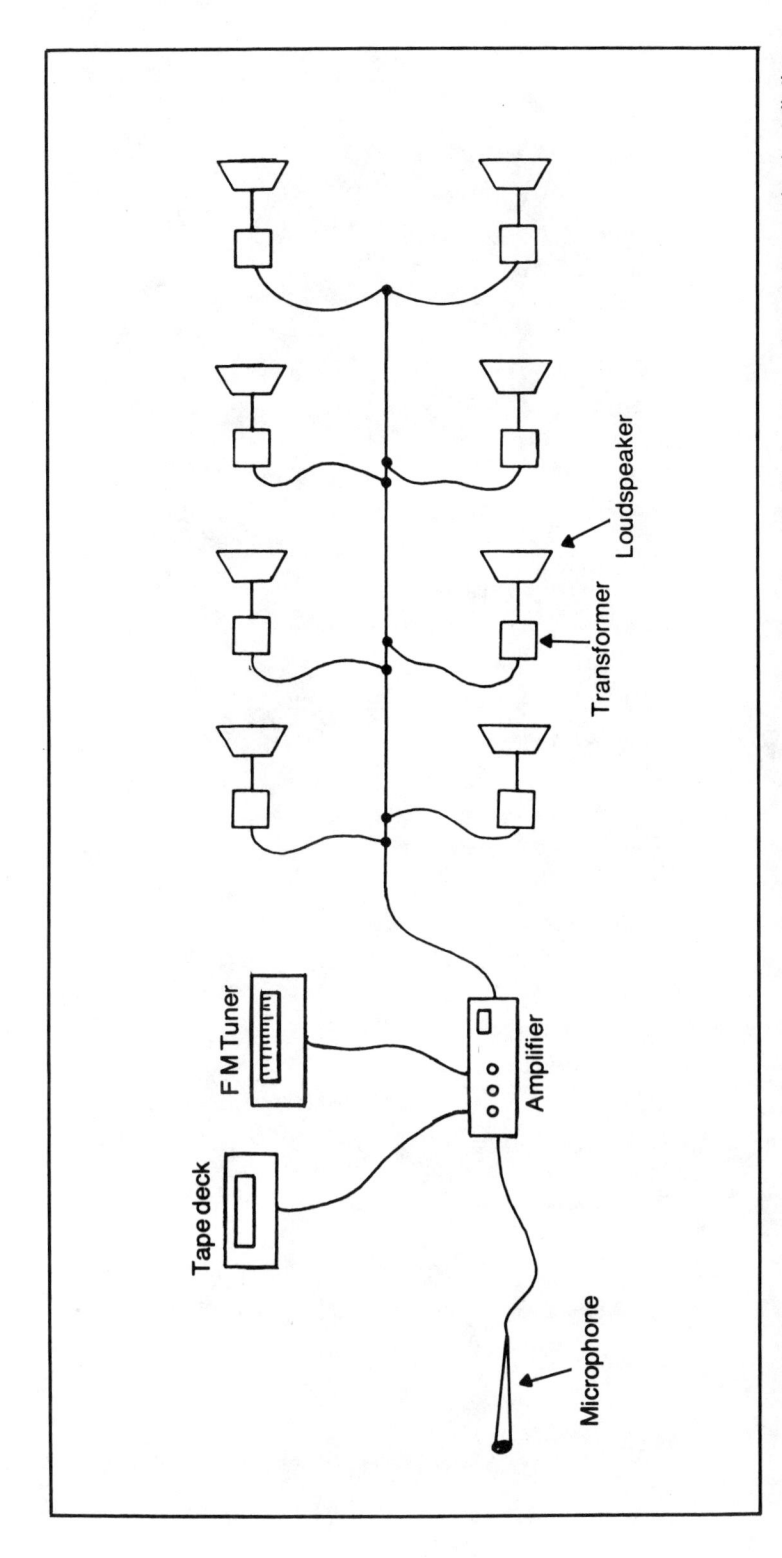

Fig. 6-2. As a system is expanded, complications increase. A mixer may be needed to accommodate the inputs, and multiple speaker installations require care in achieving correct impedance matching and phasing.

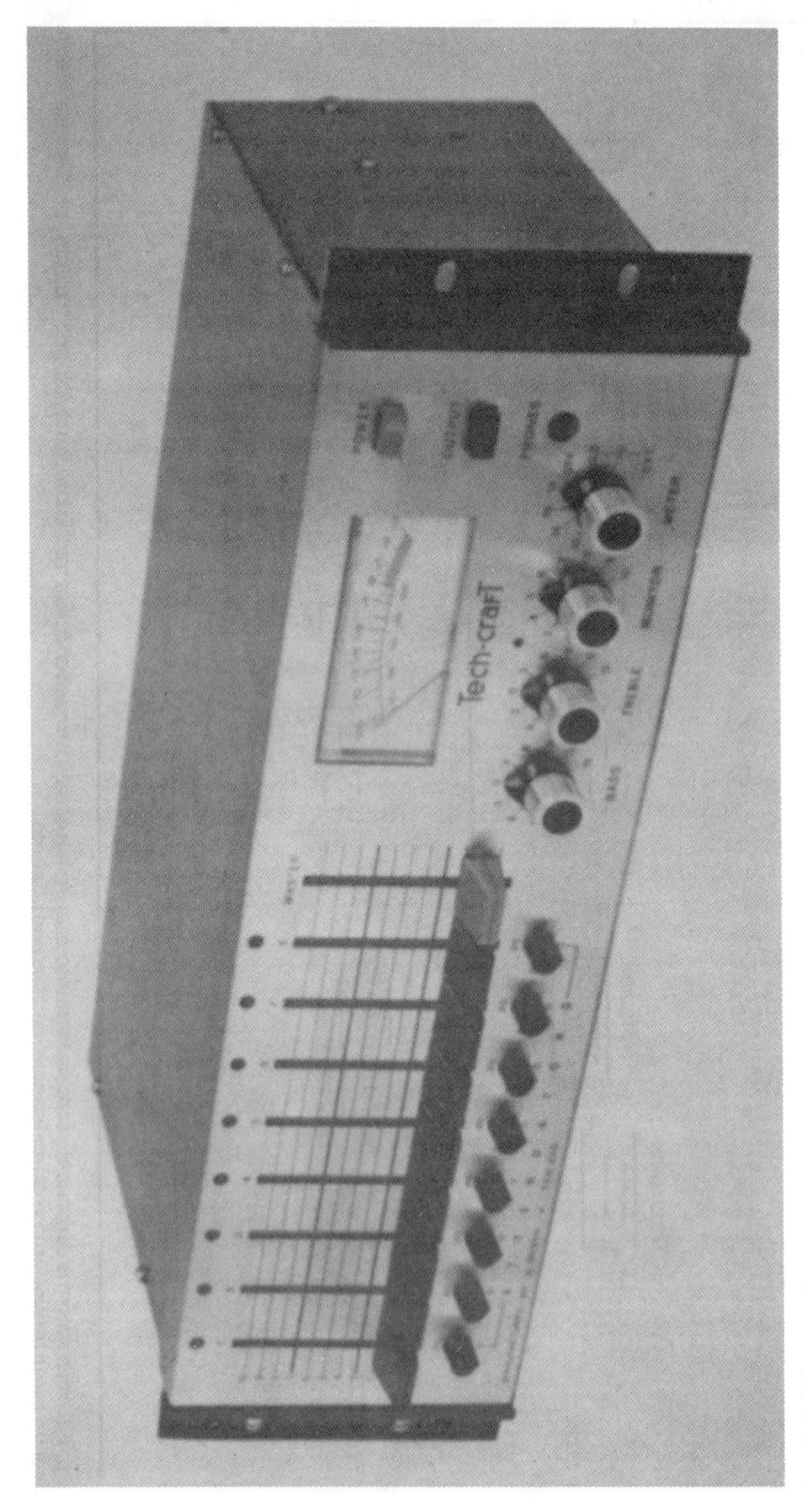

Fig. 6-3. A Bogen mixer.

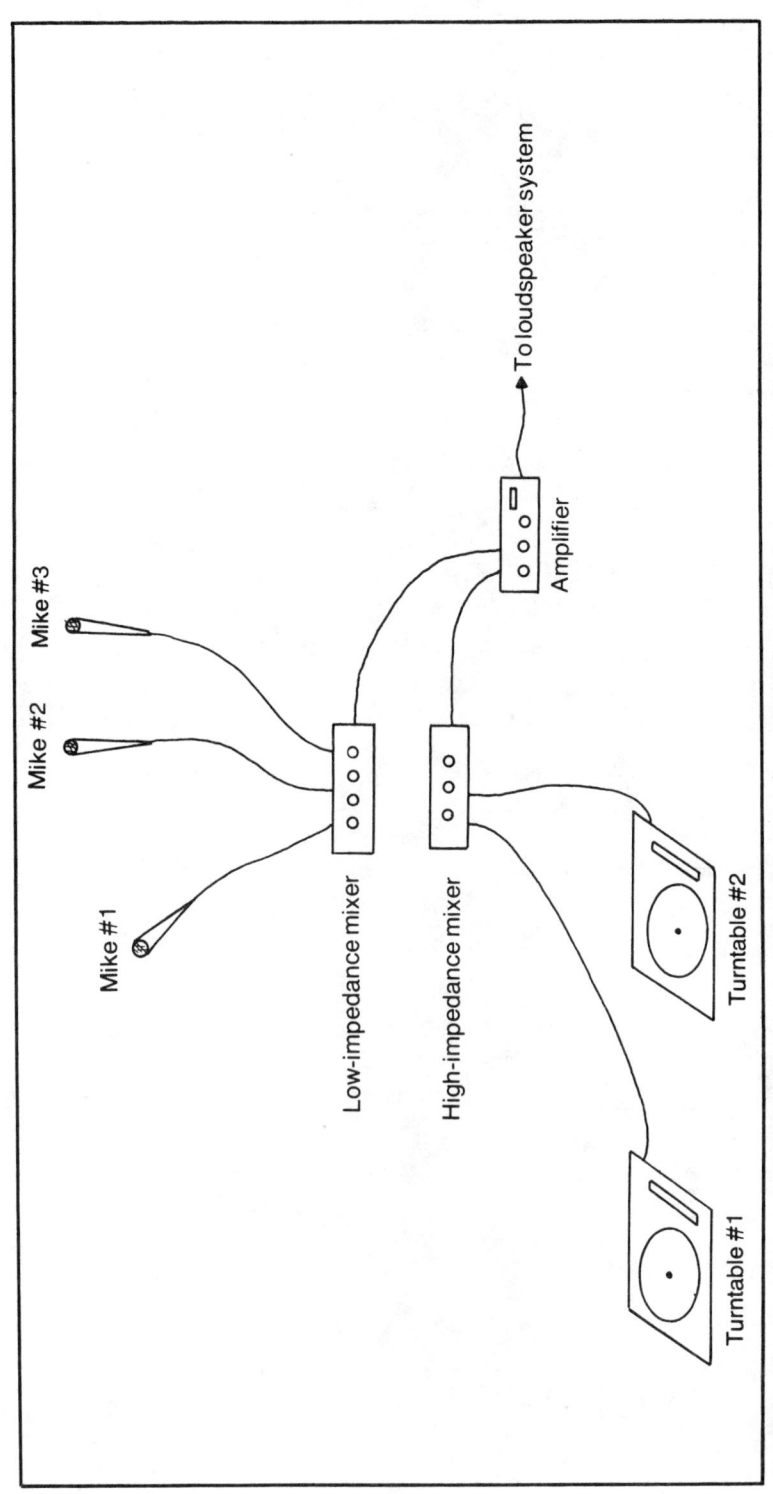

Fig. 6-4. External mixers can greatly increase the number of program sources that an amplifier can accommodate.

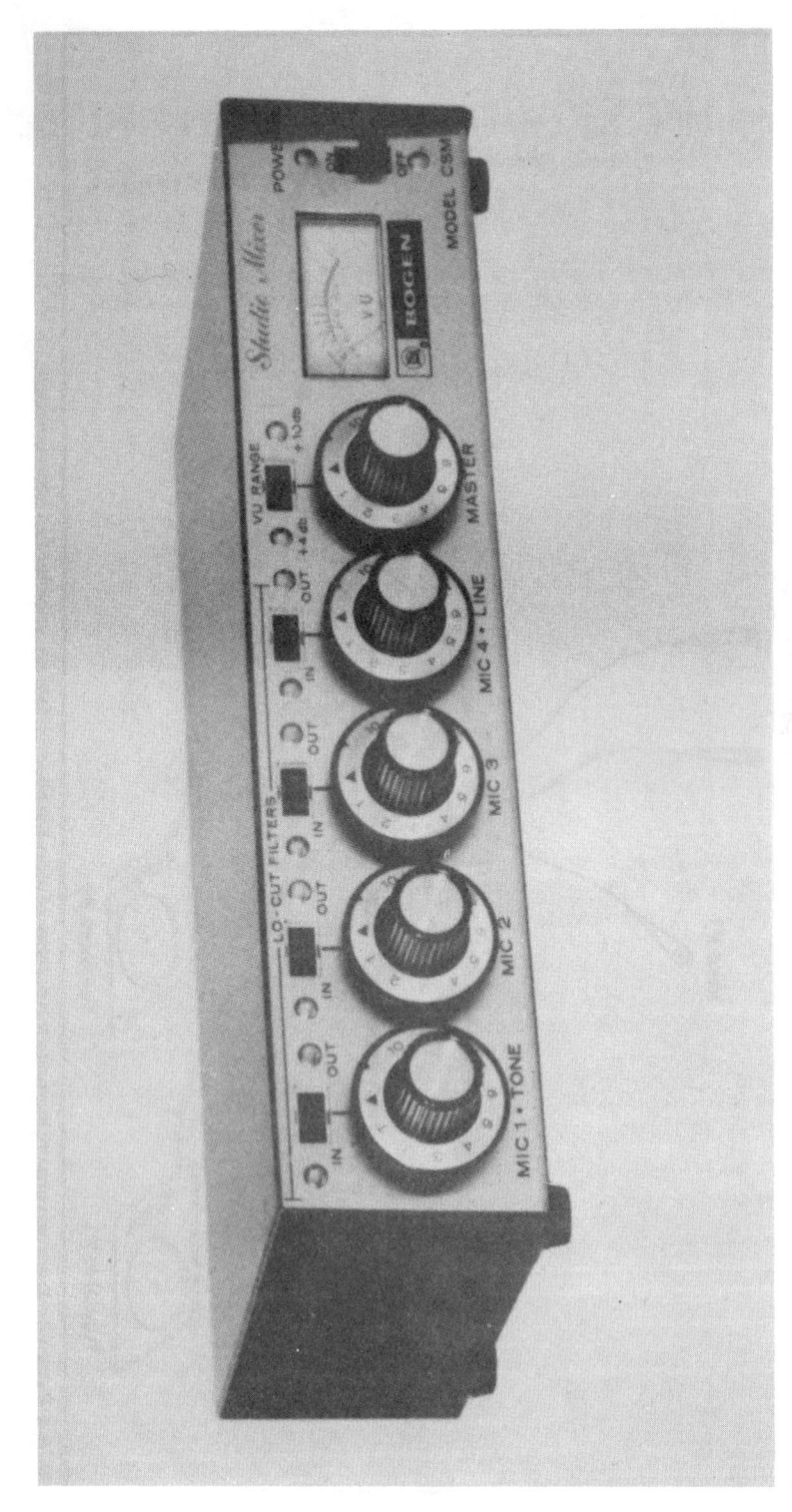

Fig. 6-5. The Bogen CSM mixer-preamplifier will combine four microphone outputs into a single amplifier input.

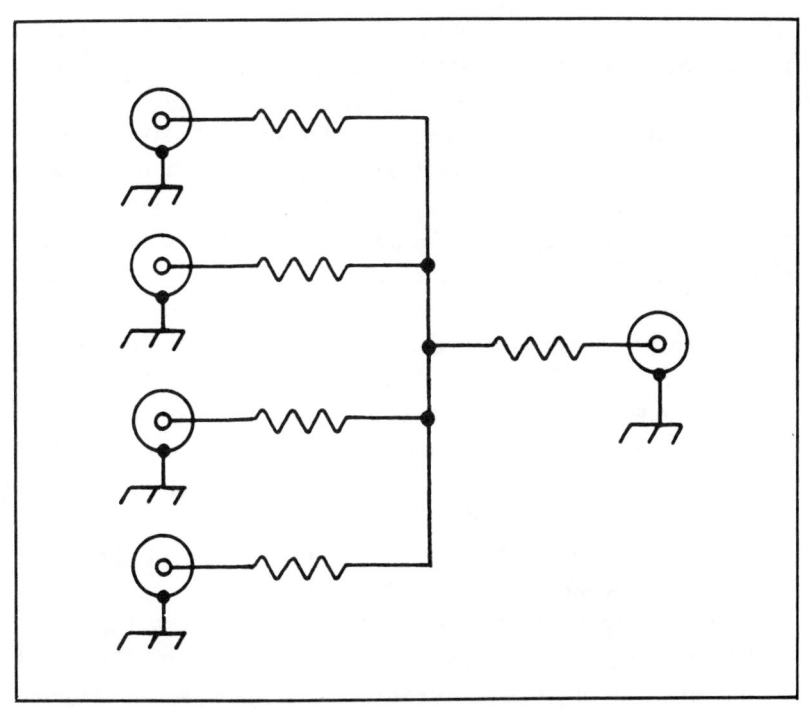

Fig. 6-6. Circuit of a simple, non-amplifying mixer.

correct impedance. Common, inexpensive carbon resistors are used and the resistance value is determinded from the following equation:

$$R = \frac{(N-2) \times Z}{N}$$

It might look complicated, but it's not that bad. R is the resistance of the resistors, N is the total number of branches, including the output, Z is the impedance of the microphones and it is assumed, of the amplifier input.

Here's how it works. Let's assume you want to mix four microphones. The mikes all have impedances of 20,000 ohms, as does the amplifier input. The total number of branches will be five (four microphones and the ouput). Set up the equation like this:

$$R = \frac{(5-2) \times 20,000}{5}$$

or

$3 \times 20,000 \div 5$

which is 12,000 ohms.

133

Five inexpensive carbon resistors, a couple of terminal strips or a piece of "perf-board" to mount them on, a small metal box, some connectors and you're all set (Fig. 6-7).

This kind of mixing network uses no power, so it doesn't amplify. It merely allows the various channels to combine without upsetting the impedance match of the circuit. It is symmetrical, that is, any branch can be used either as an input or as the output. The main disadvantage in its use, other than the lack of individual control, is that all branches must either be used or shunted with a resistor of the same value as the microphone impedance if it is to properly match the circuit impedance.

Except for the item just described, all the mixers I've ever seen have had gain controls for each of the respective channels plus a master gain control (Fig. 6-5). Generally, they also have some amount of amplification. Mixers can be obtained to work with either high- or low-impedance equipment. Some of the more expensive types offer combinations of both.

When you get into the mixing of several channels, especially for theatrical presentations, some means of monitoring the sound level of the program is advisable. In professional systems, a meter is provided on the mixing console for this purpose. Sometimes each channel is metered separately. For amateur theatrics, one meter monitoring the program line is plenty. It can either monitor the program going into the main amplifier or monitor the program going to the speakers. If there is no such meter in your system, one can easily be built, as shown in the circuit in Fig. 6-8. Small, attractive meters, calibrated in volume units, are available quite cheaply from most electronic hobby centers or supply houses. One of these, mounted in a box and provided with a potentiometer to calibrate it, is all you need.

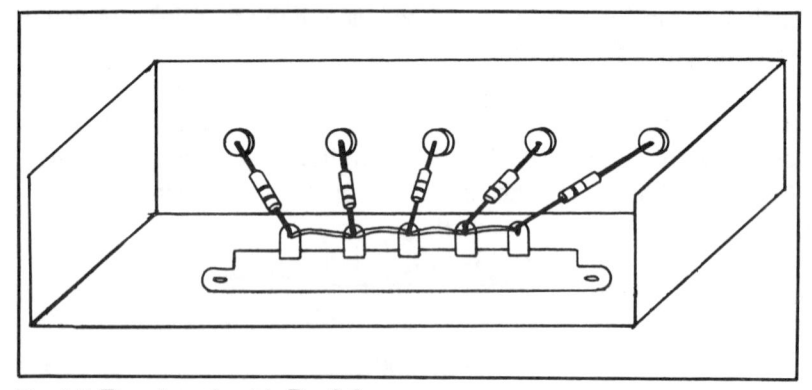

Fig. 6-7. The mixer circuit in Fig. 6-6.

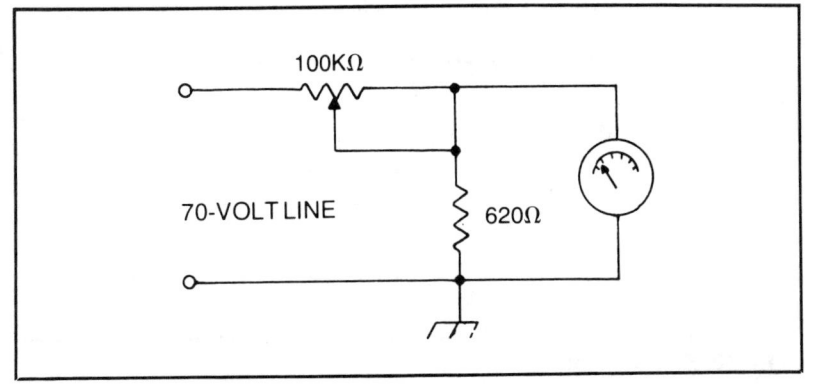

Fig. 6-8. Circuit designed to measure relative system output sound level.

To calibrate a volume level meter, set the amplifier gain (*before* the event!) so that the sound in the audience area is at a comfortable level. Then adjust the calibration potentiometer on the meter so that the reading averages 0 dB. You now have a reference level and can set any channel gain, for the same average reading during the performance.

A circuit designed to mix two channels with a little gain appears in Fig. 6-9. Any general purpose audio transistors can be used. For anything more elaborate than this, you might find it better in the long run to buy a mixer (unless you enjoy constructing equipment).

In the preceding two examples, the mixer input gain controls were deliberately left out. While a simple potentiometer connected as shown in Fig. 6-10 will control the level of the program, it will not keep the impedance of the circuit constant. The impedance

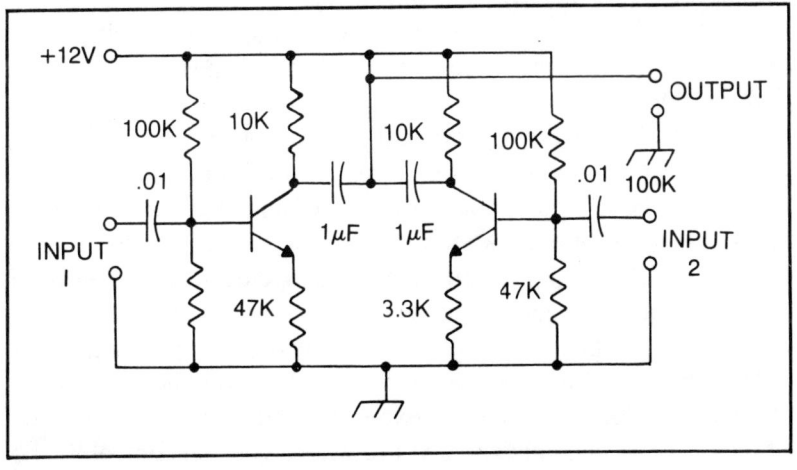

Fig. 6-9. Circuit for a two-transistor electronic mixer.

135

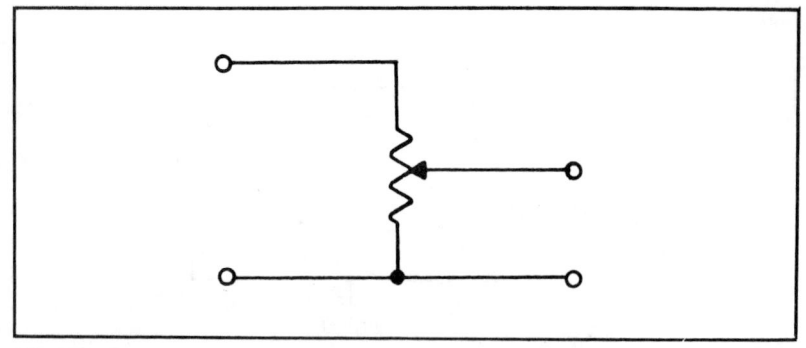

Fig. 6-10. Simplest input control circuit.

will seem fairly constant in the direction that looks across the outer terminals of the control, but even that will show a variation of at least 0.5 : 1 as the control is turned. For many amateur applications, that little technicality doesn't matter. If you want to control the level of the program while keeping the circuit impedance constant at all times, you need an attenuator.

I will discuss two kinds of attenuators: the L pad and the ladder. The L pad provides a nearly constant impedance looking in one direction while the impedance in the other direction will vary as the control is operated. It can be constructed with two potentiometers operated by a single shaft and give a continuously variable level (Fig. 6-11). The ladder attenuator (Fig. 6-12) varies the level in discreet steps, but it keeps the circuit impedance nearly constant looking in either direction. This type is used in the mixing consoles of many radio stations and recording stuios.

Resistance values for either of these attenuators is calculated for circuit impedances of 100 ohms in Table 6-1. If resistances are desired for circuits of other impedance values, simply multiply the resistance given in the table by the desired impedance divided by 100 (Z/100).

Depending on the equipment that you have available, it might sometimes become necessary to improvise. If your amplifier has only microphone inputs, but you are called upon to somehow feed a turntable or a tape deck into it, you have little choice but to improvise. The output of a turntable or a tape deck is often several times that of a microphone and you must cut the voltage down to a level that is compatible. The quickest way of accomplishing this is with a simple voltage divider circuit (Fig. 6-13). The ratio of the two resistors might have to be experimented with, but it's not too precise. If you once get the level to where you can control it, the battle's won.

You have seen one application in which the outputs of two ceramic phono pickups were patched into the 50-ohm input of a microphone mixer with very satisfactory results. A 100,000-ohm resistor offered a satisfactory load to the pickups and was connected in series with a 50-ohm resistor that matched nicely into the mixer. The level coming into the mixer was just right to offer smooth control of the level with the mixer input control. You might not always be this lucky. The same division of voltage into a 20,000-ohm input would take over 40,000,000 ohms and this is, of course, impractical. You can get approximately the same reduction of voltage, however, with a two-step arrangement as shown in Fig. 6-14. In Fig. 6-14 there are two voltage dividers in cascade. The input impedance is high—close to 800,000 ohms and the output is 20,000 ohms. The total reduction of voltage is about 2,000 to 1. Therefore an input averaging two volts will be reduced to about one millivolt and that can easily be handled by a microphone input.

I have not discussed equilization of the frequency response, and I do not intend to. Using the various improvisations described here will produce sound quality that is acceptable for most amateur puposes. Equalization networks must be designed for the individual circumstance and that requires a technical level considerably above that of this book.

By bits and pieces, I have expanded the sound system from a basic PA system into something approaching the capabilities of a professional theatre. Systems like this and even more complex systems, have been used in amateur theatrics. The old Methodist camp meeting ground of Asbury Grove in Massachusetts never was too well heeled when it came to auditorium equipment, yet they always put on amateur stage presentations that come off at an impressive level. Let's take a look at some of the conglomerations they've used.

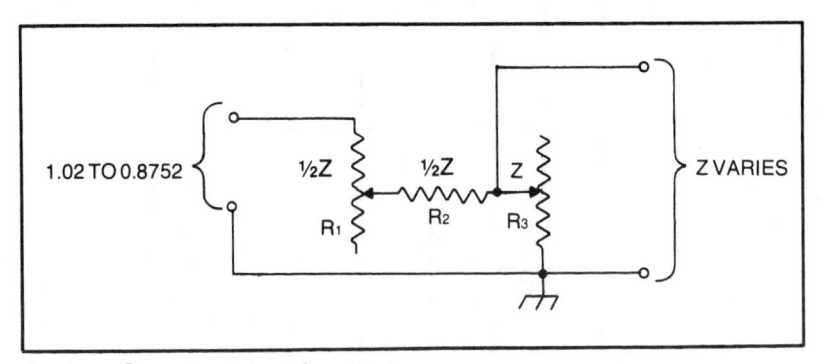

Fig. 6-11. Circuit for an L-pad attenuator.

Table 6-1. Resistance Values for the L-Pad and Ladder Attenuators.

	L-PAD	
R₁ R₂	50 OHMS	
R₃	100 OHMS	

	LADDER ATTENUATOR				
	R₁ (OHMS)	R₂ (OHMS)	R₃ (OHMS)	R₄ (OHMS)	R₅ (OHMS)
1 dB STEPS	50	94.5	11.6	870	1740
3 dB STEPS	50	85	35.2	292.5	585
6 dB STEPS	50	75	74.6	151	302

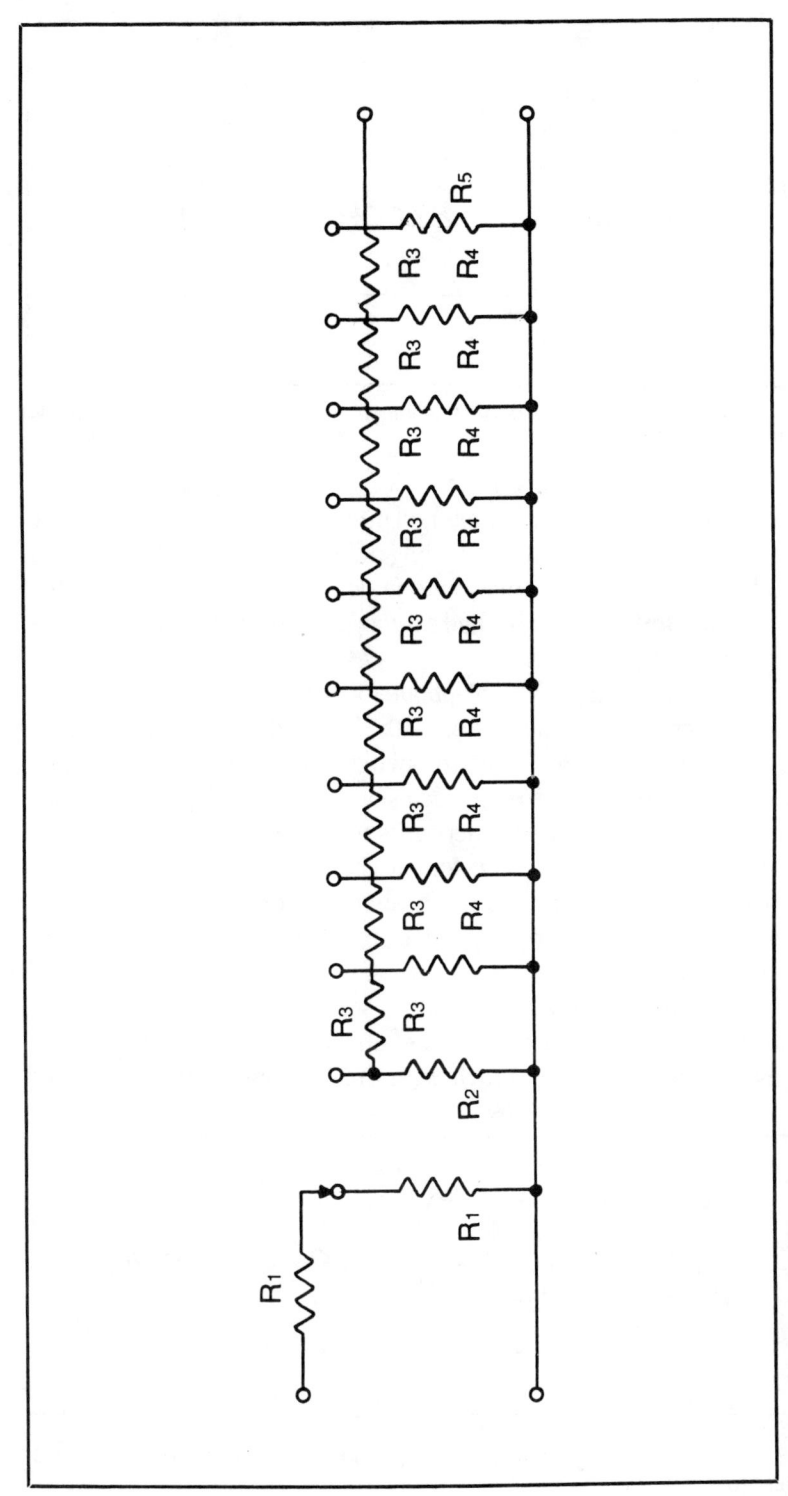

Fig. 6-12. Ladder attenuator circuit.

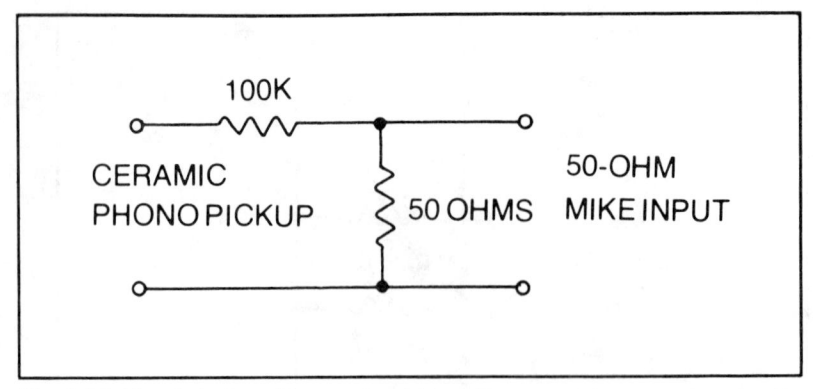

```
         100K
  o──────/\/\──────┬──────o
                   │
  CERAMIC          │       50-OHM
  PHONO PICKUP     ≶ 50 OHMS   MIKE INPUT
                   │
  o────────────────┴──────o
```

Fig. 6-13. Circuit designed to couple a high-voltage crystal or ceramic output to a microphone amplifier input.

The choral group on stage was covered by three hanging microphones which were combined into a single input with a simple resistance network. Three standing mikes on the stage took care of soloists. A backstage microphone was also available and the operator of the system also had a microphone enabling him to make announcements.

The three hanging microphones were treated as one unit and shared a channel in the mixer with one of the standing units by virtue of a double-throw selector switch (Fig. 6-15). The backstage mike and the operator's mike each shared a channel with one of the other standing mikes. This accounts for three of the four available channels in the mixer. The fourth channel was occupied by the phone turntable and a tape deck, also selected by a switch. Four available channels were expanded into eight, but only four were usable at any one time.

In addition, a separate amplifier was used to cue the tape deck and turntable. A telephone line enabled the producer of the presentation to keep in touch with the lighting technician, sound

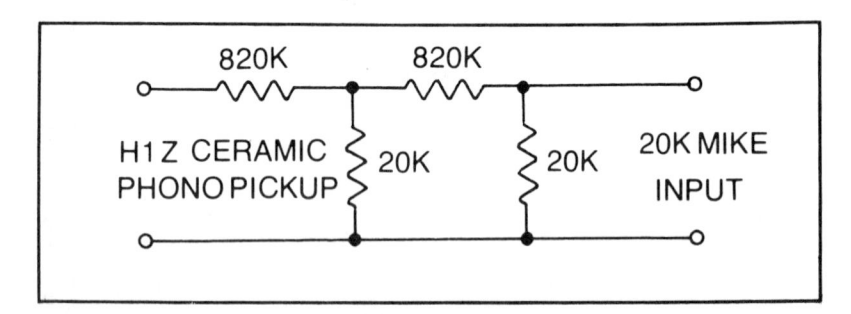

```
          820K         820K
  o──────/\/\─────┬────/\/\─────┬──────o
                  │             │
  HI Z CERAMIC    ≶ 20K         ≶ 20K    20K MIKE
  PHONO PICKUP    ≶             ≶         INPUT
                  │             │
  o───────────────┴─────────────┴──────o
```

Fig. 6-14. Circuit designed to couple a phono pickup into a high-impedance mike input.

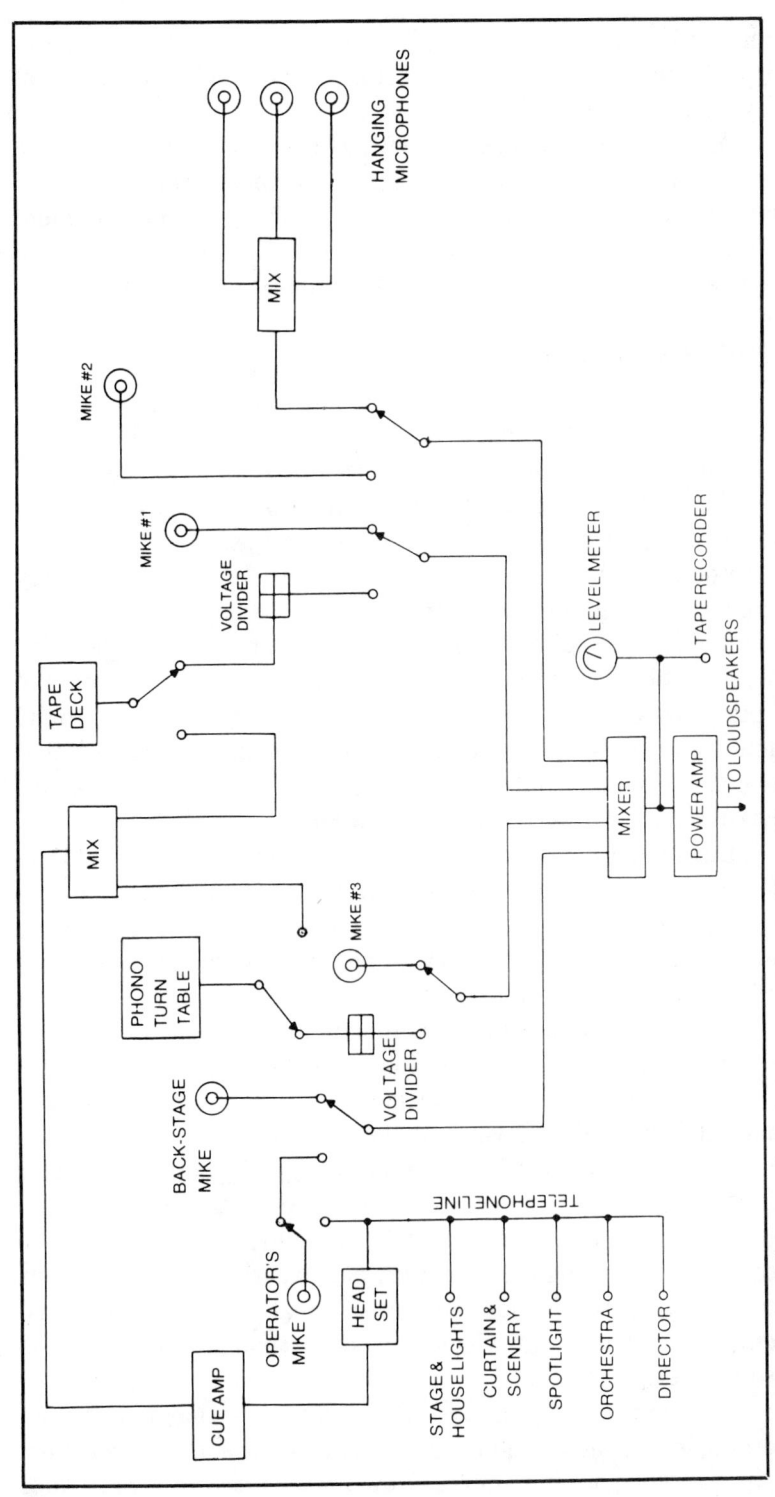

Fig. 6-15. Mixer circuit using switched inputs to combine additional program sources.

operator, curtain operator, etc. The system was a conglomeration, but there was very little a professional stage might have had that they didn't have.

All this was put together with available equipment and the junkbox of a local ham radio enthusiast. If these aren't available, every large city has rental agencies that supply sound equipment for theatrical presentations. There are even some who will set it up and operate it for you. Otherwise, all it takes is a little imagination.

OUTDOOR INSTALLATIONS

Outdoor presentations can be handled in much the same way and with equipment similar to that used indoors. The main problem is keeping the loudspeakers so orientated as not to feed back into the microphones. The complexity of this task is directly related to the surrounding terrain and the problem of echos.

For a very basic system, consider again Asbury Grove. They have a small, outdoor church there and the loudspeakers used are mounted on the roof of the bandstand that serves as a pulpit. The only microphone used is isolated from the loudspeakers by the roof of the pulpit area and the sound is directed very effectively to the audience (Fig. 6-16). The contour of the seating area is such that the sound from the loudspeakers passes over the heads of the first few rows, but reaches the back rows where it is needed.

Equipment used in this installation is not what you would call the very best high-fidelity equipment. In this application, all that is needed is to amplify the voice of the speaker. For that application, low-priced equipment suffices very nicely. One thing to remember with outdoor installations is that you need considerably more power than you would indoors. Indoor sound systems are reinforced by the natural reverberation of the room, however big. But outdoor systems are not. Furthermore, the loudspeakers are generally much farther away from the audience.

Outdoor equipment is much more ruggedly built than indoor equipment, for obvious reasons. Figure 6-17 and Fig. 6-18 are examples of battery power portable amplifiers. Care should be exercised in locating the amplifier, particularly with installations that might be used under less than ideal weather conditions. Remember, moisture provides a conductive path for electricity and so does the operator's body!

Let's examine a professional job of outdoor theatrical sound. Nothing in this country quite compares with the annual pageant put on by the Mormons in Palmyra, New York. Leaving any religious

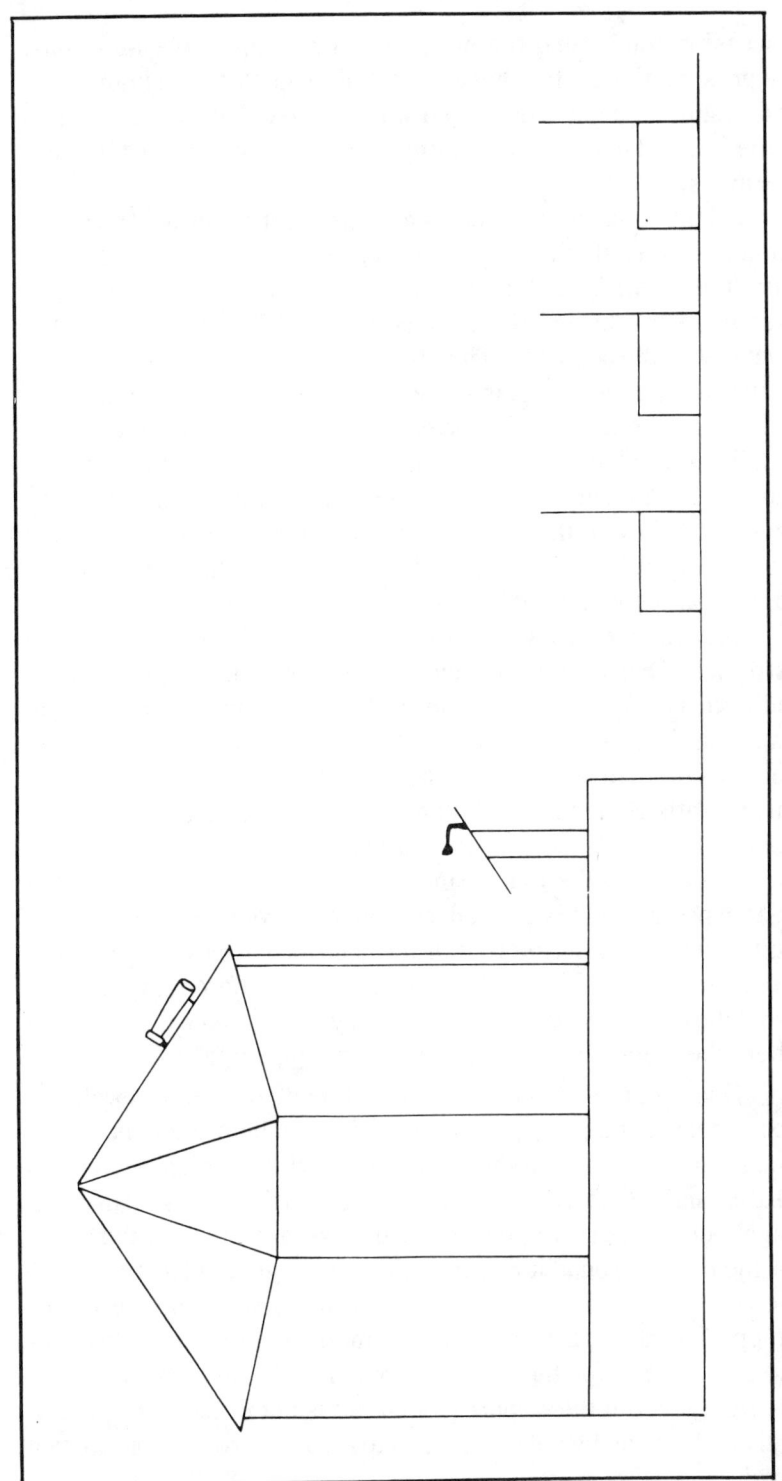

Fig. 6-16. Outdoor installation using building construction to isolate the speaker from the microphone.

143

discussion concerning the program entirely up to the Mormons, the presentation is, for sheer theatrical technology, an impressive undertaking. Sound is delivered with all the quality you might find in the finest of indoor sound systems to an audience covering nearly five acres.

All the sound for their pageant is prerecorded on a 5-track tape totaling nearly 8,000 feet. This tape is computer-synchronized with the lighting and other special effects. The loudspeaker system, over a dozen units in all, is located 200 to 300 feet from the front row of the audience. The major horn, seven feet square at the mouth by nine feet deep, is supported by three multicellular horns and six smaller units at the top of the hill. All the loudspeakers are artfully concealed in the landscaping, so as to be invisible to the audience. Of course, the average organization can hardly be expected to have either the funds or the technology of a worldwide church. However, you can glean ideas from them that might enable you to do more with what he has.

You will note that the two systems just described are opposite extremes. One is intended only to deliver human speech to an audience covering only half an acre or so. The other uses the maximum impact of faithful sound reproduction in presenting the religious dramatizations of the Mormon traditions. It delivers not only narration but music and sound effects. The sound effects range from those subtle noises one normally associates with a quiet summer night to the thundering roar of an earthquake. Even the system power itself is utilized, as your seat trembles beneath you. Quite a feat, considering your seat can be as much as 900 feet from the loudspeakers. There, then, are two very different systems for two different applications. The system you develop will depend on where, between the two extremes, your application best fits.

Once your system is installed and ready to use, it is well that you rehearse the program a couple of times before you put it on. You should, long before show time, determine the ideal audio level setting and adjust your system for that setting. This adjustment might consist merely of observing the average swing of the meter for the desired sound level. It might need slight readjustment with the auditorium full, —a minor adjustment easily made during the first performance. During the program, the operator merely opens the gain control for the desired channel until the meter indicates the right level. If the compressor circuit is not in use, the operator will need to ride the volume control to assure a program of constant level.

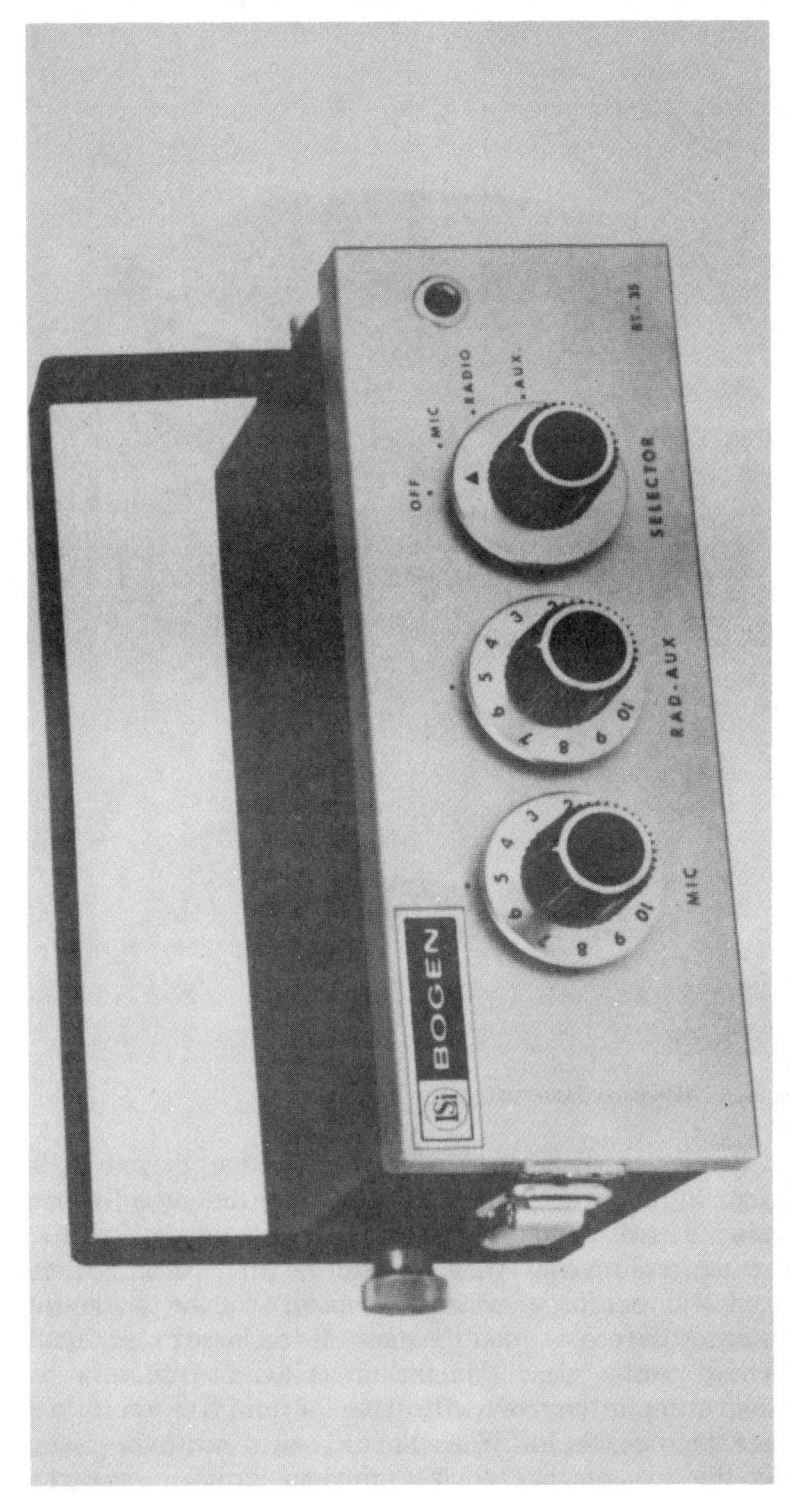

Fig. 6-17. A Bogen battery powered portable amplifier.

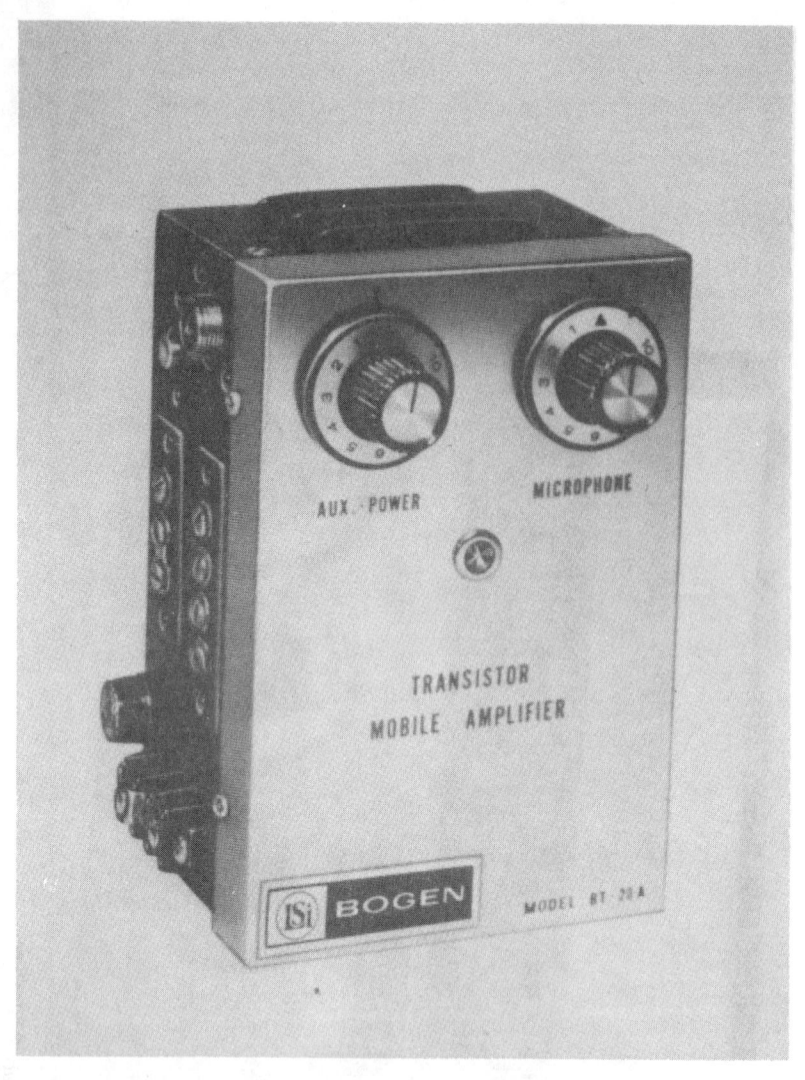

Fig. 6-18. A Bogen mobile amplifier.

Recordings should be "cued up" well before they are to be played. In broadcast stations, the following technique, or one similar, is used. With the pickup connected to the cue amplifier, start the record going. When you hear the first sound, hold the record with your finger and stop the motor. With the pickup still resting on the record, rotate the turntable backward by hand until you hear no more sound. With the turntable turned off, leave the pickup resting in the groove, at least one full turn of the record from where the sound begins. When the cue comes, switch the pickup from the cue amplifier to the program amplifier, open the appropriate gain control, and switch on the turntable. Use a similar technique to cue up a tape recording. In both cases, be sure you leave enough space between the pickup and the beginning of the sound for the record or tape to accelerate to its proper speed. Otherwise, the recording will begin with an annoying "wow."

Let's imagine a typical production. The script calls for a few bars of "canned" music, a bit of narration and then some live performance. Some recorded sound effects are included in the performance. Here's how you might do it.

Well before the production begins, cue up the music. Have the pick-up waiting in the groove, and the "hot," that is, the pick-up connected to the program amplifier.

When ready, open the gain for the music. You *did* determine the level beforehand, didn't you? After the first couple of musical phrases have played, cut the gain way back, but not off and open the narrator's mike. This will put his voice on with the music low in the background. When the narrator has said his bit, close his mike and bring the music up for another few bars. Then fade out the music and open the performer's mike.

Depending on how tight the timing is, you might want to have the sound effects cued up ahead of time. It is a good idea to have the sound effects for the entire program, in their correct sequence, on a separate tape, with a few seconds of silence between. Then you need cue up only the first one. Stopping the tape after each effect leaves it automatically cued up for the next one.

As the performer finishes, bring up the music again, if called for. In cases where a closing few bars of music are wanted, it is often the ending of a particular selection. For this effect, set the pickup ready a turn or two of the record from the point you want to cut in. As your cue approaches, monitor the record on the cue amplifier and start the turntable. On cue, switch the pick-up to the program amplifier and then open the gain control. It takes some practice, but it is very effective.

If the program is to be taped from your system, have the recorder set up and ready well beforehand. Well before the production begins, set up the record gain by playing a record on the turntable into the system and setting the level of the recorder. This should be done long in advance, before the audience enters the hall. Set the tape in place, or insert the cassette after the record gain is set. Start the tape a minute or so before the program begins. It is easy to erase any unwanted sounds and you will have your hands full with other matters once the program starts.

Only a fool would attempt to operate both a sound system and the lighting for a complex program. If the setup is relatively simple and no mixing effects are needed, you can get away with it. Otherwise, let somebody else do the lighting operation.

Chapter 7

Lighting the Stage

In any lighting system the beginning is the lamp. Three kinds of lamps are considered here: tungsten, tungsten-halogen, and arc. Carbon arc sources are also discussed, even though a carbon arc isn't necessarily a lamp. The first two types mentioned are incandescent, as opposed to arc. In an incandescent lamp, the light comes from a white-hot filament. In an arc lamp the light is produced by electrical current passing through a vapor. In the two covered here, one uses mercury vapor and the other uses a rare gas such as xenon.

TUNGSTEN INCANDESCENT LAMPS

A tungsten incandescent lamp is the everyday light bulb as we know it. A wide variety of types are available for amateur theatrical use. These might range from outdoor-type floodlamps and projection lamps for the do-it-yourselfer to professional photoflood and studio lamps. Generally speaking, tungsten is the most economical lamp to use in small installations. Since conventional fixtures available at any hardware store will accommodate them, they should be given first consideration when building your own setup.

The chief disadvantage with conventional lamps is the tendency to blacken on the inside with age. This can reduce the light output of a lamp to as much as half of what it was when new (Fig. 7-1). The blackening is caused by deterioration of the filament. In order for the lamp to be any kind of a light source, the

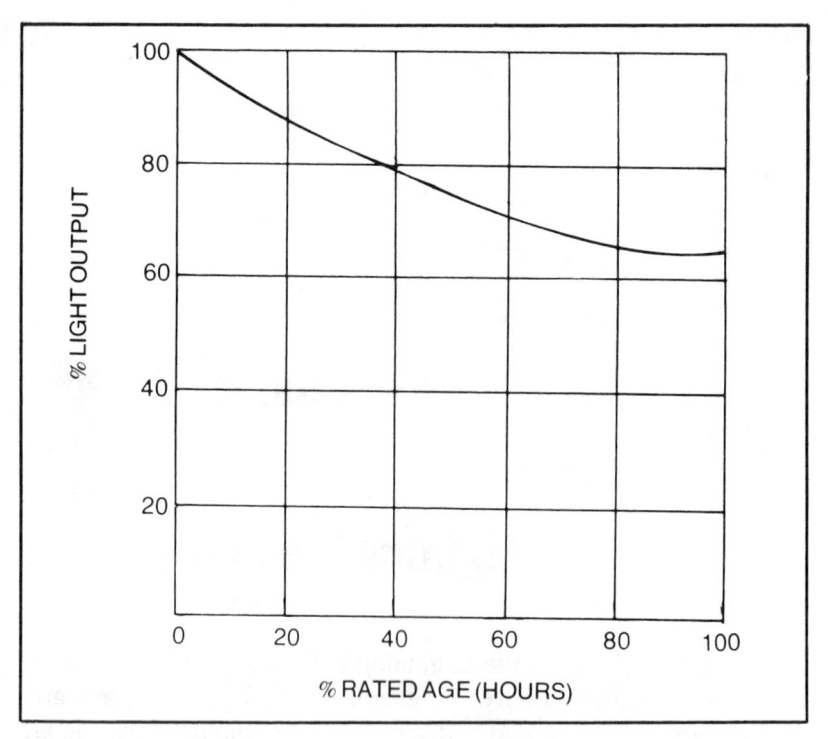

Fig. 7-1. The light output of an incandescent lamp decreases with use.

filament must be heated while hot. Even though tungsten can stand such heat without melting, some of the metal actually evaporates. Then, when the lamp cools the evaporated metal condenses on the inner surface of the glass bulb. This condensed tungsten is the blackening you see.

Tungsten lamps of the household variety are filled with a nitrogen/argon mixture to slow the evaporation of the filament. While this does improve lamp performance, an even greater improvement is achieved by adding another element. In addition to the aforementioned gases, a little iodine or similar element is introduced into the lamp. When the lamp is run hot enough, the iodine gas combines with the evaporated tungsten. Then, when the tungsten halide contacts the white hot filament, the extreme heat breaks it down, causing the tungsten to be redeposited on the filament. Therefore, the lamp maintains its brightness throughout its life and lasts a bit longer (Fig. 7-2). Iodine belongs to a chemical group known as the halogens. Therefore, the lamps are called tungsten-halogen lamps.

Tungsten-halogen lamps are run at a hotter temperature in order to maintain the chemical action inside. Consequently, special sockets are needed in order to maintain reliable operation (Fig. 7-3). Tungsten-halogen lamps are often designed to have a higher internal pressure than the non-halogen types. Being smaller in size and hotter, they often require some means of forced cooling and a heat sink to dissipate heat from the socket. The longer life and constant output level of tungsten-halogen lamps, as well as the smaller size, greatly outweighs any disadvantages.

ARC LAMPS

Arc lamps require a special power supply (Fig. 7-4 and 7-5). This is true whether you are using a mercury lamp, a flourescent lamp or a xenon flashtube. Xenon flashtubes are discussed in chapter 11.

Mercury arc lamps are used in only very limited applications in the theatre. This is due to their very limited spectral output. A mercury lamp has almost no output at the red and yellow portions of the spectrum and is very efficient at the green to ultra-violet end. It is the same greenish blue lamp that is often used for street and other outdoor lighting. While it is very efficient, so far as lumens per watt is concerned, its use on a stage would make the performers look absolutely ghastly.

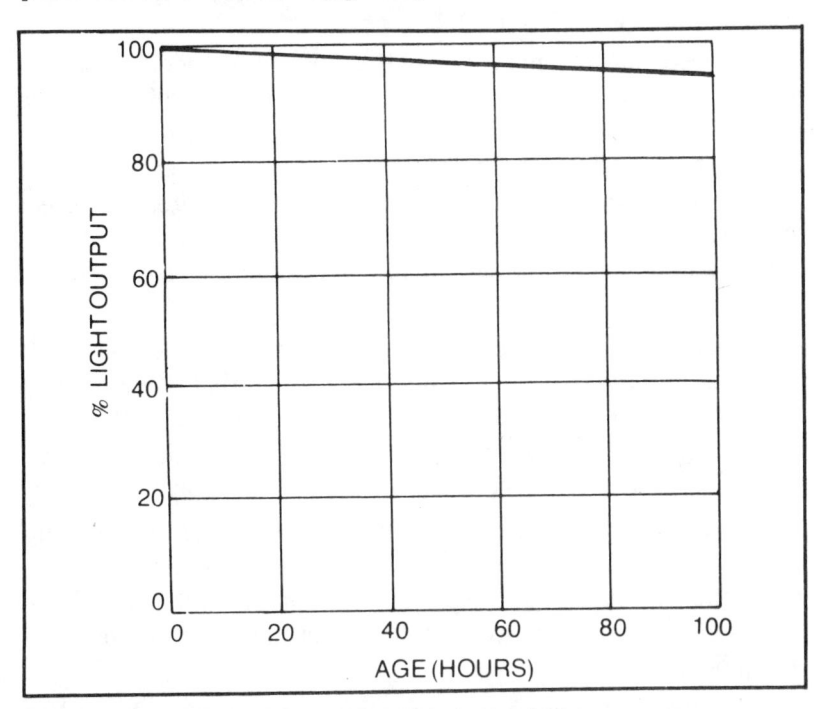

Fig. 7-2. The light output of a tungsten-halogen lamp decreases with age but to a lesser degree than conventional incandescent lamps.

Outside of application as an ultra-violet source, I know of only one instance in which a mercury lamp was used on a stage. This was in a church play. The scene was supposed to be the interior of a desert tent. Actors entering the set would push aside a cloth flap representing the tent door. The intense glare of the mercury lamp, momentarily streaming in, very effectively simulated the desert sunshine.

A mercury lamp will work quite effectively as an ultra-violet source, provided a proper filter is used. Such filters are available from the stroblite Co. (Fig. 7-5) and from other sources. If you should make your own ultra-violet source, do *not* use any lamp with a quartz envelope and do *not* use a germicide lamp unless you have it filtered through a Strobelite filter. Mercury arc lamps and germicide lamps produce ultra-violet radiations at wavelengths that can permanently damage the actor's eyes. With correct filtering, however, it is reasonably safe.

The arc in a mercury lamp is triggered with a high initial voltage, but less voltage is needed to sustain it. This is true with any kind of an arc lamp. A transformer, designed for the purpose, handles this very nicely. But an individual transformer is necessary for each lamp (Figs. 7-3 and 7-4).

The xenon arc lamp is one of the more recent additions to the family of light sources and is the most powerful light source available. It produces an intense, white light. The xenon arc operates on a principle similar to the mercury arc, except that it uses a much lower sustaining voltage and operates on direct current. The lower voltage means a very high current level for a given wattage. Also the lamp has a very high internal operating pressure.

Operating voltages generally run around 25 to 30 volts with currents in the hundreds of amperes. An external power supply provides the needed voltages and, while this makes it a bit clumsy to transport and set up, the high light output more than compensates for the inconvenience of the special power supply.

Xenon lamps increase the effective power of any lighting device in which they are used. Manufacturers of lighting equipment claim they produce up to 70% more light than a carbon arc. They are used in the more powerful follow spotlights and in projection equipment.

Fluorescent lamps are another type of mercury arc lamp. But instead of being concentrated into a relatively small area, the arc is

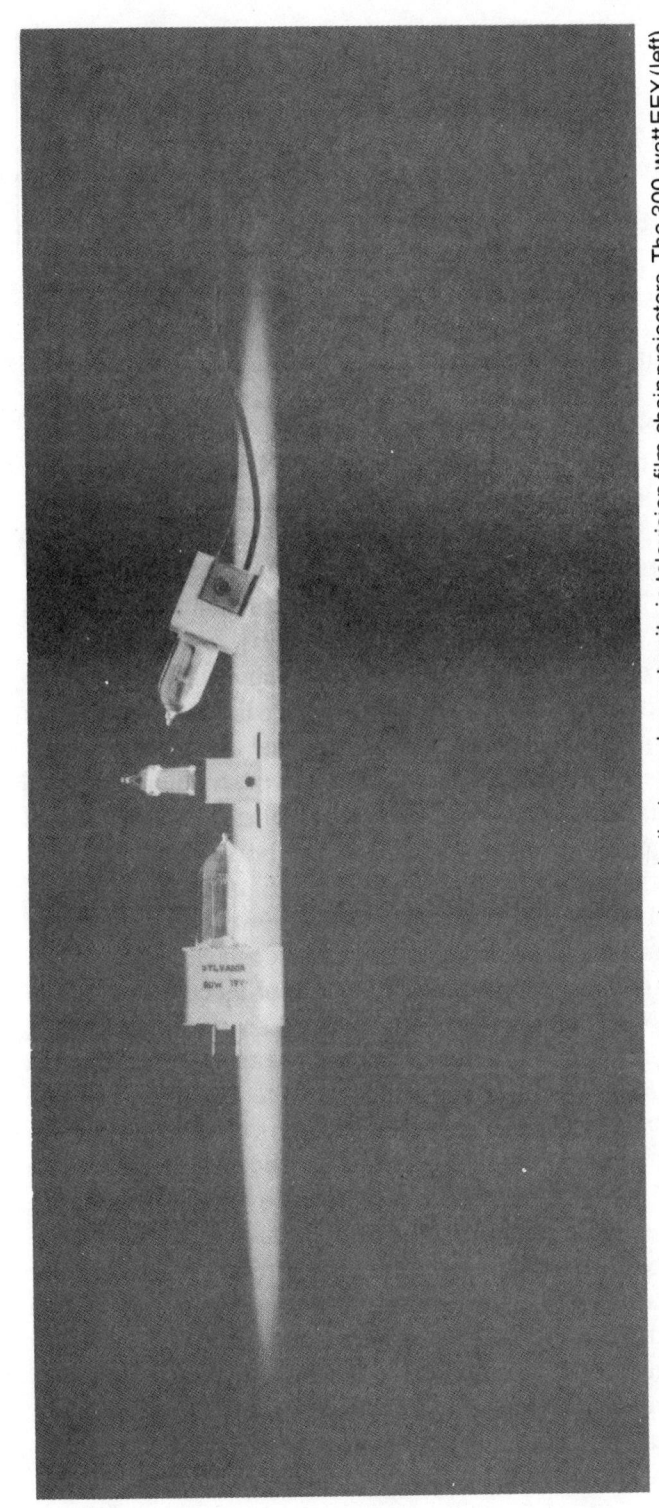

Fig. 7-3. Three tungsten-halogen lamps, designed to replace bulky incandescent units in television film-chain projectors. The 300-watt EEX (left) provides 7,200 lumens and operates at 3200° K, the 500-watt DZG (center) provides 13,000 lumens and operates at 3200° K, and the 1000-watt BTC (right) provides 31,000 lumens at 3325° K. The lamps have been designed as direct replacements for incandescent types without the use of adapters. They provide constant illumination and color temperature throughout their life and may be burned in any plane. Reflectors are built in, assuring high efficiency, and precision-aligned filaments provide exacting standards of light distribution required in television studio projectors (photo courtesy GTE Sylvania).

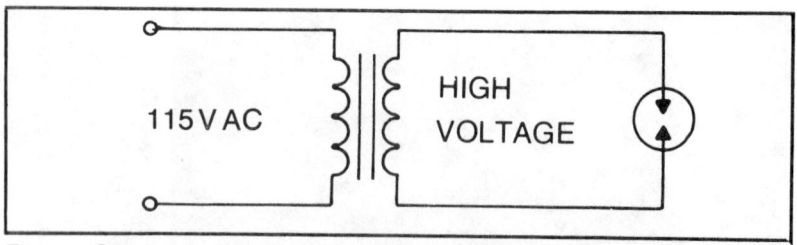

Fig. 7-4. Circuit for a mercury arc lamp. This same basic circuit is used for other types of metallic vapor lamps.

stretched out throughout the length of the lamp. Less current is used and the light produced is much less intense. The inside of the lamp is coated with a phosphor that converts the ultra-violet light produced by the arc to visible light. Lamps of this type, minus the phosphor coating and made with special glass or quartz envelopes, are often used in hospitals and laboratories for germicidal purposes. Others, made with special filter glass, are used in theatrical and familiar "black light" applications. They all use the same kind of a circuit.

In fluorescent lamps, the mercury vapor is heated by a filament at either end (Fig. 7-6). Then the arc is sustained and the filaments turned off. A ballast unit ensures that the lamp draws the correct current. Fixtures are available quite economically, pre-wired with starter and ballast. Again, if you plan to use this type of lamp for a home-made black light source, be sure to use lamps intended for that purpose.

The carbon arc is still one of the most powerful light sources known. It has been around longer than incandescent lamps. When two carbon rods are connected to a source of electric power and momentarily touched together, an electrical spark occurs as they are drawn apart. If the separation is no more than an eighth of an inch or so, the arc will sustain itself, and the electrodes will be heated to incandescence. It only takes 55 volts or so to sustain the arc, although considerable current is required. As the arc wears away the carbon rod (the positive electrode wears fastest), an electromagnet and spring arrangement advance the rod to keep the arc going. A carbon-arc lamp circuit is shown in Fig. 7-7.

Carbon arcs are used in the more powerful of follow spotlights (Fig. 7-8) and in commercial movie projectors. There are still quite a few of them around, although some of the rare gas arc lamps are gradually replacing them. They do require a bit of care in their operation, but are hard to beat for a really powerful light source. Also, a carbon arc unit does require a special power supply.

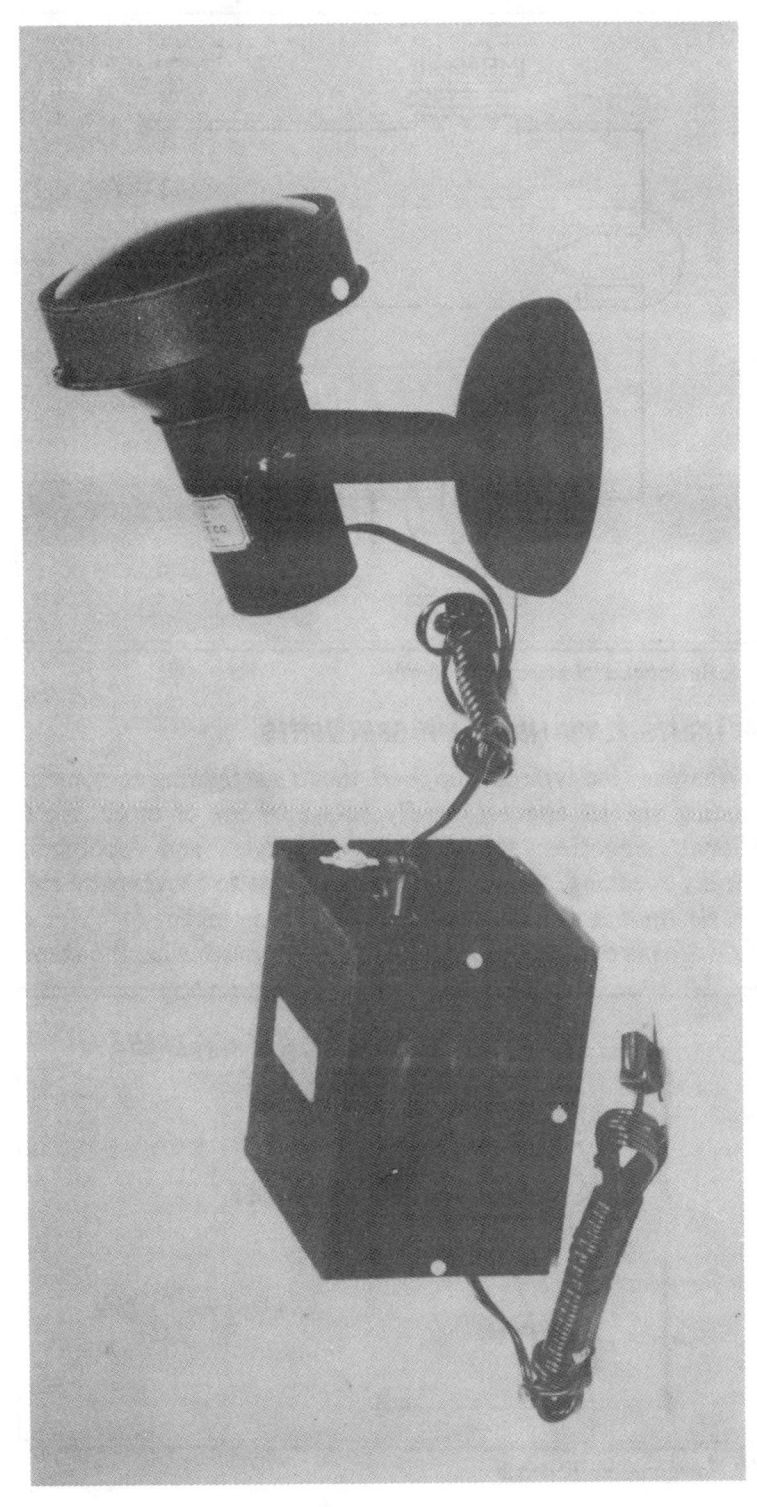

Fig. 7-5. A small ultra-violet light unit. The black box contains a transformer that supplies the mercury-arc lamp in the light unit (photo courtesy Stroblite Corp.).

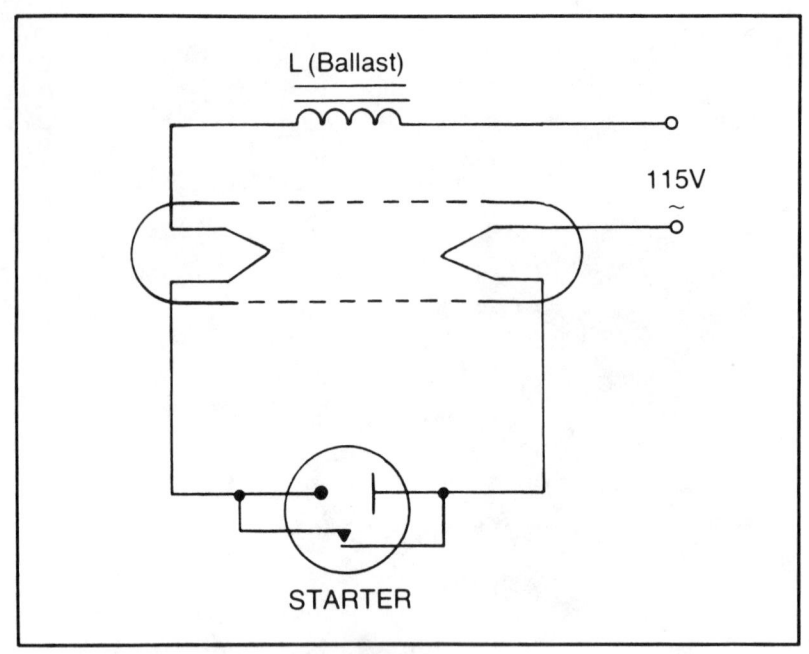

Fig. 7-6. Basic circuit of a fluorescent lamp.

STRIP LIGHTS, FLOOD LIGHTS AND SPOTLIGHTS

Whatever the type of lamp used, theatrical lighting equipment (excluding special effects) usually falls into one of three major functional categories: strip lights, flood lights and spotlights. Generally speaking, a light unit that has a lens to concentrate and direct its light is a spot, while a light that is meant to cover a general area is a flood. Strip lights are pretty much what the name

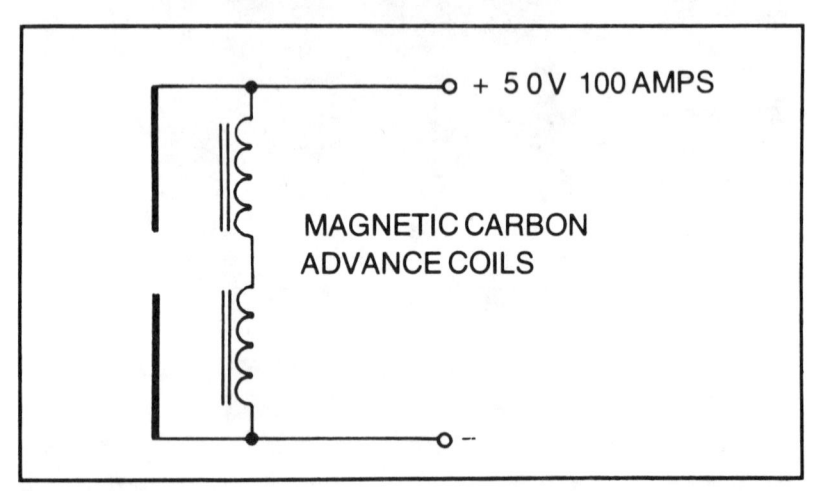

Fig. 7-7. Basic carbon arc circuit.

implies—strips of light units—generally used as border lights or foot lights.

Strip Lights

Let us pause here and become familiar with the arrangement and terms of a well planned stage (Fig. 7-9). A professional stage has easily twice as much or more floor space as is visible to the

Fig. 7-8. The Strong Trouper uses a carbon arc light source, with the power supply built into the base. It is recommended for throws up to 200 feet. At 80 feet with a 7-foot spot, it yields 280 foot candles. Levers on the top control spot size, while the set of levers at the end operate color media (photo courtesy of the Strong Co.).

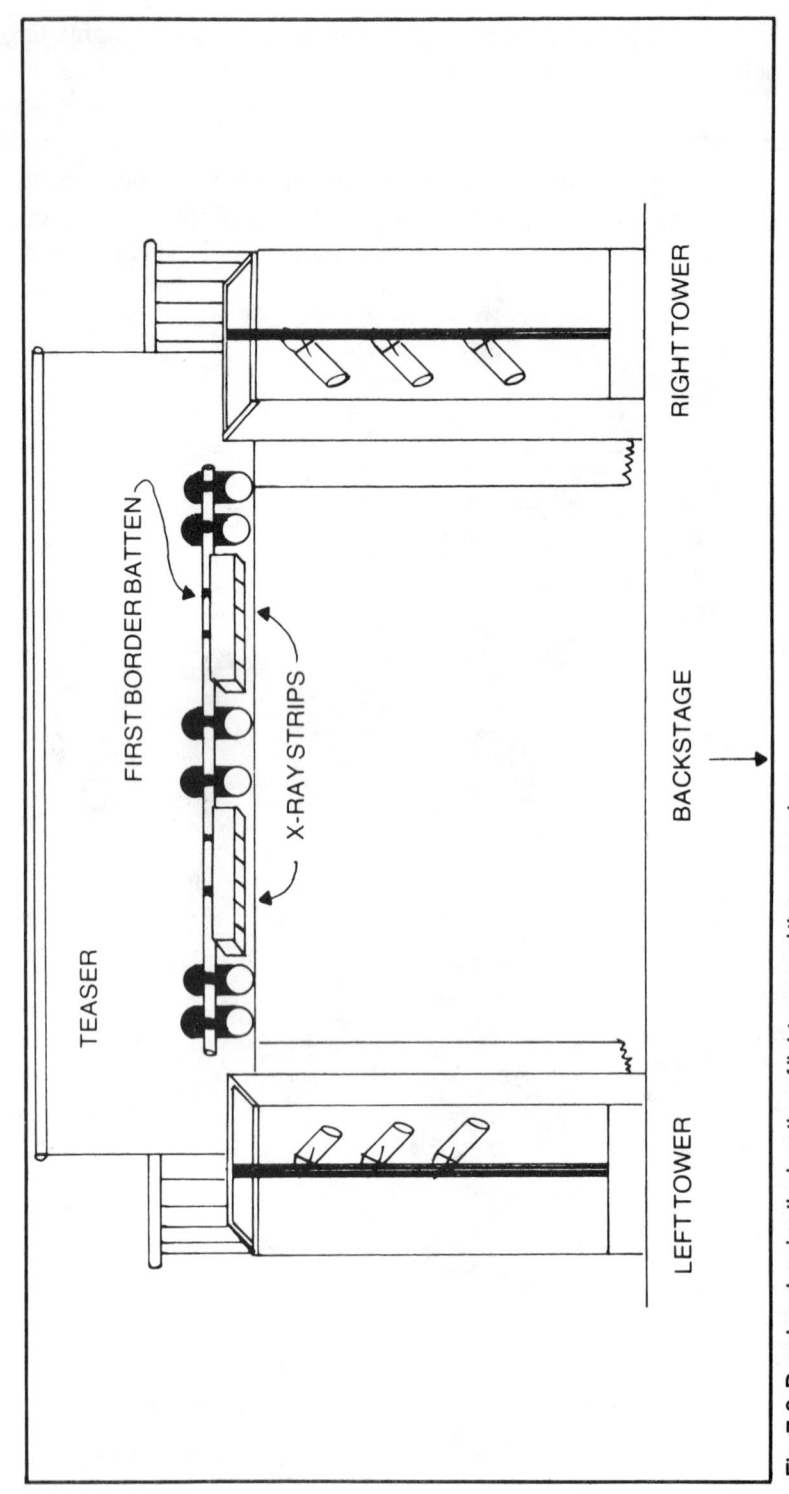

Fig. 7-9. Drawing showing the location of lights around the proscenium.

Fig. 7-10. The first border batten and teaser in a high-school auditorium. This school is better equipped than most. Here they apparently prefer individual units to strip-lights.

audience. The stage floor extends on either side of the proscenium (or stage opening) easily half again as far as the proscenium is wide. Behind the backdrop, it can extend as far as from the curtain line to the backdrop. All in all, twice as much floor space is really a conservative number.

The height above the proscenium is easily twice that of the proscenium height. At the very top is a gridiron from which all the rigging is hung. The rigging is controlled from a position at extreme stage right, that is, to the right of the performers, or to the left of the audience. The rigging is secured to a low rail, called a pin rail, close to the wall at the control position. Generally, the lighting console is also located off stage right, concentrating the backstage staff where the director can reach them.

Immediately behind the act curtain is a small strip curtain, called the teaser which forms the top border of the proscenium. The teaser is adjustable in height. Immediately behind the teaser, sometimes slung on the same rigging, are the border lights which hang on a long pole called the batten (Fig. 7-10). The border lights are those lights that are mounted overhead near the front of the stage. Depending on the size of the installation, there might be two or three sets of borders—front, middle and rear.

The border lights usually consist of at least two strips, which provide general illumination, and six or more floods. The strips consist of a row of lights, often mounted as separate units, wired into three circuits. Colored mediums, called gels, are fitted over each light unit. With three separately controlled circuits, each gelled with a different primary color, any desired color of the overall lighting can be realized.

The stage is arbitrarily divided into a number of equal areas, and a flood light is mounted on the border light batten to cover each area (Fig. 7-11). These floods can be gelled if desired and can either be controlled together or individually. Power circuits for the border lights are usually brought to outlets mounted on a batten immediately above the border light batten.

Behind the act curtain, on either side, stands a vertical structure called a light tower. The towers are wired with three or more circuits apiece and hold such additional floodlights, fixed spotlights and special effects equipment as might be needed.

Footlights are positioned on the apron, that portion of the stage in front of the act curtain. Like the others, these are wired in three circuits. Care must be taken in selecting the colors for footlights (see Chapter 10), for they are in a very sensitive position

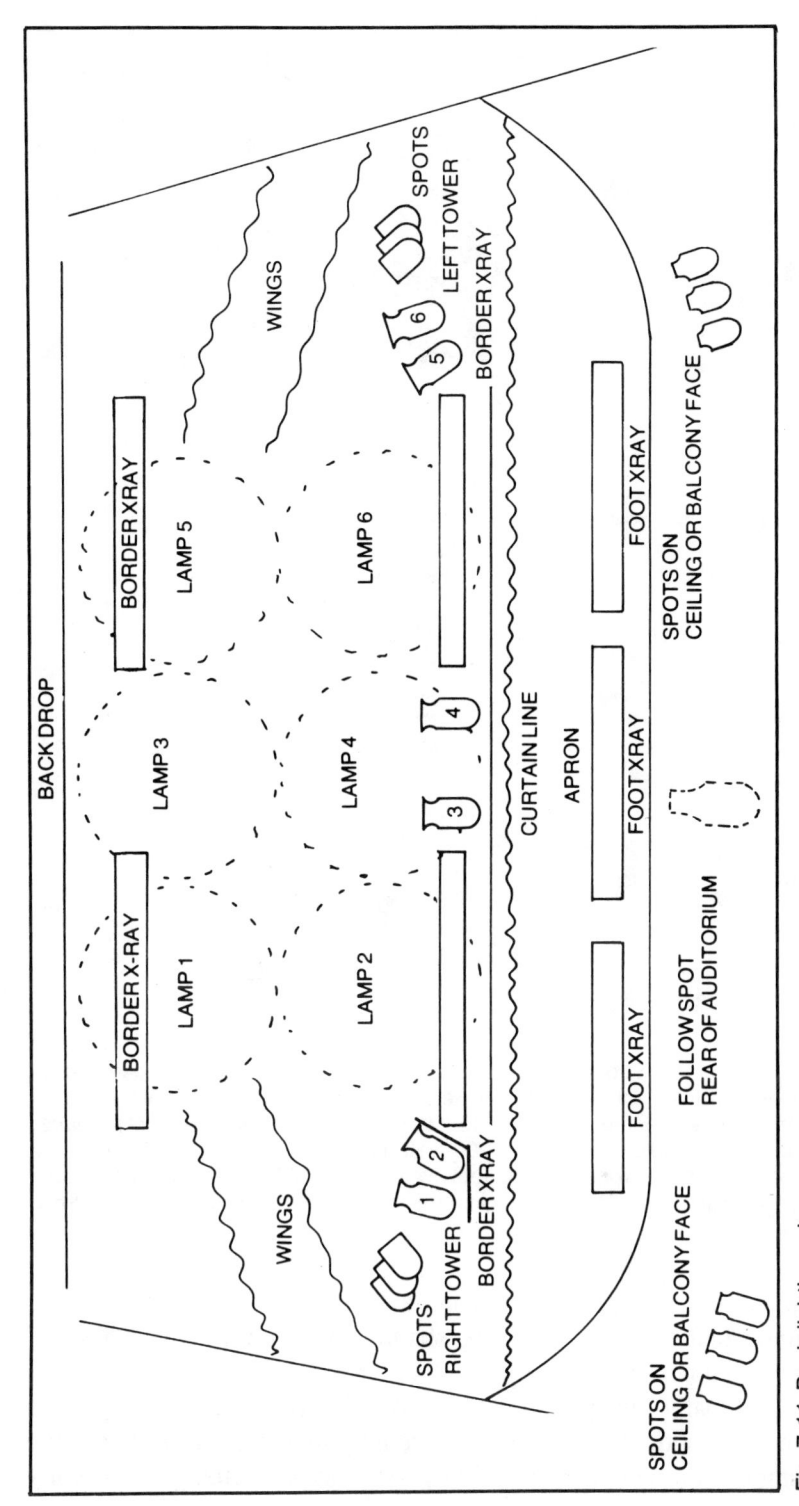

Fig. 7-11. Basic lighting scheme.

Fig. 7-12. The Strong Trouperette model is available with an incandescent quartz-bromine, or a quartz-halogen light source and is recommended for throws up to 140 feet. With a 40-foot throw, the incandescent model produces 128 foot candles, using a 1000-watt lamp. At the same distance, the quartz-bromine produces 220 foot candles with 650 watts and the quartz-halogen produces 240 foot candles with 1000 watts (photo courtesy the Strong Co.).

with respect to the performer's features. They serve a very important function in killing shadows under the chin and nose, among other things.

Finally, many installations have lighting positions either on the face of the balcony or in the ceiling immediately in front of the stage. Because of the relatively long throw, ceiling ports usually are equipped with fixed spotlights. A small school auditorium may have a fixed spot mounted on either wall aimed at the stage.

To sum it all up, theatrical lighting equipment, except for special devices, falls into three broad categories: strip, flood and spotlights. Strip lights, also called borders or X-rays, provide general, overall illumination. Flood lights illuminate a specific area, but that area is not sharply defined. Spotlights aim a beam to a particular position, object or person.

Border lights generally come in 6 and 8 foot sections, although continuous sections of almost any length can be ordered. A 6-foot

Fig. 7-13. The Strong Super Trouper with a carbon arc is recommended for throws up to 400 feet.

163

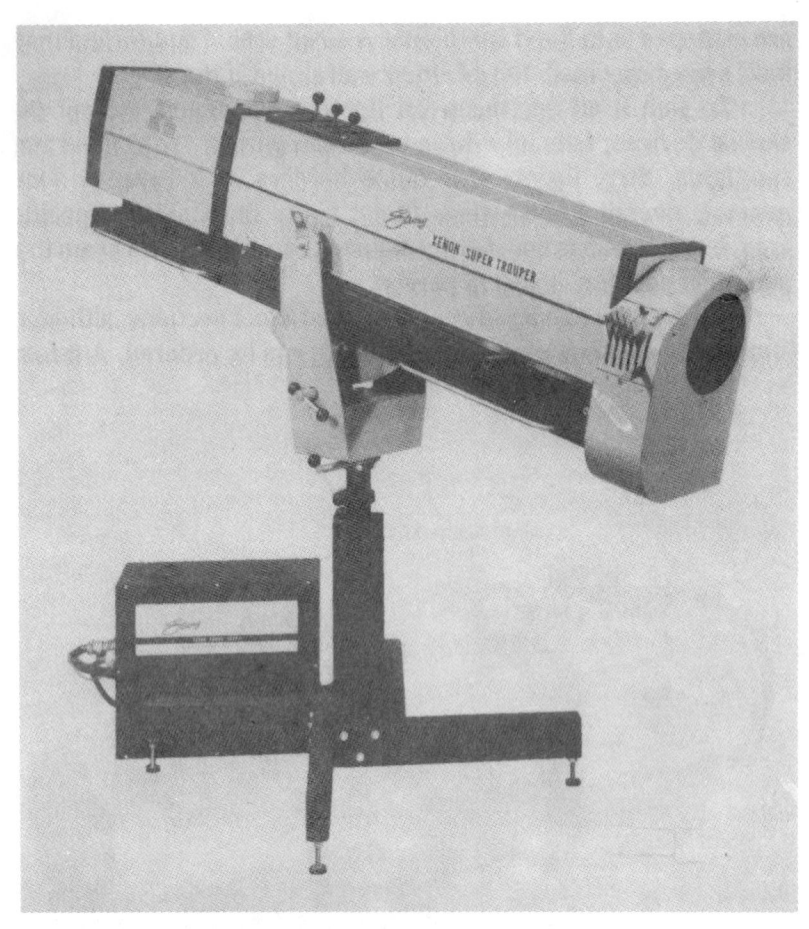

Fig. 7-14. A Strong Super Trouper with a xenon light source. It offers 70% more light output than the carbon-arc model.

section has nine light units. An 8-foot section has twelve light units. Each unit is contained in its own isolated compartment and has a frame for a color medium. Wattage can range from 100 to 300 watts per circuit, depending on the lamps used.

Floodlights

Floodlights, sometimes called beam lights, come in a variety of sizes and shapes that range from simple lamp/reflector units, similar to those used by amateur photographers, to more sophisticated devices equipped with a lens. The fancier units can be adjusted to set the width of the beam, in a fashion similar to a spotlight. Theatrical floods are usually equipped with a pipe clamp for mounting on a batten. Wattage can range from several hundred to over a thousand. Old-time units might still be found; they consist of a number of lamps clustered in a single reflector unit.

Spotlights

There are a number of types of spotlights but these fall into two general categories—fixed and follow spots. A fixed spot is intended to be aimed at one area and left there. It is generally controlled from the dimmer console. A follow spot, by far the more complex is controlled by an individual operator for each unit, and is equipped with such refinements as an iris diaphragm for adjusting the size of the spot and color filters that can be instantly flipped into

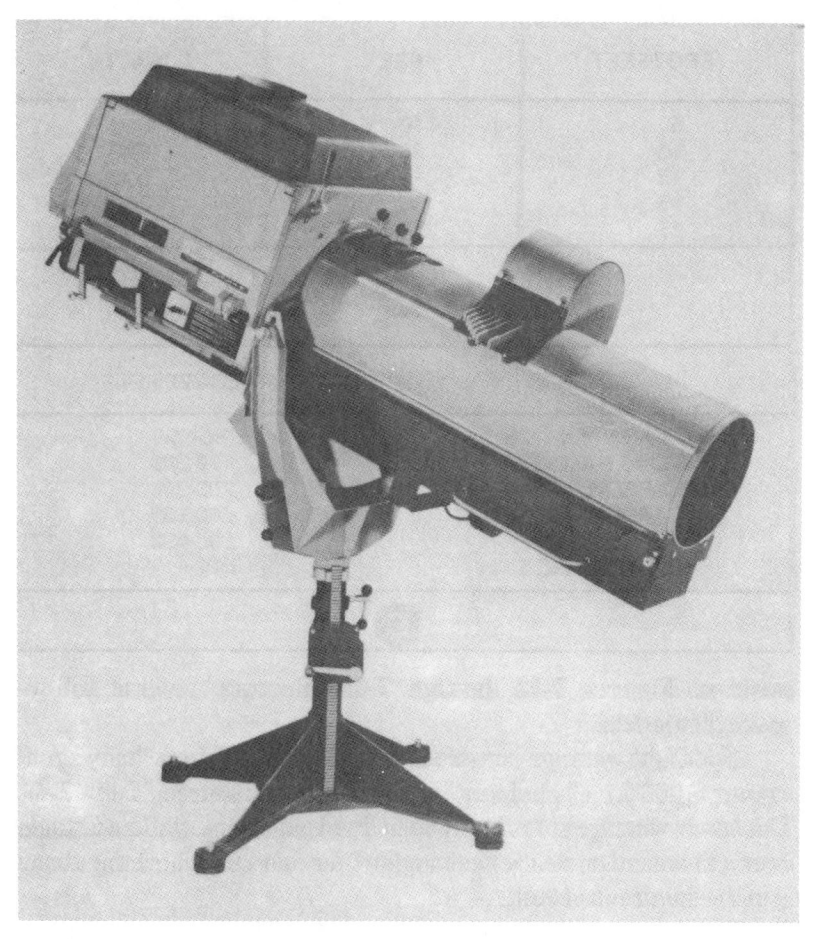

Fig. 7-15. The Strong Gladiator is advertised as the most powerful spotlight made. It has a power demand of over 5000 watts and is said to be twice as bright as the next most powerful unit available. It carries six color filters and an ultra-violet filter. Accessories are available to produce stroboscopic effects. A throw up to 600 feet isn't by any means unrealistic with this unit.

Table 7-1. Light Coverage and Intensity Tables. A: Approximate Power and Throw Required to Light an Area to 100 Foot-Candles. B: Approximate Power and Throw Required for a Fixed Spot to Light to 100 Foot-Candles. C: Approximate Throw Provided by Various Follow-Spot Light Sources.

LIGHT COVERAGE AND INTENSITY		
AREA (SQ. FT.)	FEET	WATTS
20	5	150
115	15	750
250	30	2000
A		
SPOT FEET	FEET	WATTS
5	10-15	400
10	30-40	500
15	15	500
15	30	750
15	50-70	1000
B		
SOURCE		AVERAGE FEET
TUNGSTEN 1 KW		50-100
TUNG-HALOGEN		100-200
CARBON ARC 1 KW		100-200
CARBON ARC 1.5 KW		200-350
XENON ARC		200-400
CARBON ARC 5 KW		500+
C		

position. Figures 7-12 through 7-15 illustrate several follow-spotlight models.

Spotlight wattage runs from several hundred for a "baby spot" to over 5,000 for a "gladiator" with a carbon arc source (Table 7-1). The lower wattage units are used in fixed positions, while wattages over a thousand or so are best applied outdoors or where the throw is in the hundreds of feet.

LIGHT CONTROLS

Since the advent of solid-state electronics, light dimmer units have become almost unbelievably small. It is most likely, how-

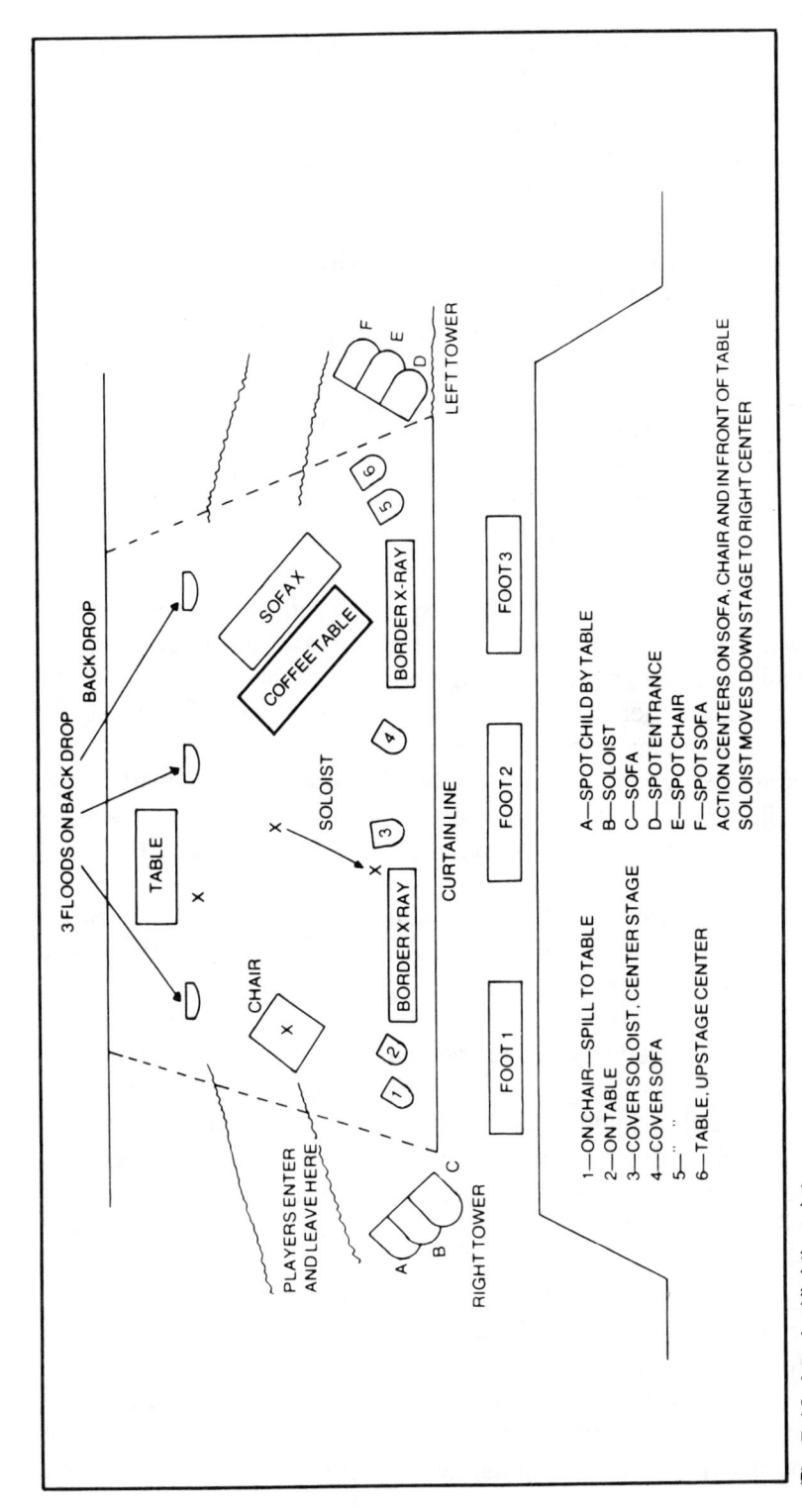

Fig. 7-16. A typical lighting plot.

ever, that the amateur will run across an older console, rather than a state-of-the-art control panel.

A lighting console can be divided into three arbitrary sections, a switchboard, a patch panel and a dimmer panel. The switchboard provides the on/off functions. The dimmer panel provides the moment-to-moment control needed during a production. The patch panel, however, is where the whole character of the console is adapted to the individual production. Power mains are connected, through appropriate breakers and main switches, to a series of outlets at the bottom of the panel. Light circuits, either from permanent lights or from lighting outlets (pockets) on stage, are brought to another series of connectors. Finally, the dimmers are wired to still another series. Short lengths of power cable with appropriate mating connectors then connect light circuits to dimmers and to mains. The scheme allows any conceivable combination of light control.

All the details in the world on lighting equipment and how it is used is but a small help once we get down to the basics of using that equipment to light the stage. Some of the old hands at it will try to tell you that there are no set rules, but that's no help. The least slip or missed timing in light control is sure to be noticed by the audience. Lighting can make or break a production, no matter how well or how poorly it is produced. Good lighting can pick up a mediocre to poor production and poor lighting can ruin a good production.

Let us say from the beginning that some kind of control is vital. Spots, floods and borders can be bought as the budget permits, but they're not much use if you can't dim them on cue. Whether you have an elaborate, expensive professional console or a simple, home-brewed one, you must have complete control over the lights.

The first thing to do, of course, is to read the script. Get together with the stage manager and wardrobe manager to determine the colors being used in each setting, where the players will stand or sit in each scene and the colors of their costumes. Then you're ready to start.

Diagram the set (Fig. 7-16), determining exactly where each prop will be and where the major action in the set will take place. You must also be aware of just where the players will enter the set.

Let the border and foot lights provide the general mood colors. Bearing in mind that certain colors should be avoided in the footlights. Use border spots, gelled to pick up the colors, to light

Fig. 7-17. Lighting and equipment towers at the Hill Cumorah outdoor production area.

each major prop in the set. For playing areas where you know people will be standing with certain color costumes, focus a border spot on each area—gelled for the costume. Bear in mind that light angle will count. It might be best to throw the light from the opposite end of the stage, rather than from nearly overhead. Also, you might want to gel a spot to cover a person's face at a particular position.

Once the border spots are set, you and you alone can determine how far to open the dimmers to the right intensity for the desired effect. Now you can set up the units on the towers to better accentuate the actors' faces. Refer to Chapter 10 with regard to color. Here again, you will want a fixed spot for each playing position. Keep in mind any effect being simulated in the script and gel your lights accordingly. Will a player be standing near a fireplace? Maybe you'll want to add a bit of red. Is it late evening or under moonlight? You have to very color conscious. Is there a door or window in the scene? Will it be used by the players? Doors, if used, will need a strip overhead behind the set. Windows will also require an overhead strip. In each case, keep the strips gelled to harmonize with the light supposed to be on the other side (sunset, etc.).

Don't forget special effects. These will need separate control. Also, if there are any props that would, in real life, produce light, let them be lights on the stage and cover them with spots wired to the same circuit.

Watch for accidental spill of one light unit into the area covered by another. It might be all right, unless the two lights are different in color. In that case, flags (gobos) will be needed on the light units to block the light spillage.

No two sets are the same, but these general ideas—which should *not* be considered sacred rules—can offer a general guideline. After that, your own artistic abilities must take over.

Outdoor settings can be an even bigger headache, unless an actual stage is built for the event. They take advantage of every natural barrier—such as rocks, bushes, etc—to conceal light units (Fig. 7-17). Main lighting, however, can be provided by follow spot units which cover the hillside from towers on either side of the pageant area. Don't hedge on power. Gladiator and Super Trouper spots are among the most powerful available. Since the setting is on a hillside, there are no border lights or battens available to hold fixed spots.

Chapter 8

Optics, Lenses and Projection

Generally speaking, any light-producing device, whether simple or complex, incorporates some means of controlling the light output. This can be either a reflector, a lens or a combination of the two. The more accurate instruments have intricate combinations of precisely formed reflectors and lenses.

REFLECTORS

A law of nature says, "The angle of incidence is equal to the angle of reflection." This law comes into play in many of the commonly used reflection devices wherein light coming from a variety of angles are all reflected into a parallel beam or spread to the exact coverage desired (Fig. 8-1).

Reflectors used in lighting equipment are generally formed into an ellipsoid or a parabaloid. The scientific definition of an ellipse describes it as a closed curve around two focus points. At any point on the curve, the sum of the distances to the two points remains a constant number (Fig. 8-2). Obviously, an ellipsoidal reflector follows only a portion of the complete ellipse. Otherwise, it would be a closed object.

A parabola is an open curve having only one focus point. It is defined as that distance from any point on the curve to the focus plus the distance from the curve to an imaginary reference line always equal a constant number (Fig. 8-3). An ellipse and a parabola are related. The difference is that one refers to two focus points while the other refers to a focus and a line.

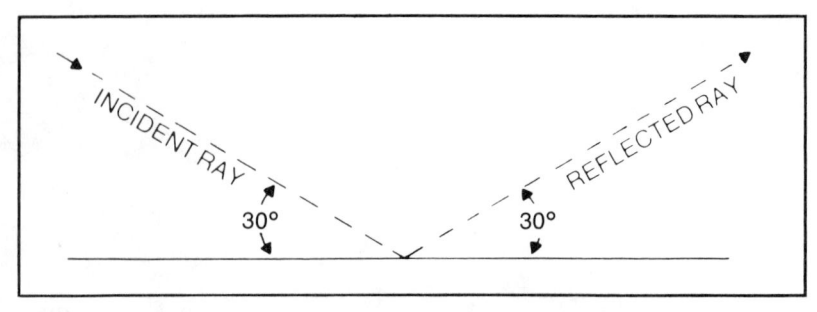

Fig. 8-1. A light beam striking a surface at a given angle will be reflected at the same angle.

Parabolic reflectors have been used for many years in all manner of lighting devices, ranging from automobile headlamps to searchlights. The parabolic curve is such that when a light source is placed at the focus the angle of incidence to any point on the reflector is just right to cause the reflected beam to follow a parallel path. By moving the light source along the axis of the parabola, the beam can be made either to spread or to converge. While there is some amount of "spill" from light passing the edges of the reflector, the bulk of the light is a parallel beam (Fig. 8-4).

An ellipsoidal reflector operates in a manner similar to a paraboloid, except that the light source can be farther out from the reflector to provide a given amount of spread of the beam. Ellipsoidal reflectors are often applied in long-throw devices such as spotlights.

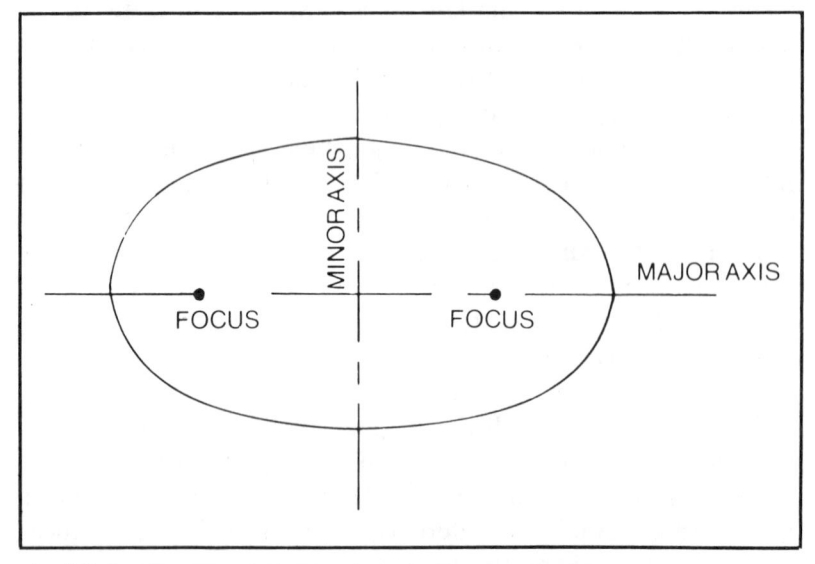

Fig. 8-2. An ellipse is a closed curve around two focus points.

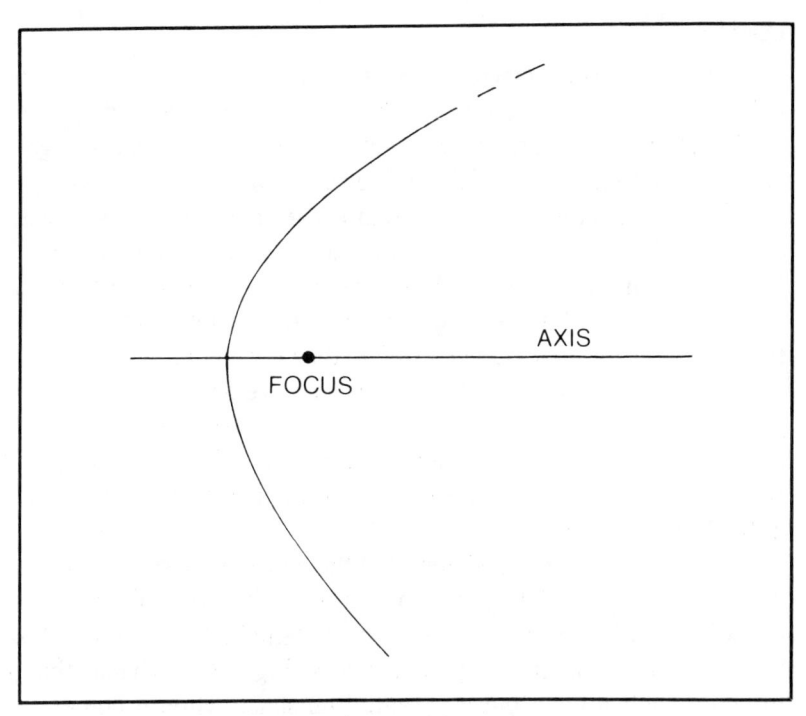

Fig. 8-3. A parabola has only one focus point.

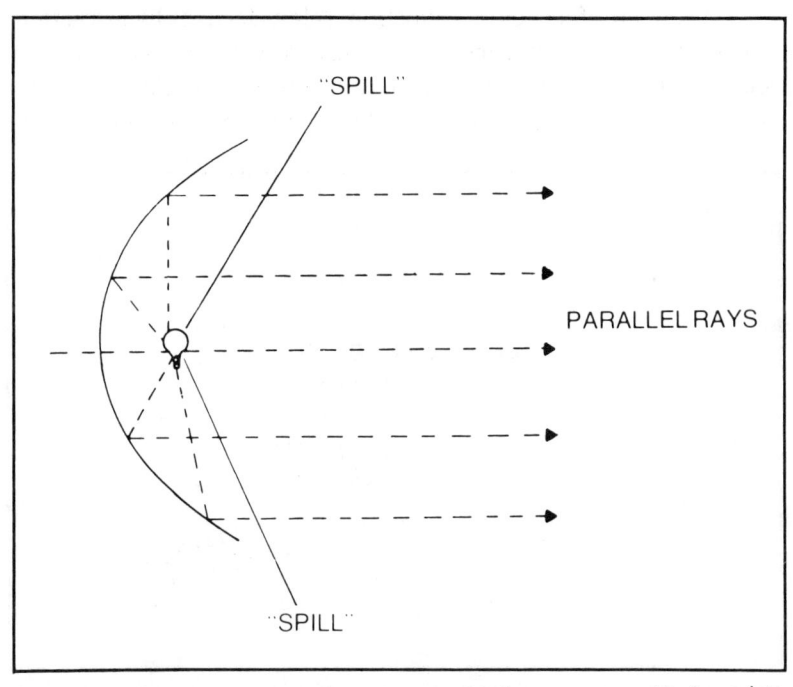

Fig. 8-4. A parabolic reflector reflects light coming from a source at its focus into a beam parallel to its axis.

173

LENSES

So far I have discussed reflection. Now let us turn to refraction, or the bending of light rays as they pass from one medium to another. If the barrier between the two media is at right angles to the path of the light, the effect is negligible. However, when the light enters the new medium at an angle, its path changes direction. Referring to Fig. 8-5, imagine you are looking down at the tops of the light waves. As they enter the new medium at an angle, point A enters first and immediately slows down. It has travelled some finite distance through the new medium by the time point B enters. Since the wave fronts must remain parallel in any given medium, you can easily see where they have taken on a new path. If the new medium is a glass prism, the light will bend again when it comes out the other side. A triangular prism, bends the light twice, each time toward the wide end.

It should be mentioned here that the wavelength of light varies with color. When white light—which is a mixture of all colors—passes through a prism, the longer wavelengths bend more. This breaks the light into its component colors (Fig. 8-6)—a handy thing in some applications, but a potential nuisance when it comes to color photography and projection.

A reflector focuses by reflection. A lens focuses by refraction. If you understand the principles of a prism, you can easily draw an analogy of a lens as two prisms placed back to back. Since the light is bent toward the wide portion of the prisms, there is a point some

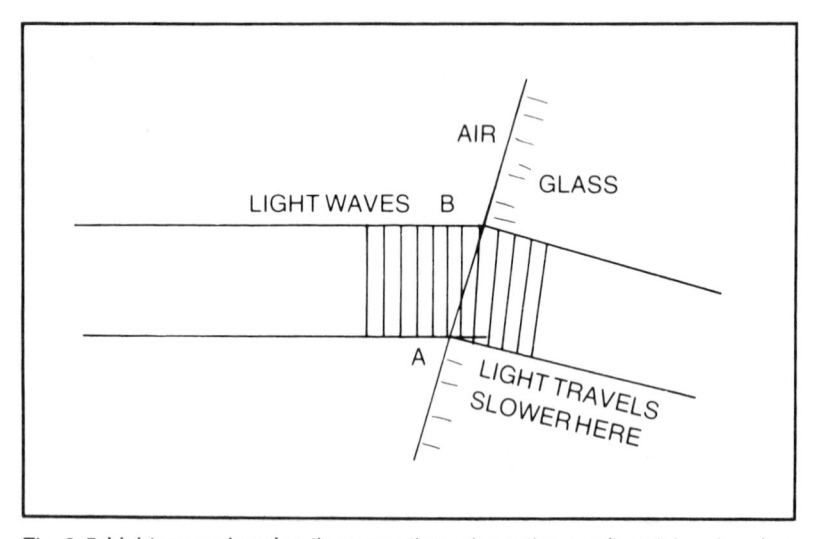

Fig. 8-5. Light waves bend as they pass through another medium (glass here) at an angle.

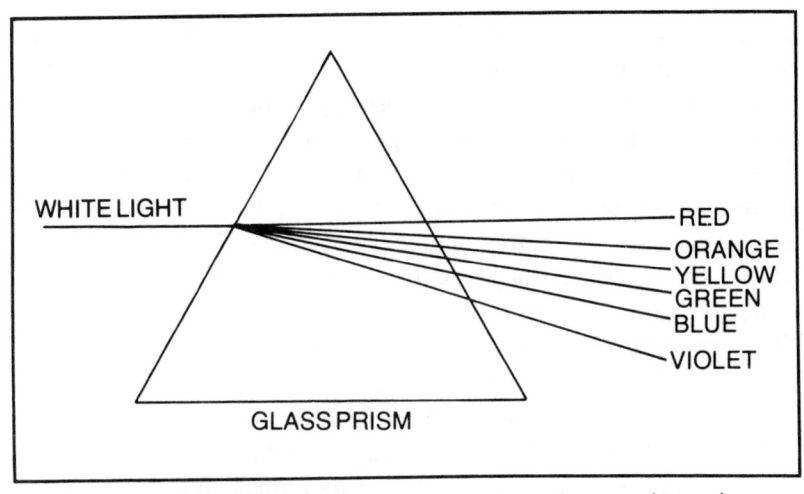

Fig. 8-6. Since some wavelengths bend more than others, a glass prism can break up a white light beam into its component colors.

distance away where the two beams of light will cross. This is known as the focus point (Fig. 8-7).

The system works the other way, too. If the light source is placed at the focus point, the diverging rays that enter the lens will come out the other side in a parallel beam. By repositioning the source slightly along the axis of the lens, the emerging light can be made to either diverge slightly or focus at any point beyond the lens. The lens depicted in Fig. 8-7 is known as a convex lens.

In Fig. 8-8 are some of the various surface configurations used to form the lens elements commonly used in optical equipment.

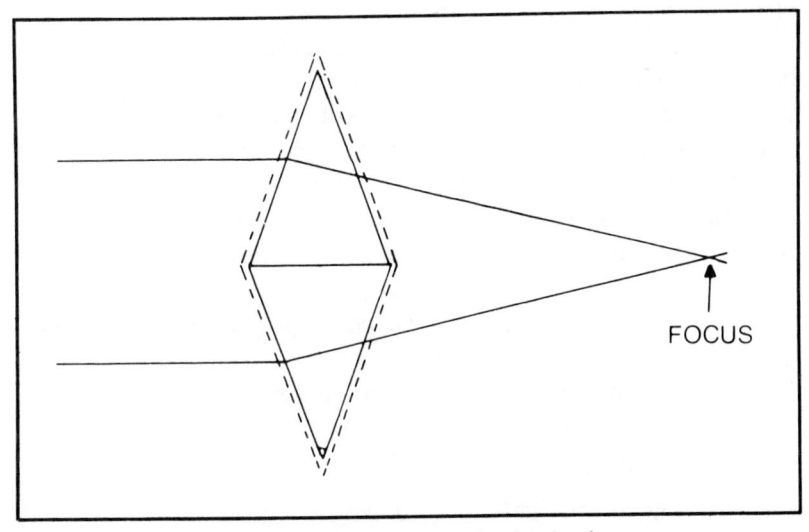

Fig. 8-7. A lens can be compared to two prisms back to back.

Each of the various types has its field of application. Without getting deep into optical engineering, I will point out a few generalities. Double concave lenses are found in inexpensive cameras, lighting equipment and generally in single-lens applications. Plano convex lenses are often seen in the condenser lens systems of projection equipment. Concave convex lenses are found everywhere from lighting equipment to cameras and projectors, where they are components of multi-element lens systems. Concave lenses will spread the light and cannot focus an image. They are often found, however, as portions of multi-lens systems, where they assist in color correction.

Perhaps the most important application of lenses is that of focusing an image. To better understand how this happens, imagine light coming from only two points, passing through the lens. Each set of light rays will come to a focus the same distance away from the lens, but in positions opposite though congruent to the respective positions of the sources (Fig. 8-9). The distance between the positions of the two images will depend on the size of the object, the distance from the object to the lens and the focal length of the lens.

A picture can be defined as an infinite number of points, each of its own characteristic color and brightness. Light from the object focuses to form an inverted image, either larger or smaller than the original object, depending on the use of the particular lens. The original object can be either a scene being photographed or a photographic transparency. The image can be cast either on a piece of film or on a projection screen.

If you give a little thought on the phenomenon of focusing, or on the behavior of a lens in general, you can arrive at the conclusion that the behavior of the lens depends not so much on the thickness of the lens as on the angle at which the light enters the lens—that is, the curvature of its surface. The thickness of the lens is merely a consequence of the necessary curvature. The Fresnel lens is one way of working around the evils of thick, heavy lenses. The lens surface is divided into a great number of circular segments, each segment containing a portion of the curve (Fig. 8-10). While some light does spill out between the segments, resulting in a softer focus than could be had with a conventional lens, theatrical lighting people consider that an advantage for many applications.

LIGHT PROJECTION

Turning now to lighting equipment, floodlights can be divided into two very broad categories: lighting units using a reflector and

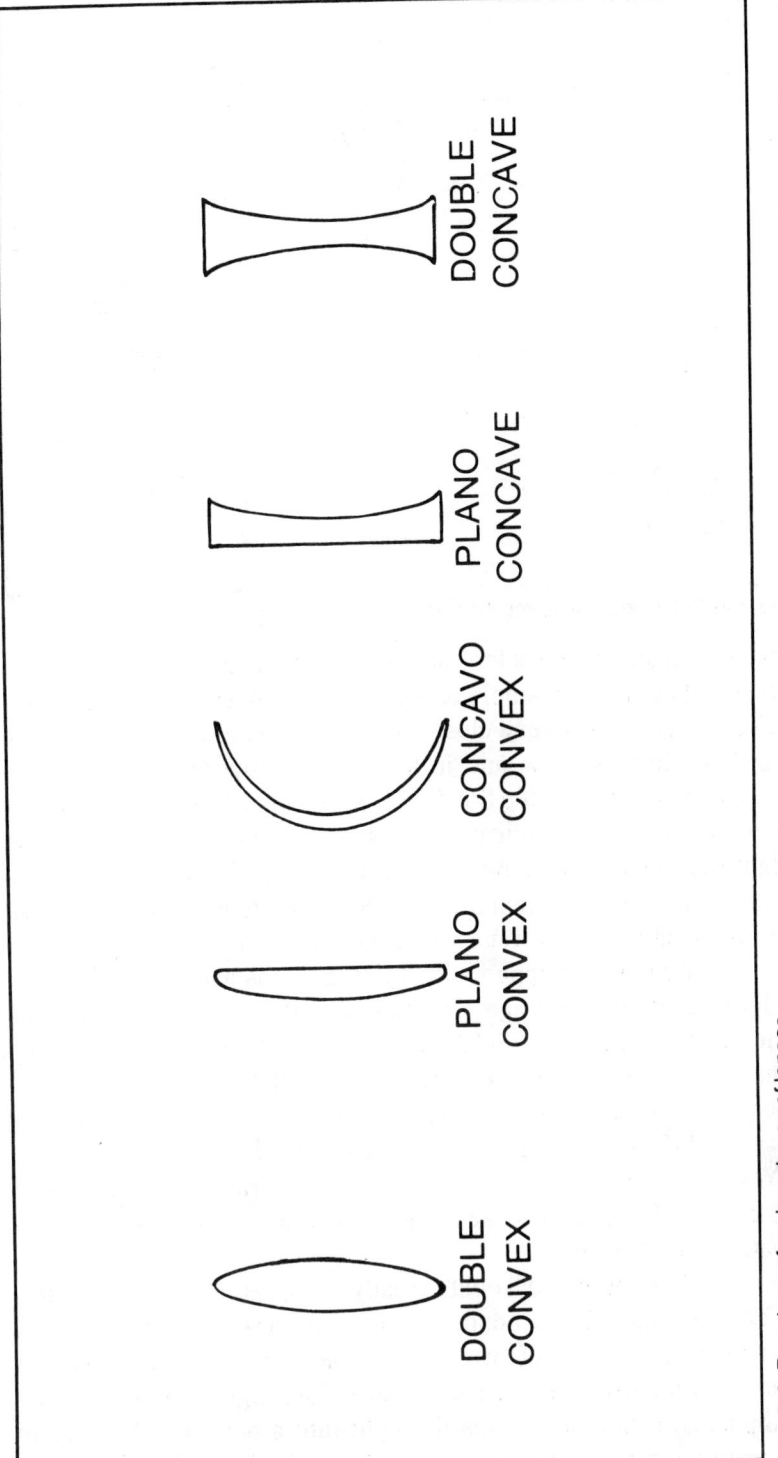

Fig. 8-8. Drawings of various types of lenses.

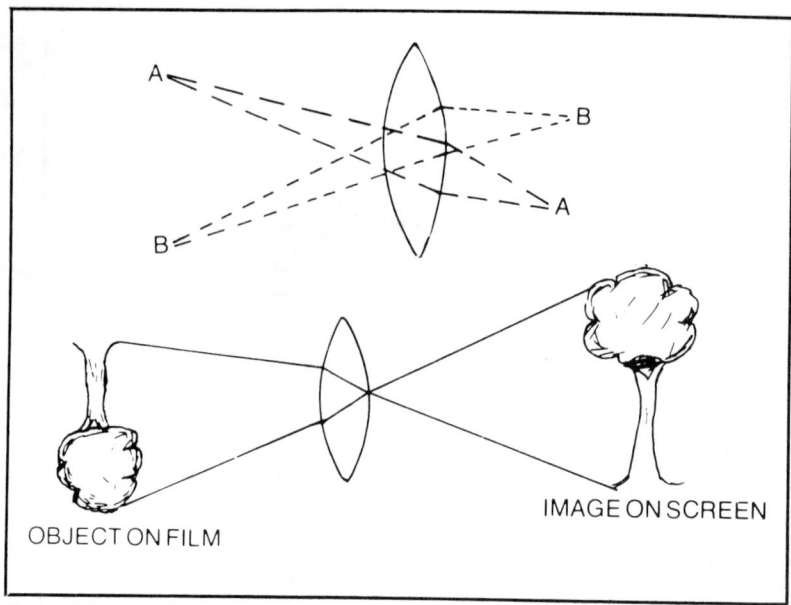

Fig. 8-9. Drawings illustrating the principles of focusing.

those with some kind of lens or lens system. The scoop floodlight is the most common example of light units employing just a reflector (Fig. 8-11). It is a very close relative to some of the floodlamps used in photo studios and in amateur productions can often be replaced by them. Scoop floodlights give a broad, soft-edged beam. This limits their application to short-throw, general-coverage lighting, such as that needed for backgrounds and cycloramas. Except for that limitation they are the most efficient of floodlights, so far as light output versus power is concerned.

Floodlights equipped with a Fresnel lens and some means of adjusting their coverage are the favorite workhorse units in theatrical lighting (Fig. 8-12). The position of the light source with respect to the lens is variable, allowing the spread of the light output to be varied from a wide beam for general coverage to a narrow beam encroaching on the characteristics of a spotlight. Fresnel lights come in a variety of sizes ranging from a lens diameter of 3 inches to 12 inches, with power ratings from 150 watts to 5,000 watts.

While an ellipsoidal light is really in the category of spotlights, it can be adjusted to produce a wide, general-coverage flood. In a sense, it is the best of two worlds. The ellipsoidal reflector and lens system produce a sharply focused, hard light (Fig. 8-13). The ellipsoidal reflector focuses the light into a point just beyond an aperture located between the lamp and the lens. The lens then

Fig. 8-10. Drawing showing how a Fresnel lens surface effectively duplicates the convex surface.

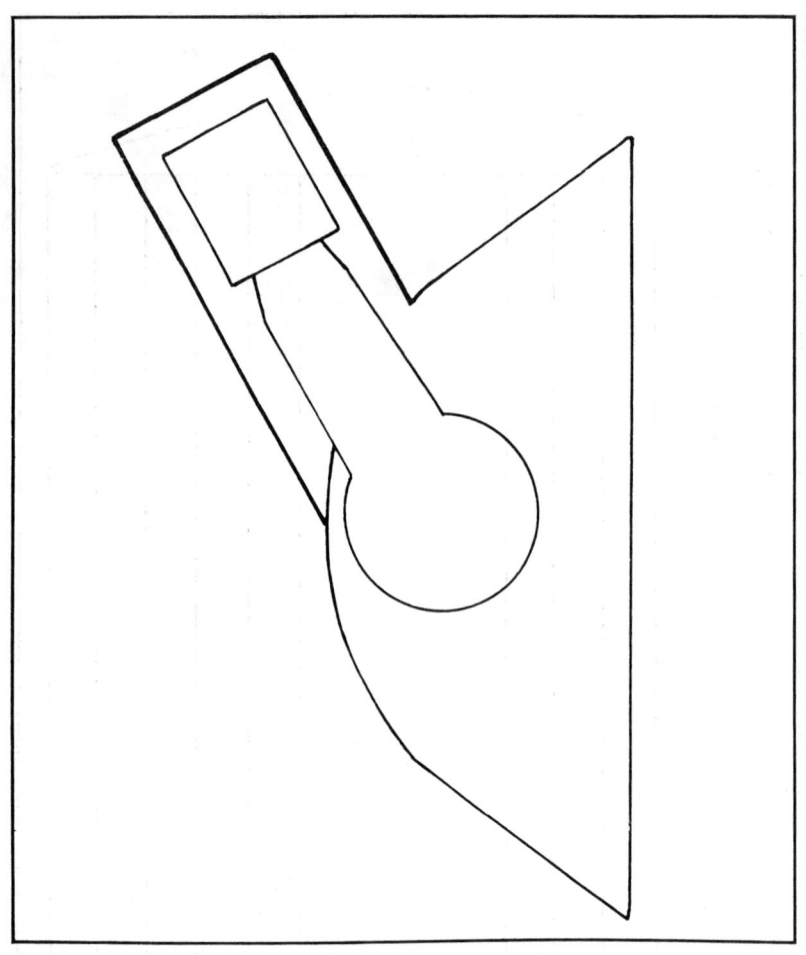

Fig. 8-11. Drawing of a scoop flood lamp, the simplest of the lighting devices.

produces the spot—which is actually an image of the aperture—onto the stage. The size of the spot depends on the focal length of the lens. This method produces a very even field of illumination.

Spotlights intended for fixed-position operation have a fixed aperture, and the size of the spot depends on the throw. Some are provided with a pattern holder for special effects. Units intended to follow the action on the stage are provided with a variable aperture, called an iris, to adjust the size of the spot. The more sophisticated ones also vary the focal length of the lens system to provide increased light intensity with a smaller spot.

A basic understanding of the principles of lighting equipment can often bring up some crude, but ingenious ideas of ways to improvise. One country church, which could no more afford a follow spotlight than I can a Rolls-Royce came up with the idea of

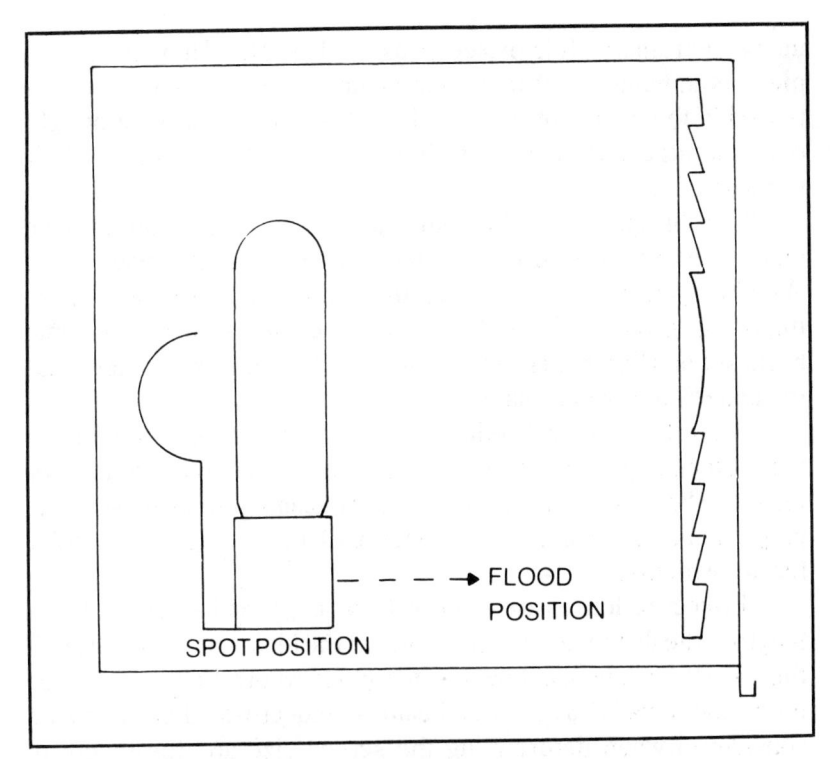

Fig. 8-12. Drawing of flood light equipped with a Fresnel lens.

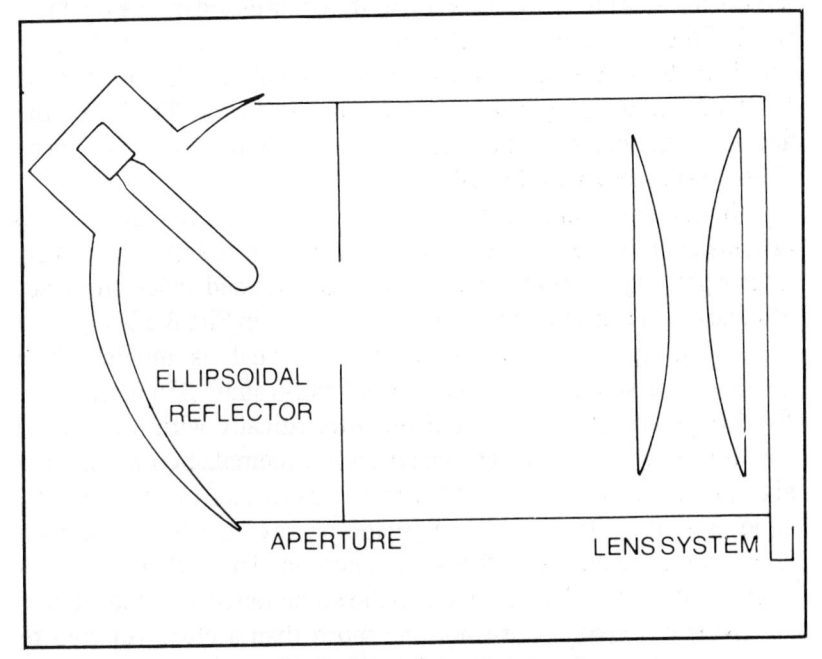

Fig. 8-13. Drawing of a spotlight with an ellipsoidal reflector.

using an ordinary slide projector as a substitute. They mounted a piece of aluminum foil in a slide mount. A small round hole was placed in the center of the foil. This threw a circular spot of light onto the stage. It was a bit clumsy to use, but it served their purpose.

This brings us into the field of projectors, a bit removed from stage lighting, but closely enough related to justify space here. Whether you are using the familiar home projector or a more imposing, professional unit, you will find they all have the same basic set up (Fig. 8-14). Some will have less of it than others, but the general idea will remain the same.

A small ellipsoidal reflector is behind the lamp—sometimes part of the lamp itself. It concentrates the beam into the condenser lenses. The latter usually consist of two plano-convex lenses. The projection lens consists of a number of elements—for better color focus correction.

Projection lenses are rated by focal length and aperture. Focal length is the distance from the center of the lens—or the aperture if the particular lens has one—to the point where light rays which enter the lens in a parallel beam would cross. This is to be considered when determining the screen size and the length of throw. The aperture determines the brightness of the picture and affects the sharpness of the picture. It is expressed in this manner, f/4.5. This is arrived at by dividing the focal length of the lens by the diameter of the aperture. Generally speaking, the shorter the focal length, the larger the picture for a given throw. The larger the aperture, the brighter the picture, but the more critical the focus (Table 8-1 through Table 8-3).

35mm slides are shot on film cut and sprocketed similarly to professional movie film. The picture format on the film, however, is at right angles to the movie frame format and twice the size. Standard still transparency formats are drawn in Fig. 8-15.

Filmstrips are shot in the same format as movies. The amateur can shoot filmstrips with a "half-frame" 35mm camera. Filmstrips are often synchronized automatically with a recorded sound program. The synchronization is accomplished by using a high-pitch tone signal to trigger the frame-advance mechanism. All slide and movie transparencies made on reversal film should be shown with the emulsion toward the screen. Those that are prints or duplicates should be shown with the emulsion toward the lamp.

Movie projectors are nothing more than a close relative to slide projectors (Fig. 8-16 and Fig. 8-17). Except for professional

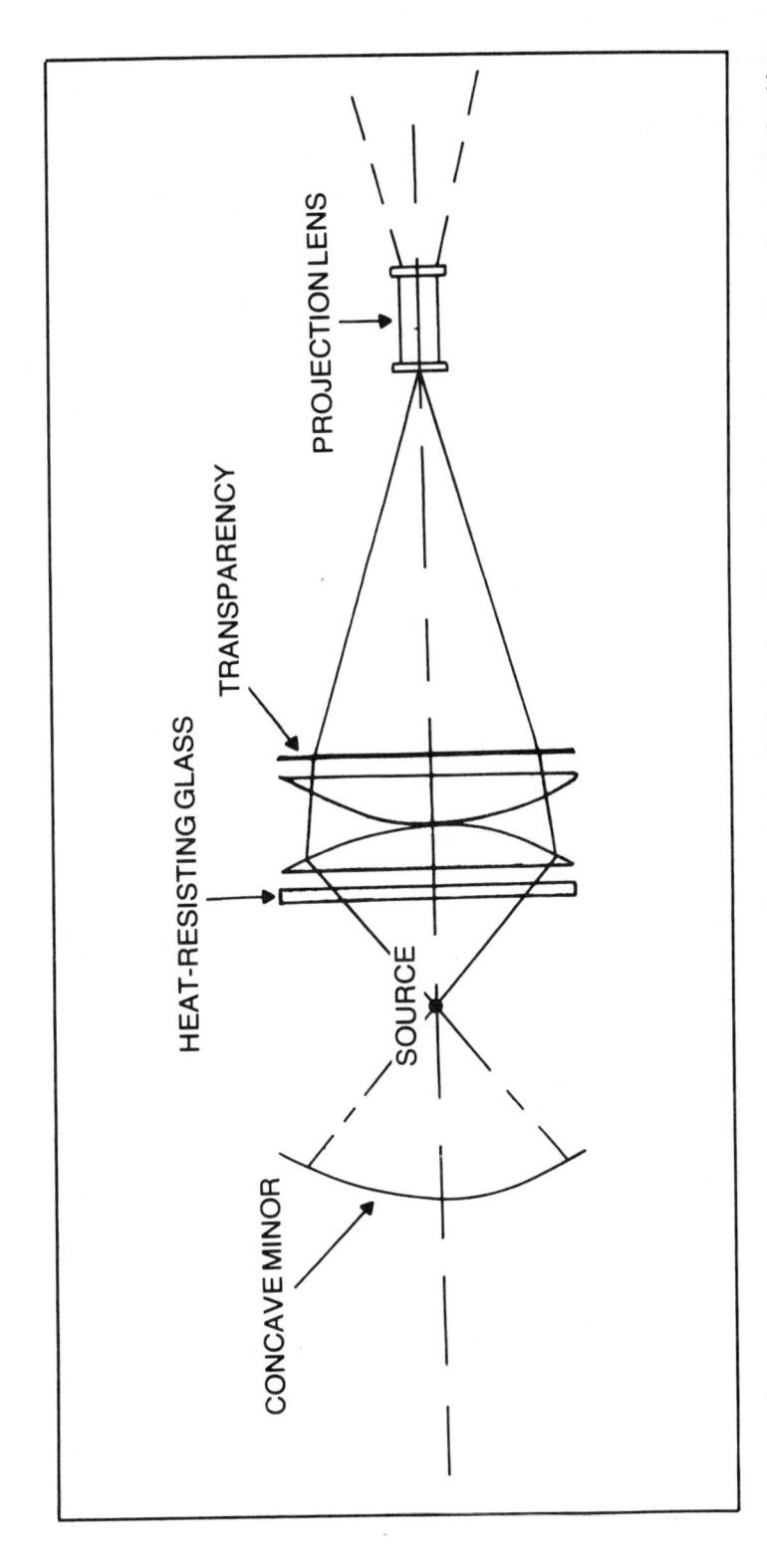

Fig. 8-14. Drawing of the optical arrangement in a typical projection device. While the size of the optical elements vary, depending on whether it's a movie projector, slide projector, or follow spotlight (in slide or movie projectors, the optical path may be folded a few times by mirrors) the general arrangement remains the same.

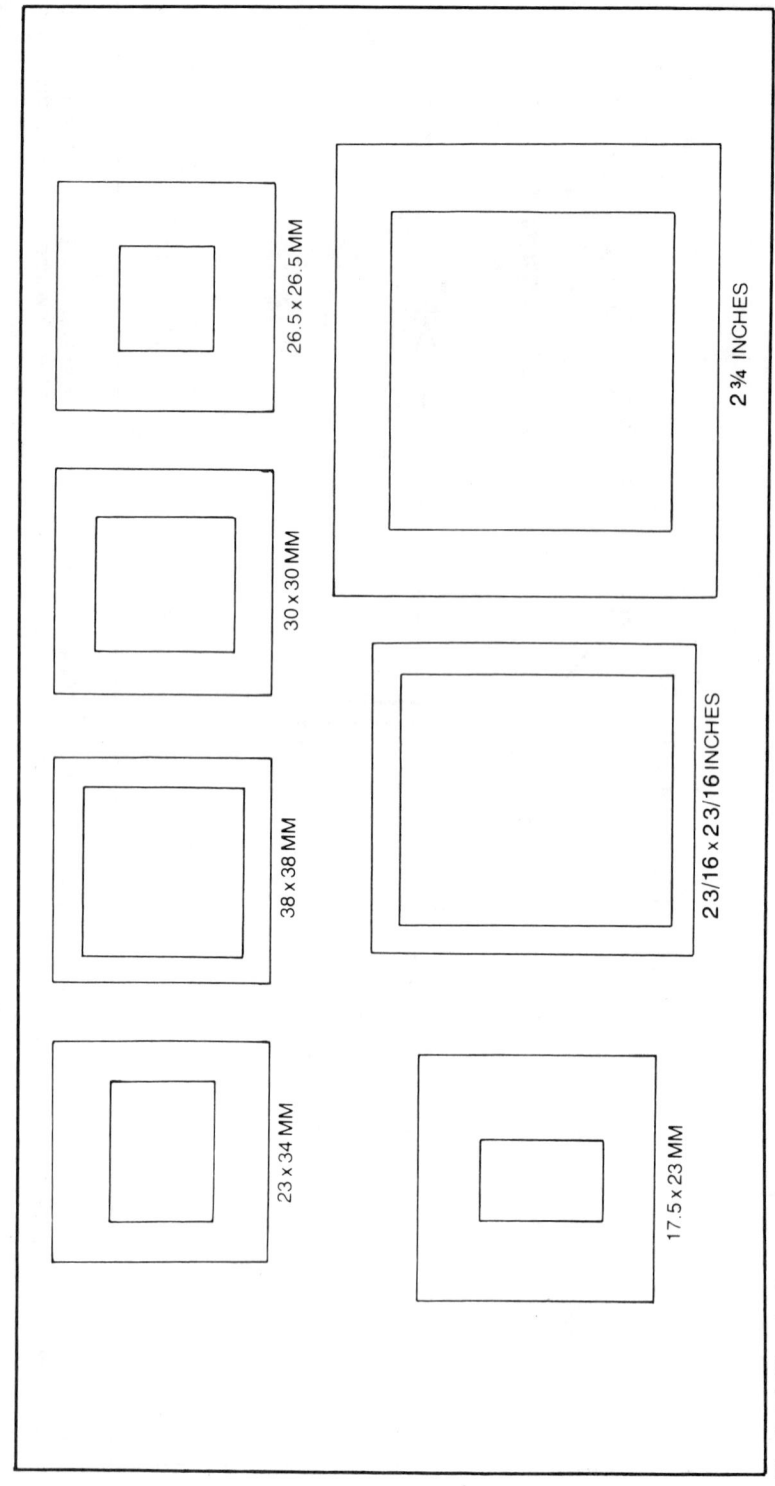

Fig. 8-15. Standard still transparency formats.

Fig. 8-16. Typical 16mm sound movie projector (photo courtesy Eastman Kodak Co.).

theatres, which use 35mm film, movies use a smaller transparency and are geared to show a great number in very rapid succession. While a revolving shutter momentarily cuts off the light, a metal claw or a sprocket advances the film. To avoid tiresome flicker, the shutter opens and closes two or three times faster than the frame rate. That is, each frame is flashed onto the screen two or three times.

Silent home movies operate at a rate of 16 frames per second; sound movies at a rate of 24 frames per second. With sound movies, the sound track replaces the sprocket holes on the inner edge of the film (Fig. 8-18). The sound image on the film, for a

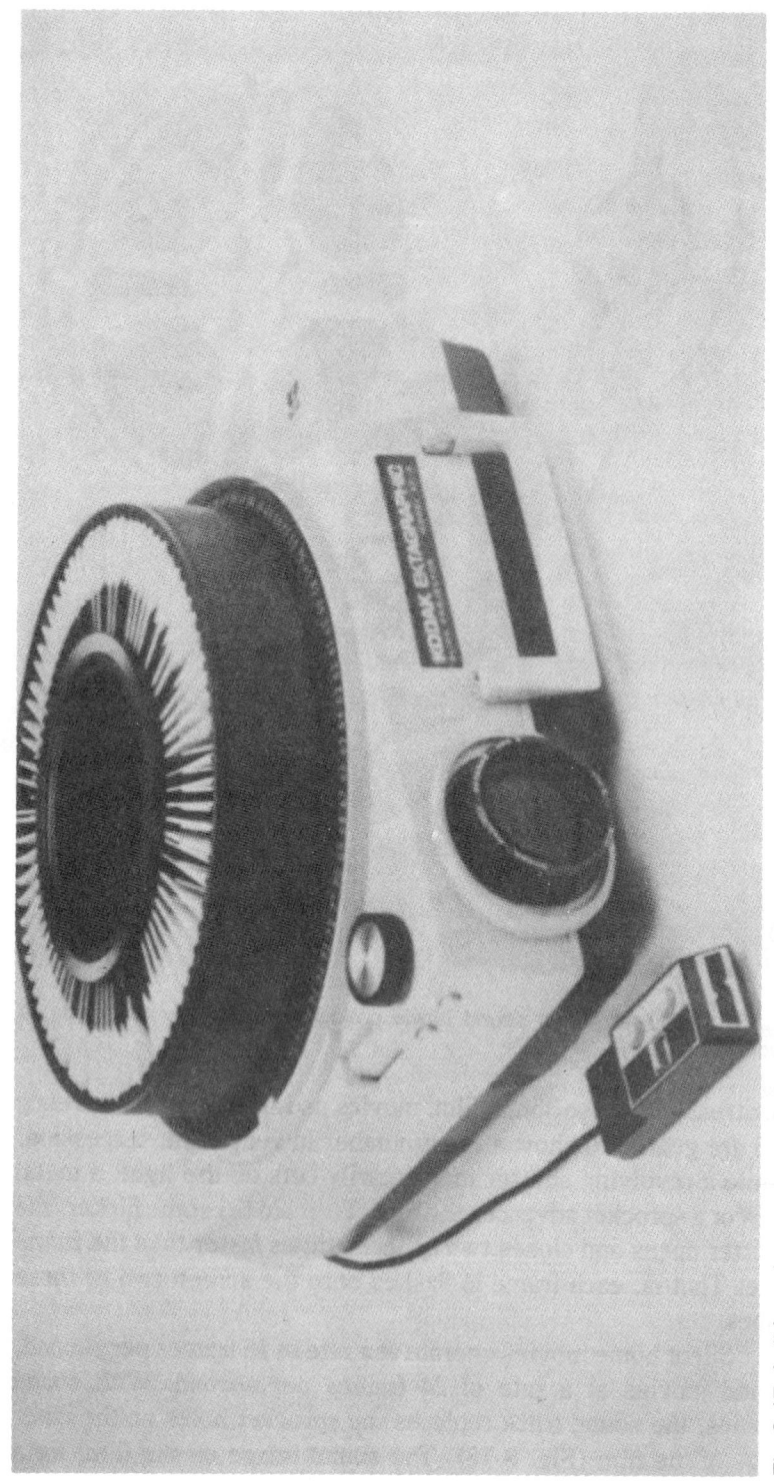

Fig. 8-17. A slide projector (photo courtesy Eastman Kodak Co.).

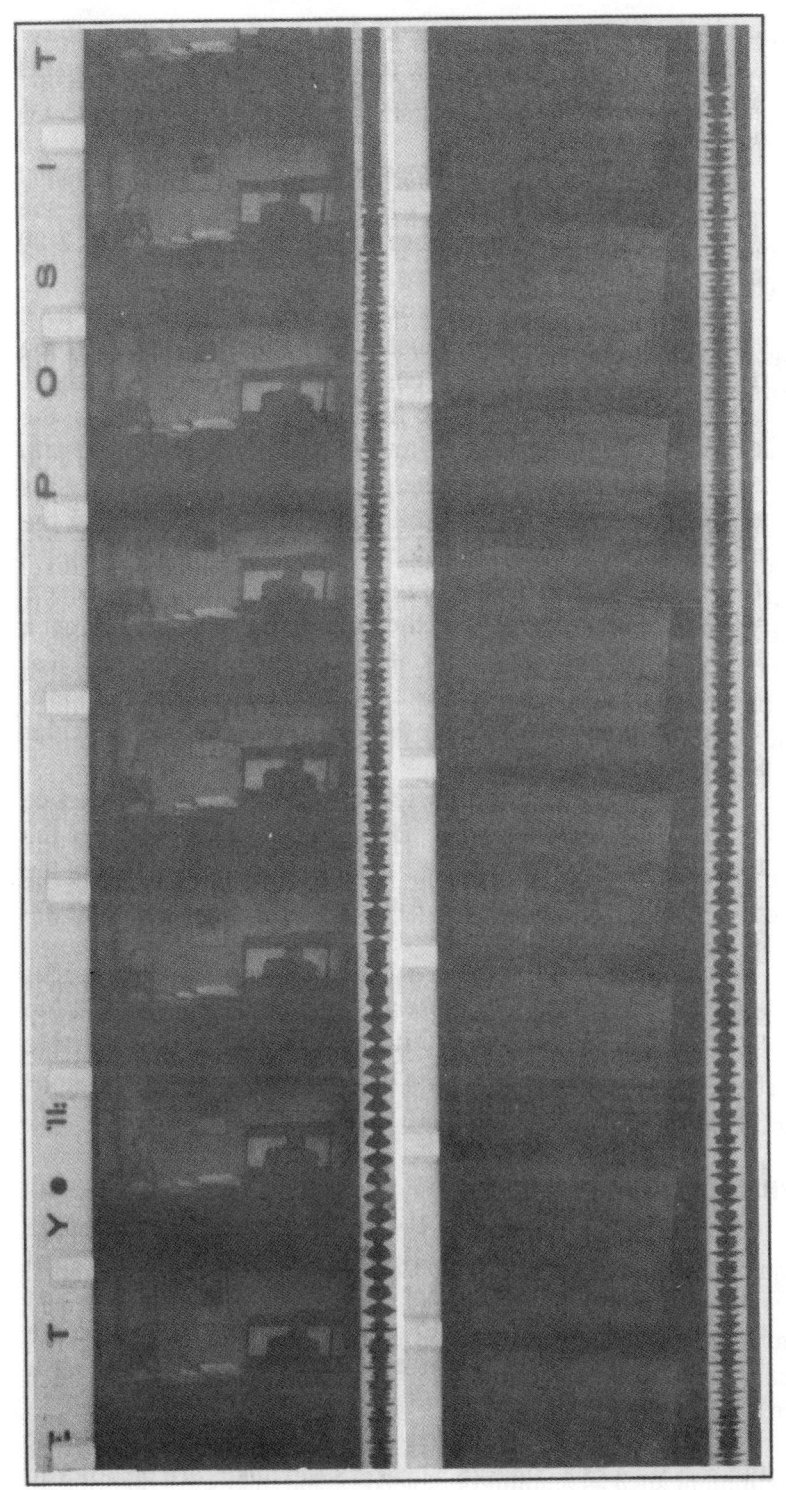

Fig. 8-18. Clip of a 16mm sound film.

given instant in the program, is 26 frames ahead of the picture. Figure 8-19 shows the threading pattern of a typical 16mm sound projector. See Table 8-1 through 8-4 for the running time for various film lengths.

Incandescent projection lamps come in wattage sizes ranging from less than a hundred to over a thousand. For large halls, movie projectors can be fitted with either a xenon light source (Fig. 8-20 through Fig. 8-22) or an arc source.

Projection screens come with a variety of surfaces and each has its own best application. Most home screens and many of the portable semiprofessional screens have a beaded-glass surface. The tiny glass beads bonded to the surface greatly increase the screen's reflectivity, enabling a lower wattage lamp to be used with a given amount of brightness. There is one disadvantage. The glass beads tend to reflect most of the light directly back toward the source. Therefore, if the projector is not at approximate eye level with the audience, a loss in efficiency is realized. Moreover, viewers off to one side or the other see nowhere near as bright a picture as those near the center. This can easily be demonstrated experimentally by projecting a picture and moving from one side to the other. A distinct loss can be noticed as little as 30° off center (Fig. 8-22).

The so-called "daylight" screens have an aluminized surface for reflectivity. This does not adversely affect the color of the picture, as the eye tends to adapt itself to the color balance of the picture. It does afford a much wider angle of view with uniform brightness.

Screens used in professional theatres have a very porous appearance when examined close up. This allows the speakers to be mounted behind the screen. With amateur setups using portable screens, the speaker is most effective when placed directly below the center of the screen.

WHEN YOU HAVE TO MAKE DO

Sooner or later, there is bound to be a time when proper equipment just isn't available. Perhaps there won't be a rental agency within reach, or perhaps your particular operation just won't have the funds available to rent or buy. Such a situation is a real test of your ingenuity. More than one person has, in such times, surprised themselves.

At this point, I will discuss lighting equipment. Electronic equipment such as amplifiers, speakers and mikes are plentiful all

Table 8-1. Table for Calculating Focal Length and Throw for Various Image Sizes (courtesy Eastman Kodak Co.).

LENS FOCAL LENGTHS (in./mm)				ZOOM				SCREEN-IMAGE DIMENSIONS (in./m)			
2½	3	4	5	6	7			135	126	SUPER-SLIDE	110
65	76	102	127	152	180						
PROJECTION DISTANCES (ft/m)											
6½	8	10½	13	16	18½			27 x 40 in.	31 sq	44½ sq	14 x 18½ in.
8	10	13	16½	19½	23			33½ x 50	38½ sq	55½ sq	17½ x 23
9½	11½	15½	19½	23½	27			40 x 60	46½ sq	66½ sq	21 x 27½
11½	13½	18	22½	27	31½			47 x 70	54 sq	77½ sq	24½ x 32½
15½	18½	24½	30½	36½	43			64½ x 96	74½ sq	106½ sq	33½ x 44½
2.0	2.3	3.1	3.9	4.7	5.6			.67 x 1 m	0.77 sq	1.11 sq	.35 x .46 m
3.5	4.0	5.3	6.6	8.0	9.6			1.17 x 1.75	1.36 sq	1.94 sq	.61 x .81

Projection distances are approximate and are measured from projector gate to screen.

Table 8-2. Factors for Computing Projection Distances, Image Sizes and Required Lens Focal Lengths (courtesy Eastman Kodak Co.).

FORMAT	SUPER 8 ZOOM					LENS FOCAL LENGTH (in. mm)						SLIDE ZOOM				
	0.6	0.875	1.2	1½	1⅝	2	2½	3	4	5	6	7	9	10	11
	15	22	30	38	41	50	65	76	102	127	152	180	230	255	280
135-size slides				1.1	1.2	1.5	1.9	2.2	2.9	3.7	4.4	5.3	6.7	7.5	8.2
126-size slides				1.4	1.5	1.9	2.5	2.8	3.8	4.7	5.7	6.8	8.7	9.6	10.6
Super-slide				1.0	1.1	1.3	1.7	2.0	2.6	3.3	3.9	4.7	6.1	6.7	7.4
110-size slides				2.4	2.6	3.2*	4.1	4.7*	6.3	7.9	9.5	11.4	14.6	16.1	17.7
Filmstrip				1.7	1.8	2.2	2.9	3.3	4.4	5.6	6.7	8.0	10.2	11.3	12.4
16 mm MP	1.6	2.3	3.1	3.9	4.2	5.2	6.7	7.8	10.4	13.0	15.5				
Super 8 MP	2.8	4.1	5.6	7.2	7.7	9.4	12.2	14.1							

Table 8-3. Additional Information for Computing Factors.

TO FIND:	DO THIS:
Image width for given projection distance	1. Find type of format at left. 2. Read across to factor, under lens focal length. 3. Divide projection distance* by factor. The result is image width.
Projection distance for given image width	1. Find type of format at left. 2. Read across to factor, under lens focal length. 3. Multiply image width* desired by factor to obtain projection distance.
Lens to use for specified image width and projection distance	1. Divide projection distance* by image width to obtain necessary factor. 2. Find type of format at left; read across to factor nearest that needed. 3. Find lens focal length required at top of column.

*Use the same dimensional units in multiplying and dividing (all inches, all feet, all meters, etc.). Values determined by this approximate method may not agree with values in the tables, particularly for long focal length lenses.

Table 8-4. Running Time for Various Length 16mm and Super 8 Films (courtesy Eastman Kodak Co.).

FILM LENGTH		RUNNING TIMES (Minutes and Seconds)			
FEET	APPROX. METERS	16 mm		SUPER 8	
		24 fps	18 fps	24 fps	18 fps
50	15	1:23	1:51	2:30	3:20
100	30	2:47	3:42	5:00	6:40
200	60	5:33	7:24	10:00	13:20
220	67	6:07	8:09	11:00	14:40
400	121	11:07	14:49	20:00	26:40
1200	366	33:20	44:27	60:00	80:00
1600	488	44:27	59:16	80:00	106:40

RUNNING TIMES			LENGTH OF FILM REQUIRED			
			16 mm		SUPER 8	
			24 fps	18 fps	24 fps	18 fps
S E C O N D S	1	in. mm	7.2 183	5.4 137	4 102	3 76
	10	ft m	6 1.83	4½ 1.37	3⅓ 1.02	2½ .76
	20	ft m	12 3.66	9 2.74	6⅔ 2.03	5 1.52
	30	ft m	18 5.49	13½ 4.11	10 3.05	7½ 2.29
	1	ft m	36 10.97	27 8.23	20 6.10	15 4.57
	5	ft m	180 54.86	135 41.15	100 30.48	75 22.86
	10	ft m	360 109.73	270 82.30	200 60.96	150 45.72
	15	ft m	540 164.59	405 123.44	300 91.44	225 68.58
	30	ft m	1080 329.18	810 246.89	600 182.88	450 137.16

16 mm film
40 frames per foot; 131.234 frames per meter; optical sound—26 frames in advance of picture; magnetic—28 frames advance

Super 8 film
72 frames per foot; 236.2205 frames per meter; magnetic sound—18 frames advance

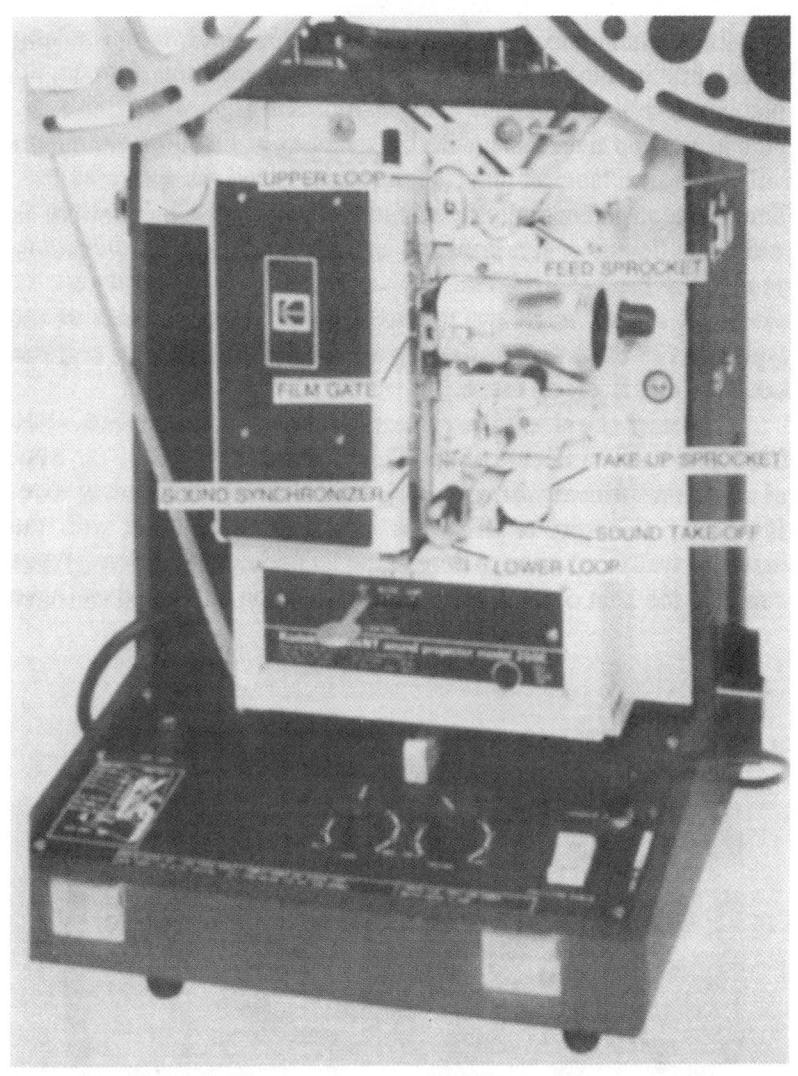

Fig. 8-19. Threading pattern of a typical 16mm sound movie projector (photo courtesy Eastman Kodak Co.).

over the country. However, lighting equipment is rather specialized in this art and improvising can be difficult.

Before you do too much to provide light units, be sure you have something to hang them on. A light batten can be improvised with a length of 1-inch iron pipe. Power can be provided by clamping a piece of one-by-three board to the pipe and running a temporary wire along it. Heavy screw-eyes allow fastening small pulleys. Both are available at hardware stores. Clothesline is sufficient to rig through the pulleys for hanging (Fig. 8-24).

Earlier amateur theatrics included techniques for improvising floodlights by mounting lamp sockets inside anything from an old dishpan to a bucket. Don't use plastic! See Figs. 8-25 and 8-26. This is now not necessary with the quantity of clamp-on aluminum reflectors available at most supermarkets and hardware stores. These are all independently adjustable and can be used either as individual floods or in a group as a striplight. For color mediums, you might have a problem. However, a well run hardware or electrical supply store can probably supply colored bulbs of the type used in advertising. Keep your color format simple and you can get along fine with these.

You might be able to buy sheets of colored transparent acetate from an art and handicraft shop. This can be fastened over the front of a light unit with anything ranging from clothespins to baling wire. If you try this sort of thing, be sure you experiment with the material well in advance to determine its flammability. Some types can take the heat of the lamp, some can't. You might find you have

Fig. 8-20. The Lume-X can illuminate screens up to 52 feet wide (courtesy Strong Electric Corp.).

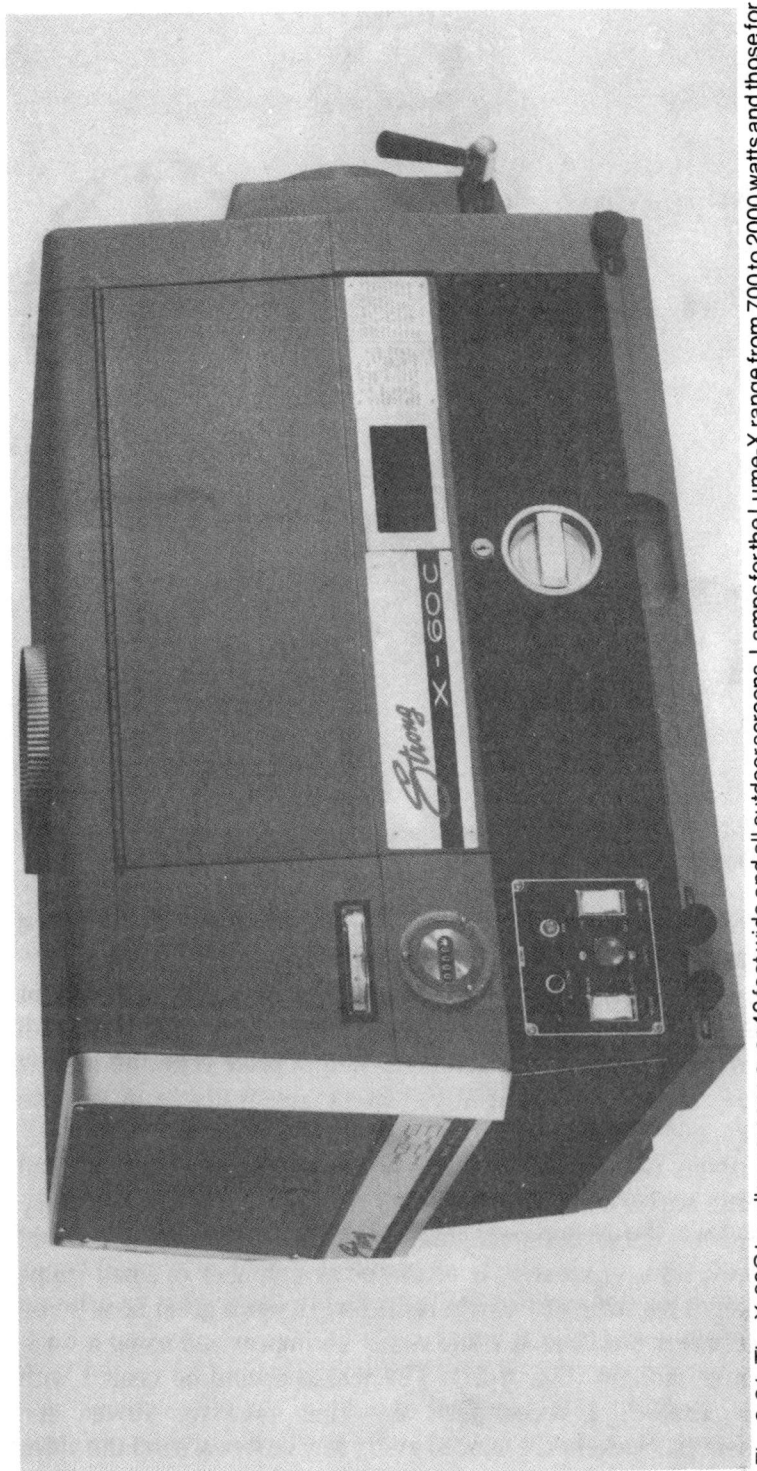

Fig. 8-21. The X-60C handles screens over 40 feet wide and all outdoor screens. Lamps for the Lume-X range from 700 to 2000 watts and those for the X-60C run 3000 to 4000 watts (courtesy Strong Electric Corp.).

Fig. 8-22. The Xenon Light Source can be adapted to projectors (photo courtesy Strong Electric Corp.).

to re-gel the lights after each performance. Don't worry. I've heard of situations where the gels had to be changed after each act.

Fixed lamps can also be improvised on a more permanent basis by using outdoor light fixtures. Some of these are made with an adjustable swivel that can be locked in place once the light is aimed. Lamps with built-in reflectors are available in diverse colors, especially around Christmas time.

When you need a lot of light power and high-power bulbs and sockets are hard to get, you can improvise by using an old hickory not seen in the professional stage for years. This monster is called a bunch light, or cluster. It consisted of a number of small lamps clustered together in a single reflector. It was a great favorite on the amateur stage, as it could easily be improvised using a wash basin or dishpan (Fig. 8-27). The inside should be coated with white enamel. I recommend the kind used for stoves and appliances. Sockets are spaced every few inches around the sides of the dishpan and wired, either in a single circuit or in several circuits for multi-color work. The unit is mounted by means of angle brackets or any method you can improvise. Be sure the wire you use is heavy enough to handle *all* the power.

For all homemade light units, white enamel is the best reflective coating. It is 80 percent reflective as compared to 70 percent for flat white paint. Shiny tin is only 35 percent reflective. You might want to go modern and investigate some of the highly reflective paints used for traffic signs. I would suggest experimenting beforehand with paints containing glass beads to see how it will take the heat.

It has also been suggested that guttering can be used to form the reflectors for strip lights or footlights. However, I haven't run into anybody who has done this.

Oldtimers in amateur show biz have universally spoken with great fondness of the stove pipe spotlight. A followspot made from a stove pipe has always drawn chuckles and snide remarks, but it also has always worked.

Take a 3-foot length of stove pipe (large size) and enamel it white on the inside to within a few inches of one end (Fig. 8-26). Leave this end black to prevent excessive light spill. For a reflector, the oldtimers used to use an old auto headlight reflector. However, these are hard to come by nowadays. Some people have used a small aluminum plate. Others have purchased reflectors from Edmund Scientific or some similar company. Those lucky enough to get one have also mounted a lens inside the output end. However, this requires some trial and error to get the right focus.

Mount a porcelain socket a few inches in front of the reflector and ventilate the pipe above it as shown. Use a photo flood or other high-output lamp. A color medium frame can be fashioned as shown and both sides should be painted flat black. Sheet-metal masks to control the spot size can be cut to fit the color medium frame.

To mount the stove pipe spot, many means from hanging on wires to any number of cleverly crafted brackets have been described. The nicest I've heard of consisted of a solid metal block welded to the bottom near the balance point. A threaded hole big enough to receive a tripod screw was made in the center of the block and the spotlight was mounted on a photographer's tripod. This allowed easy movement and a means of locking it in place.

PROJECTED SCENERY

In situations where the budget is really low, scenery can be improvised by projecting slides onto a smooth, blank background.

A

GOOD VIEWING AREA

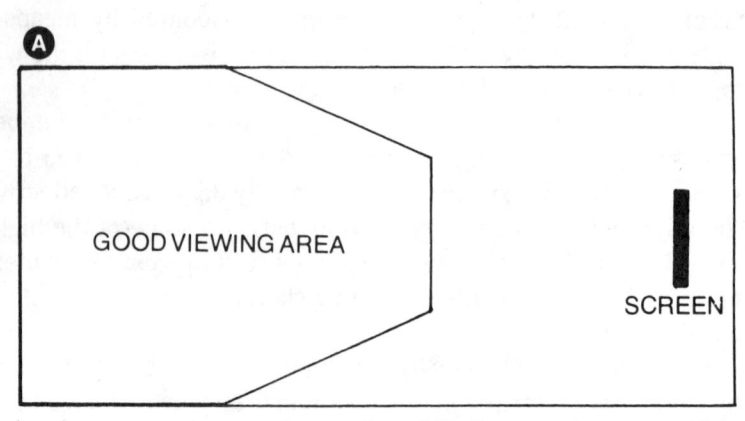

SCREEN

In a long, narrow room (more than 1 ½ times as long as wide), the best arrangement is usually that shown above. A beaded screen or other narrow-angle screen is suitable

B

GOOD VIEWING AREA

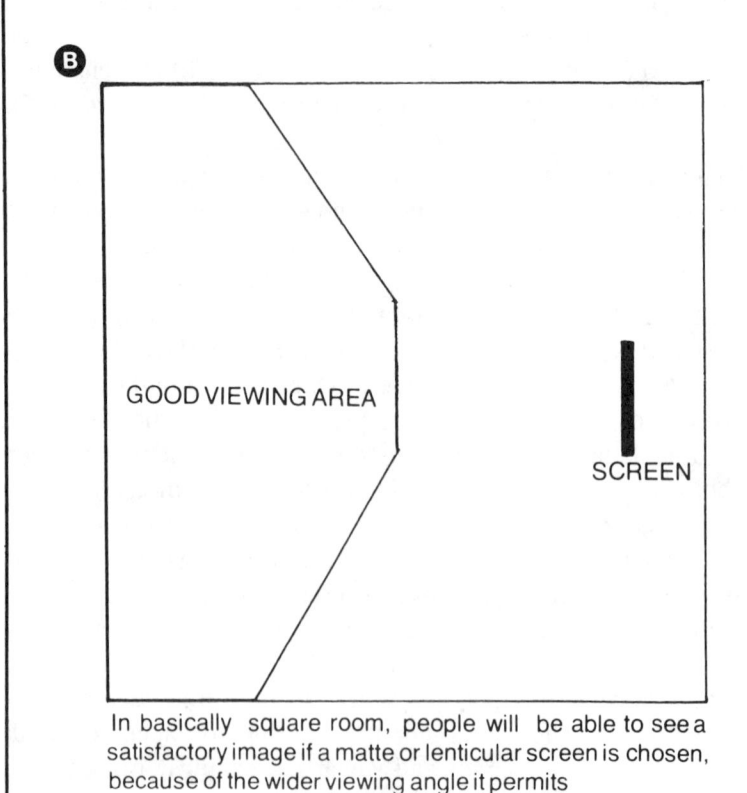

SCREEN

In basically square room, people will be able to see a satisfactory image if a matte or lenticular screen is chosen, because of the wider viewing angle it permits

Fig. 8-23. Good viewing areas for various screen sizes and types (courtesy Eastman Kodak Co.).

C

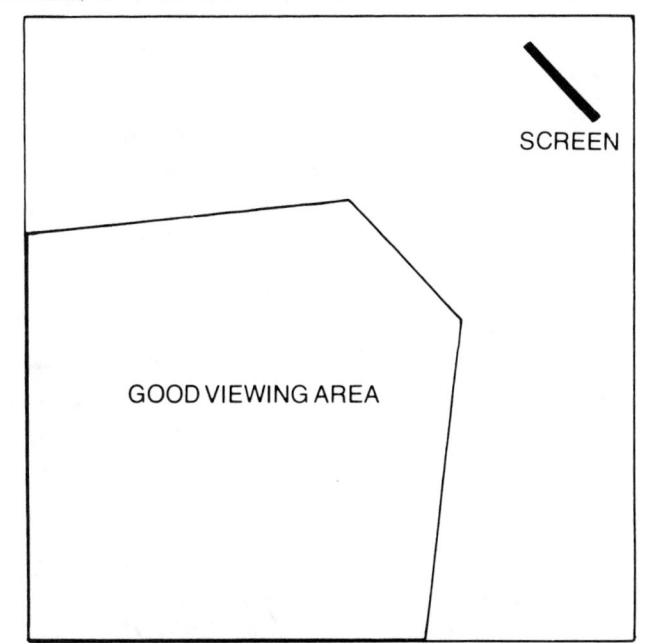

In basically square rooms, often more people can sit in the good viewing area if projection is diagonal. A slightly larger screen may be needed because of the greater maximum viewing distance

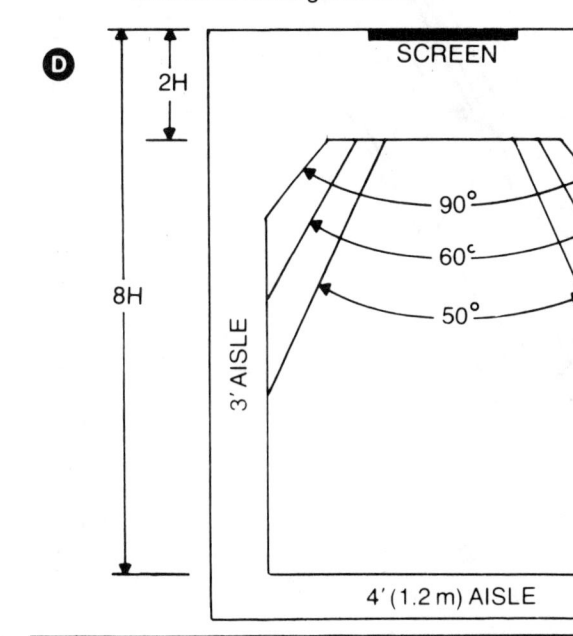

D

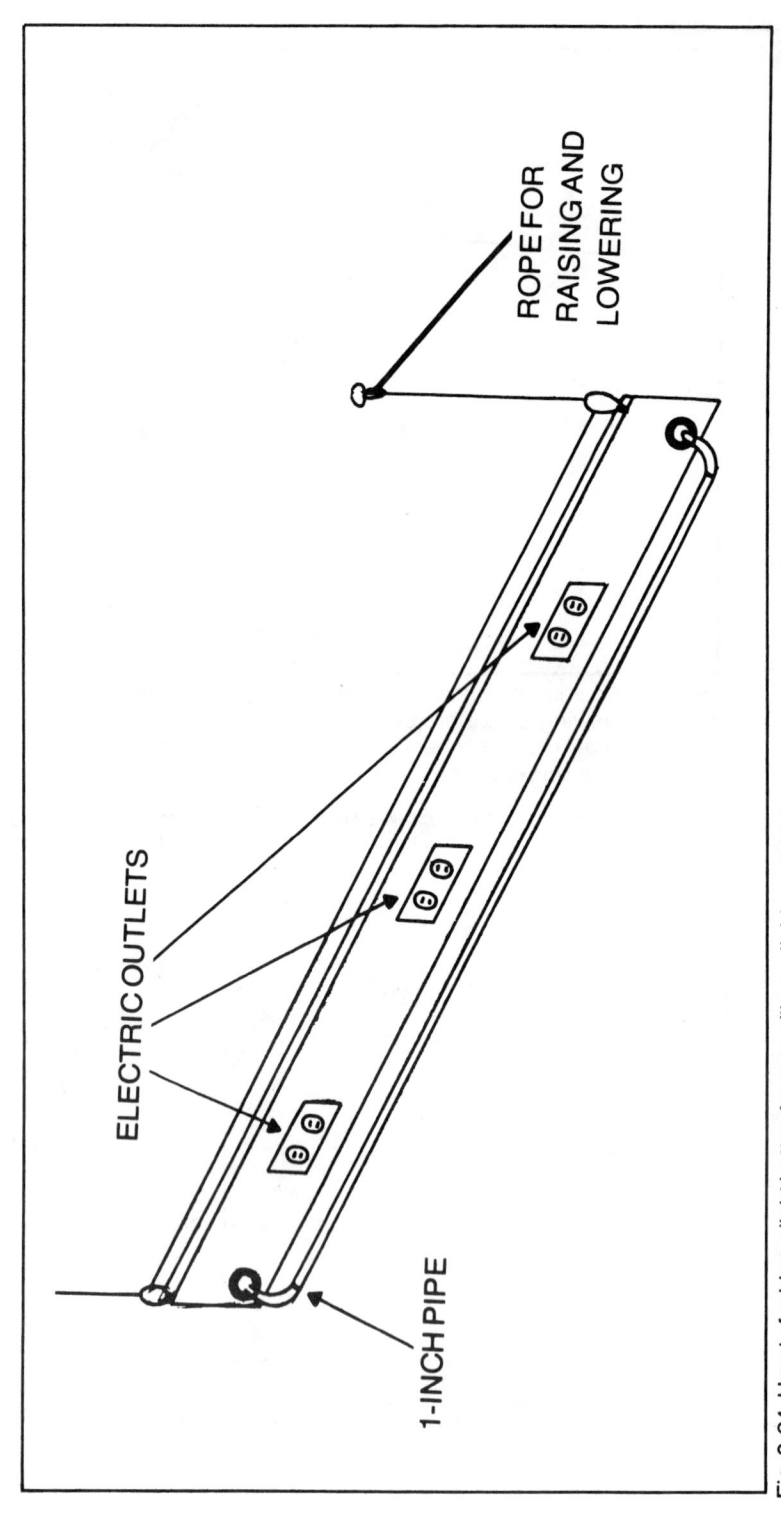

Fig. 8-24. How to fashion a light batten from readily available materials.

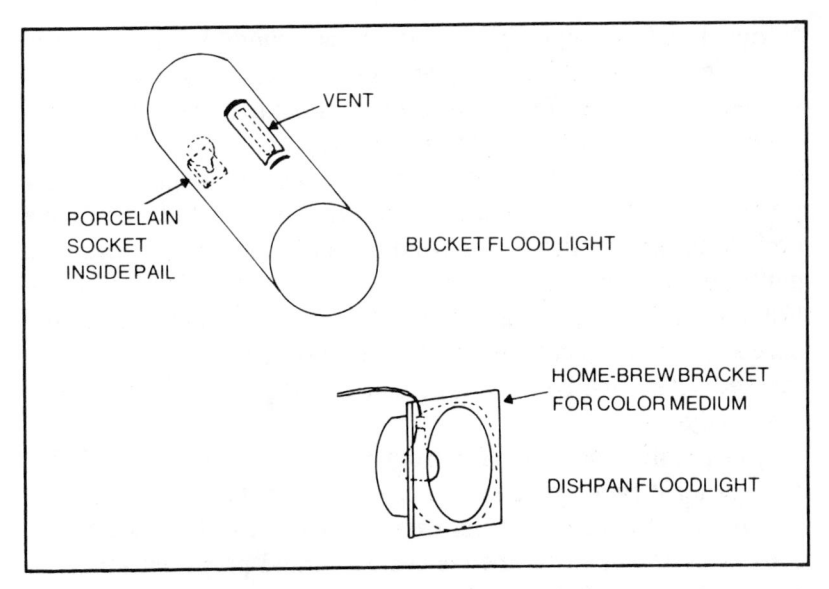

Fig. 8-25. Flood lights can be made from a bucket or a dishpan.

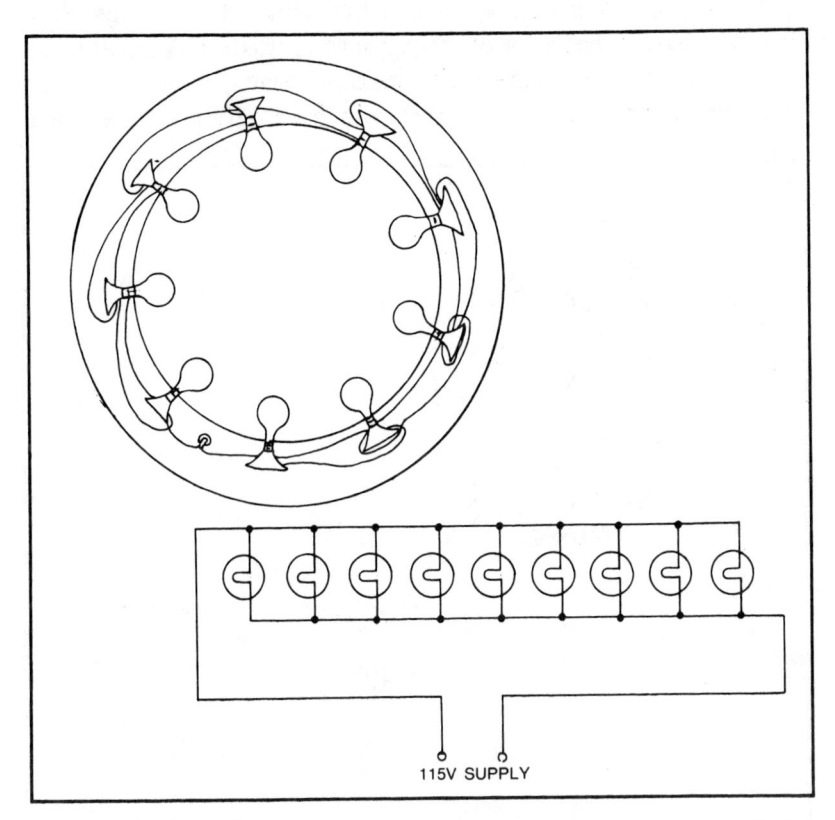

Fig. 8-26. Wiring scheme for a multiple-light dishpan flood light, usually called a bunch light or cluster.

201

Notice I did not specify a white background. Interesting and effective results can be had by projecting a light, solid color onto a screen. In fact, the effects can be very similar to that of using lights of one color only with conventional scenery.

It is relatively seldom that sufficient space is available for rear projection to the size needed, even with the widest of wide-angle projection lenses. Projecting from in front, however, brings on a multitude of problems otherwise unheard of. You don't want the shadows of the players appearing on the scenery—magnified by the spread of the projector beam. This means having the stage floor marked where the beam will go and keeping all performers well downstage.

Generally speaking, for front projection you will probably need at least two projectors so oriented that their pictures abutt one another to make a single, extra-wide picture (Fig. 8-28). The projectors themselves are concealed behind props on stage. A cyclorama arrangement is ideal for projected scenery, particularly with the beams crossing each other (Fig. 8-29). The main disadvantage is that a lot of stage space is wasted. A small-town high school created some truly amazing results, using projected scenery, in a production of *South Pacific*. Four different slides were

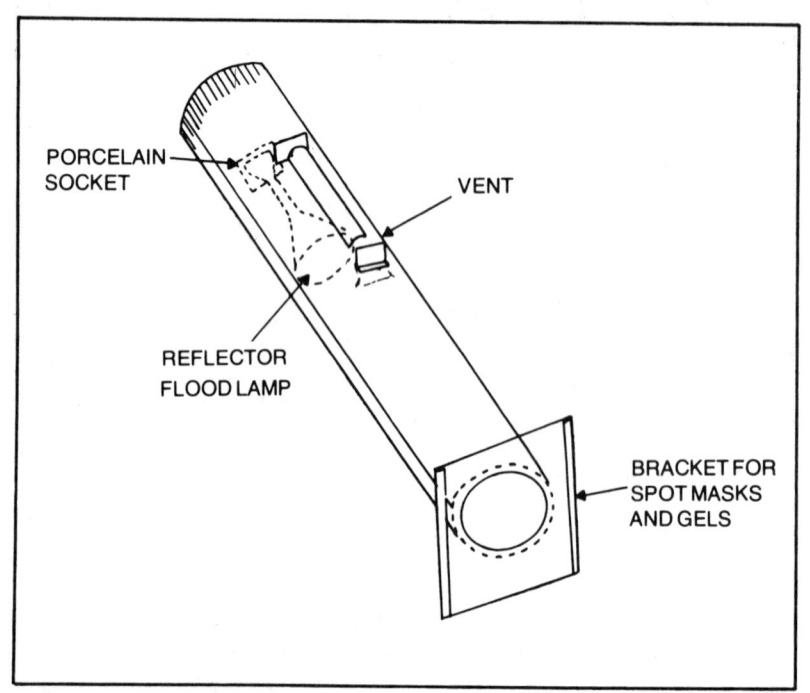

Fig. 8-27. Follow-spotlight made from a length of stove pipe.

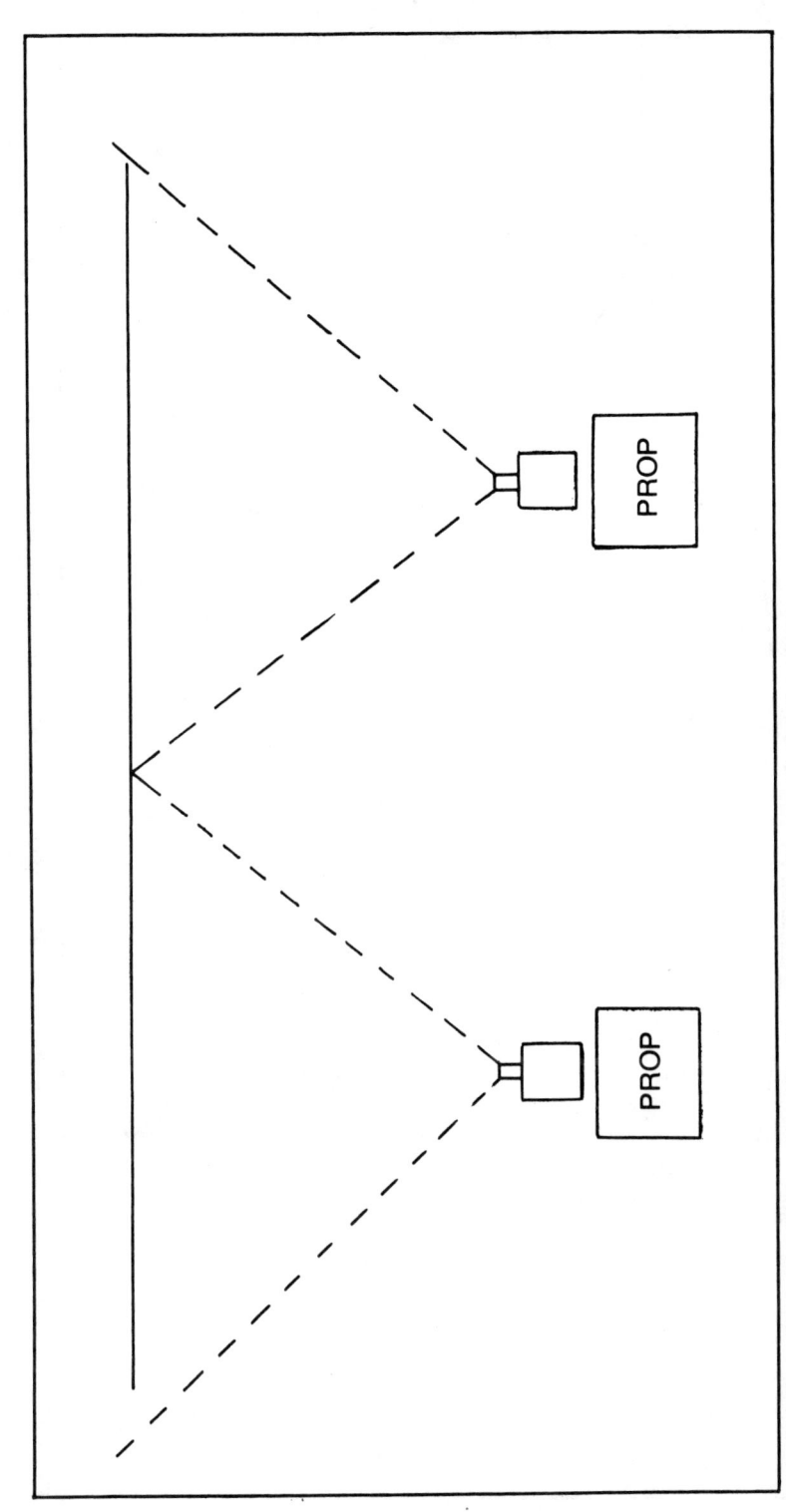

Fig. 8-28. Two slide projectors used to project two side-by-side images on a background.

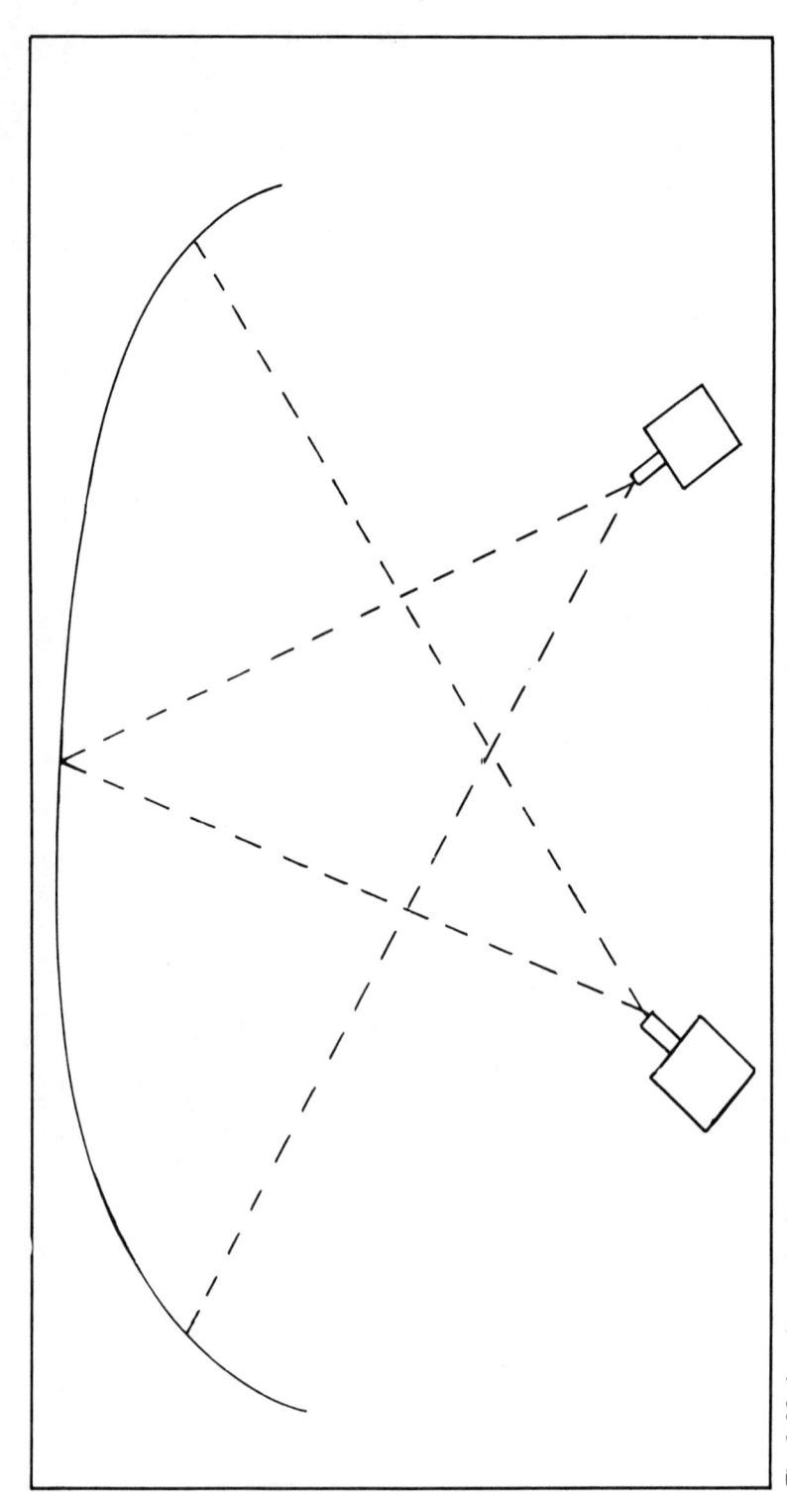

Fig. 8-29. A cyclorama background is provided by two slide projectors with beams crossing each other.

projected simultaneously, superimposing a seascape, palm trees, tropical flowers and sky effects. These were projected onto fine netting instead of a solid screen. A fan was provided to keep the netting in motion while Bloody Mary sang *Bali Hai*, for a very dream-like effect.

In another production, shadows, which are usually taboo with projected scenery—were used to advantage. Dracula's entrance was preceded by a huge bat silhouette which appeared to grow until it all but blacked out the set. The silhouette was a paper cutout held in front of the projector lens. As it was moved closer, it appeared to grow.

Finally, in a production of Dickens' Christmas Carol, Scrooge sat in his chair well downstage, while Marley stayed close to the screen. Marley wore a light colored costume. By remaining close to the screen, shadows were kept at a minimum. The projected scenery on his costume made him appear transparent. It all goes to show you, even when the rules are broken, the possibilities with projected scenery are virtually unlimited.

Chapter 9

Electrical Power Distribution

Electrical power requirements vary with the scope and complexity of a stage setting. Electrical wiring codes vary from one locality to the other. In many places the wiring can only be done by a licensed electrician if the building's insurance is not to be voided.

In a very small auditorium, such as might be found in a church, stage equipment, including lighting, is minimal. Often the stage is lighted by turning on one switch backstage, while the house lights are controlled by a dimmer near the main entrance. This is a far cry from a professional theatre. Most school auditoriums fall somewhere between the two extremes, depending on the size and affluence of the institution.

TYPICAL ELECTRICAL REQUIREMENTS

In a professional theatre, all lighting, including the house lights, is controlled from a console located backstage. This console contains switches and dimmers for each of the circuits and a patch panel where the final connections between the dimmers and the circuits they are to control are made.

The stage wiring is composed of a half dozen or more circuits, all controlled independently. "Work lights" are provided to enable stage hands to do their job when the main stage lighting is off. Each of the several sets of lights has at least three circuits, one for each primary color. For additional lighting and special effects, service outlets or "pockets" are provided on stage. These are controlled independently. Still other circuits service sound and projection systems. A typical stage wiring diagram appears in Fig. 9-1.

If you intend to add anything to the existing wiring, it is important that you check on local wiring codes. There are restrictions relating to wire size and the types of wiring allowed for your particular facility. To avoid possible complications later, find out what you can do as opposed to what must be done by a licensed electrician. Illegal wiring can void fire insurance, especially on a building that is open to the general public.

Determine first what equipment will be used and ascertain its power consumption. Table 9-1 is a partial list of typical power demands of some of the more popular lighting devices. Total power demand for a given circuit is determined by adding the power demand of each of the several pieces of equipment or lights to be

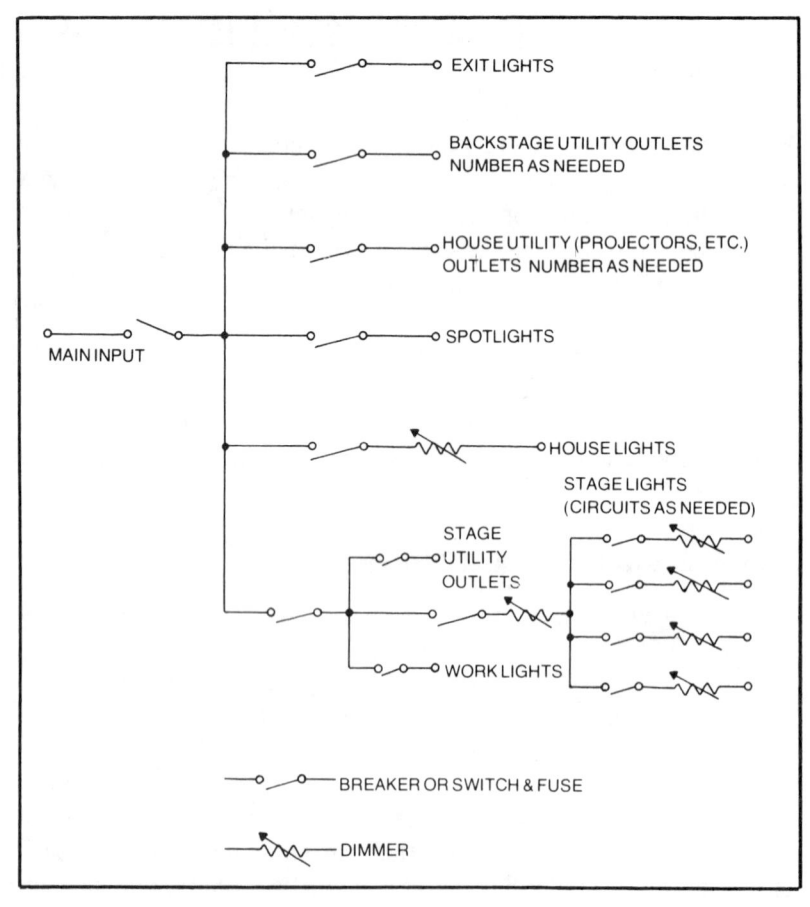

Fig. 9-1. Basic wiring diagram of a typical theatre. For simplicity, the patch panel has been omitted.

operated from the circuit under consideration. Where several circuits combine into one main line, its wiring must be big enough to handle the power required by all the combined circuits. Generally, power demand is expressed in watts rather than in amperes. To convert from watts to amperes, simply divide watts by the line voltage. Once the current to be drawn from a given circuit is known, the correct wire size can be determined from Table 9-2.

It is always a good idea to add 25 percent or so as a safety factor in calculating circuit loads. Never make it a practice to run a circuit at its absolute limit. Once you know the size of conductors you will need, you have only to determine the type of wiring cable you will use. This depends, of course, on the particular kind of installation and on what's already in the building. There are presently four principle types of wiring material in general use. Three types appear in the installation pictured in Fig. 9-2.

NON-METALLIC SHEATHED CABLE

Sometimes referred to as "Roamex," this is the least expensive of the four principle types of cable. It is very often used in farm wiring, and it is ideal for special wiring of scenery, etc. It is not suitable for outdoor use, nor should it be buried in the ground. Furthermore, it is vulnerable to mechanical damage. It consists of two main conductors and sometimes a bare ground conductor wrapped in a damp-proofed woven fabric sheath. It is very easy to work with and the economy of this material suits it for quick installations.

PLASTIC-SHEATHED CABLE

Also called "outdoor Roamex," this is the most attractive of the several types of wiring. It can be used either indoors or out, or buried in the ground with no additional protection. Indoors, it can be fully exposed without necessarily being unattractive. It can even be painted to match its surroundings. Plastic-sheathed Roamex has exceptionally high resistance to fire, rodents, weather or other kinds of abuse. Prior to the invention of this versatile cable, underground wiring had to be encased in lead.

Plastic-sheathed Roamex consists of two conductors, with a third ground conductor usually included, bound together with a molded plastic sheath. The sheath has an attractive white color, which is responsible for its popularity in exposed-wiring installa-

Table 9-1. Typical Equipment and Lighting Power Demands.

Follow Spots		Projection Systems		Incandescent Lamps		Sound Systems	
Trouperette II Quartz-Bromine Lamp 115v	5-6 AMPS	Slide or Movie with Xenon Source	15-20 AMPS	All Types For each 100 Watts	0.9 AMPS	Average PA System	1-3 AMPS
Trouperette Trouperette III Trouper (carbon arc) 115v	8.5-10 AMPS	16 mm Movie (conventional, with 1000-watt Lamp)	8-12 AMPS			Electric Guitar	2-4 AMPS
Super Trouper (carbon arc)	20 AMP	Conventional Slide Projector	5-10 AMPS			Tape Deck	1-2 AMPS
Gladiator 220v	23.5 AMPS						

Table 9-2. Wire Size Versus Current-Carrying Capacity.

WIRE SIZE AND CURRENT CAPACITY						
WIRE SIZE	#14	#12	#10	#8	#6	CURRENT-HANDLING CAPABILITY
	15 AMP	20 AMP	30 AMP	40 AMP	55 AMP	
WIRE SIZE	#4	#2	#1	#0	#000	CURRENT-HANDLING CAPABILITY
	70 AMP	95 AMP	110 AMP	125 AMP	165 AMP	

tion. Its flat, oval shape makes it very easy to work. The cost is only slightly higher than its indoor-only counterpart.

FLEXIBLE ARMORED CABLE

Often called "BX cable," this rugged material is the modern-day descendant of an old favorite dating back to the early '40s. The

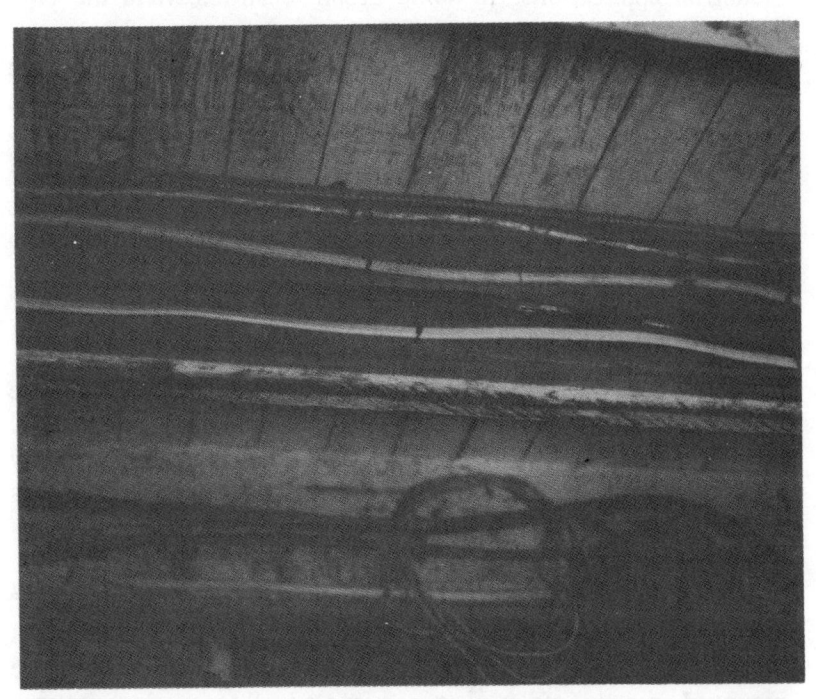

Fig. 9-2. Here are three of the most popular types of power cable. Metallic-sheathed cable (BX) appears at the top of the beam, followed by two runs of low-cost Roamex. Plastic-jacketed Roamex is located at the bottom.

older variety had an inherent defect that, under certain conditions, made it a fire hazard. That defect has been eliminated in the present-day version and it is out and away a favorite where both flexibility and protection from mechanical damage is required. BX cable must be used only with steel outlet and junction boxes—never plastic. When properly installed, it is acceptable in almost all locations.

BX cable consists of two or three conductors and a ground wire encased in a heavy, galvanized steel cover. It is more expensive than Roamex, and a bit more difficult for the beginner to work with. It is not recommended for burial or for outdoor use. However, indoors under dry conditions, it can be imbedded in a plaster or cement wall. When installing, be sure to connect the ground wire to the box and to the fixture's ground terminal at both ends.

THIN-WALL CONDUIT

This is the most expensive but also the safest and most widely accepted system of wiring. It is used almost exclusively in industrial applications. In some urban localities, it is the only accepted method.

It consists of thin-walled, steel tubing (called conduit), which is fastened to the walls or ceilings as needed. The wiring is drawn through by means of a long "fish wire" (called a snake). Mechanically it is far superior to other forms of wiring. The only disadvantage is that more general labor and special tools are required to install it. Because of these disadvantages, conduit is seldom used for temporary installations.

FIXTURES AND WIRING DEVICES

Surface-mounting bakelite fixtures are available in a wide variety for temporary exposed-wiring installations. Generally, however, steel outlet and junction boxes are preferred in virtually all professional installations. These boxes have (knockout) holes for cable entrances and adaptors are available to fit these entrances to any one of the four wiring methods used.

Light fixtures and junctions are usually housed in square boxes, while outlets, dimmers and switches use rectangular boxes equivalent each to one half of a square box. All boxes can be mounted on a surface or recessed into a wall for flush mounting. Specially designed clamps are available to flushmount outlet and switch boxes onto existing panelled walls.

INSTALLATION OF CABLE

In exposed installations non-metallic sheathed cable should be run along some supporting surface, such as framework or studding. When run across studs, attach it to a "running board," usually 1 × 2-inch strapping. Use steel strapping—never staples—with this kind of cable and support it at least every three feet or so and one foot from each outlet or switch box.

Boxes are made specifically for this or plastic sheathed cable or you can use any standard box, provided each box entrance hole used is fitted with the proper entrance clamps. Take care that the cable is protected from mechanical damage and moisture.

Plastic-sheathed cable—called "dual-purpose" because it can be used indoors or out—should be supported along cable runs in the same manner as its more economical counterpart. Staples can be used with this kind of cable with less danger of damage and it can be buried directly in the ground. When used in exposed wiring runs, it can be painted to match its surroundings.

Armored cable used under indoor, dry-environment conditions can be run and supported in the same manner as non-metallic sheathed cable. It is, however, considerably more rugged than other cable. It should be supported every 4½ feet and within 1 foot of each outlet or switch box. Armored cable can be anchored by means of either staples or straps.

Use only steel outlet and switch boxes—never bakelite or porcelain—with armored cable. Whenever the cable is cut, insert a bushing into the end of the armor to protect the wires from the cut end of the armor. Special boxes with built-in cable clamps for this kind of cable might be used or separate clamps might be purchased and used with standard boxes. All splices must be made inside a junction box.

When cutting armored cable, first cut through one section of the armor with an ordinary hacksaw. Be careful not to cut through the insulation of the wires. Then draw the cut ends of the armor apart, allowing at least 8 inches of wire to protrude beyond each half of the cut armor. *Be sure to insert a bushing to protect the cut end.* This is required in wiring codes.

Thin-walled conduit is best installed by a professional electrician. The tubing is expensive and not very forgiving of mistakes in measurement. All junction, outlet and switch boxes must be mounted and tubing installed first. Half-inch conduit carries four #14 wires or three #12; ¾-inch conduit carries four #10 or 12 or three #8; 1¼-inch conduit carries four #6, three #4 or three #2;

1½-inch conduit carries three #1 wires; 2-inch conduit carries three 1/0 or three 3/0.

The tubing comes in 10-foot lengths which are joined by couplings, if necessary. Connector clamps are used at all box entrances. The tubing can be cut with a hacksaw. The cut ends must be de-burred with a file. A special tubing bender is needed to fabricate corners or other bends. When conduit is installed, it should be anchored with a pipe strap every six feet in exposed installations or every 10 feet in concealed work.

After the tubing and boxes are installed, the wire must be inserted. This is done by means of a stiff fish wire (snake). To do it right when long runs are involved, two people are needed. Push the snake into one end of the tubing until it comes out the other end then fasten the wires by bending and hooking the wires into the end of the fish wire. Then, with one person pulling and the other guiding the wires smoothly into the conduit, draw the conductors through until at least 8 inches extend beyond the conduit for making connections. If the run of conduit is longer than the snake, open a coupling partway along the run, draw the wire halfway there, then insert the snake at the end to draw the wire the rest of the way. Once the wire is in, be sure to close the coupling.

Whatever kind of wiring you use, one wire will be white, the other either black or red. If there is a third wire, it will probably be green. The white wire is usually the *neutral*, the wire electrically closest to ground, and the dark wire is *hot*. Green wires are used to ground all fixtures together. Each fixture will have a white metal contact screw, a brass screw, and, if a third one is used, it will be marked with a drop of green paint. When installing switches, always open the *hot* wire—after shutting off the power. When installing outlets, connect the white wire to the white metal screw. Connect the dark wire to the brass screw. Connect the green wire to the screw marked with green paint.

All the foregoing applies to installations that are indoors. Outdoor installations are an entirely different matter. Each is done according to the individual designer's ideas. Of all the outdoor theatrical installations to this author's knowledge, none can come close to that used by the Church of Jesus Christ of Latter-Day Saints for their annual pageant at Palmyra, NY. They use the entire side of the hill to present their dramatizations, using no less than 25 separate outdoor stages. Each stage has local lighting available. Several towers along the sidelines support spotlights that cover any part of the area in use. Three dozen outdoor weatherproof

Fig. 9-3. A weatherproof multiple-outlet box used for lighting equipment at the Mormon outdoor theatre.

boxes (Fig. 9-3), distributed about the hill contain outlets for nearly 200 circuits, served by five miles of buried wiring.

All circuits except those used for the spots are switched from a central control point. Spotlight circuits are hot all the time, leaving their control up to the operators. Outlets are of the weatherproof type and are housed in specially built, steel boxes. Individual stages are locally floodlighted from their local outlet boxes. Spots are perched on top of towers where they can command a view of any part of the hill. All in all, it is an enviable feat.

The reader can, by reading "between the lines" in the descriptions of the Hill Cummorah installation, or by examining other outdoor installations, easily observe that the prime requisite for outdoor installations is simply waterproofing. For any outdoor installation, the prime enemy is dampness. Waterproof wiring, waterproof outlet boxes and waterproof fixtures are all you need over and above the supplies used for indoor installations.

Cable that is buried directly should be of the molded-plastic type. There should be no splices underground. If a junction is absolutely necessary in the field, bring the wire up to a water-

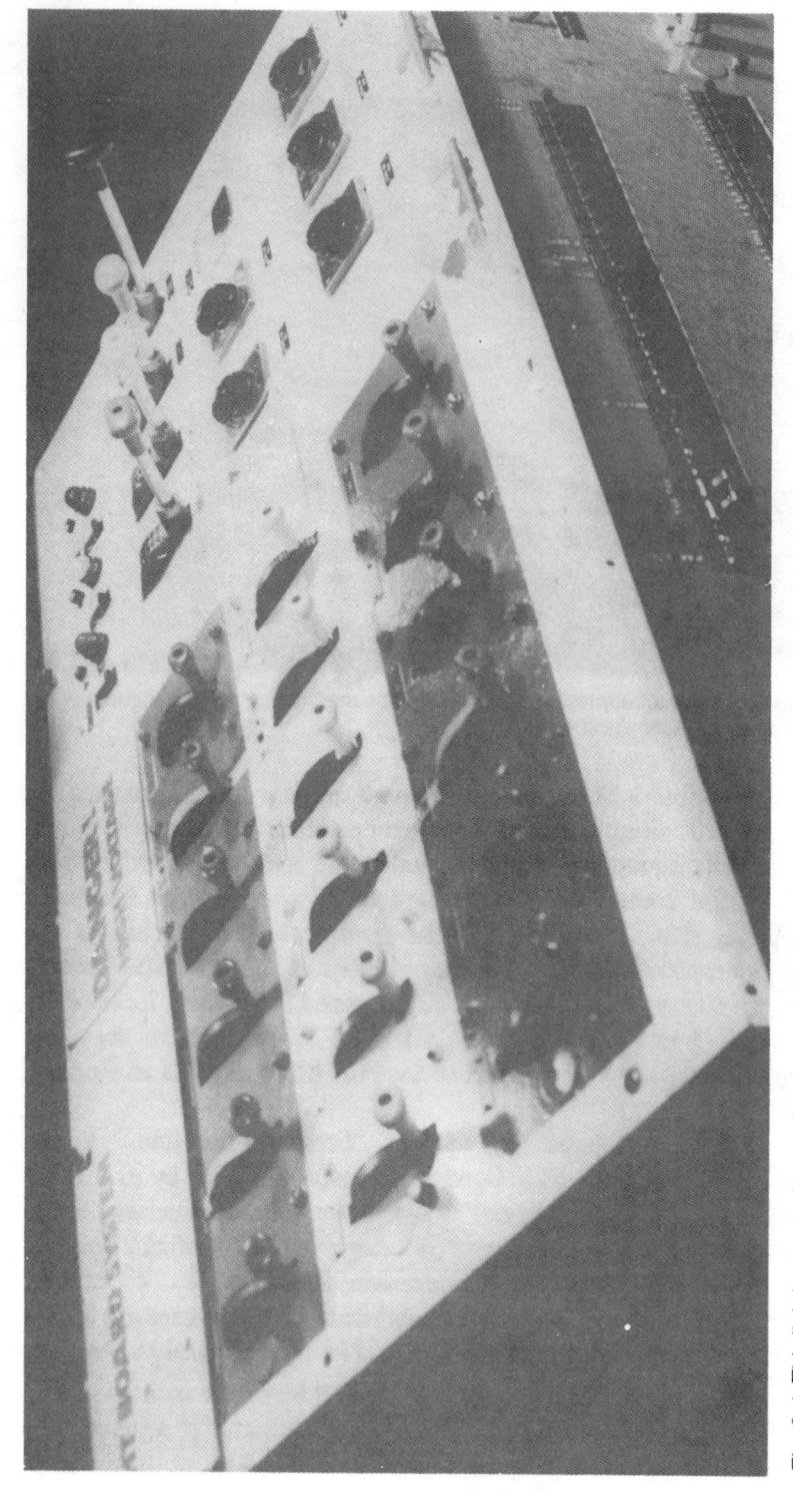

Fig. 9-4. This lighting control console was purchased by a high school. Dimmers are on the top panel.

Fig. 9-5. Circuit breakers are on the front panel.

Fig. 9-6. The patch is immediately beneath the circuit breakers.

Fig. 9-7. Lighting control cabinet in a small high school auditorium. The PA amplifier (on the shelf) is also under the control of the lighting technician.

proof junction box. Make your splice and then seal the box with hot tar or other suitable waterproofing material.

If conduit is used underground, it should be either a single piece or all underground couplings should be waterproofed. Lay the conduit so as to provide one point lower than the rest of the system. Let it drain into a small dry well. Be sure any outlet or junction boxes are entirely closed and weatherproof. I have heard more than one story of systems being thrown out of service by field mice, squirrels, rats, etc. that make their way

219

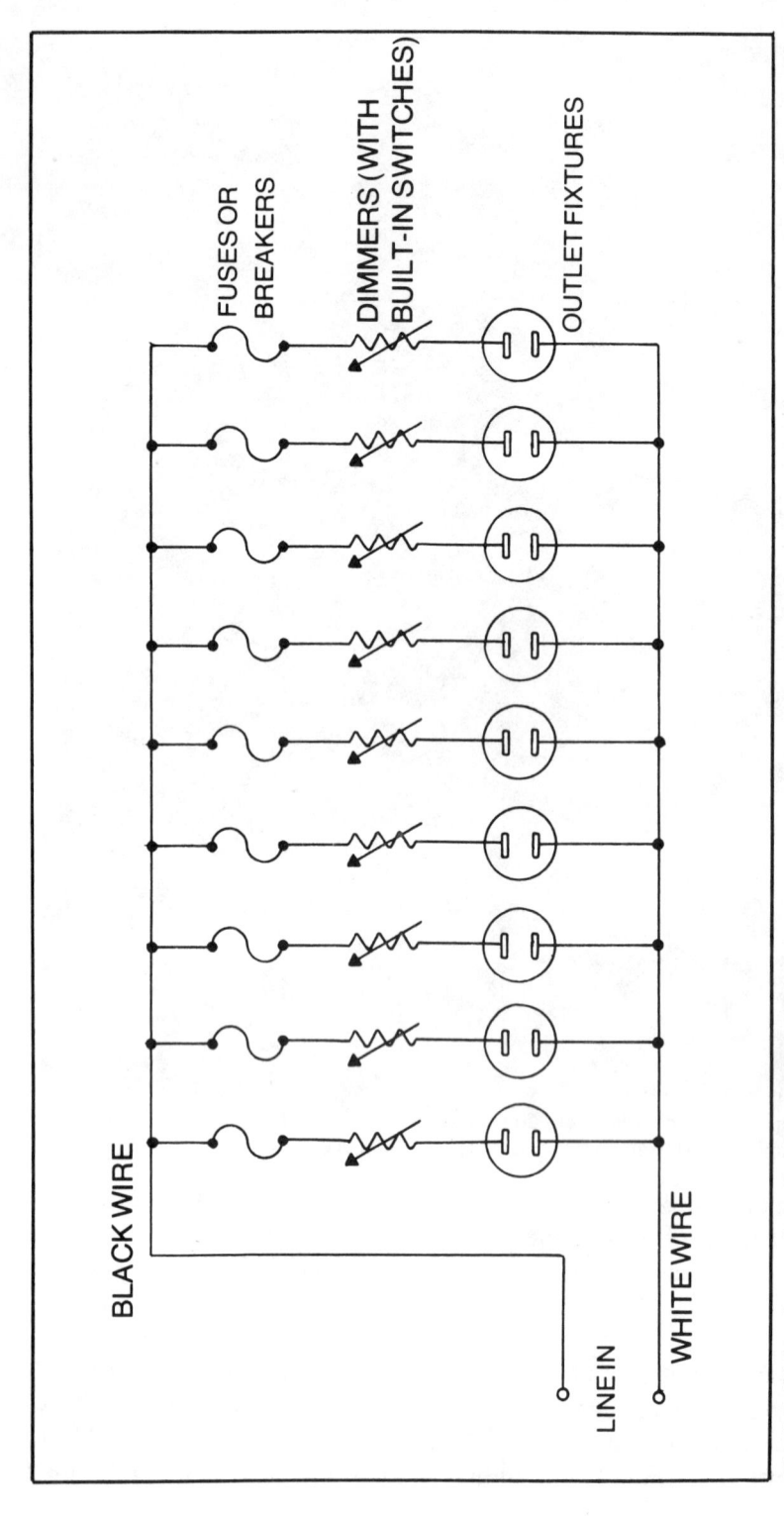

Fig. 9-8. Wiring diagram for a 9-outlet 110-volt lighting system.

into the boxes and then chew the wires. Control housings, switch boxes, etc. can also be protected by leaving a box of D-Con or something similar inside.

Be sure you take adequate steps to prevent access to outlet and switch boxes by unauthorized persons. Even if there wasn't the danger of your being sued by somebody who shouldn't have been there in the first place, nobody wants to see any one killed or injured by a system he or she installed, even if it happens to be the fault of the victim.

CONTROL SYSTEMS

Since no two systems are alike, it would be difficult to offer a control panel that would handle all jobs. However, the ideas to follow can easily be adapted to handle your situation. Commercially made panels are certainly available (Figs. 9-4, Fig. 9-5, Fig. 9-6 and Fig. 9-7), but their cost is frequently out of reach of the small-time operator. However, a very satisfactory homemade system can be built from parts readily available in any hardware store.

It is best to build your control system on metal panels which can then be mounted in a cabinet of a form to suit your taste. Panels should be of 1/16-inch to 1/8-inch sheet metal. Dimmers used are the solid-state kind sold in most hardware or home-improvement supply houses. They have built-in switches for on/off functions and can dim circuits up to 600 watts power demand. Electrical supply stores also have dimmers that handle power levels up to 3,600 watts. For anything bigger than that, you will have to turn to commercial equipment and a professional electrician.

The solid-state dimmers are made to mount in place of standard wall switches and can easily be attractively mounted. Each circuit should have its own dimmer and should be separately fused. It might be more convenient to mount the outlet sockets on a rear or side panel than on the same panel as the dimmers. Wiring diagrams are shown for a 9-outlet panel (Fig. 9-8) feeding from a 115-volt line and a 10-outlet panel (Fig. 9-9) feeding from a 3-wire, 220-volt line. If a master dimmer or fuse is desired, it is inserted between the power source and the feed point of the panel. While the wiring is shown for 2-wire ungrounded sockets, there should be no problem adding the ground wire if you want.

Ordinary extension cords can be used to connect the lamps to the control console, provided they are not too long and are of heavy

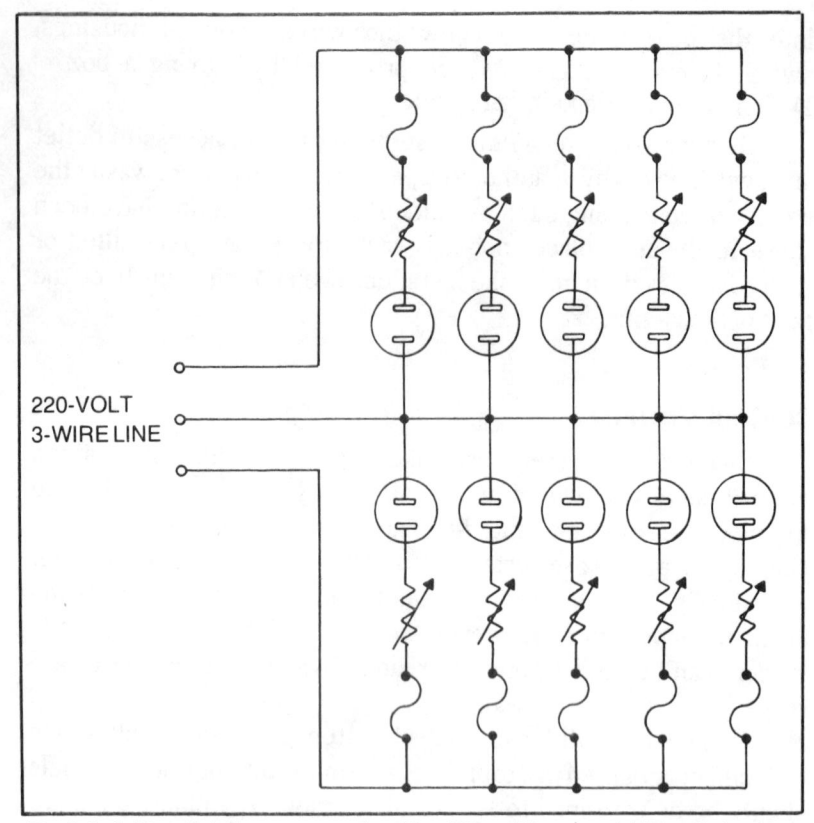

Fig. 9-9. A 10-outlet dimmer console with a 220-volt input and 115-volt circuits.

enough gauge to handle the load. For loads over 500 watts or so, you might prefer to make an extension cord of #14 or #16 Roamex, with the receptacle mounted in a standard outlet box. This box can either be unmounted or attached to a nearby permanent prop.

Chapter 10

Color and Its Magic

The use of color in theatrical lighting is an art all in itself. By working in subtle differences in color and intensity, moods can be worked into a scene and even changed without making any difference that is visible to any but a trained eye. Makeshift scenery can be enhanced or the finest in scenery can be downgraded, depending on how well it is lighted. Little wonder, then, that the professionals refer to various phases of the art as "painting with light." I will discuss some of the principles and give just a few examples of how they might be applied. From there it's up to you and your own artistic taste.

THE LIGHT SPECTRUM

Light and radio waves are comprised of the same type of energy—electromagnetic radiation. The only difference is the wavelength. Radio waves range in wavelength from hundreds of meters to a few millimeters and shorter (Fig. 10-1). Light waves range in lengths so short they are measured in angstroms. An angstrom is one ten-millionth of a millimeter. The longest light waves are deep red and have a wavelength of about 8,000 angstroms. The shortest are deep violet and are approximately 4,000 angstroms long. All the colors of the rainbow are between these extremes and other colors are mixtures of these. Wavelengths just outside the range of the visible spectrum are called infra-red (longer) and ultra-violet (shorter). These, espe-

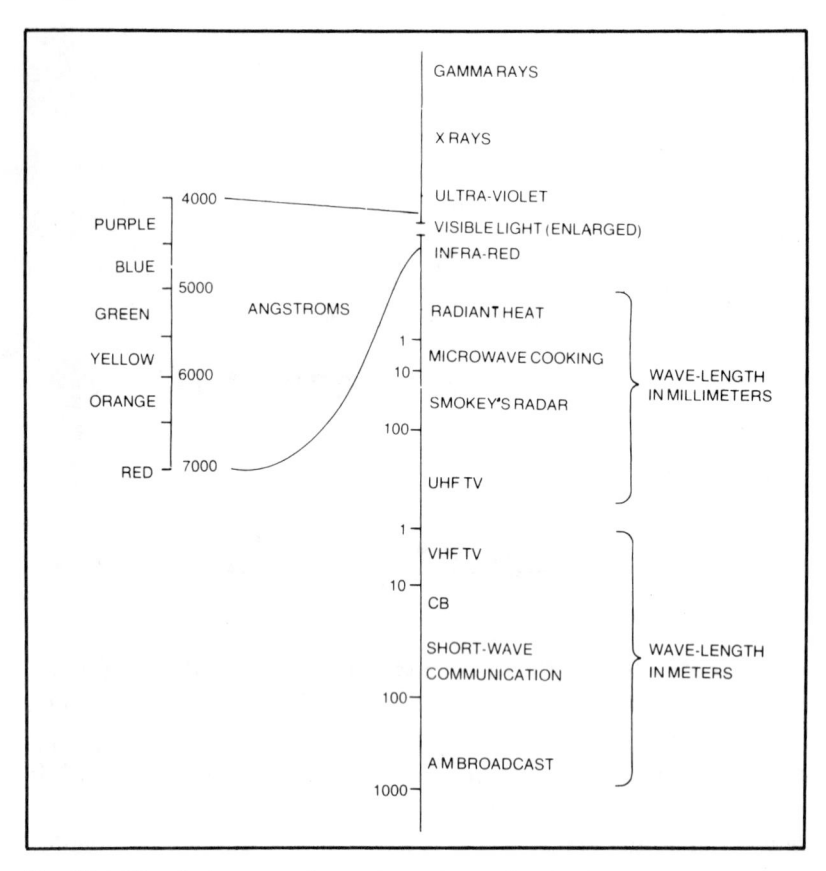

```
                        GAMMA RAYS

                        X RAYS

           4000         ULTRA-VIOLET
   PURPLE               VISIBLE LIGHT (ENLARGED)
   BLUE                 INFRA-RED
           5000
   GREEN       ANGSTROMS       RADIANT HEAT
   YELLOW                1
           6000        10  MICROWAVE COOKING     WAVE-LENGTH
   ORANGE                                        IN MILLIMETERS
                            SMOKEY'S RADAR
                       100
   RED     7000
                            UHF TV

                        1
                            VHF TV
                       10
                            CB

                            SHORT-WAVE            WAVE-LENGTH
                            COMMUNICATION         IN METERS
                       100

                            A M BROADCAST
                      1000
```

Fig. 10-1. The electromagnetic wave spectrum, showing how light waves relate to other forms of radiation.

cially ultra-violet, are often referred to as "black light." Infra-red has no application in the theatrical field. Ultra-violet is often used for special effects. More on that in Chapter 11.

HOW THE HUMAN EYE RESPONDS TO COLOR

The human eye responds to and discriminates between the various light wavelengths between 8,000 and 4,000 angstroms. The human eye perceives color by three sets of color receptors, each sensitive to a slightly different portion of the visible spectrum. One is most sensitive to wavelengths between 4,000 and 5,000 angstroms (numbers are approximate) with peak efficiency at 4,500 and is said to be *blue* sensitive. The second receptor functions in the range between (roughly) 4800 to 6200 with a peak at 5,500 angstroms and is said to be *green* sensitive. The third responds to light waves between 4,800 to 8000 angstroms with a peak at about 6,000 angstroms and is said to be *red* sensitive. You will note that the green and red receptor sensitivities overlap one another considerably in their response ranges (Fig. 10-2). They are equally sensitive at about 5,500 angstroms, which is a greenish yellow color. This point is the color most humans see most easily. It is the peak of visual response, which explains the reason for the yellow sodium-vapor lamps used for highway lighting—they offer the greatest visual aid with the least expenditure of power.

THE ADDITION AND SUBTRACTION OF LIGHT

What is called "white" is not a separate color. Rather, white is a mixture of all colors, equally stimulating to all three color receptors in our eyes. The colors to which the individual receptors are most sensitive are known as the *primary colors*. Any third-grader will tell you that the primary colors are red, yellow and blue. Here green is used instead of yellow. I am referring to a different kind of color mixing, that which is accomplished by adding colors together. What you did in elementary school was subtractive mixing. I will get to that shortly.

If you darken the room and then shine a red light and a green light onto the same white surface, you will see a yellow spot. If you then shine a blue light onto that same spot and experiment with the brilliance of the three lights, you will end up with a white spot of light. You began with a dark room (absence of light). You turned on a red light and then added green light to that. This stimulated the red and green color receptors of your eye equally and your brain told you it was yellow. Then you added blue light and your brain received signals from all three receptors, interpreting it as white (Fig. 10-3). Additive mixing sees much use in the theatrical world and in color television. Examine a color TV picture with a high-power magnifier, and you will see millions of tiny red, green and blue dots.

The color mixing that is done with paints—which you did in the third grade—is known as subtractive mixing. You were told that the primaries were red, yellow and blue and that was close enough for what you were doing. However, if you ever get into color photography or printing you will learn differently. Instead of red, the first subtractive primary is magenta, a reddish-purple color. Instead of blue, the third subtractive primary is cyan, greenish-blue. Magenta stimulates the red and blue receptors equally and is formed by subtracting green from a white light. Cyan

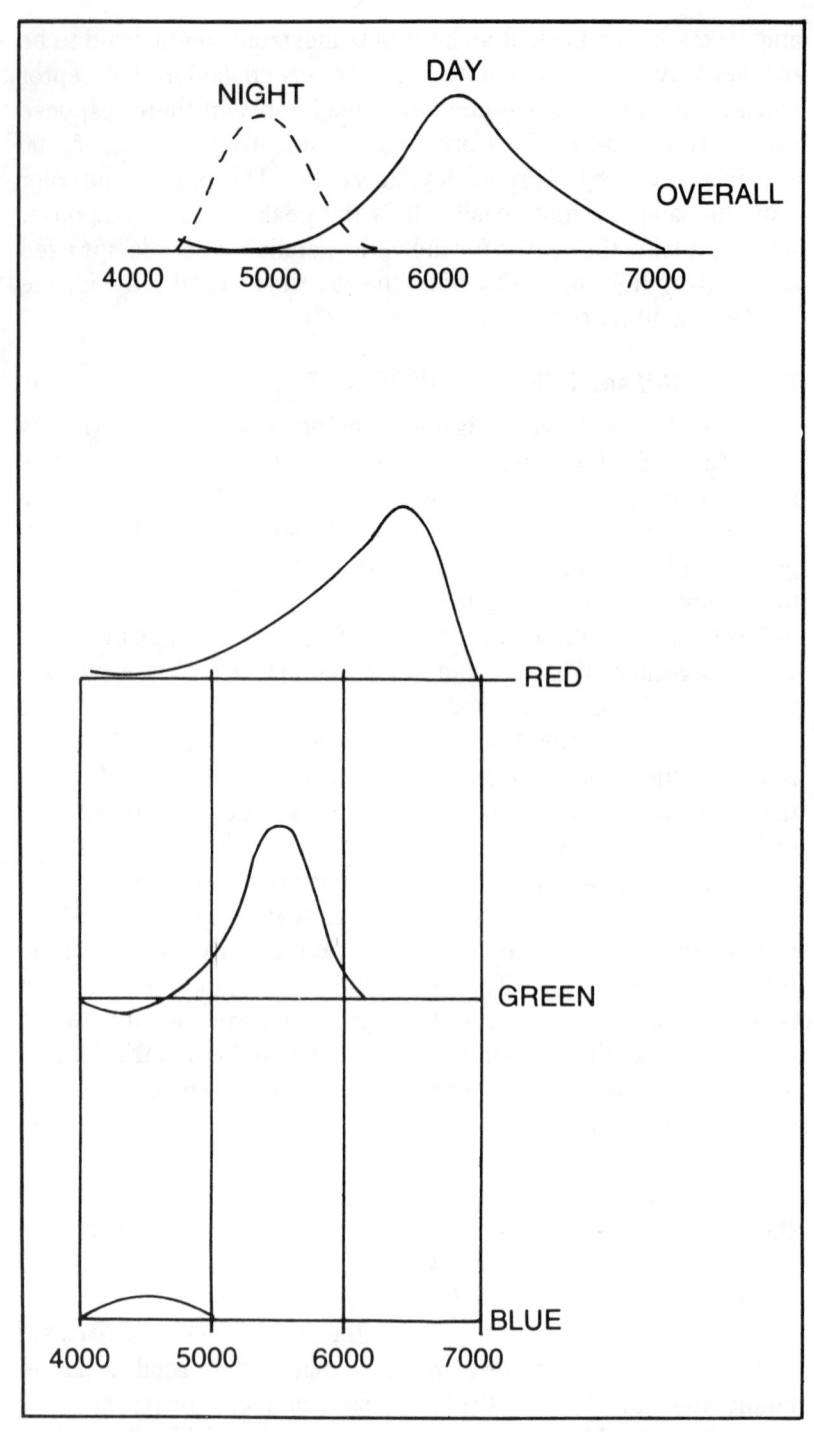

Fig. 10-2. Curves showing average color receptor response and over all color response of the human eye.

226

stimulates the green and blue receptors equally and is formed by subtracting red from a white light. Yellow is perceived by stimulation of the red and green receptors in the eye and is formed by subtracting blue from white light.

When an artist paints a spot of color on his canvas, he or she is changing the surface to make it reflect only the wavelength or mixture of wavelengths he wants. The artist *subtracts* all unwanted colors from the light illuminating the canvas. If the artist paints cyan, the surface of his canvas is altered so that it will reflect only green and blue—subtracting the red. Yellow paint will reflect only red and green, minus blue. If the artist paints yellow over cyan, one pigment subtracts red, the other subtracts blue. All that is left is green. You did that in primary school.

Subtractive mixing sees its theatrical application in the coloring of costumes and scenery and in the coloring of light. Practically all colored lights derive color by starting with a white or nearly white source and passing the light through the proper filters to subtract all but the wanted colors. Quite often, the resulting colors will be again mixed as they shine together on the scenery and performers. It seems complicated, but it does give the maximum control over the light.

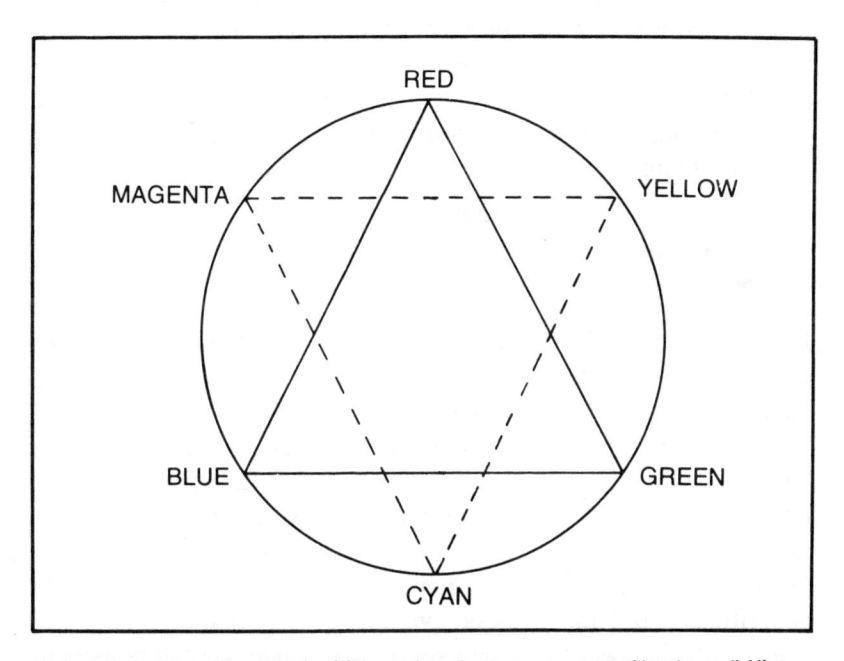

Fig. 10-3. In this color wheel additive primaries are connected by the solid lines, while the complementary subtractive primaries are connected by the dotted lines. The complement of any color is directly across the wheel.

Table 10-1. Use This Table for Mixing Colors.

% RED	% BLUE	% GREEN	RESULT
100	0	0	RED
43	24	33	LIGHT RED
48	43	9	MAGENTA
51	10	39	ORANGE
40	12	48	YELLOW
0	0	100	GREEN
0	50	50	CYAN
0	100	0	BLUE
28	52	20	PURPLE
33.3	33.3	33.3	WHITE

You can produce any color you want by using either the additive or the subtractive primaries or by using both together. For example, if a yellow prop on a stage is illuminated by a red spotlight, the yellow will reflect the red and the prop will appear red to the audience. At the right moment if the red spot is changed to green, the result will be that the prop will change color right before the eyes of the audience.

When two or more light sources of different additive primary colors are beamed together onto the same object, they will mix to form new colors:

- red and green mix to form yellow.
- blue and green mix to form cyan.
- red and blue mix to form magenta.

By using dimmers on the lights and controlling the proportions of each color, a wide range of colors can be produced. Some guidelines appear in Table 10-1.

Two qualities of light must be considered. So far I have discussed only color. You must not forget saturation. By saturation I mean the extent to which a color is diluted with white. While fully saturated colors are often used to create special effects, the majority of theatrical lighting uses color in much more subtle quantities. Often an untrained eye might not notice the individual colors, yet their presence will serve to enhance the colors used in costumes and scenery or to help set the mood required for the scene.

MOODS AND SPECIAL EFFECTS

Color, either saturated or diluted, is of great importance in setting a mood. Color can bring an otherwise drab scene to life. Here are a few basics:
- Steel blue or light green simulates moonlight.
- Magenta suggests late sunset or early sunrise.
- Red or amber simulates firelight.
- Peacock blue is generally used on sky backdrops.
- Deep green is a favorite for horror scenes.
- Amber or rose is good for lighting the face.

Lights used to set a mood are generally of low saturation, except in very extreme cases. Here are a few mood color ideas:
- Red suggests anger, danger, war, and sex.
- Blue suggests peace.
- Yellow suggests gaiety, a "party" atmosphere.
- Orange is hot, stifling.
- Violet is gloomy, melancholy.

There is some danger in taking these ideas too literally. For example, just because red might suggest anger, you shouldn't expect the audience to get mad at the villain just because you bathe him with a red light. They'll only get mad at you! On the other hand, working some red into the scene when he's at the height of his villainy will heighten the sense of danger or perhaps strengthen the sense of anger displayed by the lynch-mob when they go after him.

A Few Do's and Don'ts. When you use light to set a mood, be aware of the color of the props. Color can either enhance a particular prop or spoil its effect altogether. For example, a red prop against a white background can be softened by a little red illumination or it can become nearly invisible as the saturation of the red is increased.

Don't use too much amber in a scene containing a lot of blue. Amber light makes blue objects look muddy.

Use white or amber in the footlights. Too much red coming from below will mottle the performer's face. If red is needed, use it in the overhead lights or in the spots—never in the footlights.

Use white, amber, blue, and green in the border lights with just a few reds.

COLORED LIGHT ON COLORED OBJECTS

The illumination on a colored object will reflect a color dependent on the color of the light and the subtractive color of the object. For example, a yellow object will reflect red, yellow or

Table 10-2. Table Listing the result of Illuminating Colored Objects with Colored Light. Find the Color of the Light in the Vertical, Left-Hand Column. Move Across the Chart Until You Reach the Column Under the Color of the Object.

MATERIAL → LIGHT ↓	RED	ORANGE	YELLOW	GREEN	BLUE	VIOLET
RED ORANGE YELLOW GREEN BLUE VIOLET AMBER	RED RED-ORANGE ORANGE MUDDY VIOLET DEEP RED RED	RED-ORANGE ORANGE YELLOW-ORANGE YELLOW-GREEN BROWN LIGHT RED ORANGE	ORANGE ORANGE-YELLOW YELLOW YELLOW-GREEN GREEN MUDDY RED YELLOW	MUDDY RED YELLOW-GREEN YELLOW-GREEN GREEN CYAN LIGHT PURPLE MUDDY	VIOLET BROWNISH GREEN INTENSE GREEN BLUE BLUE-VIOLET MUDDY	DEEP PURPLE LIGHT RED MUDDY MUDDY GREEN BLUE-VIOLET VIOLET MUDDY

green light. When illuminated with magenta, it will reflect red. When illuminated with cyan, it will reflect green. Under blue light, it will appear dark grey. Straw light tends to soften most colors, as does frost. Table 10-2 is a chart of the effects of various colors of light on colored material.

CROSSING LIGHTS

By crossing, I mean that light of one color is beamed onto a prop from one direction while light of a second color is beamed from another. This produces a striking effect from the combined additive and subtractive mixing that occurs with the two source colors and the prop color. Highlights stand out in one color while shadows can be either of two other colors. This is especially outstanding when used with draperies. It's an old trick, but effective. Table 10-3 gives some of the effects that can be achieved using various colors against white draperies.

SPECIAL EFFECTS

The number of special effects that can be achieved using the phenomena of additive and subtractive color mixing is limited only by the imagination. I will offer a couple of examples and let you take it from there.

In the play, *Aladdin's Lamp*, a scene takes place deep in a cave where Aladdin comes upon the repository of the lamp. The niche in which the lamp was placed had a white background and the lamp itself was yellow. At first, it was lighted with highly saturated green light. The yellow lamp and the white background both reflected green light equally well, so the lamp was invisible to the audience. At the right moment, the lighting on the lamp was faded from green to blue. The white background reflected the blue light as easily as it had the green, but the yellow lamp could not reflect blue, so it now contrasted with the background. The effect was that, as the light faded from green to blue, the lamp appeared in the niche as if it materialized by magic.

In another production, two scenes were painted on a single drop, a pastoral scene in red and an ocean scene in blue. The background, lighted separately from the performer, was lighted in deeply saturated red. This made the pastoral scene invisible while the ocean scene stood out. As the performer "dreamed" of home, the background lights were faded from red to blue. The ocean scene became invisible, while the pastoral scene stood out. At the

Table 10-3. Table of Effects Achieved with Light Crossing.

LIGHT #1	LIGHT #2	EFFECT
BLUE	YELLOW	White highlights, blue, yellow, green shadows
RED	GREEN	Yellow highlights, orange red, & green shadows
RED	BLUE	Purple highlights, blue, red, & green shadows
BLUE	VIOLET	Purple highlights, green fog in shadows
GREEN	(45°) MAGENTA	White highlights multicolored shadows

end of the number, the lights were faded back to make the ocean scene visible—his return to reality.

These are just two of a great many possibilities. Back in the days when movies were new, 3-dimensional effects were achieved by using two projectors with different colored lights and letting the audience view them through glasses containing one red and one green lens. This was, of course, outmoded with the discovery of polarized light.

MAKEUP

When you're using colored lights on human faces, be careful. One small mistake with the makeup and a person will look pretty weird under the lights. If you're using color in the lights, let the performer apply makeup under similar lighting conditions and then check it from a distance—stage-to-audience, if possible. Do this well in advance of performance time, to allow for any adjustments.

Makeup should be a bit on the florid side to look natural under amber light. With blue or green light, use no rouge on the face and just a touch on the lips. A red surface looks purple or brown under blue or green light and that certainly does not flatter one's face. On the other hand, no amount of rouge is visible under red light, so the

Table 10-4. Table of Colors Achieved by Using Two Dye Colors.

Dye #1	Dye #2	Result
RED	YELLOW	ORANGE
YELLOW	BLUE	GREEN
RED	BLUE	VIOLET
ORANGE	GREEN	CITRON
GREEN	VIOLET	OLIVE
VIOLET	ORANGE	RUSSET
CITRON	OLIVE	SAGE
OLIVE	RUSSET	PLUM
RUSSET	CITRON	BUFF

decision to use or not to use rouge must depend on the lighting of other scenes.

COSTUMES

When you use colored light, especially the three primaries, you can get away with an awful lot, if you dye the material properly. Cheesecloth can replace silk. Unbleached muslin can replace taffeta and flannel can be used in place of velvet. The secret is to dye it with a broken surface. By this I mean that you dye it, not with a pure color, but with the proper combination of subtractive primaries used one at a time. Don't mix the dyes themselves. For example, if you want a green garment, first put it in yellow dye, then in blue. Table 10-4 lists the colors resulting from various color combinations.

One last caution—never use a simulated material on the same stage as the real thing. If you improvise, you must be consistent throughout the production.

SCENERY

With colored light, scenery can be made of very inexpensive material. Kalsomined newspaper, painted wrapping paper, or painted burlap appear very substantial. This is the nicest part of the magic of color—it makes beauty out of commonplace materials.

Chapter 11

Psychedelic and Special Lighting Devices

The so-called psychedelic effects that come from flashing lights and ultra-violet light are not necessarily, as one might suppose, confined to the drug culture and "way out" societies. Indeed, any effect that might be devised, psychedelic or not, can have its place in theatrical applications if used imaginatively.

Much attention has been given to the stroboscope—not to be confused with Strobolite, which is a brand name of ultra-violet products. A stroboscope, long-used in industry, is a special kind of lighting device, described by one writer as "lightning in a bottle." However recent its application in theatrical circles may be, it has been used in industry and in photography for many years.

FLASHTUBES

A flashtube is the heart of a stroboscope. It consists of a small, glass or quartz tube that is filled with a rare gas such as xenon. As with neon or other rare gasses, a high electric potential will cause the gas to ionize. The instant the gas ionizes, it becomes a low-resistance path and, as current flows, it glows brilliantly.

Flashtubes are not meant to give a sustained light. If steady current were supplied to them, they would probably explode. The current supplied is momentary, and it is supplied from a charged capacitor. While the instantaneous wattage is in the order of hundreds of thousands of watts, the duration is so short that the number of watt-seconds is in the order of a hundred or so. The brilliant, brief flash of light has the effect of freezing the fastest motion. Repetitive flashes can make a spinning fan appear to stand still or move backwards. It can make the water from a dripping faucet appear to be going up from the sink to the faucet. If the correct repetition rate is selected it can produce an effect that will confuse even the most stable observer.

The voltage required to make the tube flash is usually much higher than the supply voltage. As long as the supply voltage remains below the minimum ionization voltage, nothing will happen. The instant the minimum ionization voltage is exceeded, however, the resistance of the gas within the tube drops to near zero ohms and a very large current flows.

In practical applications, a third electrode, called the trigger, is used to flash the tube. The trigger might consist of a very thin wire touching the outside of the tube or it might even be the metal reflector—as is the case in some of the popular, low-priced photoflash units. A flashtube is shown schematically in Fig. 11-1. Ionization voltage on the trigger electrode is usually provided by discharging a small capacitor through a transformer. The resulting voltage pulse is very high and short in duration. This provides uniform, instantaneous flashing.

The power supply for a flashtube need deliver only a relatively small current. Power is built up gradually and stored by charging a large capacitor through a series resistor. A large current surge can be supplied through the flashtube with only a small but steady drain on the primary power source (Fig. 11-2). The primary power source can be either a transformer/rectifier arrangement for taking power from the house wiring or it can consist of a battery and inverter. An inverter is a transistor oscillator circuit that takes a direct current input and produces alternating current. This is then raised to the desired voltage by means of a transformer. The transformer is often the same one used to provide the necessary feedback in the oscillator circuit (Fig. 11-3).

In units that produce repetitive flashes, the rate at which the trigger voltage is applied is determined by a variable-frequency oscillator which closes the capacitor discharge circuit to the trigger transformer by means of a transistor switch (Fig. 11-4). In order to build up the supply voltage quickly, the resistor in series with the supply capacitors is relatively small. Therefore, the capacitors recharge quicker after each flash, but the current drain from the primary power source is greater. Flash units that flash only once

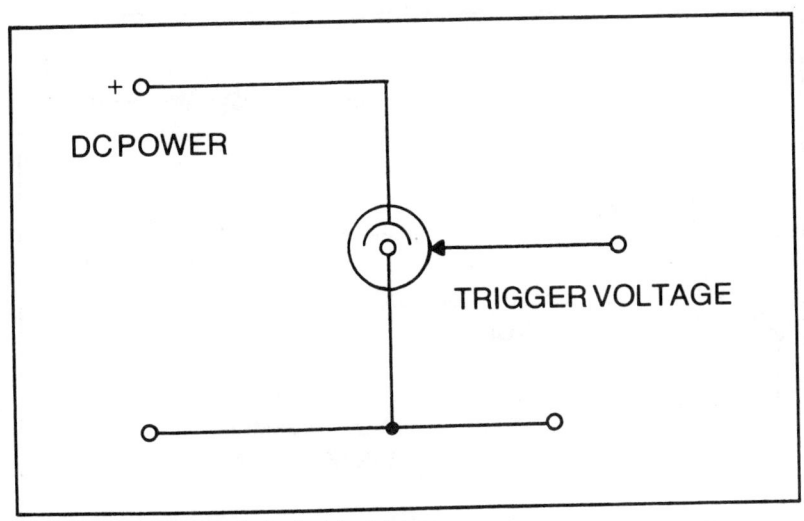

Fig. 11-1. Schematic of a typical flashtube.

every minute or so can produce a brighter flash and draw less current than units that flash several hundred times a second.

You should realize, of course, that the particular flashtube used for one application might not operate too well in another. There are a great many different types of different power ratings, recovery rate, etc. Some are designed to give a relatively low-intensity flash with a very high rate of repetition. Others give an intense flash but must "rest" a few seconds before flashing again. Some have a flash duration of several thousandths of a second. Others have a flash duration measured in microseconds.

The amount of power consumed by a flashtube is usually expressed in watt-seconds. That is, the number of watts consumed by the flashtube multiplied by the number of seconds the lamp is on. The latter figure is usually a very small fractional number. As an illustration, I might point out that the average small photoflash

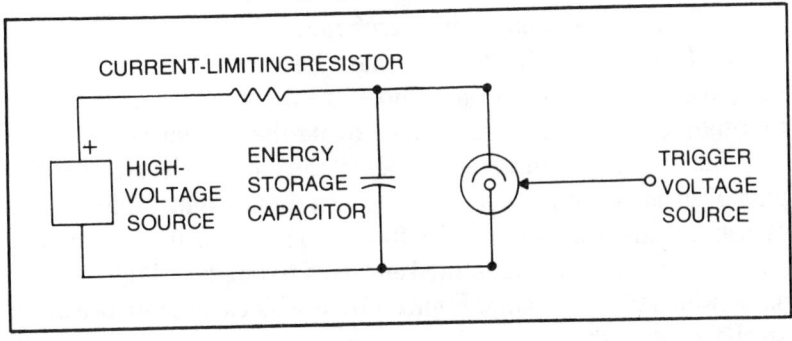

Fig. 11-2. Basic flashtube power supply circuit.

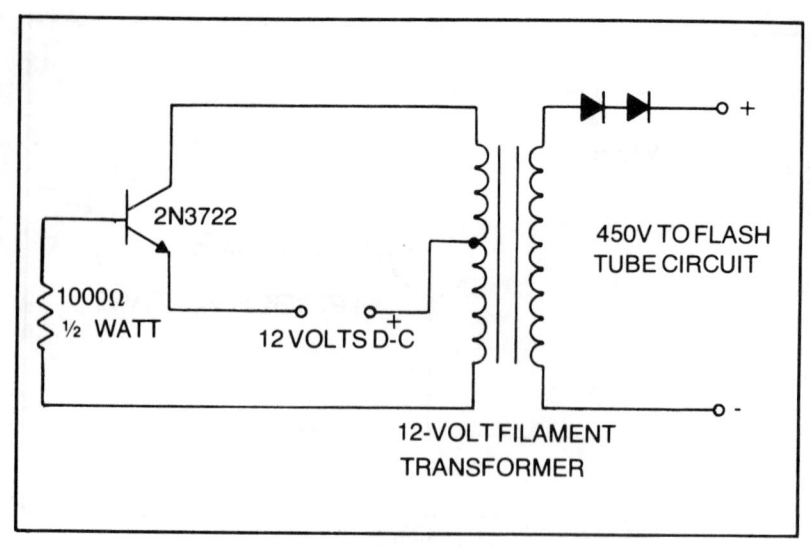

Fig. 11-3. Simple inverter circuit for flashtubes.

unit is rated around 25 watt-seconds. The lamp consumes a power of 100,000 watts for 0.00025 seconds or 250 microseconds.

Light output is measured in beam candlepower seconds—the intensity of the center of the beam at a given distance multiplied by the flash duration. Amateur photoflash units average 1000 BCPS. This means that for the 250 microseconds that the lamp is lighted, it has a light intensity of four million candle power.

The watt-second rating of a flash unit is dependent not only on the lamp's ratings—which only tell the maximum it can deliver—but on the electrical values of the capacitors within the power supply and the voltage applied. There is a mathematical formula to determine the amount of energy available to the flashtube:

$$J = \tfrac{1}{2} E^2 C$$

Where: J is the charge in watt-seconds,
E is the applied voltage in thousands of volts,
C is the capacity in microfarads.

The circuits shown so far have been primarily those used for photographic applications. Those are the most basic. If a basic flashtube circuit is changed by removing the trigger transformer and connecting the trigger electrode of the lamp to the No. 1 spark plug of an automobile engine, you have a timing light. This is but a skip and a jump from a theatrical flasher. The signal from a variable frequency oscillator is amplified and used to trigger a high-voltage pulse which fires the lamp. Figure 11-5 is a block diagram of a basic stroboscope flash unit.

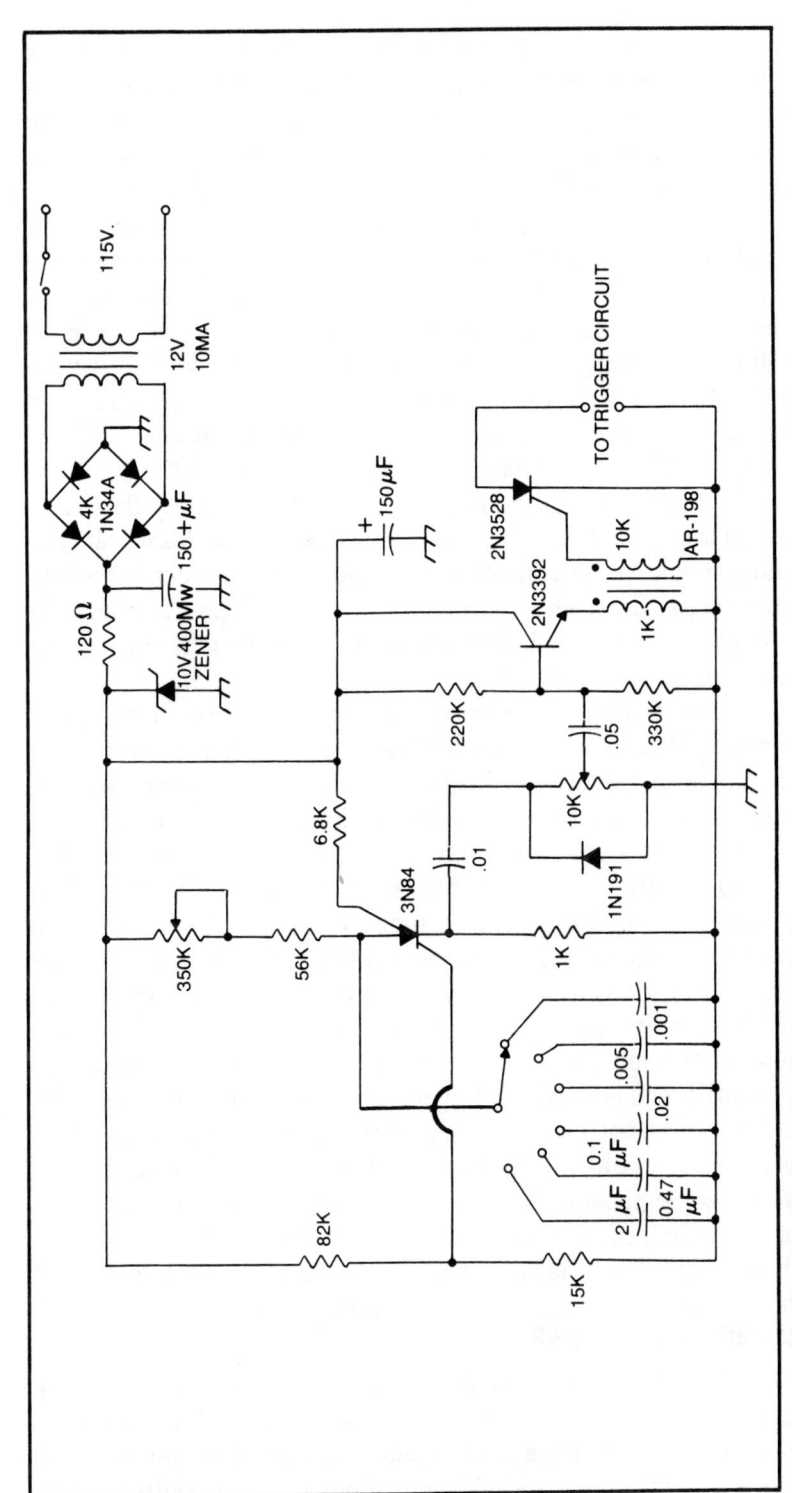

Fig. 11-4. Schematic of a variable rate flash control circuit.

Theatrical use of flashtubes, while gaining in popularity, is still greatly limited. The mind-boggling, rapid-fire flashing in a disco is by no means its only application. The stark, bluish-white color of the light has an eerie effect all its own. Wherever you might want to introduce a shock factor, it is well worth considering.

There is a natural rhythm in the impulses of the brain somewhere in the neighborhood of 10 to 15 pulses per second that is easily jogged by brilliant flashes of light. A stroboscope operating near this rate can greatly accentuate moods such as confusion or anxiety. This was the basis of one very effective application of a flasher in an amateur play depicting a man's dream of a trip to the moon. As the last scene of the dream was ending, a voice, modified by a strong echo, called him from off stage. This was the cue to fade out the regular stage lights and use a flasher as the major illumination. The stop-action effect of the flashes and the echoing voice called from off stage would have to be seen to be fully appreciated. The flash rate was slowed to zero. After a few seconds of darkness, the stage lights were raised, showing the man being awakened by his wife.

Other flasher applications include science-fiction, ghost scenes and I've even seen it used in a modernistic ballet. Be careful not to overdo it, however. Prolonged flashing in an otherwise dark hall can have undesirable side effects, especially on epileptics.

There was an application of non-repetitive flashtubes that drew a lot of attention around the end of the 1950s. This was called subliminal advertising. It was supposed to enable one to work directly into the subconscious mind of the audience. It worked this way. During the course of a movie show, a slide projector, using a flashtube for its light source, would project a picture of the item being advertised, say a box of popcorn, onto the screen for about a thousandth of a second once every five or ten minutes. While the audience was not aware of seeing the picture, due to its short duration, it would nontheless register in the subconscious and sales were supposed to boom. It is said that a preacher used the same method, projecting a picture of the Savior. This method of advertising was outlawed because the audience had no way of knowing they were being subjected to advertising.

FLUORESCENT LIGHTING

While stop-action flashing lights have entered the theatrical scene largely through the sudden popularity of psychodelia, fluorescent effects have been around for a much longer time and have seen a far wider range of application. When tastefully applied,

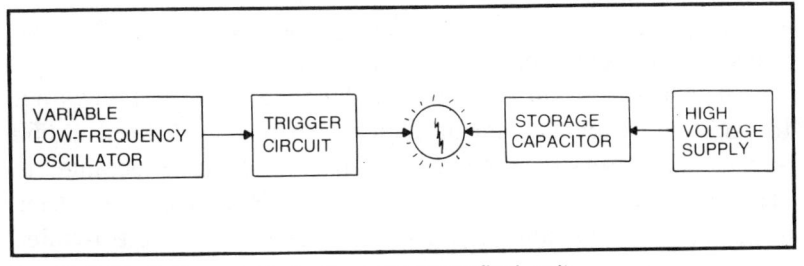

Fig. 11-5. Block diagram of a basic stroboscope flash unit.

fluorescence can be impressively beautiful in almost any phase of theatrics.

Fluorescence is a natural phenomenon whereby certain materials absorb radiant energy of one wavelength and re-radiate it at a longer wavelength. A great many materials will absorb visible light and radiate heat, but there are certain substances that absorb energy in the extreme violet and low ultra-violet region of the spectrum and radiate visible light. It is the latter of these two in which we are interested.

In order to achieve any fluorescent effect, it is first necessary to provide a source of ultra-violet light, generally ultra-violet without any visible light accompanying it. All electric lamps produce some ultra-violet. The most common sources for theatrical applications, however, are halogen-arc or mercury lamps. Both types have a spectrum that is rich in ultra-violet. The only thing necessary is to isolate the particular wavelength (spectrum line) needed.

The do-it-yourselfer might be tempted at this point to try using germicide lamps which are commonly available and work in a standard fluorescent lamp fixture. Beware! Germicide lamps, if used, must be provided with a filter to isolate the correct wavelength. Otherwise, personnel on stage could suffer eye damage. The spectrum line used for germicidal work is much more powerful than that used for theatrical work; therefore, it can severely burn the surface of the eye. Theatrical ultra-violet sources use a longer wavelength, in the region of 3,650 angstroms, which is harmless and very effective.

Any light source can be used as an ultra-violet generator, although regular incandescent lamps are very inefficient when used this way. All that is needed is a suitable filter to isolate the ultra-violet from the visible light. Quartz-halogen spots or blacklight lamps that resemble fluorescent lamps and work in standard fluorescent fixtures are the two most popular. A follow spot has the advantage that it can select a single person or object, while the black light tubes are best to cover a general area.

If you make your own source, be sure your filter does not transmit wavelengths much shorter than the desired 3,650 angstroms. Filters designed for theatrical use can be obtained in standard sizes from the Stroblite Co. in New York City (See Appendix C for the address). They also have a line of ultra-violet light sources and fluorescent materials including costume material, paint and makeup (Fig. 11-6).

Fluorescent poster colors are commonly available in most discount stores, as are "day glow" fluorescent paints. Most fabric stores, particularly those that cater to the theatrical world or to dancing schools, regularly stock fluorescent cloth. Fluorescent ribbon can often be found in any department store sewing department, as it is considered to be a useful safety device to put on childrens' clothing. Any white cotton garments that have been laundered a few times will fluoresce a brilliant blue without any further treatment. Professional fluorescent materials, such as makeup, can usually be obtained from any well stocked theatrical supply house or by mail from the Stroblite people.

The application of ultra-violet is far more versatile than the application of stroboscopic flashers. Dancing schools (in their annual recitals, etc.) can cover up a multitude of sins by putting their youthful students under black light. The audience is usually so impressed by the spectacular effect of the fluorescence that they fail to notice the many mistakes that inevitably creep in.

Using ultra-violet simply as a cover up, however, is a poor excuse for having it. Let's examine a few of the other applications. In an "outer space" scene, a moonscape comes alive when highlighted with ultra-violet. Stars painted on the sky backdrop in fluorescent colors appear to be giving their own light which, in a way, they are.

In a mystery play, a white, nonfluorescent door was painted with a ghost, using paint that is white under visible light but fluoresces blue under ultra-violet. With the stage lights up, it was just a plain old door. However, when the night scene came on and the stage lights were faded to blue—there was sufficient ultra-violet in them to make the ghost appear. Then, when the door was spotlighted under ultra-violet, the ghost stood out eerie and "alive."

A dancer had the upper part of her costume made of conventional material and the lower half of fluorescent material. A

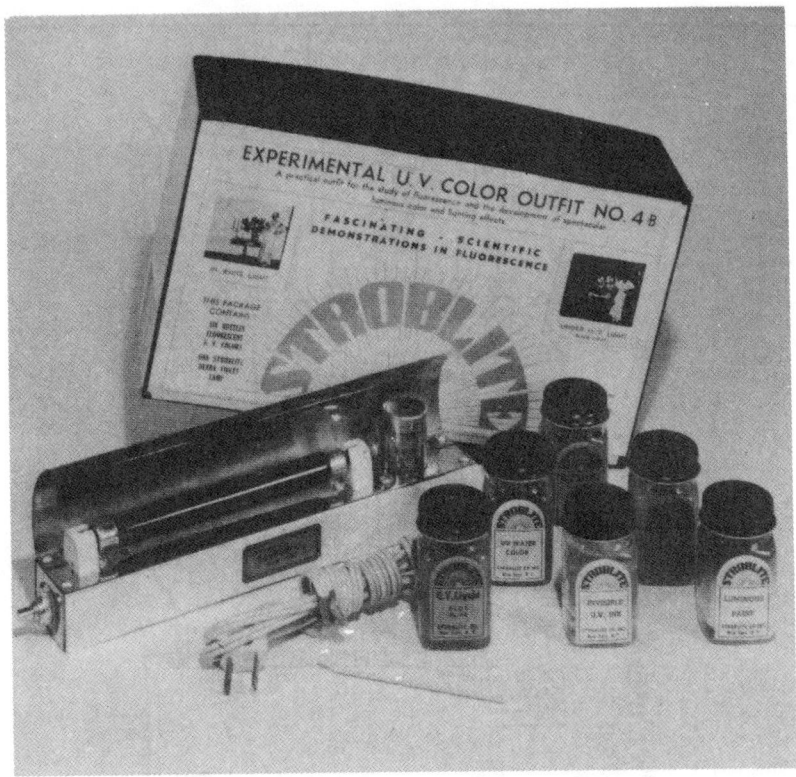

Fig. 11-6. This experimenter kit enables the amateur producer to try out various combinations before investing in large amounts of materials (photo courtesy Strobolite Co.).

second dancer hid behind a prop. The lower half of his costume was made of conventional material and the upper half of fluorescent material, otherwise both costumes were identical. As the first dancer circled about the stage, she momentarily stepped behind the prop. At that instant, all stage lights went from visible to ultra-violet and both dancers stepped from behind the prop. The effect was that the dancer seemed to have split in two—her top half here and her bottom half there. The white makeup area of characters in a minstrel show were covered with fluorescent makeup. Their white cotton shirts and white gloves were naturally fluorescent, although ultra-violet fabric colors should be used to make the effect uniform.

Orchestral numbers can be made very dramatic by outlining the instruments with fluorescent paint. If you do this, however, be sure it's a number the musicians can play without having to look at their sheet music. Otherwise, when the lights go out, you'll have a very confused number and a few very angry musicians!

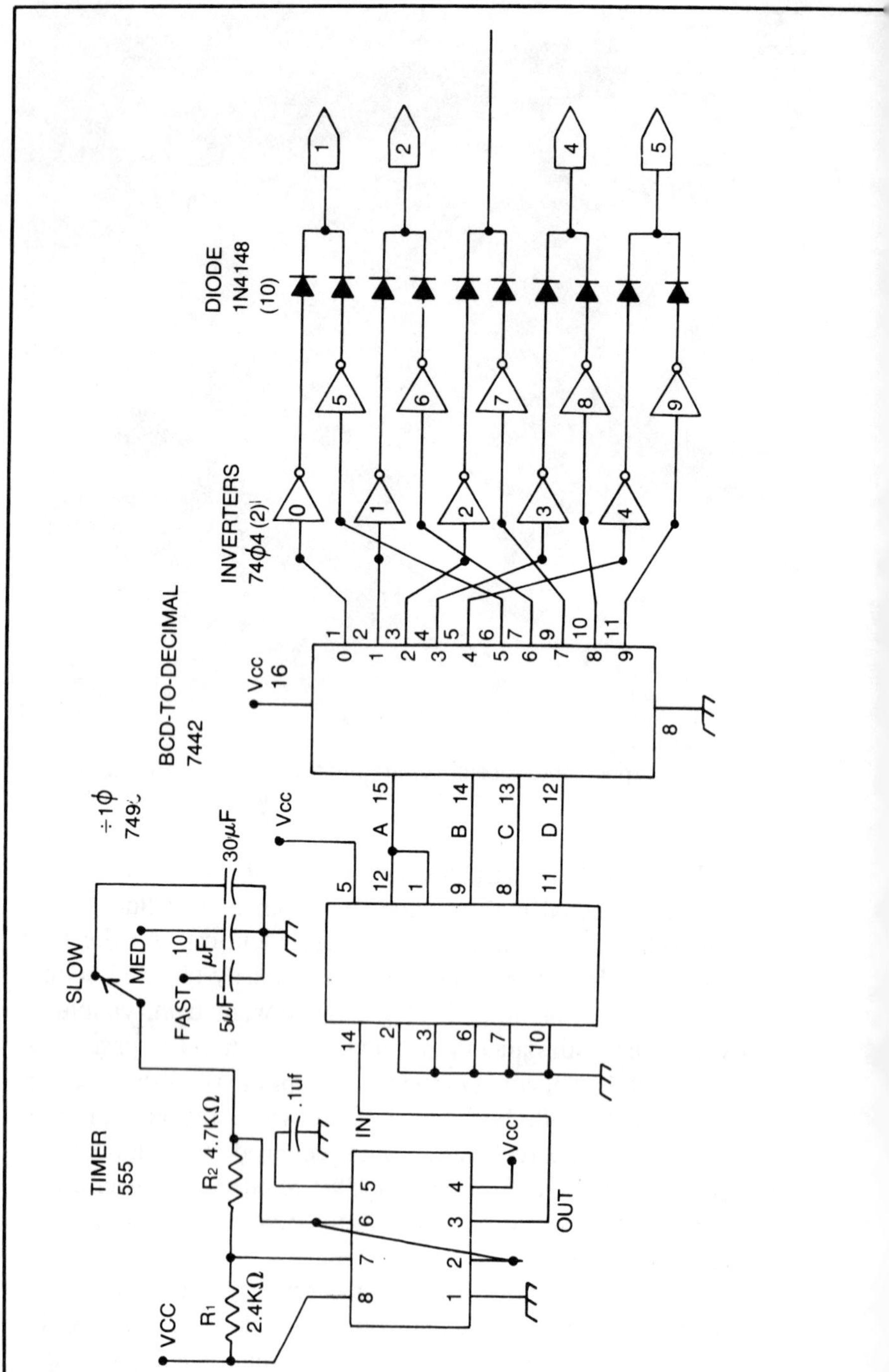
TIMER
555
VCC
R1
2.4KΩ
R2 4.7KΩ
.1uf
IN
OUT
Vcc
SLOW
MED
FAST
5uF
10
μF
30μF
Vcc
BCD-TO-DECIMAL
7442
Vcc
16
A
B
C
D
INVERTERS
74Φ4 (2)
DIODE
1N4148
(10)

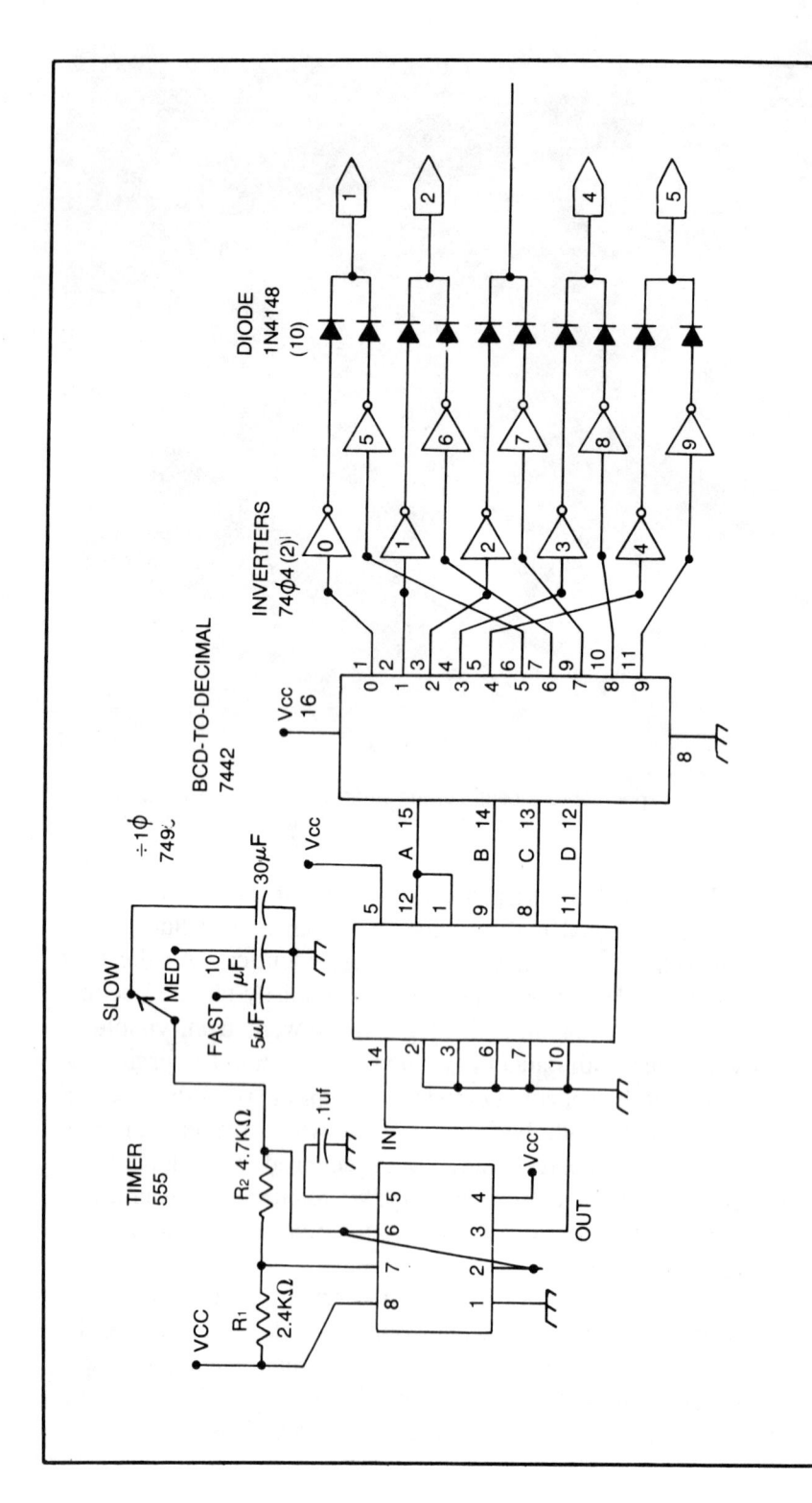

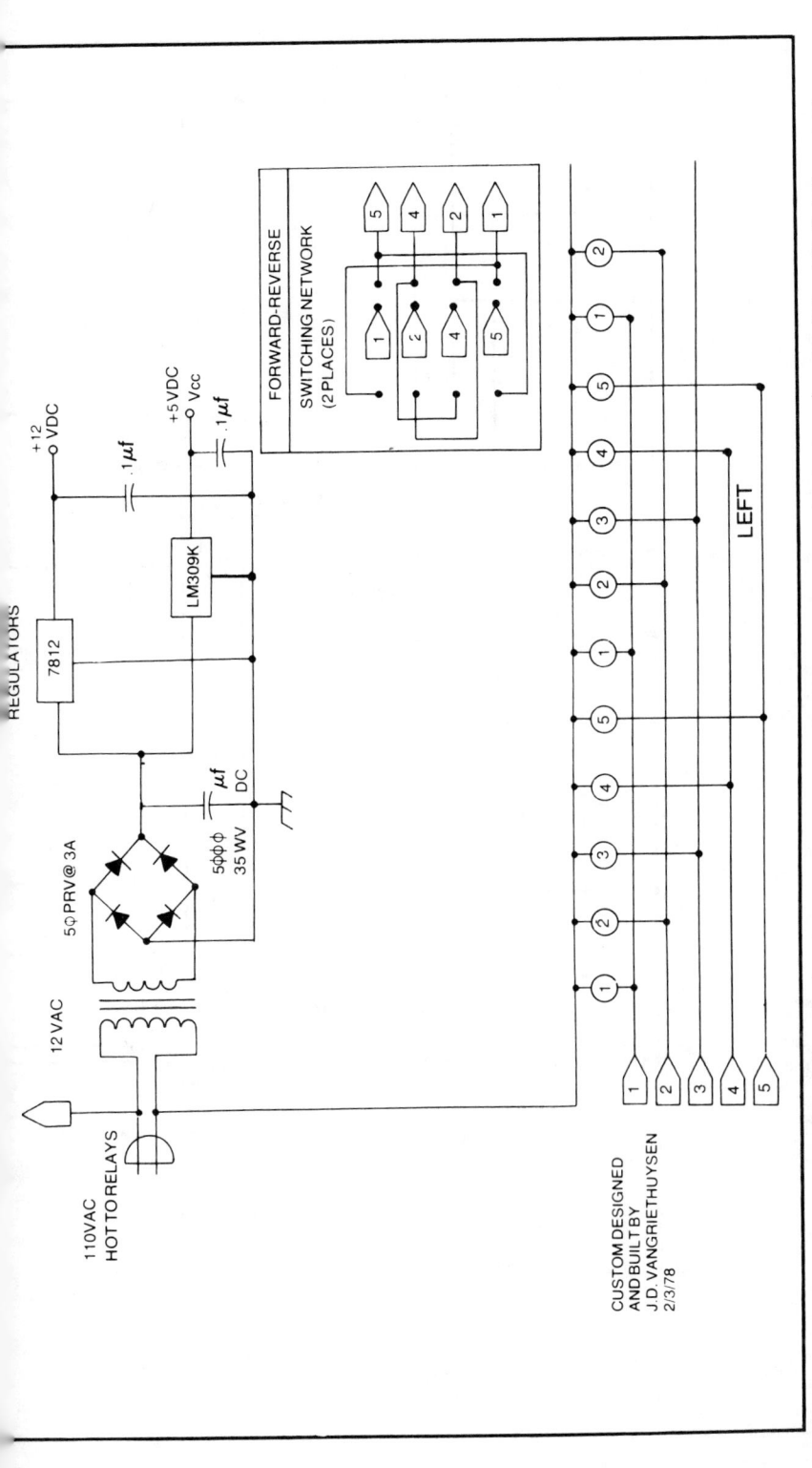

Fig. 11-7. Schematic of a special-effects repetitive-flash system for incandescent lights (custom designed and built by J.D. Griethuysen.).

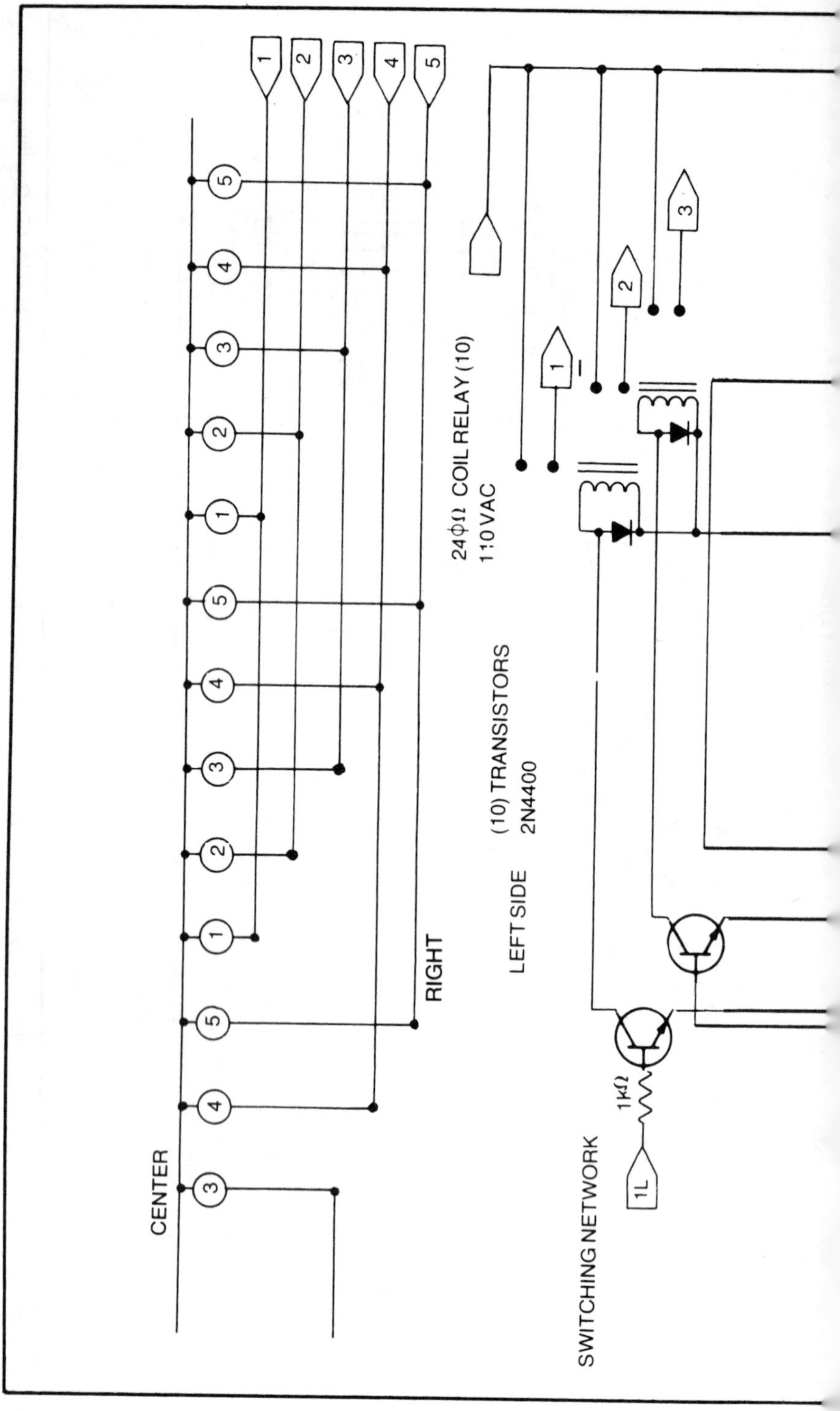
240Ω COIL RELAY (10)
110 VAC
(10) TRANSISTORS
2N4400
LEFT SIDE
SWITCHING NETWORK
1KΩ
1L
CENTER
RIGHT

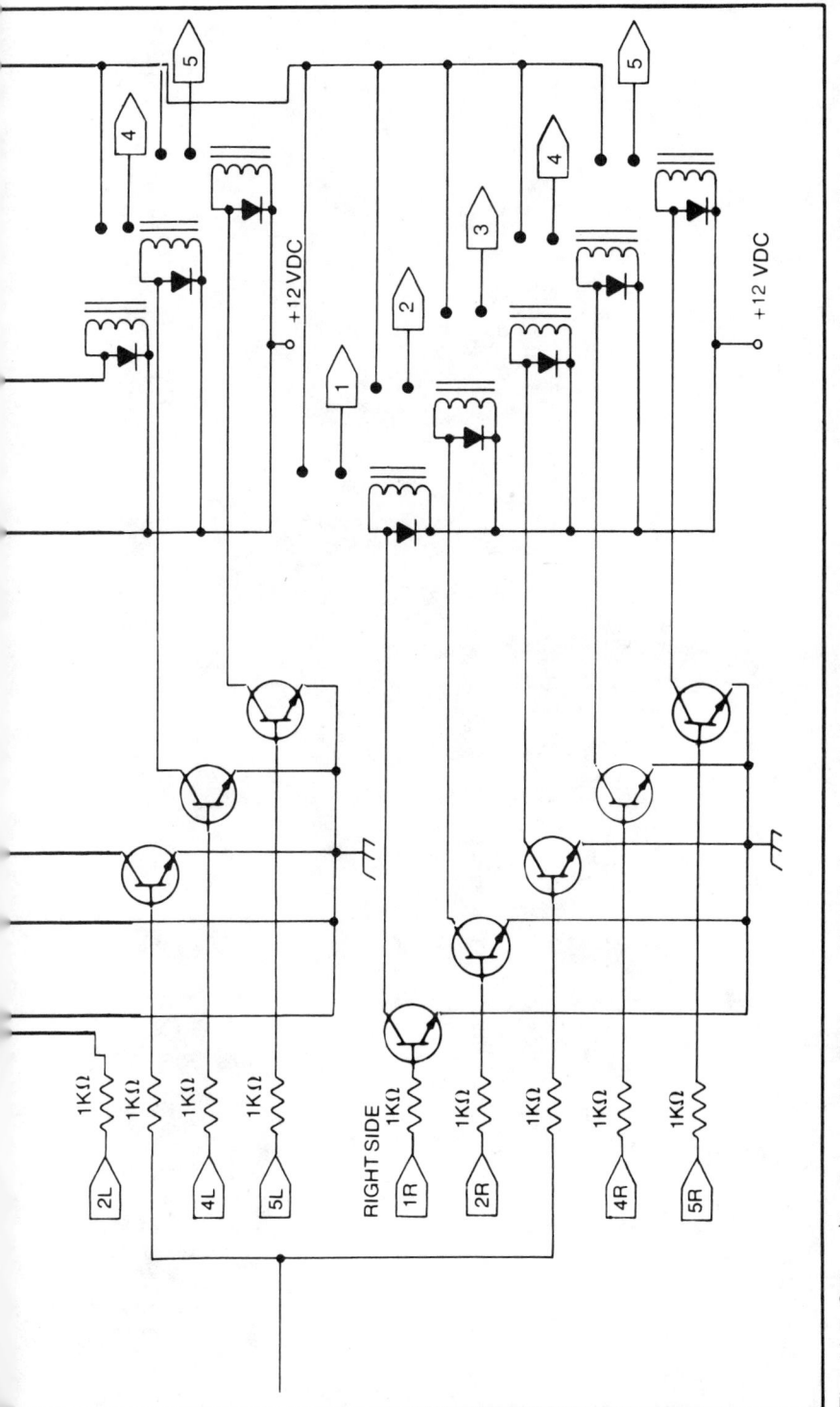

Fig. 11-7. Schematic of a special-effects repetitive-flash system for incandescent lights (custom designed and built by J.D. Griethuysen.). (cont.)

Fig. 11-8. The repetitive flasher shown schematically in Fig. 11-7.

Finally, one application that does not involve the audience is the marking of the stage floor. This means simply making fluorescent indications of the locations of props, scenery, etc. When the stage is blacked out between scenes, except for a little ultra-violet, stage hands can see the markings. But the audience sees nothing.

These are but a few of the possibilities. With a little imagination, coupled with an understanding of the phenomenon, you can use ultra-violet in ways I might not even think of—depending on the needs of your particular production.

In the professional circles, where special effects are called for, it is frequently customary to perfect the design of the set using a miniature mockup. This saves a lot of grief, expense and hard work that might be experienced if the full-sized set had to be altered using the relatively expensive ultra-violet paints.

Amateur groups planning ultra-violet scenery would do well to invest in an "experimenter" outfit such as the Stroblite Demonstration kits. In 1977, these were going for $15. Each kit included an ultra-violet source and six bottles of fluorescent lacquer. If you have a small ultra-violet lamp already, you can get kits of various fluorescent-color paint or lacquer for five to $80. Then, once you've determined exactly what will be needed in the way of fluorescent props or scenery, you will be better able to purchase the needed materials with a minimum expenditure.

SEQUENTIAL FLASHING LIGHTS

A great variety of special effects can be produced with sequential flashing lights. The devices to make the lights flash are as many and as varied as the effects. Some are mechanical, utilizing a rotating cam. Others are electronic. In Fig. 11-7 is a circuit the electronics enthusiast might enjoy building. It was used by a group of high school players in their production of *Hello Dolly* at the Greece-Olympia High School near Rochester, NY, early in 1978.

The circuit uses integrated-circuit chips and, while it can be made with a printed circuit, it was simply haywired together for the production. The timer chip is an oscillator, the frequency of which is set with a 3-position switch. The output of the oscillator is fed into a counter module which in turn feeds into a BCD-to-decimal decoder. The decoded outputs are gated together, giving a repeating count of one to five. This count feeds the relay drivers which operate the relays to flash the lamps. The relays could have been replaced with solid-state switches, but the builder had run out of funds and had to use what he had.

Two banks are used and, depending on the phase in which they are fed, the lights can appear to progress along in a line—move from the ends in to the center or vice versa. It was crude, but effective. The relays made a loud clatter and had to be enclosed in an insulated box to deaden the sound. Other than that, there was no problem and the number *When the Parade Passes By* was very nicely enhanced by the parade of lights along the front of the stage.

Glossary

absorption. The property of being able to absorb rather than to reflect sound waves. It is used to compute the acoustic properties of rooms. The standard of absorption is that an open window absorbs sound 100% because of all the sound reaching the area of wall occupied by an open window is absorbed by a corresponding area of wall, the wall is said to have 50% absorption.

acoustic. Pertaining to the behavior of sound.

acoustic dipole. A name given to an open-backed loudspeaker, particularly if it is mounted on a flat baffle. Because sound waves originate from both sides of the cone, or diaphragm, but are out of phase, one pushing when the other is pulling, the kind of waves it radiates have similarities with the waves radiated in radio by a dipole antenna, thus the name.

acoustic filter. When the internal construction of a loudspeaker cabinet or box is designed to behave like an electrical filter would on the frequency response of the system, but the effect is achieved by working on the acoustic waves generated inside the loudspeaker, the part of the loudspeaker that does this is called an acoustic filter.

acoustic labrynth. A form of loudspeaker cabinet with internal partitions and passages designed to prevent cabinet resonance difficulties.

acoustic lens. The essential features of an acoustic lens are that it is built of channels whose width is much smaller than the highest frequency's wavelength, and that those channels make the sound travel further than they would in free air without the channels. The extra time taken traversing this extra distance has the effect of forming a sound wave, just as an optical lens forms the waves propagated by light.

acoustic loading. When the radiation of a sound wave produces loading on a loudspeaker diaphragm, that part of the energy used to drive the diaphragm is called acoustic loading. More particularly, it is applied where the arrangement of the system increases that loading on the diaphragm, as when multiple units produce such loading on one another, or where restriction, as in the throat of a horn, increases the loading.

acoustic suspension. A word used to describe a system designed so that the main controlling force on the diaphragm is the compression and expansion of air inside a sealed loudspeaker box.

acoustical transparency. Many light, open-weave fabrics, or types of expanded metal or plastic, that allow sound to pass through virtually unimpeded, although they are not optically transparent. Such substances are called acoustically transparent.

act drop. The curtain that opens and closes between acts.

active filter. An electronic filter with internal amplifying electronics. It needs an external power supply to operate.

alternating current. Electric current that periodically changes direction. Standard for the domestic power supply.

ambience. Primarily the background sound present in a room in which you listen to program sound. It can include extraneous sounds, such as audience noises, reverberation of the programs sound, and any other components that would normally be present in background sound.

ampere. The basic unit for measuring electric current.

amplification. Increasing the level of a signal.

amplitude. The magnitude of a signal.

amplitude modulation. A process for putting intelligence onto a radio signal wherein the amplitude of the carrier is modulated or varied. Standard for radio broadcasting.

anechoic room. A specially constructed room in which all of the walls, including ceiling and floor, are made highly absorbent to

anechoic room—back-up

sound throughout most of the audible range, so that there are no reflections or echoes. It is not a natural listening environment, but is useful for conducting measurements on loudspeakers or microphones.

angle set. A stage setting in which the rear wall is not parallel to the footlights.

anode. That element in a transistor, diode, or vacuum tube that receives the positive polarity of the power.

antiresonance. The opposite of a resonance. An antiresonance is a frequency at which a system absorbs, or fails to radiate, the normal amount of sound.

arc. A luminous electrical discharge, either through air, other gasses, or vacuum.

attack. Part of a program sound that begins with a sudden component that is louder than the rest of the sound. Applied to a system, the capability of satisfactorily reproducing or rendering such a sound.

attenuation. Reducing the level of a signal.

audio. Pertaining to those frequencies capable of being heard by an average human ear.

audio salon. A showroom designed for prospective customers to audition loudspeakers and other system components before purchase. In using one, you need to verify that its acoustic properties—size and treatment—are as close to being like the room for which you want the components as possible.

autotransformer. A transformer having only one winding.

AWG. American Wire Gauge. The common notation in the United States for measuring wire diameter.

baby spot. A spotlight of less than 500 watts.

back light. Illumination of a subject from behind.

back stage. That portion of the stage area not enclosed by the set.

backing. A small piece of scenery used to cover a door, window, or other opening in a set.

back-loaded horn. A type of folded horn in which the back of the loudspeaker diaphragm or cone feeds into a horn designed to handle the lower frequencies, while the front of the diaphragm radiates the middle and upper frequencies, either as a direct radiator or with a smaller front-loaded horn.

back-up. A spare sound or lighting system intended to suffice in the event of failure of the main system.

baffle. Primarily any device designed to prevent air movement from the front of a loudspeaker cone or diaphragm from having easy access to the rear. In its simplest form, it is a flat board with a hole in it of a size suitable to accommodate the loudspeaker unit for which it will be used. See *Infinite Baffle*.

balanced circuit. A circuit in which both conductors are the same electrical potential away from a common or ground point.

bandpass filter. A filter that passes a predetermined range of signal frequencies but attenuates all others.

bandwidth. That portion of the electrical spectrum needed to transmit the necessary intelligence.

barn doors. Flaps attached to the front of a light unit to control the shape of the beam.

bass. The lowest frequencies that a sound system is called upon to handle. In music it will be the major frequencies produced by instruments classified as bass instruments, as opposed to tenor, alto, or soprano. In sound reproduction it will be the frequencies handled by the biggest unit of a multiway system. In a single-unit system, it applies to the lowest frequencies the system reproduces. Also the region between the collector and the emitter of a transistor.

bass reflex. A loudspeaker system in which the lowest frequencies reproduced are reinforced by an acoustic combination that phase-reverses pressure from the back of the diaphragm so that it emerges in phase with sound waves from the front. Also called vented baffle. A loudspeaker cabinet in which the sound waves from the back of the speaker are brought out the front.

batten. A pole or pipe suspended overhead as a support for lighting equipment.

beam angle. The spread of a light beam within which the illumination level is not less than 10% of that at the center.

beam projector. A light unit equipped with a parabolic reflector oriented to concentrate most of the light in a nearly parallel beam.

beaming sound. Any of a variety of methods of concentrating the direction of sound into wanted areas, where an audience is or may be listening, while restricting it from radiating into areas where excessive reflection could cause confusion or excessive reverberation.

beta. A measure of the current gain of a transistor.

biamplification or triamplification. A system using two-way or multiway loudspeakers, in which separation of the frequencies is achieved before final power amplification so that each unit of the system is driven by a separate power amplifier.

bias. Voltage or current applied to the input element of a tube or transistor to establish its operational reference level.

binaural. Two-channel stereo.

binaural listening. A property about the way any person with two normal ears listens, enabling him to readily determine the direction from which sounds reach him. The human hearing faculty processes the combined sounds received by each ear to determine time and intensity differences, from which information about direction of the arriving sound is conveyed to the listener.

binaural recording. A form of recording that uses two channels of sound, a little differently from stereo. It is designed primarily to be used with headphones so that the binaural listening faculty gives an accurate reproduction of the illusion that would have been conveyed to the listener had he been present at the original performance.

black body. A theoretically perfect light source, or one in which the color of the light output is dependent only on temperature.

black light. Ultra-violet light.

bookshelf speaker. One of a variety of loudspeaker designs, in which more than the usual bass response is obtained from a much smaller unit, of a size suitable for placing on a bookshelf.

boom. A pole, usually horizontally mounted, on which a microphone is hung.

border light. A row of lighting equipment suspended above the acting area.

bridge. A small platform suspended above the acting area. Also, a 4-element circuit for precise electrical measurement.

bridge rectifier. A 4-diode rectifier circuit.

breaker. A device that automatically switches off an electrical circuit in the event of overload.

bus. A heavy section of electric conductor to which one side of all the branch lines are connected.

button. A carbon microphone element.

buzz. A sound, usually generated mechanically, that is spurious to the program sound. A typical source of such sound would be the diaphragm tapping against the grill cloth on high-amplitude bass response. It could also be due to vibration effects producing spurious sounds in parts of the cabinet that are not solidly secured. Occasionally, a similar sound may be produced in the electronic part of the system by a form of intermodulation.

BX cable. Electric power cable protected by a flexible armored sheath.

cameo. A lighting situation in which only the action is lighted and the background kept black. (See also: limbo)

candlepower. The basic unit of light level.

capacitance. That electrical property which permits the storage of an electric charge.

capacitor. An electronic component consisting of two conductors separated by an insulator.

capstan. The rotating shaft in a tape drive that imparts motion to the tape.

cardioid. A heart-shaped curve; the pickup pattern of a cardioid dynamic microphone.

cathode. The negative element in a diode, transistor, or vacuum tube.

choke. A component (coil) having a known amount of inductance.

chip. An integrated circuit (slang).

classic stereo. In the early days of stereo, to get the correct illusion the listener was required to sit at an equal distance from the two loudspeakers reproducing left- and right-channel sound. Now stereo for which that would be a requirement, or seating oneself in such a position, is referred to as classic stereo.

closed pipe. Part of an acoustic system built by analogy with a closed, or stopped, organ pipe. It is characterized by providing emphasis of frequencies such that their wavelengths make the closed pipe an odd number of quarter-wavelengths long.

coloration. A property of a loudspeaker, or other part of a system, that changes the relative intensity and response to certain groups of frequencies in such a way as to give the sound a different character, or color. The objective, in any good reproduction, should be to make the reproduced sound audibly indistinguishable from the original sound. Usually, the telltale differences constitute a form of coloration.

column speaker. A composite loudspeaker system made up of a line of units all working in unison with the result that sound is concentrated in a cylindrical pattern, of which the line of column

column speaker—constant-voltage distribution

is the axis. Column speakers are a convenient way of beaming sound.

collector. The element in a transistor through which the primary flow of carriers leaves the interelement region.

collimate. To concentrate light into a parallel beam.

color code. A standard means of identifying the electrical value of components.

color temperature. The temperature at which a black body produces light of a color with the closest *visual* match to the light source under consideration.

compatability. Whenever a new system is introduced, such as stereo in the days of mono, or quadraphonic in the days of stereo, one of the problems encountered is that a compatability: old systems should be able to reproduce a new program acceptably, and new systems should be able to reproduce old program acceptably, each in addition to the new system being able to do its best with the new program.

complementary colors. Colors that are chromatic opposites: red; cyan; green magenta; blue yellow.

compliance. Another word for elasticity. It applies to the restoring force used to bring the diaphragm back to its normal position after reproduction of a sound wave has moved it away from that position. The lower the restoring force, the greater the compliance. An everyday word that conveys the same intent is springiness.

compression. Reducing the range of output level variation of an amplifier with respect to input level variations.

concentrated arc. A low-voltage arc lamp having non-vaporizing electrodes sealed in an environment of inert gas. It produces a small, brilliantly incandescent cathode spot.

concert border. Border lights mounted immediately behind the proscenium.

conduit. Lightweight metal tubing through which electric power wiring is run.

cone. The vibrating element of a loudspeaker.

conical horn. A horn with uniform flare.

console. A desk-like cabinet containing either lighting or sound controls.

constant-voltage distribution. A system in which the voltage delivered to all loudspeaker units in the system is the same, and the relative power taken by each is controlled by changing the impedance presented to the system by that individual unit. Constant voltage refers to the maximum or peak voltage reached when the system is momentarily delivering full power.

contact microphone. A microphone that picks up sound by direct contact. Often used as an inexpensive way of electrifying instruments.

control grid. The grid nearest the cathode of a vacuum tube.

corner horn. A type of horn loudspeaker unit designed to be placed in the corner of a room, and in which the two walls and floor that constitute the corner provide the completion of the horn for the purposes of getting the lowest frequencies out into the room.

counter. An electronic device or circuit that gives an output impulse for a fixed number of input pulses.

cover spot. A spotlight hanging on the first border batten, intended to illuminate a particular area of the stage.

crossover frequency. The precise frequency in a crossover at which each unit receives equal power. At lower frequencies most of the power goes to one unit, and at higher frequencies most of the power goes to the other unit.

crossovers. Electrical networks or filters, the purpose of which is to see that the correct frequencies get delivered to the various units of a multiway system.

crystal. In this application, a piece of quartz between two electrodes. It produces electrical impulses when mechanically vibrated and vibrates when electrically excited. It is used for microphones, phono pickups and similar devices.

cucoloris. Also called *cookie* or *cuke*. An opaque material with cutouts to pass light, used to project special effects such as clouds.

cyc strip. A striplight mounted at the top or bottom of a cyclorama to provide smooth lighting.

cycle. Two complete reversals of alternating current.

cylindrical wave. A form of sound radiation in which sound moves out like an expanding cylinder. If you think of a can, or cylinder, very little sound goes out along the axis of the cylinder or can, most of it moves outward from the curved surface.

cyclorama. A large semicircular drop with sides extending well downstage. Used to enclose the acting area and to provide a sky background for outdoor scenes.

damping factor. A property of amplifiers designed to stop

dampening factor—diode

spurious movement of loudspeaker diaphragms when reproducing complex sound waves that include transients. It does so by providing a braking force on the diaphragm whenever the active driving force suddenly terminates. If the internal resistance of the amplifier is one-tenth of the nominal loudspeaker impedance to receive rated power, the amplifier is said to have a damping factor of ten.

dB levels. A system of rated levels of sound with reference to the threshold of audibility or hearing. See *Decibel.*

DC. Abbreviation for direct current.

Darlington amplifier. A sequence of two or more emitter-follower transistor stages.

dead room. A room with more than average absorbent surfaces so that sound does not tend to bounce around or reverberate in it.

dead spot. Any position where acoustical characteristics from different directions interfere with one another.

decibel. A unit of loudness difference. Changes in apparent loudness depend on the ratio or factor by which the sound energy producing them is changed. Thus increasing sound energy by ten times produces a loudness difference of 10 decibels. A decibel is a barely discernible loudness difference, such that ten of them represent an increase of sound energy by ten times.

diaphragm. The moving part of a loudspeaker unit, usually conical or similar in form, that is responsible for producing the air movements that eventually form a sound wave.

dielectric. The insulating material in a capacitor.

diffuse. A reflecting or transmitting medium that scatters the light. When used in reference to the light itself, the term indicates soft light.

diffusion. The capability of a loudspeaker to send sound waves out relatively uniformly in all directions.

dimmer. Any device to control the light output of a luminaire. It might be a variable resistance, autotransformer, magnetic amplifier, solid-state circuit, thyratron, or mechanical iris.

dimmer curve. A graph of the light output of a dimmer, showing light output versus position.

dimmer room. The place where remotely controlled dimmers are housed.

diode. A 2-element electronic device, either a vacuum tube or solid-state. It allows current to flow in only one direction.

dipole. See *Acoustic Dipole*.

direct current. Electric current that flows in only one direction.

directive listening. The human capability of concentrating attention on sounds coming from a specific direction. As the listener has no power to change the sound waves reaching his head, and thus his ears, the power of directive listening is totally within the auditory interpretive faculty of a person's brain.

directivity, loudspeaker. The capability of a loudspeaker to concentrate sound radiated to certain directions and to the exclusion or reduction of others.

direct radiator. Any loudspeaker in which the diaphragm radiates sound waves directly into the surrounding air rather than, for example, through a horn.

displacement, acoustic. The total movement of air accompanying the radiation of a given sound wave. Sometimes also called volume displacement.

displacement, mechanical. The total movement accompanying the radiation of a given sound wave, for example, of the diaphragm. It would thus be the total distance moved by the diaphragm when radiating a sound wave of given frequency and intensity.

discharge lamp. A low-power gas arc lamp.

discharge tube. An electronic device very similar to a discharge lamp. Used to regulate DC voltage.

door flat. A piece of scenery with a rectangular opening, often fitted with a door frame.

down stage. That portion of the stage nearest the audience or in a direction toward the audience.

drone cone. In some of the reflex units, a cone mounted in an opening that is not electrically driven, but free to move as part of the radiation system for some of the lowest frequencies the system handles.

drop. A large curtain used as a background, distinguished from a cyclorama in that it is straight while the other is curved.

duct. Part of a loudspeaker enclosure, usually in the form of a tube, circular or rectangular in shape, through which air moves or escapes, particularly at the lowest frequency the loudspeaker unit handles. See also *Port* and *Vent*.

echo. The reflection of sound from solid objects or surfaces.

efficiency. The amount of acoustic energy radiated as a sound wave, expressed as a fraction, or percentage, of the electrical energy required to produce it. Loudspeakers are not inherently high-efficiency devices, by their very nature. The highest efficiency systems ever built were a little over 50%2 efficient. What is commonly called a high-efficiency unit may be between 10% and 20% efficient. Low-efficiency units have efficiencies well below 1%.

electrolytic capacitor. A capacitor in which the dielectric is formed by the action of the applied voltage on a liquid (electrolyte).

electromotive force. The electrical pressure or voltage in a circuit.

electronic crossover. A crossover for use with biamplification. Instead of using reactances, such as inductors and capacitors, it uses active devices, such as transistors, to achieve the necessary frequency response. It should be noted that the combination of amplitude and phase response produced by an electronic crossover is identical with that of a prototype crossover of the nonelectronic type. There are other misconceptions about their use discussed in preceding chapters.

electrostatic. Referring to the action of voltage rather than current, or to the action of electrical force without the presence of moving currents.

ellipse. A closed curve referenced to two focus points in such a way that the sum of the distances from any point on the curve to the foci is always a constant number.

ellipsoidal spotlight. A spotlight with an ellipsoidal reflector.

emitter. That element of a transistor through which the primary flow of carriers enters the interelement area.

enclosure. A general word for the box in which a loudspeaker unit is installed.

equivalent duct length. The effect of a duct in a loudspeaker system that is due to the air column that moves through it. As the air in motion includes that approaching and leaving at the ends of the tube itself, this means the equivalent length is always longer than its physical measurements.

exciter lamp. The lamp which provides the light to operate the sound-track detection phototube in a sound movie projector.

exponential horn. A horn in which the expansion rate, or flare, is such that its cross-sectional area doubles at a regular distance

exponential horn—flare factor

interval along its length. It has a cutoff frequencies above the cutoff frequency but not below it.

extension speaker. A loudspeaker installed in a different room or location from the main loudspeaker. It may be for use at the same time as the main loudspeaker, or separately. Connecting it for best use depends on just how it will be used, requiring care in figuring how to do it.

faders. In professional systems, relative volume levels from different sound sources are controlled by faders. Originally intended for programs where such sources could be faded in and out, these controls are really well-designed step switches, giving a change in level of about 1 dB for each step. A typical fader may have from 30 to 60 steps.

farad. The basic unit of capacitance. It is so big that capacitors are generally expressed in terms of microfarads (millionths of a farad), and micro microfarads or picofarads.

feedback. Any condition in which some of the output of an electronic system finds its way back to the input. It is the cause of howl in PA systems.

female connector. A connector whose contacts are recessed intended to mate with a plug. Also called a jack.

FET. Field-effect transistor. A transistor in which the resistance between two terminals (the source and the drain) is controlled by the field from a voltage applied to a third terminal (gate).

field angle. The deviation from the center of a light beam wherein the light level is within 10% that of the center. See also: beam angle.

field magnet. The magnet in a loudspeaker which provides a steady magnetic field in which the voice coil operates.

filament. The element of a vacuum tube that heats the cathode, causing it to emit electrons. Also, the main element of an incandescent lamp.

fill light. Illumination to reduce shadows.

filter. An electronic network that passes certain frequencies and rejects others.

fixture. Light unit. Also, an electric power connector.

flag. A piece of opaque material hung a short distance in front of a light unit to mask the light from certain areas.

flare factor. The rate of change in the diameter of a horn with respect to length.

flare rate. The rate at which an exponential horn expands the sound wave. The professional formula uses a coefficient in the exponent of ϵ to represent flare rate. For quick and easy calculations, a good substitute is the distance along the horn at which area doubles. In inches this can be taken as 700 divided by the horn cutoff frequency. Thus for a 100 hertz cutoff, the area doubles every 7 inches.

flasher. Any electronic or mechanical device that causes a light to flash.

flashtube. A gas-discharge lamp designed to produce a brief but brilliant burst of light.

flat. A canvas-covered framework; the basic unit of scenery.

flat pack. An integrated circuit in a low-profile case or package.

flat radiator. A type of loudspeaker using a slim-line unit mounted in a flat baffle, and used as an acoustic dipole. For certain types of rooms, a pair of flat radiators can give very good stereo reproduction.

Fletcher-Munson Curves. A group of curves graphing the relative intensity of sound as heard by the human ear between the threshold of hearing and the threshold of feeling.

flies. The space above the stage.

flipper. A narrow piece of scenery, often a foot or less wide.

flood. A light unit without a lens intended to light a general area.

fluorescent. Capable of emitting light of one wavelength when excited by light of another wavelength.

flush mounting. As with anything, flush mounting means mounting the article so its front edge is flush with the surface in which it is mounted. However, in loudspeaker installation, flush mounting requires careful attention to see that it is acoustically flush so that no cavities produce spurious effects not desired.

FM. See: frequency modulation.

FM multiplex. A system for transmitting two channels of stereo or, by further adaptation, four channels of quadraphonic, over a single FM carrier. In essence it uses a 38 kilohertz switching frequency to carry alternate samples of left and right program. The 38 kilohertz frequency itself is not transmitted, but a 19 kilohertz pilot frequency is transmitted to provide a means of synchronizing the switching at the receiver to coincide with that at the transmitter.

focal point. That point where parallel rays of light passing through a lens system cross. Also, to adjust a projection lens for the

focal point—hard surface

desired image.

focal length. The distance from the center of a lens to the focal point.

focus. The reference points in an ellipse or a parabola.

folded horn. A way of reducing the space occupied by a horn. The usual way turns the horn back on itself so the sound path divides into multiple channels, or an expanding channel, covering distance down the horn without requiring the same physical distance from throat to mouth. See *Horn* and *Back-Loaded Horn*.

forward current. The current that flows through a diode in the direction of greatest conductivity.

frequency. The rate of vibration that is responsible for the characteristic of sound known as pitch. The more rapidly the vibrations occur, thus the higher the frequency, the higher the pitch of the sound heard. Human hearing is sensitive to a range of frequencies from approximately 20 hertz, or vibrations per second, to approaching 20,000 hertz.

frequency modulation (FM). The process of putting intelligence onto a signal by modulating or varying the carrier frequency; the amplitude remains constant.

fresnel lens. A lens of nearly constant thickness, having the characteristics of a plano-convex lens.

fresnel spotlight. A spotlight employing a fresnel lens.

frost. A piece of colorless, light-transmitting material with a diffusing surface; it is used to diffuse the light from a luminaire.

funnel. A metal tube on the front of a spotlight, used to cut off stray light. Also called a snoot.

gate. The controlling element of a field-effect transistor. Also, a digital electronics device employing several inputs and one output.

gel. Also called: color medium. A piece of colored transparent material mounted on a luminaire to impart color to the light.

gobo. A large freestanding flag.

gray scale. A system of classifying the brightness values of a TV or movie image.

grid. A vacuum tube element with greatest influence on electron flow within the tube

hard light. Light that produces sharp shadows.

hard surface. A term used in acoustics to indicate a high degree of

sound reflection. A surface that is hard acoustically may or may not be very hard in the physical sense because air, the medium through which sound normally travels, is very soft by comparison.

harmonics. The pitch of a note is determined by its fundamental frequency. Most sound sources produce multiples of the fundamental frequency, which are called harmonics. The second harmonic (which in music is known as the first overtone) is twice the fundamental frequency, the third three times, and so on. The term harmonics is used by audio engineers, while musicians prefer overtones.

hearing faculty. While human ears are a vital part of a person's hearing faculty, what we hear is determined more by the processing center in the brain. This compares the nerve impulses corresponding to sounds received by the two ears, and from them conveys to our consciousness, within limits, whatever we want to hear.

Hertz. The basic unit of frequency; equal to one cycle per second.

high-key lighting. Lighting at a level that does not allow many dark areas in the scene.

hole in the middle. In a stereo system, when the left and right loudspeakers are too widely separated for the room in which they are installed, sounds that should appear to come from center lose their identity, and an impression is conveyed that there is a "hole in the middle." Some systems overcome this by providing a mix between left and right to obtain a center channel, which is fed to a center loudspeaker. Modern stereo techniques have rendered this unnecessary in most instances.

horn. Before the advent of loudspeakers, the musical instrument family known as horns produced families of notes, based on resonant properties of the horns. For a loudspeaker, a special development of the shape is intended to amplify all frequencies within the horn's range uniformly (see *Exponential Horn*). Other special developments are designed to distribute the sound in special ways (see *Multicellular Horn*).

house lights. The lights that illuminate the audience area.

impedance. The property about a loudspeaker that determines the ratio of voltage to current that it draws from the amplifier to produce sound. Impedance is given a nominal value, such as 8 ohms. However, impedance varies at different frequencies, with consequences discussed more fully in preceding chapters.

inductance. The electromagnetic property of a coil that causes it to oppose the flow of alternating current.

infinite baffle. A baffle is more effective, the larger it is. An infinite baffle totally encloses the back of the loudspeaker cone or diaphragm in a sealed box so there is no acoustic path from the front to the back of the diaphragm, thus the baffle is effectively infinite in size. It does, however, have other limitations.

input. The signal fed into an electronic device. Also, the connection or circuit through the signal is fed in.

insulator. Any material that is incapable of conducting electricity.

integrated circuit. A solid-state electronic device in which several transistors, diodes, and associated parts are microminiaturized in a single, small package.

intensity. The amplitude of a signal or level of a light beam.

integrated design. A design in which the enclosure and the unit to work in it are designed to go together, such as the acoustic suspension or loaded reflex types. With such designs, neither will work correctly unless the other is used with it.

intermodulation. A form of distortion that occurs only when more than one frequency is present in the reproduced sound. It occurs due to interaction between two or more frequencies. Two main forms are distinguishable. In one a relatively low frequency modulates much higher frequencies, causing a sound resembling gargling, as if the higher frequencies come through a "throat" being gargled at the lower frequency. In the other, two higher frequencies produce a spurious note of lower frequency that resembles a buzz.

intimacy. A property about program sound that conveys the impression of a small, intimate group, of which the listener is a part. It should be marked by a relatively low reverberation and a frequency balance that suggests closeness, rather than distance.

inverse square law. "The power of a signal varies inversely with the square of the distance from its source."

iris. A diaphragm similar to that of a camera in which the diameter of an opening can be varied. This permits variation in the size of a spot or variations in the brightness of the beam if the iris is correctly positioned with respect to the lens system.

jack. A means of keeping a flat piece of scenery standing upright. Also a female connector.

joule. The basic, quantitative unit of energy.

junction. The point within a transistor or diode where N-type and P-type germanium meet.

key light. That light which establishes the character of a scene.

kicker. A side or back light used in movie or TV work to rim face and profile shots.

kilo. A prefix meaning 1000; one kiloHertz equals one thousand Hertz.

ladder attenuator. An attenuator employing series and parallel resistances. The series resistances are in both circuit conductors.

lag. Fall behind.

lead. Pull ahead.

leader. A length of film or tape that serves no purpose except to pull the recorded tape through the recorder or pull the film program into the projector.

lens. A piece of transparent material having uniformly curved surfaces to cause a controlled convergence or divergence of light.

light spectrum. That portion of the radiation spectrum that includes the visible wavelengths.

listening. Paying auditory attention. This involves not only sound reaching the ears of a listener, but the listener's using his hearing faculty to critically examine the sounds heard for whatever purpose. With speech, this could be the gathering of information. With music, it could be solely for enjoyment.

live room. A term used to describe a room, in which most surfaces reflect more sound than they absorb. From the view-point of installing effective loudspeaker systems, the live room presents more problems than the dead room because ways must be found to use its liveness, rather than have the liveness create confusion in sound.

limbo. A completely black background, void of detail.

Linnebach. A lensless projector that uses a point source of light. It makes a very soft focused image.

load. Anything connected to the output of an amplifier or similar device which consumes power.

loaded reflex. A variety of modifications to the bass reflex that

loaded reflex—micro

extend its low-frequency capability, at the expense of efficiency, in a manner similar to the way acoustic suspension extends the capability of the infinite baffle.

loudspeaker directivity. Any difference in the way a loudspeaker delivers sound in different directions. This may be a situation in which some frequencies (usually the highs) are delivered more directly than others (the lows), or it may be a situation in which careful design has enabled all or most frequencies to be delivered in similar directional fashion.

low-key lighting. Lighting at a level that produces relatively few highlights.

luminaire. Any complete piece of lighting equipment.

luminous. Able to produce light by itself.

lumped parameters. Used as a description of any system in which different parts of the system utilize the parameters of the air—its compressibility and mass—separately, as opposed to a system in which the propagation velocity of sound is an essential ingredient in the design. Notably, in a system that uses lumped parameters, the important feature of air inside a box is its compressibility, not the time taken for sound to travel the distance across it; the important feature of air in a duct is its mass, rather than the time taken for sound to traverse its length.

masking. A situation in which a louder sound prevents you from hearing a quieter one. Because the quieter sound is not heard, the listener is usually not conscious that masking occurs. For this reason the effect can have a great many results that the average listener does not suspect. Possibly the most noteworthy is the change in apparent threshold of hearing, or audibility. However it can also affect apparent loudness of sounds well within audible limits under varying ambient conditions.

mass. In the case of a loudspeaker diaphragm, or cone, mass is simply its weight, usually measured in grams. However acoustic mass is more complex. Primarily it refers to the density of air in weight per unit volume. But in loudspeaker usage, it can refer to the mass effects in a port or duct, which vary in rather complicated fashion with the dimensions of the opening.

mat (matte). A dull or diffuse surface. Any device attached to the front of a light unit to shape the beam.

micro. One millionth; a microfarad is a millionth of a farad, a micro-microfarad is one millionth of a microfarad.

microphone. An instrument for picking up sound. While beyond the scope of this book, microphone techniques are inseparably connected with the problems of reproduced or reinforced sound. Microphones have similarities and differences from those properties discussed in this book relative to loudspeakers.

midrange. Frequencies between the low, usually handled by the woofer, and the high, usually handled by the tweeter. The name given to the unit that handles these frequencies.

milli. One thousandth. A milliamp is one thousandth of an amp.

mixer. A device that combines several audio channels into a single channel.

modulation. The process of varying either the amplitude or the frequency of a signal in order to make it carry another.

module. A subassembly of a complete system that is in itself a complete device.

monaural. Single channel.

monitor. A separate amplifier equipped with either a pair of headphones or a small loudspeaker to enable the sound technician to hear the audio program. Also, in TV, its video counterpart.

mono. Short for monophonic. Sound from a single channel or source. At one time called monaural, this term was discarded because it does not mean the listener hears with only one ear. While for many purposes stereo or quadraphonic reproduction provides more satisfaction, mono still has its uses, especially for aligning the more complicated systems.

monochrome. One-color; in movies or TV a black-and-white picture.

mouth. The end of a horn loudspeaker from which sound emerges into the air. Its dimensions are important for determining the low-frequency cutoff of the horn. A useful formula is that the dimension across the mouth needs to be at least 4000 inches, divided by the cutoff frequency in hertz. Thus a horn with 100 hertz cutoff should have a mouth at least 40 inches across.

multimeter. A general purpose testing device for measuring voltage, current, and resistance.

multicellular horns. A type of horn in which the throat divides the sound channel into a number of separate channels, each of which feeds its own individual horn. These are usually arranged in clusters to provide solid coverage for the frequencies

multicellular horns — nonlinearity

delivered by the horns, over an appropriate angle, proportionate to the number of horns into which that angle is divided.

multiple unit systems. A type of loudspeaker (of which the column speaker is an example) in which a number of small units are used, instead of a single larger one. Such a system has the advantage that it can handle lower frequencies, somewhat after the manner of a single larger unit, while at the same time handling higher frequencies, the same as each individual unit in the multiple unit system can.

multiway systems. A type of loudspeaker employing some or all of the following elements: a woofer, tweeter, a midrange, a superwoofer, a supertweeter, and suitable crossovers or biamplification to feed them all correctly.

music. From the viewpoint of sound reproduction or reinforcement, music is defined as sound in which individual components heard are identified primarily by their frequencies as having various differences in pitch. While, esthetically, one man's music is another man's noise, from the viewpoint of loudspeaker installation, this is the important distinction from sounds generally classified as voice.

music power rating. A method of rating the output capability of an amplifier. Because peaks in music are often of relatively short duration, so that the amplifier would be required to deliver if the peak music power were sustained, instead of existing only for instant now and then during the program material.

NAB. Abbreviation for National Association of Broadcasters.

National Electric Code. A code of standard practices adopted by the board of fire underwriters for safety purposes.

negative. A type of electric charge produced by a surplus of electrons.

negative feedback. Feedback that opposes the input signal.

N-germanium. Germanium that has been doped with a controlled amount of impurity, resulting in an atomic structure where electrons are the major conductive current carriers.

non-dim circuit. An electric power circuit having only off/on control.

nonlinearity. A general expression to mean a variety of defects in performance. Nonlinearity in frequency response means that the system does not reproduce all frequencies uniformly. More generally, nonlinearity means that the cone or diaphragm movement does not uniformly correspond to the driving force, or the electrical output from the amplifier. The consequence of nonlinearity is that the system produces harmonic distortion, the introduction of harmonics not present in the original sound, and intermodulation.

octave. The basic unit of the musical scale, that interrelates frequency and pitch. In frequency, each octave doubles or halves frequency. In pitch, an octave interval is twelve semitones, and one that provides the only perfect unison when two notes are sounded together.

off-stage. That portion of the stage outside the set and unseen by the audience.

on-stage. That portion of the stage within the set and seen by the audience.

omnidirectional speakers. Literally, any type of loudspeaker that delivers sound uniformly in all directions. More specifically, a type that delivers sound uniformly in all horizontal directions. Most units so designated consist of units mounted facing vertically upwards in a piller type enclosure with a shaped piece over the unit to assist in dispersing the sound horizontally in all directions.

outdoor effect. Sounds produced indoors are accompanied by much more reverberation than is characteristic of sounds produced outdoors, especially if the indoor space is large, such as a sound stage. Outdoor effect consists of using microphone techniques and other processing to give the illusion that the sound is outdoors. Even more specifically, low-frequency sounds such as a foghorn can have directionality outdoors, which it is virtually impossible to reproduce indoors.

overtones. The musicians' name for what loudspeaker designers and engineers call harmonics. However, the second harmonic, which is twice the fundamental frequency, is called the first overtone, the third harmonic becomes the second overtone, and so on. The first harmonic becomes the second overtone, and so on. The first harmonic is the fundamental.

P-germanium. Germanium that has been doped with a controlled amount of impurity, resulting in an atomic structure where holes are the prime conductive current carriers.

pantograph. A light hanger having a mechanical scissor action allowing the position of the light to be adjusted.

parabola. A curve so oriented that the sum of the distances from a given point to the focus and to a reference line perpendicular to its axis is always a constant number.

parallel connection. A method of connecting loudspeaker units, crossover filter inputs, or whatever, so that all of the items so connected share the same voltage, and distribute the current between them. Thus, while they all receive the same voltage, the current into all of them is the sum total of the individual currents into each of them. Parallel connection is most advantageous for applying an amplifier's damping factor to every unit in the system.

particle velocity. The maximum velocity at which particles of air move during the passage of a particular sound wave due to the passage of that sound wave. This should not be confused with propagation velocity. For a single frequency of sound, particle velocity reaches alternate maxima in each direction, normally along the direction of propagation, although in the case of flat radiators or dipoles particle velocity has components transverse to the direction of propagation, and may even follow circular or elliptical paths.

passive filter. A filter circuit requiring no power to operate.

patch cable. A cable equipped with the proper connectors to connect two otherwise independent devices together.

patch panel. A portion of a control console equipped with connectors to enable the operator to insert or remove circuits from any control on the console.

peak power. The maximum momentary power represented, during reproduction of sound, roughly corresponding to a moment of maximum compression or expansion of air in the waves produced by the loudspeaker. In a single frequency sine wave, peak power is always just twice the average power, often as much as 10 or 100 times average power.

peak-to-peak voltage. The potential difference from peak positive level to peak negative.

peak voltage. In alternating current measurements, the absolute maximum potential of either polarity.

pentode. A vacuum tube having five or more elements.

phantom load. A resistance applied to the output of some resistance dimmers to keep them under constant minimum load, thus preventing breakdowns.

phase. A way of representing the different parts of a wave, or of a

phase—plane wave

combination of waves, where a designated angle describes the relative timing. Such a phase angle must always have a reference, or point in relative time corresponding to the wave being measured, to which other points are compared. A complete cycle, or period of vibration is always 360 degrees, and parts of a cycle, or wave, are designated proportionately.

phasing. Attention to the way various units in a system are connected so that the correct combination of waves shall be radiated at all frequencies by the whole system. This can apply to different units within a multiway system, or a multiple unit system, to different loudspeakers on a monophonic system, to loudspeakers on a stereo or quadraphonic system, and to combinations of all these. In order to phase a whole system other than monophonic, it is best to use monophonic program to avoid confusion due to phase differences between channels of a stereo or quad system.

phase angle. The difference (in degrees) between the time of occurrence of related events; the relative phase of voltage versus current, for example.

piezo electric. The property of certain elements to produce electric voltages when mechanically stressed, and to vibrate at a fixed rate when electrically stressed.

ping-pong effect. The use of a stereo system and its program to produce extreme separation by having first a sound reproduced from the left channel, then the right, then back to the left, and so on, with virtually no inbetween. While it is a dramatic demonstration of stereo, it does not achieve the advantage for which stereo is capable and has now been discontinued by most producers of programs.

pipe, open or closed. Unlike a duct, in which air acts mainly by its mass, the use of an acoustic pipe is based on organ pipe technology. A pipe open at one end, closed at the other, emphasizes resonances at frequencies for which the pipe is an odd number of quarter-wavelengths long. A pipe open at both ends emphasizes resonances at frequencies for which the pipe is any number of half-wavelengths long.

pitch. The quality of musical sounds that corresponds to frequency. See *Octave* and *Semitone*.

plane wave. A sound wave that travels forward without expanding appreciably. A small section of a sound wave at a considerable distance from its source always approximates a plane wave although, strictly, it may be part of a spherical or cylindrical wave. Alternatively, a plane wave may be created deliberately by use of a special kind of sound source.

plano-convex. A lens that is flat on one side, convex (curved outward) on the other. A spotlight employing a plano-convex lens.

plot. A diagram of the stage setting showing the lighting scheme.

plug. A male electrical connector. Also, a small piece of scenery used to fill openings in door and window flats.

pocket. A depression in the stage floor or wall in which a number of power service outlets are housed.

point source. A source of light in which the source of light is very small but bright.

polarity. The arrangement of positive and negative terminals in a circuit.

port. In a bass reflex or similar enclosure, an opening that does not have a duct attached. See *Duct* and *Vent*.

power. Energy being produced or reproduced in any form. It is measured in watts. However, energy and power are measured over time, whereas in the production and propagation of sound waves, these quantities are changing at a very rapid rate. This leads to the need for specifying such quantities as average power, peak power, maximum power, and so forth.

power distribution. A system of connections to enable the power delivered by an amplifier to be distributed properly to the various loudspeaker units it has to drive so that sound is properly distributed.

practical. Any part of the set, such as a door or a window, that is actually operational.

pre-emphasis. Accentuation of certain frequencies prior to recording or broadcasting.

pressure, sound. The maximum variation in pressure of air from its average (barometric) value due to the passage of a sound wave. Maximum sound levels may produce measurable variation from barometric pressure. However, sound levels closer to the limit of audibility (threshold of hearing) have sound pressures that are about one-millionth of maximum, so special means are needed to detect and measure them. Sound power is the product of multiplying sound pressure and particle velocity, both of which, in a normal sound wave, vary proportionately.

primary. The winding of a transformer to which the input power is connected.

primary color. Any of the three additive or three subtractive colors which when combined in correct proportions can produce any known hue.

printed circuit. A piece of phenolic or fiberglass board with copper lines etched on one or both sides.

propagation. The process by which a sound wave propels itself forward. Momentary sound pressure and momentary particle velocity, each mutually produce the other, which results in the propagation of sound waves.

propagation velocity. The characteristic velocity at which sound waves propagate. In air, this is about 1080 feet per second. In water, and in most solids or liquids, it is at least five times as fast as that. Propagation velocity depends on the density (or mass per unit volume) and elasticity (or compressibility) of the medium through which the sound is traveling.

proscenium. The opening through which the audience sees the stage.

psychoacoustics. The study of the effect that sounds people hear have on them. Relative to sound reproduction and reinforcement, it pertains more specifically to determining what they can hear and to how they tell differences between various sounds, according to the source of such sounds and the environment in which they are heard.

push-pull. An arrangement of two tubes or transistors wherein only one conducts at a time, alternating with each half cycle.

quad. Short for quadraphonic. Any of a variety of systems, in which four channels of sound are presented with the aid of at least four loudspeakers in order to enhance the realism of sound reproduction. In most quad systems, two such channels handle essentially direct sound, coming from the original sound sources, while the other two reproduce ambience from the original sound with the purpose of reproducing the original environment.

radio frequency. All frequencies capable of radiating.

reactance. One of two kinds of elements used in crossovers: inductance and capacitance. The essential feature of any reactance is that its value changes with frequency, enabling a crossover built of such reactances to deliver different frequencies presented to its input to different outputs, to which different loudspeakers, such as woofers, and tweeters, are connected.

reflex, bass. See Bass Reflex.

reflex, loaded. See *Loaded Reflex*.

reinforcement, sound. A system in which the purpose of a loudspeaker system is to make sound more audible in parts of a room or auditorium where the original sound is produced. This introduces quite different requirements for the system than for sound reproduction, mainly because the original sound and the reinforced sound have the possibility of interfering with one another.

reproduction, sound. A system in which the purpose of a loudspeaker system is to reproduce sound in a location different in place and time, or both, from that where the original sound was produced. The characteristic difference from sound reinforcement is that there is no direct connection, acoustically, between the original sound and the reproduced sound.

resistor. A device that introduces a controlled amount of resistance into a circuit.

resistor color code. A system of identifying the value of resistors by color.

resonance. A property of a system that emphasizes one particular frequency, or a narrow band of frequencies. Because it depends on a number of elements or factors, the frequency at which it occurs can vary when changes are made in the system. Thus a loudspeaker unit resonance may change considerably, according to whether it is mounted or unmounted, as well as with how it is mounted.

resonator. A combination of elements to produce resonance. The best known example of a resonator is the Helmholtz resonator, in which the elements are the air inside a bottle with the air in a comparatively narrow neck that the bottle has.

reverberation. In one sense, a fancy word for echo. However, where echo usually refers to a single, and quite distinct repetition of the original sound, reverberation more generally refers to a much more confused multiplicity of such repetitions, sometimes with insufficient time difference to be discernible as a separate entity, although their presence changes the nature of the sound heard.

reverberation time. This is one measure of reverberation, being the time taken for sound level to drop by 60 dB after a source of continuous sound (to fill the room with reverberant sound) is abruptly discontinued. But this simple measure of reverberation time gives only a very rough idea of how much reverberation a room or auditorium possesses, giving virtually no idea at all about its character.

reverse bias. Application of power in the opposite polarity to that normally used.

root mean square (RMS). A measurement of the effective value of alternating current. It is the square root of the average of the squares of all the values taken over a complete cycle.

roamex. Semi-flat plastic or fabric sheathed electrical cable used for power wiring.

saturation. A measure of the degree to which colored light is diluted with white light.

screen grid. The accelerator grid in a vacuum tube.

sealing. A very necessary procedure with any loudspeaker enclosure that is enclosed at the back to prevent leaks and spurious sounds.

secondary. The winding in a transformer to which the output is connected.

sectoral horn. A rectangular horn with two parallel sides and two flared sides.

semiconductor. A material whose electrical properties permit electron flow in one direction and resist it in the opposite direction.

semitone. A unit on the Western musical scale, being one-twelfth of an octave. The ratio of one semitone frequency to the next is 1.059463:1. To illustrate what this means, suppose we start from a note of 1000 hertz (this is not a musical tone in any standard scale): the frequencies from that note up one whole octave would be: 1000, 1059.63, 1122.46, 1189.21, 1259.92, 1334.84, 1414.21, 1498.31, 1587.40, 1681.79, 1781.80, 1887.75, 2000.

separation, stereo. This can have two meanings: (1) a performance spec, which might say that separation is, say 40 dB. This would mean that, if some program is supposed to be 100% from the left channel, only 1% leaks through to the right channel; (2) an indication of how well the separation sounds to an average listener.

series connection. A method of connecting loudspeaker units, crossover inputs, or whatever, so that they receive the same input current. The total voltage is shared between them, so they each get a part of it. Thus they each get a part of the total voltage, while sharing the same current. This method of connection may be the best available in multiple unit operation, but it is not recommended if parallel can be used.

set. All the scenery, props, etc. of a scene taken collectively.

set light. Lighting equipment that is used only on one particular set.

set piece. A unit of scenery that stands by itself.

shunt. Two circuit elements connected in parallel.

snoot. See: *funnel*.

soft light. Diffused light, casting no sharp shadows.

soft surface. A surface that has good absorbency for acoustic or sound waves. As with hard surfaces, this is not necessarily related to its physical characteristics otherwise. For example, a well-designed acoustic tile may have an acoustically soft surface, while being quite hard physically.

sound pressure. See *Pressure, Sound*.

sound reinforcement and reproduction. See *Reinforcement* and *Reproduction*.

sound track. A sound recording, either optical or magnetic, carried at the edge of a movie film.

spectrum. The sequential arrangement of a specific segment of radiational frequencies.

spherical wave. The most basic form of acoustic wave that radiates outward from a single, central source. So called, because each expanding shell of instantaneously equal sound pressure is spherical in form. While this is the most basic form, a perfect spherical wave is actually rare, only approximated in real life.

spider. A light flexible member used in a loudspeaker to keep the voice coil centered over the magnet.

spotlight. A light unit that employs a lens.

stage left. To the left of the actor as he faces the audience.

stage right. To the right of the actor as he faces the audience.

standing waves. A form of wave that does not appear to move. To produce it requires a steady source of sound at the frequency of the wave in a room with reflecting walls such that reflections cause a steady pattern to build up with nodes and antinodes of sound pressure all over the room. A pipe produces the simplest form of standing wave in a single direction along the pipe.

stereo. Short for stereophonic sound, which means literally "solid sound." By using two or more reproducing sources (loudspeakers) stereo can create an illusion of sound sources distributed about the room, other than where the loudspeakers are located, that to some extent reproduces the positions of the original sound sources as picked up by the microphones.

stereo record. A variety of phonograph record in which the groove, and thus the stylus that follows it, moves in a variety of directions as the record rotates. The easiest way to visualize how a single groove can thus carry two channels of program sound is to think of the left channel as being recorded by undulations on the left wall of the groove, while the right channel is recorded by undulations on the right wall of the groove. Program representing sound at front center, comes from a groove in which the groove moves purely from left to right, with no vertical motion at all, so that both walls of the groove have equal undulations on them.

stereo separation. See *Separation, Stereo.*

strip light. A row of lights, usually hung above the stage as part of the border lights.

strobe. Also see: stroboscope. A device that produces a rapid sequence of short flashes of light.

Stroblite. A brand name for theatrical ultra-violet lighting equipment.

successive decoupling. Design of a loudspeaker cone or diaphragm, so that at progressively higher frequencies, less of the cone moves. At the lowest frequencies the whole cone moves, flexing at the outer surround. As frequency moves up, outer rings of the cone gradually stop moving, as parts of the cone itself start to flex, allowing the inner rings to move at these frequencies without the outer ones. Properly designed, this makes for a more uniform frequency response.

supertweeters. Extra precision, tiny units designed to reproduce the very high frequencies, above those where ordinary tweeters start to become somewhat erratic in their response.

superwoofer. An extra large, heavy-duty woofer, designed to reproduce only the very lowest frequencies. A secondary purpose for such a unit, in some instances, is to reproduce airborne vibrations that are too low to be considered audible

sound. For example, to produce effects for a movie such as *Earthquake*.

surround. That portion of a loudspeaker cone that connects it to the frame.

susceptance. The reciprocal of reactance.

suspension. The part of a loudspeaker that provides the restoring force to keep the voice coil and cone in its normal position from which it should move to reproduce sound symmetrically. Parts of a loudspeaker suspension consist of the spider that holds the voice coil centered in the magnetic air gap, the corrugated surround that allows the cone to flex at its outside edge, and the air cushion behind the cone, in the case of a closed box such as an infinite baffle or acoustic suspension type.

sustain. An effect where a tone dies away slowly instead of abruptly. This is a feature that is often built into an electronic organ, but is usually an undesirable feature in a loudspeaker intended for sound reproduction or reinforcement.

threshold of hearing. A sound level that is barely audible to the average listener against a background of complete silence. If any ambient sound is present, the apparent threshold of hearing is raised in level. However, the average true threshold of hearing (the average taken of a number of people with normal hearing) is used as the reference level, against which various sound levels are measured.

throat. The end of a horn to which the diaphragm of a compression driver or other loudspeaker unit attaches. Its area is smaller than the diaphragm that drives it to provide matching between the mass of the diaphragm and the column of air in the throat of the horn.

throw. The distance light from a projector or spotlight travels to its target.

timbre. A musician's word for the character of a musical sound. It is related to its overtone or harmonic structure or makeup the way the sound builds up and decays and various other properties of the sound that enable the listener to recognize what kind of instrument it is, or what kind of instrument's sound is being reproduced.

tinning joints. In making soldered connections in wiring, tinning the joints before they are made is vital. This means making sure that both parts to be connected are thoroughly "wet," or covered with melted solder, so that when the solder is applied

to the joint together, it makes a secure joint.
tower. An upright structure at either side of the proscenium to support lighting equipment.
transducer. The part of a loudspeaker, microphone, or any device that transforms program sound from one form to another. In the case of a loudspeaker, the moving coil converts the electrical currents and voltages from the amplifier into drive force and movement of the cone or diaphragm that moves air to form sound waves. Thus the moving-coil element, with its associated magnet system, constitutes the transducer of a loudspeaker.
transients. Applied to reproducing sound, transients means sounds that are changing. While any changing sound is a transient, it particularly refers to sudden changes in sound, such as percussive sounds from drums, cymbals, etc.
transluscent. Capable of transmitting light, but not as an image.
transparency, acoustical. See *Acoustical Transparency.*
transparent. Capable of transmitting light with no distortion.
traveler. The track on which a draw curtain operates.
treble. In music, sounds above middle C on the concert-pitch scale, which is approximately 260 hertz. In sound reproduction the word has a somewhat more flexible meaning. Middle C is about the middle of what is usually called midrange, so treble is usually taken to begin at a somewhat higher frequency, such as 500 or 1000 hertz.
Triac. A solid-state device, often used to switch or control alternating current.
ultrasonic. Sound waves just above the range of human hearing.
ultra-violet. Light of too short a wavelength to be seen; between 200 and 400 angstroms.
unbalanced. A circuit with one side grounded.
undirectional. Sensitive to onlh one direction.
unit. General term applied to any complete piece of lighting equipment.
upstage. That part of the stage away from the audience, or in a direction away from the audience.
Variac. A variable autotransformer trade name, made by General Radio; very popular in light control.
velocity. A fancy word meaning speed of movement. See *Particle Velocity* and *Propagation Velocity.*
vent. A general word to cover secondary openings in boxes used to
visible spectrum. All radiations capable of being seen.

281

voice. One time more commonly called speech. However, to distinguish from music forms of program, the word voice is preferred. For example in two-way communication systems where the people talking change the direction of communication, the device that activates the change is called a voice-operated relay. Speech more accurately describes what the program consists of, while voice describes the characteristics that distinguish it, as in voice prints.

volume. At one time, this word was used to describe what is now more commonly called loudness. In the design of loudspeakers, volume applies to the interior content, or space, which is usually calculated in cubic inches or cubic feet as appropriate.

wavelength. The length of a wave, as propagated in air space, from one pressure maximum to the next pressure maximum, for example, at an instant in time. Wavelength is important, because a loudspeaker has to produce waves of various frequencies, and the wavelength corresponding to any specific frequency depends on the propagation velocity and the frequency. Thus with propagation velocity at 1080 feet per second, the wavelength corresponding to 40 hertz is $1080 \div 40 = 27$ feet.

white. A mixture of equal amounts of all colors.

white noise. Noise that contains all audible frequencies.

woofer. A loudspeaker intended to reproduce only the low end of the audio spectrum.

work lights. Lights that illuminate the stage between scenes to enable the stage hands to work.

working voltage. The voltage at which a capacitor is designed to be used.

X-ray. Border striplights.

xenon. A rare gas commonly used in high-intensity arc lamps and flashtubes.

zener diode. A diode designed to conduct at a specific voltage when reverse biased. Used for voltage regulation.

Appendices

Appendix A
Electronic Symbols

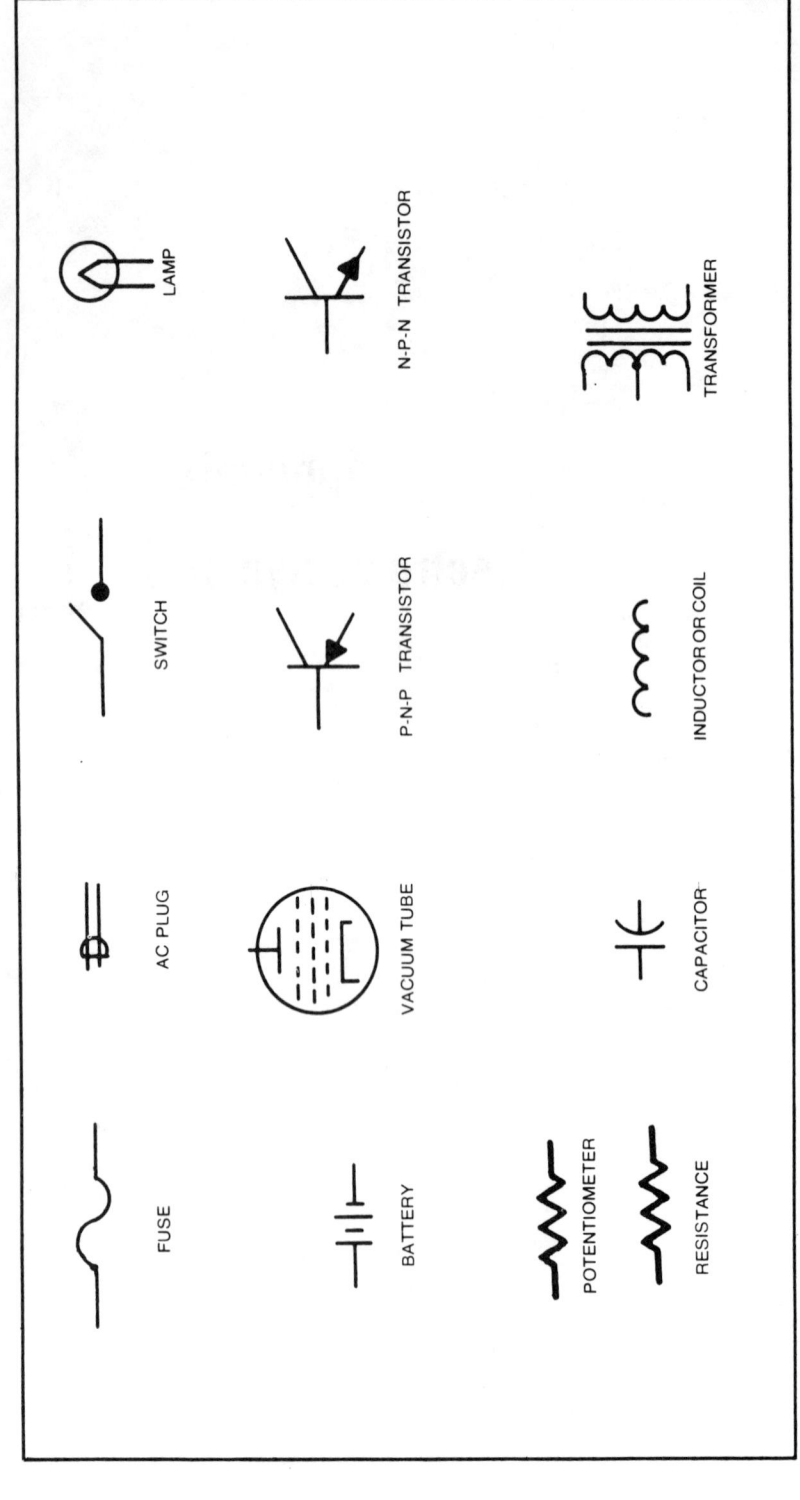

FUSE	AC PLUG	SWITCH	LAMP
BATTERY	VACUUM TUBE	P-N-P TRANSISTOR	N-P-N TRANSISTOR
POTENTIOMETER	CAPACITOR	INDUCTOR OR COIL	TRANSFORMER
RESISTANCE			

287

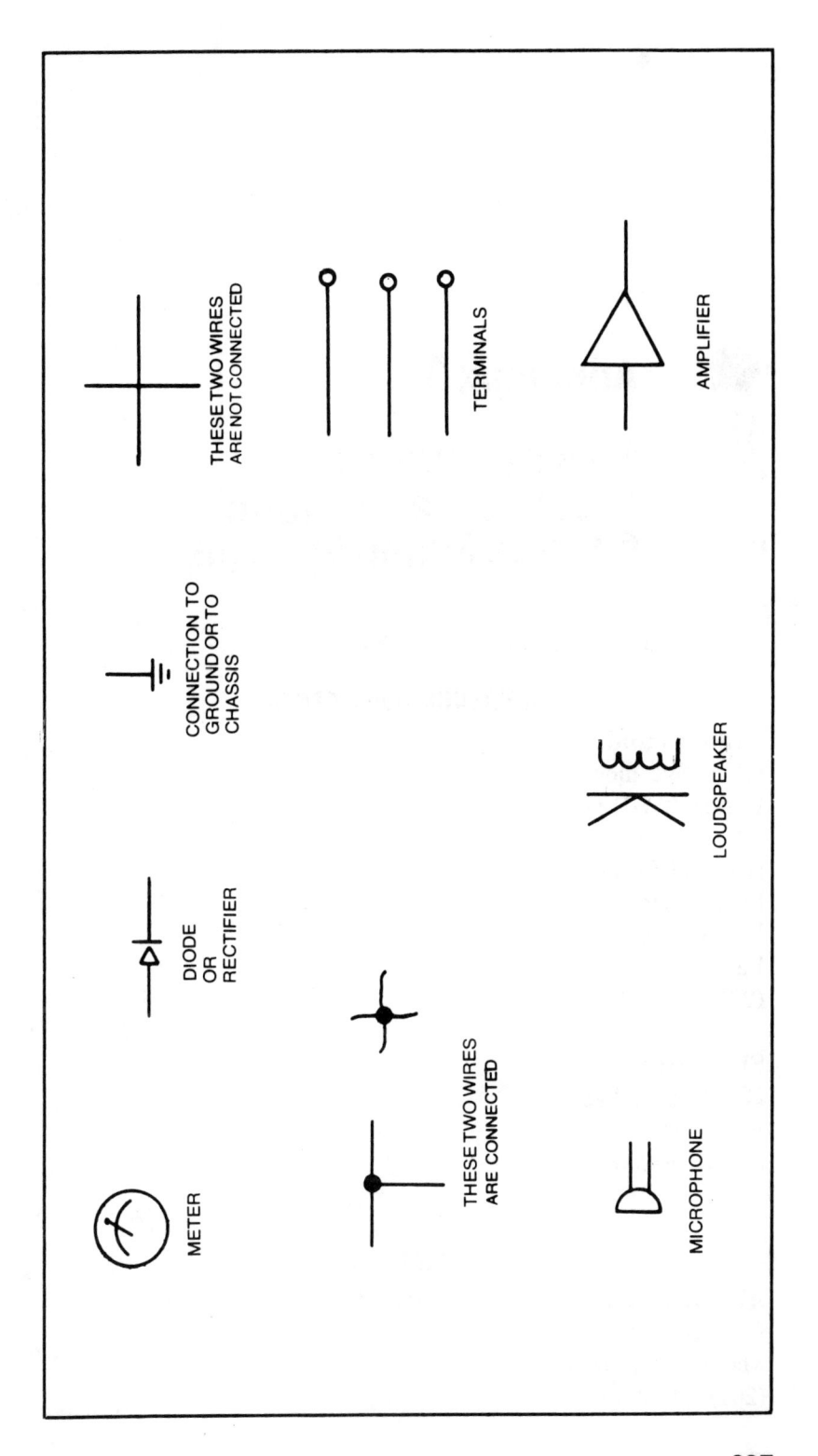

Appendix B

Manufacturers of Theatrical and Public Address Sound Systems

These listings are by no means exclusive.

SOUND EQUIPMENT, GENERAL

Argos Sound
600 S. Sycamore St.
Genoa, IL 60135

Bogen Division
Lear Siegler, Inc.
PO Box 500
Paramus, NJ 07652
(201) 343-5700

Shure Brothers
222 Hartney Ave.
Evanston, IL 60204
(312) 328-9000

MICROPHONES

AKG Acoustics
91 McKee Drive
Mahwah, NJ 07430
(201) 529-5900

Electro-Voice Inc.
600 Cecil St.
Buchanan, MI 49107

Shure Brothers
222 Hartley Ave.
Evanston, IL 60204
(312) 328-9000

LOUDSPEAKERS

Altec Sound Products
1515 S. Manchester Ave.
Anaheim, CA 92803

Argos Sound
600 S. Sycamore St.
Genoa, IL 60135

Electro-Voice
600 Cecil St.
Buchanan, MI 49107

James B. Lansing Sound Inc.
Professional Division
3249 Casitas Ave.
Los Angeles, CA 90039

Yak Stak
Box 184
Wenham, MA 01984

Appendix C

Manufacturers of Theatrical Lighting Equipment

This list is not by any means exclusive.

DIMMER CONSOLES

Capitol Stage Lighting
509 W. 56th St.
New York, NY 10019

Hunt Electronics
2617 Andjon St.
Dallas, TX 75220
(214) 352-8421

Kliegl Brothers
32-32 48th Ave.
Long Island City, NY 11101
(212) 786-7474

FOLLOW SPOTS

Capitol Stage Lighting
509 W. 56th St.
New York, NY 10019

Strong Electric Corp.
PO Box 1003
87 City Park Ave.
Toledo, OH 43697
(419) 248-3741

LAMPS

General Electric Supply Co.
1260 Boston Ave.
Bridgeport, CT 06609
(203) 334-1012

GTE Sylvania
10 Endicott St.
Danvers, MA 01923
(617) 777-1900

LENSES AND REFLECTORS

Edmund Scientific Co.
300 Edscorp Building, Dept. ED
Barrington, NJ 08007

LUMINAIRES IN GENERAL

Capitol Stage Lighting
509 W. 56th St.
New York, NY 10019

Strand-Century Inc.
20 Bushes Lane
Elmwood Park, NJ 07407
(201) 291-7000

or

5432 W. 102nd Street
Los Angeles, CA 90045
(213) 776-4600

ULTRA-VIOLET AND SPECIAL EFFECT EQUIPMENT

Capitol Stage Lighting
509 W. 56th St.
New York, NY 10019

Stroblite Co. Inc.
10 East 23rd Street
New York, NY 10010
(212) 677-9220

XENON PROJECTION LIGHT SOURCES

Strong Electric Corp.
PO Box 1003
87 City Park Ave.
Toledo, OH 43697
(419) 248-3741

LIGHTING CONTROL EQUIPMENT

Theatre Techniques Inc.
60 Connolly Parkway
Hamden, CT 06514
(203) 281-6111

Appendix D

Dealers in Theatrical Sound and Lighting Equipment

The following is a partial listing of companies known to be dealing in the sale or rental of lighting and sound equipment. It is far from being all inclusive, especially in those cities where live theater activity is high. If you see no listing convenient to your locality, refer to the yellow pages for the nearest large city under "Theatrical Equipment and Supplies" or "Theatrical Lighting and Sound Equipment."

ALBANY, NEW YORK

Albany Theatre Supply Co.
443 N. Pearl
Albany, NY
465-8894

ALBUQUERQUE, NEW MEXICO

Mixed Media Productions Ltd.
12204 Palm Springs Ct. NE
Albuquerque, NM
298-9600

ANCHORAGE, ALASKA

Alaska Stagecraft Inc.
1207 W. 47th Ave.
Anchorage, Alaska
276-5671

ANN ARBOR, MICHIGAN

Nayco Engineering
3800 Packard Road
Ann Arbor, MI
971-8795

ATLANTA, GEORGIA

Lighting & Production Equipment Corp.
1081 Memorial Drive SE
Atlanta, GA
681-0130

BIRMINGHAM, ALABAMA

American Lighting & Electric Supply Co. Inc.
229 Distribution Drive
Birmingham, AL
942-2975

BOSTON, MASSACHUSETTS

Major Theatre Equipment Corp.
28 Piedmont St.
Boston, MA
542-0445

K & L Sound Service Co.
75 N. Beacon
Watertown, MA
375-6008

BUFFALO, NEW YORK

Litelab Corp.
LaSalle St.
Angola, NY
549-5544

Unistage Inc.
330 Genesee St.
Buffalo, NY
853-6500

CHARLOTTE, NORTH CAROLINA

Atlantic Stage Equipment
1517 Central Ave.
Charlotte, NC
375-1438

Standard Theatre Supply Co.
1624 W. Independence Blvd.
Charlotte, NC
375-6008

CHICAGO, ILLINOIS

Grand Stage Lighting Co.
630 W. Lake St.
Chicago, IL
332-5611

Chicago Stage Contractors Inc.
7031 N. Greenview
Chicago, IL
764-4128

Tech Theatre
4724 Main St.
Lisle, IL
971-0885

CLEVELAND, OHIO

AAA Lighting & Sound Co.
1660 East 55th
Cleveland, OH
932-6000

L & M Stagecraft Inc.
2110 Superior
Cleveland, OH
621-0754

COLUMBUS, OHIO

Brite Lites
4135 Westward Ave.
Columbus, OH
272-1404

Schell Scenic Studio
841 S. Front Street
Columbus, OH
444-9550

DENVER, COLORADO
Capitol Stage Lighting
(Western Service & Supply Inc.)
2100 Stout
Denver, CO
534-7611

DETROIT, MICHIGAN
Albert E. Runnel Scenery Studio
4767 14th St.
Detroit, MI
898-4266

DISTRICT OF COLUMBIA
City Lights
1332 9th St. NW
Washington, D.C.
483-7090

Kinetic Artistry
7216 Carroll Ave.
Tacoma Park, MD
270-6666

DES MOINES, IOWA
Rose's Theatrical Supply
2721 Euclid
Des Moines, Iowa
277-3808

HARRISBURG, PENNSYLVANIA
Illusion House
2617 Herr St.
Harrisburg, PA
233-8848

HARTFORD, CONNECTICUT

Show Lighting Corp.
26 S. George St.
Meridan, CT
238-2000

Conn Theatre Supply
119 Ann
Hartford, CT
289-5732

JACKSON, MISSISSIPPI

Mississippi Stage Lighting Equipment Co.
5468 N. State
Jackson, MIS
366-5171

JACKSONVILLE, FLORIDA

Jacksonville Stage Lighting
629 Cassat Ave.
Jacksonville, FL
387-3298

JEFFERSON, INDIANA

Richard I. Mix Assoc. Inc.
1120 Meigs Avers
Jefferson, IN
283-7901

KANSAS CITY, MISSOURI

Allied Theatre Craft Corp.
224 W. 5th
Kansas City, MO
421-3980

ATC Theatrical Supplies
307 W. 80th
Kansas City, MO
523-1655

LAS VEGAS, NEVADA

AC & DC Inc.
3049 Regal Ave.
Las Vegas, NV
873-3115

LITTLE ROCK, ARKANSAS

Back Stage Inc.
7509 Cantrell
Little Rock, AR
664-1980

Bylites
2015 Scott
Little Rock, AR
372-4535

LOS ANGELES, CALIFORNIA

Four Star Stage Lighting Inc.
3935 N. Mission Road
Los Angeles, CA
221-5114

LOUISVILLE, KENTUCKY

McDonalds Sound Goods
4129 Shelbyville Road
Louisville, KY
895-4226

MIAMI, FLORIDA

Stage Equipment & Lighting Inc.
12231 NE 13 Ct.
Miami, FL
891-2010

MILWAUKEE, WISCONSIN

Hunt-Vern Stage Equipment
2044 N. 3rd St.
Milwaukee, WI
562-2320

NEW HAVEN, CONNECTICUT
Stage Lighting Rental Service
170 Gilbert Ave.
New Haven, CT
787-3484

NEW ORLEANS, LOUISIANA
Moon Sound Inc.
6251 General Diaz
New Orleans, LA
486-5577

NEW YORK CITY, NEW YORK
Times Square Theatrical & Studio Supply Corp.
318 W. 47th St.
New York, NY
245-4115

OAHU, HAWAII
Hawaii Stage & Lighting Rentals
690 G, Kakoi
Oahu, HI
847-4891

OKLAHOMA CITY, OKLAHOMA
Capitol Stage Equipment Co.
3121 N. Penn
Oklahoma City, OK
542-9552

OMAHA, NEBRASKA
Metropolitan Stage Equipment
2451 St. Mary's
Omaha, NE
341-3568

PHILADELPHIA, PENNSYLVANIA

Aladdin Stage Lighting
919 East Passyunk Ave.
Philadelphia, PA
467-7550

PHOENIX, ARIZONA

ABC Theatrical Rental & Sales
825 N. 7th Street
Phoenix, AZ
258-5204

PORTLAND, OREGON

Hollywood Lights Inc.
0625 SW Florida
Portland, OR
249-5808

RICHMOND, VIRGINIA

Backstage Inc.
3427 Ellwood Ave.
Richmond, VA
355-1440

Tidewater Lighting
Norfolk, VA
855-2983

SACRAMENTO, CALIFORNIA

Sacramento Theatrical Lighting
212 13th Street
Sacramento, CA
447-3258

ST. LOUIS, MISSOURI

City Stage Lighting Co.
1724 Olive
St. Louis, MO
231-2633

ST. PAUL—MINNEAPOLIS, MINNESOTA

Narcostco-Northwestern Costume
3203 N. Hwy 100
Minneapolis, MIN
533-2791

SALT LAKE CITY, UTAH

Universal Theatre Supply
264 East 100 S.
Salt Lake City, UT
328-1641

SAN FRANCISCO, CALIFORNIA

Western Theatrical Equipment
187 Golden Gate Ave.
San Francisco, CA
861-7571

SEATTLE, WASHINGTON

Pacific Northwest Theatre Assoc.
316 Westlake N.
Seattle, WA
622-7850

WICHITA, KANSAS

Theatrical Services Inc.
123 E. Douglas
Wichita, KS
263-4415

WILMINGTON, DELAWARE

American Scenic Co.
830 Dawson Dr.
Wilmington, DE
731-9585

YONKERS, NEW YORK

Altman Stage Lighting Co.
57 Alexander
Yonker, NY
476-9787

YPSILANTI, MICHIGAN

Fantasee Lighting
2828 Stommel
Ypsilanti, MI
428-6565

Index

A
AC	18
Acoustical Labyrinth	69
Acoustics	39
Addition of light	225
Alternating current	18
Amperes	14
Amplifier inputs	85
outputs	97
ARC lamps	151

B
Baffles	67
Basics lighting and optics	27
Bars	110
Block diagram	9
BX cable	211

C
Carbon microphone	110
Cardioid microphones	116
Cathode	79
Ceramic microphone	111
Choosing your equipment	107
Collector	80
Colored light on colored objects	229
Condenser microphones	114
Control systems	221
Costumes	233
Crossing lights	231
Cross-over networks	72
Crystal microphone	111

D
DC	18
Direct current	18
Dynamic microphone	112

E
Electrical measurements	12
requirements - typical	207
Emitter	80

F
Filament	79
Filters	75
Fixtures and wiring devices	212
Flashtubes	235
Flexible armored cable	211
Flood lights	164
Flourescent lighting	240

G
Gain controls	87

H
Hertz	18
Horn installations	70
How the human eye responds to color	224
How to read an electrical diagram	9
Human hearing	33
Hum	100

303

I

Impedance	20
Installation of cable	213

L

Lenses	174
Light controls	166
projection	176
spectrum	223
Loss of signal	101
Loudness controls	76
Loudspeaker types	57
Low gain	101

M

Makeup	232
Microbars	110
Microphone types & their applications	110
Milliamperes	14
Moods & special effects	229

N

Non-metallic sheathed cable	209

O

Ohms	14
Outdoor installations	142
Roamex cable	209
Output level	110

P

Parallel circuits	17
resistance	24
Phase	20
Plastic-sheathed cable	209
Power supply	98
Program mixers	128
Projected scenery	197

R

Radio interference	102
Rectifier	19
Reflectors	171
Replacing transistors	102
Roamex cable	209

S

Scenery	233
Schematic diagram	9
Selecting a microphone	120
Sequential flashing lights	249
Series circuits	17
resistance	24
Sound propagation	35
Source resistance	18
Speaker installation	44
location	42
phasing	45
wiring	49
Special effects	231
Spotlights	165
Strip lights	156, 157
Subtraction of light	225

T

Thin-wall conduit	212
Tone controls	89
Transformers	24
Troubleshooting	100
Tungsten incandescent lamps	149

U

Using a microphone	120

V

Vacuum tube versus solid-state equipment	79
Velocity microphones	114
Volts	14
Volume controls	87